# IMPERIAL INDIA

# IMPERIAL INDIA

## AN ARTIST'S JOURNALS

ILLUSTRATED BY NUMEROUS SKETCHES TAKEN AT
THE COURTS OF THE PRINCIPAL CHIEFS
IN INDIA

BY

**VAL. C. PRINSEP, A.R.A.**

SECOND EDITION, REVISED

GYAN

*Published by*

Gyan Publishing House
5, Ansari Road
Daryaganj, New Delhi-110002
Phone: 011-47034999, 9811692060
E-mail: books@gyanbooks.com

*Distribution Network*
gyanbooks.com
India, USA, Canada, UK, Australia, France



ISBN : 978-81-212-3571-6 (PB)
First Published, 1879

2nd Impression 2020

*Printed at:* Gyan Press, Delhi.



**Imperial India**
Author: Val. C. Prinsep, A.R.A.

# IMPERIAL INDIA

*AN ARTIST'S JOURNALS*

ILLUSTRATED BY NUMEROUS SKETCHES TAKEN AT THE COURTS OF THE PRINCIPAL CHIEFS IN INDIA.

BY

VAL. C. PRINSEP, A.R.A.

*SECOND EDITION, REVISED.*

LONDON:

CHAPMAN AND HALL, 193 PICCADILLY, W.

1879.

# Dedication.

TO

THE MEMORY OF MY FATHER,

ONE OF THOSE MEMBERS

OF THE

HONOURABLE EAST INDIA COMPANY'S CIVIL SERVICE,

WHO HAVE MADE OUR INDIAN EMPIRE

WHAT IT IS,

I DEDICATE

ALL THAT IS GOOD IN THIS BOOK.

VAL. C. PRINSEP.

# LIST OF ILLUSTRATIONS.

# CONTENTS.

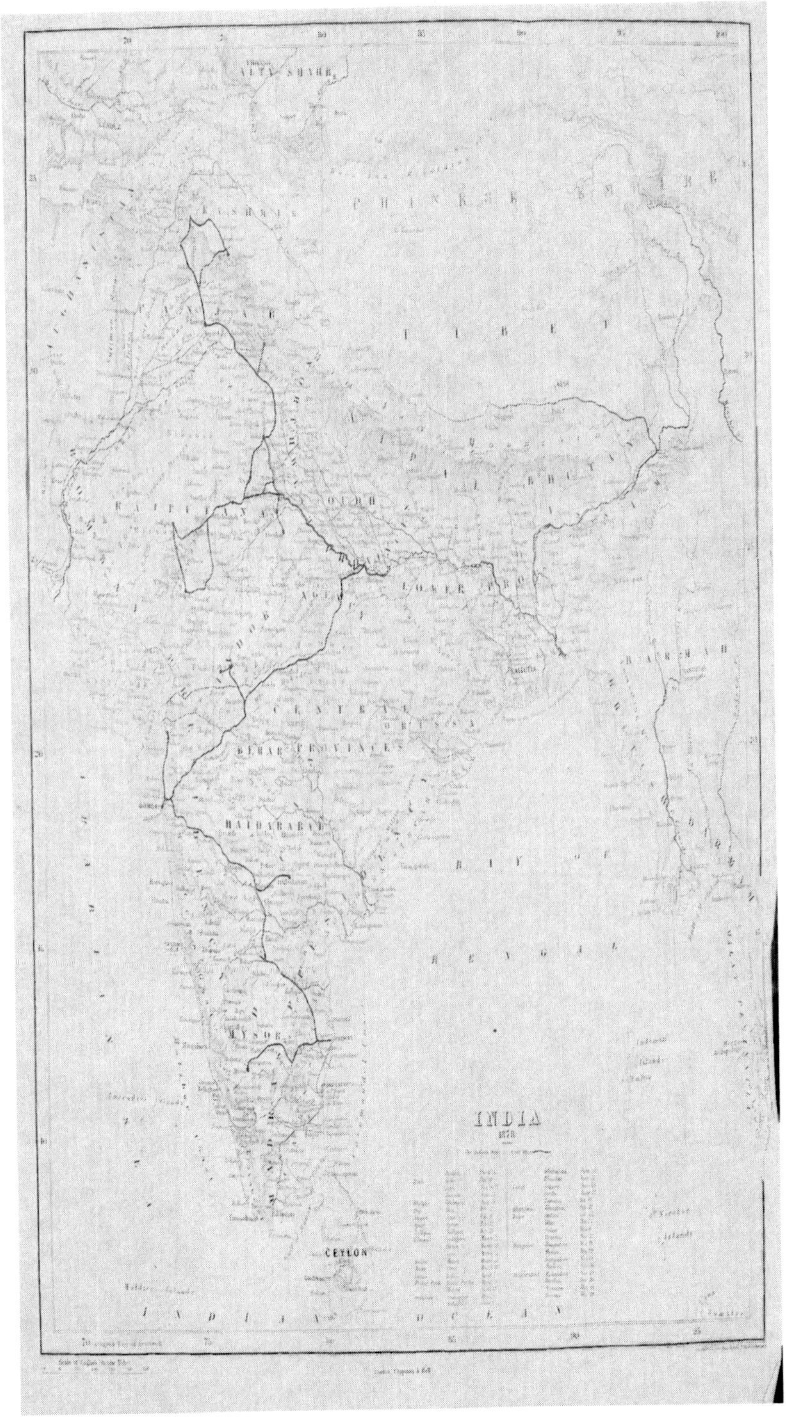
INDIA
CEYLON

# IMPERIAL INDIA.

## CHAPTER I.

### INTRODUCTORY.

TOWARDS the end of the month of October, 1876, I received, somewhat unexpectedly, a commission to paint a picture for the Indian Government, as a present to her Majesty the Queen on the occasion of the assumption of the title of Empress of India. The subject was to be the Imperial Assemblage of Delhi.

I had to make my arrangements at once, for I was obliged to leave England early in November, so that I might be sure of reaching Delhi before Christmas.

Such a commission would naturally fill the mind of an artist with anxiety, not so much from the magnitude of the picture to be produced as from the vast amount of necessary memoranda which would have to be collected from a country artistically unknown. The time required for this preliminary labour was most uncertain, and the climate and its evil effects on the constitution of a person not inured to it were much to be dreaded.

To many artists the latter consideration would have caused much apprehension, but I had the advantage of belonging to what is called an Indian family. India was the land of my birth, and, although I left Calcutta at an early age, I was still connected with Hindostan by many ties.

My grandfather left his father's vicarage in Warwickshire for the distant East more than one hundred years ago. I have still by me a letter of warning to the country parson, not to send his boy to India, as "Clive was the very devil." Notwithstanding the diabolic character of the ruler of the country, the boy throve there; while his father, with the seven remaining children, were all swept off by typhus in a few days!

Of the next generation no less than seven were in India at the same time. Of these the best known was the fifth son, James, to whom was erected the *ghât* or landing-place where travellers first put foot on Indian soil at Calcutta. It was James who first started a feeling for historical research in India.

My father was the third son, and arrived in Calcutta in the year 1809. Of his career of thirty-three years' service, during which he occupied many important offices, rising to be Member of Council in India, it is not for me, his son, to speak. Returning home, he was quickly elected a Director of the East India Company, and at the abolition of that Direction was elected again into the Indian Council, which took its place. Finally, after sixty-five years' service, he retired. His honoured days were spared to welcome my return from India; but a fortnight after my arrival he fell asleep in the fulness of years, leaving for us, his children, and for his many friends, an example of that unselfish devotion to duty and unassuming ability found in many of those who have by their unrecognized labours made India what it is. One of the things most remarkable in my father was his vast knowledge of everything connected with the East. You might turn to him as to an encyclopædia, with the certainty of receiving every information on any Indian subject. Persian, Hindostani, and Arabic were familiar languages to him; and with the literature, especially that of Persia, no one was better acquainted. From my earliest years I have heard tales of the East, and my boyish imagination was excited by many of these which my father had turned into ballads. I was also not quite ignorant of Indian literature, for I was intended for the Indian Civil Service, and, although I gave up my appointment to take to the art of painting before I had completed my two years' residence at Haileybury, my studies for that service were of great use to me. I found, too, on my arrival in the East, my contemporaries of Haileybury already high up in the service, while the honour of the old Indian name of Prinsep was sustained by two brothers and several near relations.

When, therefore, it was settled that I was to go to India, I was unexpectedly afforded an opportunity for realizing a hope that I had long cherished. But I was familiar enough with things Indian to be aware of the vastness of the undertaking. Lord Lytton's idea (conveyed in a telegram), "that I should be able to make all the necessary memoranda during the week the Assemblage was to last," was, I knew well, a delusion. I expected to have much travelling to perform, to have to track the rajah to his lair, and there "fix" him. But how many rajahs were to be "fixed" I did not know: I could form little idea of the distances I had to travel, or of the time required to cover those distances. In this my father could not help me, as in his time to travel merely from Calcutta to Delhi occupied two months! I allowed, however, six months for my travels. The sequel will show that I was more than double that time in India.

Meanwhile I determined to keep a journal, and it is this journal that I now submit with all humility to the public. I found the undertaking in which I had embarked was so much more vast than I anticipated, that I had to deny myself any deviations from the line of journey I was forced to take. The reader will therefore find no thrilling adventures of the chase, and but few hairbreadth 'scapes by flood and field. Where, however, I have come across any information about the peoples and countries in which I was sojourning, I have ventured to borrow from books such tales and descriptions as I thought would interest the public. Especially am I indebted to Tod's "Rajasthan" and Pinkerton's "Voyages." The first, like most English books on India, is so bulky as to frighten the ordinary reader. It is written in the redundant style of the first part of this century, and contains many repetitions and much confusion. It is, however, the best authority on the history of the Rajpoots, and that history furnishes almost all that is poetical in the chronicles of Hindostan. In Pinkerton I found the travels of Sir T. Roe (A.D. 1616) and Bernier (A.D. 1664), besides much information from Hamilton and Buchanan. I am also much indebted to Malcolm's "Central India" and Grant Duff's "History of the Mahrattas," both books of high standing.

I think much of the lamentable ignorance of India found even in educated circles in England comes from the forbidding aspect of the old authorities on Indian matters. Why are most Indian books ponderous quartos? And who is bold enough to tackle the many, and, I fear I must say it, dry volumes of Mill's "British India"? Surely some readable and at the same time authoritative writer might undertake the history of this empire, and produce something that would carry a knowledge of India to the homes and firesides of the mass of educated English. At present Indian history, up to the time of the Mutiny, seems to be the property of *savants* who devote themselves to those parts of history which would please the "Dryasdusts" of Mr. Carlyle, or philologists who content themselves with lengthy reproductions of the vast epics of Hindoo mythology.

In my travels I have as much as possible avoided the mention of things English. Through want of time I left unvisited Cawnpore and Lucknow—those places hallowed in our recollection by the sufferings and deeds of our countrymen and countrywomen. I have mentioned but casually the siege operations of Delhi, though the taking of that city was one of the greatest achievements of our army. Such scenes, and the localities where they happened, have been described over and over again by worthier writers. I do not set up as an historian, and only strive to represent in indifferent prose the picturesque things that have caught my eye, both in nature and history; and surely, in dealing with the picturesque, one may fairly leave English history and manners out of sight. Neither is my journal by any means complete. I could have wished to pay a visit to Mandu, the ancient Moslem capital of Malwa, and Oojein, a still more ancient city, both of which places were within a few miles of towns that I visited. Bejapore and Madura were not far from my line of route, while to examine the Caves of Ellora Sir Salar Jung offered me every facility. But to see all these places I must have turned aside, and my work, doing it as quickly as I could, occupied double the time I had originally assigned to it. I have, however, seen more of India than almost any one man, and, moreover, seen it under the most favourable circumstances, and it is with the hope of conveying some impression of what I have seen to the general reader that I submit my journals to the public.

I have thought it better to preserve the familiar and somewhat idiomatic language of my original manuscript, fearing to lose in freshness, if I gained in style, were I to improve and polish the somewhat abrupt utterances of a traveller. The narrative contained in a journal must necessarily be somewhat personal; and though I have as much as possible avoided personal description, I may unwittingly have given offence to some of my friends, either native or English. If I have done so, I humbly apologize, and beg to assure any that I may have offended that no offence is intended. I have received so much kindness and courtesy from both European and native, that my heart is full of kindly feeling for all things Indian; and although I have spoken out in some matters, I cannot think that anything in this book can irritate even the most thin-skinned.

Some stories of rajahs and their families I have inserted, as such stories are public property and matters of history. When a person is raised so much above others as is a rajah, he must expect the full blaze of the Eastern sun to shine upon him and his doings. In publishing such tales as I found current I may be doing wrong. The very fact of giving publicity to the doings of the great in India is a novelty; but to prove to a rajah that he and his doings are not above public criticism will perhaps cause some improvement in his goings on. If once native chiefs become convinced of this, and the light of publicity can be made to fall on the shades of the Zenana, a great public good will be achieved. I confess I have hesitated before I decided to print some of the tales which appear in these journals, and which may be thought to be in bad taste, and an evil return for kindness shown; but I plead guilty only to telling the truth, which I fear has been too often suppressed.

The reader will find many sketches mentioned in the journals which it has been found impossible to reproduce among the illustrations. The exigencies of the publishers have necessitated a selection, and this selection was somewhat a difficulty to me. I brought back thirty-four sketches of natives—mostly rajahs—and nearly fifty landscape studies. I have been limited to twenty-four woodcuts. I have, however, made a selection of those I think most interesting to the general public.

In the great question of spelling that has agitated, and still agitates, the Anglo-Indian public, I have found it impossible to confine myself to what has received official sanction. I am not singular in my objection to the new spelling. A high official, on being expostulated with for not adopting the new method, said, "You may do as you please, but I cannot bring myself to spell 'tub' with an 'a.'" I could no more force myself to spell Hyderabad *Haidarabad*, than I could pronounce Calais and Paris in the proper way while speaking English. I have no doubt I am wrong, and have already received a tacit reproof from my good friend the publisher, who has supplied me with a map wherein the names are spelt in the orthodox fashion. To enable those who wish to follow my route to find the places I have mentioned in the map, I have supplied at the side a list of names with the date of my arrival, all spelt correctly.

In conclusion, let me hope I may, from my descriptions, excite some who do not wish merely to kill tigers and bears, to stick pigs and see *nautches*, to follow in my footsteps. The Nimrods as form the mass of the unofficial travellers of India are no doubt the pioneers of civilization. They scale the rocky mountains, they traverse primæval jungle, they even penetrate the heart of Africa. Heat and cold do not deter them, and hardships are rather an incentive. Now, I do not wish to run down sport, for a feeling for sport is a part of the being of an

Englishman, and has tended to develop our nation into what we are. Neither am I myself without the taste for slaying, as I know from the reluctance I experienced in having to refuse more than one invitation to join in pleasant sporting excursions. But India has many objects of more interest to the rational Englishman than its tigers, bears, and pigs: while Italy, Spain, Egypt, Syria, and even distant Babylon and Bagdad, have attractions for intelligent tourists, it seems hard that India should remain unvisited. Not that I should wish our Eastern empire to be overrun with Mr. Cook's scamperers, whose only object seems to be to say that they have been in a place; but I would wish the natives to see some of our great nation who are not on the look-out for profitable investments, or separated from ordinary mortals by the brand of officialism. Such intelligent travellers would do more to create a kindly feeling between natives and their rulers than any Minutes of Council or Acts of the Legislature.

## CHAPTER II.

### VOYAGE OUT—ADEN—BOMBAY TO DELHI.

*Aden, 29th November, 1876.*

I HAD originally intended to defer the commencement of my diary till my landing in Bombay, thinking that the outward overland journey had been so often described from the time of Albert Smith, that however vivid might be my impressions, I should but re-echo what had been already written. One touch, however, of the real East, and I changed my mind. Not that what I have seen is very different from what I had seen described. But the bustle and appearance of an Egyptian bazaar, with its wonderful commingling and harmony of colour, the strange fantastic figures met each moment, the very brats in the streets with their sore eyes and horrid squalor, seem to impel me to do something as a memorial, if only to myself, and of my feelings. And as I have not time to make any studies in colour, I must essay a description in writing, even though it should be the veriest prose.

Of the voyage from London to Brindisi nothing need be written, since even I care not to remember any of its details. One long journey by rail is much like another, one *coupé* resembles another outwardly at least, and the engineer, seeking always level ground, contrives to make his line as little interesting as possible. From Brindisi, however, things changed, for we passed down the coast of Greece, and even where no land is in sight the Mediterranean under a blue sky will, as the advertisers say, well repay perusal. The Albanian coast was most beautiful, all sorts of shades blue and purple rising from the vigorous tones of the sea, while across the hills rolled long lines of wonderfully drawn clouds, through which, again, the peaks of the more distant mountains reappeared. The whole day was an artistic treat, finishing with the greatest as the sun set amid the most delicate rose-coloured clouds. On the 21st November there was a strong head wind, and the afternoon ended in rain. The heat during the night and day was fearful, as the ports had to be closed. November 22nd was again beautiful. Another wonderful sunset, with curious rags of purple amongst the general gold and crimson, and a moonset of the quarter moon "on her back," sinking like an enormous pig of orange into the sea.

My fellow-passengers were not very interesting, with the exception of an English family going to Alexandria, of whom the father was most intelligent and well informed, and the daughter, just fresh from school, good-looking and delightfully *naïve* and pleasant; of the other *voyageurs* there is not much to be said: there were some of all kinds. In the matter of bores—and there is always a bore—let me describe the one on board, if only to get rid of my pent-up feelings, for she now sits opposite to me against the golden sunset. She is exactly like that fearful "Marquise" in Robertson's play of "Caste." There is a general greyness that pervades her appearance—hair, eyes, everything—which would suggest general negativeness, and this is made intolerable by her husband being an official somewhere, which causes her to give herself young-lady airs—ugh! I shudder, but I will be ill-natured no more. The others were inoffensive. There was a fat man and a speckly man, and a Bohemian nobleman going to Egypt for consumption, and a man who was dreadfully ill, and whom my American declared to be a missionary, and we believed it so firmly that at last our parson (did I say we had a parson?—where is there not one?) went up to greet his fellow-clergyman.

"Sir," said the other, indignantly, "I am not a clergyman; I am a lawyer."

Then there is my friend and fellow-traveller, an American of youthful appearance but consummate self-possession, with a "smile childlike and bland," but with the shrewdness of his nation. Then let me not forget myself: stout, large, and, I am happy to say, in rude health. The cabin does not suit my height, which is considerably beyond six feet, and the narrowness of the sleeping-berths makes it difficult to perch thereon my vast bulk. I fancy when I am in bed I must look like a large volume on a narrow shelf, part of it being outside; but nevertheless here I am, like Mark Tapley, very jolly.

We sighted Alexandria by midday on Thursday the 23rd, and as the train did not start till 7 p.m. we had time for a run on shore, and here I got my first impression of the East. Every one says Alexandria is not to be compared to Cairo. I do not know, as I have not seen Cairo; but all I can say is that to one arriving from Europe, even Alexandria seems wonderful. The weather was fine, of course, and the bazaars were crowded: the noise of strange oaths, the very smells were fascinating and original. Two fellows by the custom house amused me much; they were disputing and quarrelling. First they rowed each other, both speaking at once, then each turned to a bystander and told his case, which was listened to gravely; then back they went at each other, with a vehemence which in England would have ended in blows, but here means nothing. Sometimes they would walk apart a little way, then come together with a rush; and so wrangling and arguing we left them. The train started at 7 p.m., and arrived at Suez at 4 a.m. We seem to bring English weather with us, for we found a thick cold fog at Suez, so thick that we were told the *Siam*, our ship, could not possibly get out of the Canal, and that we should have to wait. I did not grudge the delay, for all around was most interesting. The Arabs had their heads wrapped up with white draperies, swathed in most wonderful folds. They did not seem to feel the cold as we Europeans did. The porter at the hotel, "a fine buck nigger," as my Yankee called him, told me his ears were cold, while on his body he had nothing but the thinnest cotton garment. We had on thick great-coats. Presently the fog cleared off; then what an enchanting view! All around rose strawberry-cream-coloured hills divinely drawn, while in the foreground was a collection of all the tribes of Afric: tall Nubians in long white robes, looking like splendid statues with their faces newly blacked; donkey-boys, brilliant, shrieking, jabbering, and offensive both to ear and nose; Bedouins, silent and filthy, but most picturesque; every sort of Egyptian official and donkey. I had a ride on one of these quadrupeds, and I regret to say he gave way beneath my weight. Happily it was only my dignity that suffered, but to find the donkey gradually sinking head-foremost, amid the jeers of my fellow-travellers, was embarrassing. And so the day passed, and at last the good ship *Siam* was seen in the distance coming through the Canal. After many tiresome delays, all the more tiresome from the fact that they could have been avoided, we finally embarked, in the midst of a glorious sunset—great bars of dark clouds, golden sky, and purple hills. Such things I have seen before in England, but never so vivid and so powerful as here in Suez. I have always heard this place described as a hole, but so far as I saw, it is one of the most picturesque places I ever was in.

The voyage down the Gulf of Suez was indescribably lovely; on either side stretched the same wonderfully coloured hills we saw at Suez, fading into a sky of warm blue, but so faint and delicate in colour that the one seemed to melt into the other, the tops only being faintly and beautifully drawn by delicious lilac shadows. Indeed, when you half shut your eyes, the whole seemed of the same tone, with here and there a stronger spot. The Arabian hills were most fantastic in their forms, being cut and scarred all over, with lines of sand right up the sides. The Egyptian mountains were more in peaks.

You will no doubt think me too general in my admiration. No doubt everything I have seen I have admired: there is, however a reverse to the medal. One's cabin, with port closed and the thermometer at 110°, is simply awful. We have been experiencing the delight of a strong head wind, which has delayed us somewhat; but Perim is passed, and Aden will be reached to-night, and then I shall ship home this scrawl, which has been written under considerable difficulties on deck and in the said wind. I cannot stand the cabin, and would rather my writing should suffer, than that I should be put to the discomfort of writing in Purgatory, or worse.

The lower part of the Red Sea is not to be compared to the upper part. I am getting out my paint-box to have a try at Aden, if we only arrive in time.

It was rather droll at first to see how the Southampton passengers, who were of course quite at home on board when we arrived, kept aloof from the Brindisi passengers, and what little jealousies have sprung up about chairs and places at table. We are, however, now on speaking terms, and getting sociable.

There are of course quantities of children on board. The hot weather makes them very cross, and sleeping on deck and other discomforts try the tempers even of the ladies. Nevertheless we have got on very well, though my Yankee says it is very different from the ocean steamers, where "tears round" seem to be the order of the day. "This," said he, "is the slowest place on God's footstool!" The Red Sea produces a kind of languor, which prevents much fun, and also easily reconciles one to idleness generally. I have done absolutely nothing but loaf. Let us hope I have been laying in ideas!

*Bombay, 10th December, 1876.*

Aden, which has the reputation of being the most detestable of holes, is quite delightful by moonlight, as I saw it. Nevertheless, there is a smell of hot dusty heat which would lead one to suppose that, on further acquaintance, it would not belie its reputation. On arrival the ship was surrounded by crowds of native boats, manned by creatures who looked like the supers in a pantomime. They had long white rags hanging from nowhere in particular, long frizzled hair, and black forms. Their hair was dyed all kinds of colours, and the movements of their attenuated limbs were so weird and uncanny that one rather felt as though one had entered a kind of Pandemonium, to which indeed the Red Sea forms a fitting channel. It being night, nothing much of Aden was to be seen. I did not go to the celebrated tanks or see the lions generally, thinking I would wait till daylight and my next visit to do them justice. Before daybreak we cleared out, and by the time I got to deck, half-past six, Aden was in the blue distance.

Our week across the Indian Ocean was a great success. The weather was simply perfect, only slightly too warm. We reclined on the deck, and "do-nothingism" was the order of the day. There was much spooning among the passengers from Southampton, so that there was many an aching heart by the time we reached Bombay. One of the officers (No. 5) said he had never felt so before, and, poor boy! sought his consolation in brandy and water. As usual I was the general confidant, and to keep up my character for discretion I will write no more. We reached Bombay on Wednesday, 5th December.

Anybody who has made a journey will remember with a shudder the rush of strange forms, faces, and figures in a strange land; the jabber of unknown tongues, the banging of boxes, the good byes to fellow-travellers, &c., &c. But of all noisy places commend me to Bombay. There are two *bunders* or landing-places some four miles apart by land, both equally noisy and objectionable.

The only thing that relieved the monotony of this Babel was the shooting by accident of one of the passengers—the man we called the missionary, whom I think I mentioned before. The poor fellow cannot have a very brilliant *souvenir* of Bombay. He is an Australian, and last year travelled with his wife and two daughters through India. On arriving in Bombay they all felt unwell, sent for the doctor, and were told they had the small-pox. One of the girls died, and the two old people were frightfully marked, the lady losing one of her eyes. Well, they come back to Bombay to put up a tombstone to their dead daughter, and, at the very first moment of arrival, the man gets shot through the calf by the awkwardness of a custom-house officer. Truly, some people are not so lucky as others!

My friend Melvill sent to meet me, and after much squabbling and row, his *peons* got me and my luggage through the custom house. What a sight the bazaars of Bombay present to the artistic eye! All sorts of Indian forms, from black to white;

all sorts of dresses, from nothing at all to tinsel and *kincaub;* colours of the most entrancing originality, and forms of the wildest beauty. Every day since my arrival have I been wandering through these streets, and yet I feel quite dazed and have done absolutely nothing. The infinite variety and "rummyness" of the whole thing quite unhinges one. I trust, however, to come round before long.

The hospitality of an Indian bungalow is proverbial. This house of Melvill's is one of the best in Bombay. It faces the sea, and has the usual verandah, open to all the winds that blow, only about double the depth of the ordinary verandah. Here we all sit and live, only feeding within doors. There are five other people besides myself stopping in the house, and it is pleasant enough. Life here, however, is much too like the country-house life of England; it is very pleasant, but not conducive to work, and so I have made up my mind to rough it in the travellers' bungalow for the future. I had rather be a traveller in the bungalow of the friendless than live in the house of the civilian. The fact is that people are so intensely polite and hospitable, that you never have a chance of seeing the Indian at home. And to see him I have come, so I must give up comfort and prawn curries, and travel with a *rezai* and pillow. This morning, Sunday, I have been out to see Walkeshwar, where there is an old temple with a tank, of which I hope to make a sketch before I leave. We passed also the Governor's house at Malabar Point, and saw in the distance the Towers of Silence. Here the dead Parsees are taken by their weeping relations. At the door of the tower the priests receive the body, and it is placed on a grating over a large pit in the tower, which is open to the sky. The head priest then gives a cut with a kind of hook at the clothes, shuts the iron door with a bang, and in two hours the bones are picked clean by the vultures. No one but the priest is allowed in the tower, and strangers are not permitted to approach. I confess the whole thing fascinates me much, and I should when dead like to be so picked myself, feeling that I should at least be doing some creature some good after death.

A very enjoyable life this of loafing. To-day is Sunday; crows caw and pick about. A pedlar is exposing his goods. A general drowsy feeling is coming on me, for it is hot. I kick the pedlar out, resign myself to my fate, and sleep to dream of home.

On Tuesday, 12th December, I first opened my paint-box. I started at half-past six to Walkeshwar to make a study of the sacred tank.

Among the things that most strike a stranger in this warm climate are the glorious sunrises. Perhaps this comes from the fact of our rarely seeing the sun rise in England, partly through laziness, and partly from the sun so seldom having fair play in our damp climate. Here one is always up at sunrise, and each morning Aurora appears flushed and ruddy, preparing the way for the Sun God. Alas! she hurries too quickly by, and then comes the red and angry sun. Up he starts, impatient to assert his supremacy over all. No tenderness here. The gold of the heavenly alchemist is alloyed with copper. But there it is each morning, and surely the blessings and thanks of the artist are due to old Phœbus for a constancy unknown in our country. Such a sunrise awaited me at Walkeshwar, a most picturesque place, and one to which more time ought to have been given.

A *puttewallah*, or "belt-bearer," of the High Court, lent by Melvill, took my things down to the steps, and was of great use to keep off the crowd of young Brahmins; but I had no sooner begun than the local policeman, with many salaams, intimated to me that I must not stop there, and a learned Brahmin, more or less nude, who happily spoke English, told me that Christians were not allowed near the water. "Religious prejudice," said he. It was a case of "friend, go up higher," and I had to go. Imagine steps cut down to the tank, with temples all round. On the brink of the water, which is bright green, are crowds of devotees: some are shouting what I conjecture to be their morning prayers, some are washing their clothes, some their black persons, others are taking a swim. A pleasant hum of voices, a wonderful mingling of form and colour, and the sun striking obliquely across, making long shadows. Surely a place for an artist to linger. But, no; I must be back to *hazree* (breakfast) to bid adieu to my kind hosts; so I have only time to make a hasty dab, and leave just as it is becoming hot.

Bombay people are rather proud of their climate. During the four days I was there it was delightfully warm; yet this is the cold weather. I shall probably have further experience of Bombay and its climate, as I must pass through it in going from Hindostan to the Deccan. The first term is properly applied to the broad part of the leg-of-mutton-shaped peninsula we call India, while the Deccan is the narrowing scrag, comprising Hyderabad and the neighbouring states.

Bombay is, as everybody knows, the first foothold we acquired in India, and formed part of the marriage portion Charles II. received with Catherine of Braganza. Hamilton, who lived and travelled in these seas, A.D. 1688 to 1723, thus gives a description of the taking possession: "After the marriage, King Charles sent my Lord Malberry with four or five ships to take possession of it (Bombay); and the King of Portugal sent a Viceroy to deliver it and all its royalties to the said lord, and Sir Abraham Shipman was ordered to be Governor for King Charles. They arrived at Bombay, 1663; but the Church withstood the Crown, nor would they acknowledge the Viceroy unless he would come into their measures, which, rather than lose his new dignity, he did, and in January, 1664, my lord went back to England, carrying two ships with him, and left Sir Abraham with the rest to pass the westerly monsoon in some port on the coast; but being unacquainted, chose a desolate island called Aujadiva to winter at. The island is barren, but has some springs of good water. Here they stayed from April to October, in which time they buried above two hundred of their men! *

"When the monsoons were over the squadron put to sea, and put into Bombay to try if the Church had considered on the obedience due to the King of Portugal's orders. . . . At length

* The occupation of Cyprus rather recalls this waste of life. As history repeats itself, may the occupation of Cyprus lead to as great results as that of Bombay!

their holy zeal abated, and they were content to admit of a treaty. But before the treaty was concluded Sir Abraham died, and one Mr. Humphrey Cook, who was next in commission, continued the treaty, and articled that the inhabitants should enjoy their lands and religion under the King of England, but forgot to insert the royalties appending on Bombay, which reached as far as Vessera, in Salset, which omission has been a bone of contention to both parties ever since."

To this Mr. Humphrey Cook Bombay owes its fort, which now is not much used for military purposes, but contains all the large warehouses and shops of the city.

Our luck in India has been wonderful. We began with blunders and bad management enough! Here in Bombay there was a certain Sir John Child, who was as great a tyrant as Aurungzebe himself. He was succeeded by a certain Mr. Vaux, who had originally been sent out as supercargo of a vessel by Sir Josiah Child. On his finally being appointed a Judge, he wrote to Sir Josiah, who I suppose was omnipotent in the East Indian Company, to say "that he would acquit himself with all the integrity and justice he was capable of, and that the laws of his country should be the rule he designed to walk by." In answer, Sir Josiah "wrote roundly to Mr. Vaux that he expected his orders were to be his rules, and not the laws of England, which were a heap of nonsense compiled by a few ignorant country gentlemen that hardly knew how to make laws for the good government of their own private families, much less for the regulating of companies and foreign commerce!"

Thus was justice administered at first, when bribery and corruption, extortion and tyranny were common enough. Sickness and disease were rife. "Of seven or eight hundred English that inhabited Bombay before the war, there were not sixty left by the sword and plague; and Bombay, that was one of the pleasantest places in India, was brought to be one of the most dismal deserts." Yet fate and the genius of one or two men like Clive have overcome all obstacles, and from the time when Lord Malberry was refused Bombay, we have steadily advanced till our empire exceeds by a great deal that of Aurungzebe, who wrote to Sir John Child: "At the arrival of my phirmaund (firman), receive it with great respect, acknowledging the great glory you have in receiving the same."

The train started at nightfall, so we missed seeing the famous *ghâts*. We were quickly made aware by the change of temperature that we were rising to a higher level; a couple of hours in the rail brings you to the cold, and we were glad of *rezais*, rugs, and coats the very first night out of Bombay. We intended stopping at Jubbulpore (twenty-eight hours from starting), but once in the train I determined to push on for Delhi. It was a happy idea, I found afterwards. The country crossed, with the exception of an hour or two while the train is passing the Nagpore Hills, is flat in the extreme; and all the way from Khundwa to Delhi it is most of it like a billiard-table. I like the long plain, seemingly without limit, studded with mud-walled villages and tufts of trees. Here and there we passed herds of cattle and buffaloes, and many times we flushed troops of antelopes, which went bounding through the country. Blue jays, storks, and cranes we saw in abundance, and flights of green paroquets, and even monkeys. On we steam past Jubbulpore to Allahabad, where we arrive four hours late, at 9 on Thursday, the 14th December, and where, by a stupid arrangement of trains, we are forced to wait twelve hours. I did not regret it. What I saw of Allahabad was most picturesque, and yet I only saw a part of the bazaar, as I drove down to the sacred Jumna, first of the Indian rivers I had seen. The shops are small and low, and arched over with Moorish arches, with many ornaments done in plaster, of most artistic design. Allahabad must be seen again, I inwardly determine. At 9 p.m. Thursday we continue our journey, and arrive at Delhi, four hours late again, at 7.30 p.m. Friday. At the station, Allahabad, we have our first taste of the Indian rajah. While we are waiting for the train, suddenly hoarse cries echo through the station, torches gleam and redden, *chowries* flash, and behold the Maharajah of Rewah! A stout, burly man is Rewah, painted bright red, for all the ruling family are afflicted with a skin disease.

He is carried aloft on the shoulders of his bearers, in a silver throne with wonderful green velvet lining and cushions. As he moves along, he sucks the mouthpiece of a *hookah* carried by an attendant, while other servants brush away imaginary flies with silver-headed *chowries.* Before him are certain loud-voiced retainers, who shout his titles; around are a ragged lot of nobles (I suppose), armed with every sort of weapon used in war or chase. One man proudly shoulders an enormous elephant-gun; some have spears, most *tulwars* with silver hilts. Rewah has come to meet Holkar at the railway. Our train is shunted, for the Maharajah is due. Presently Holkar arrives, and the place is filled with swarms of the oddest-looking fellows imaginable. Holkar then appears, led by the hand of some official. He is in white, with a white turban, and a magnificent string of emeralds is his only ornament. Rewah, on the contrary, is all gold and green, and has his red face tied up in a kind of gold pocket-handkerchief, to keep his whiskers up, for they should bristle upwards like a tiger's. The rajahs meet and embrace, and probably say that each is dearer to the other than his stomach, which is the dearest portion of a native's body. Each is then borne off to his own camp, and gradually, amid yells and flashing torches, the crowd also scatters. Palanquins come for the women, orange stuffs are spread from the railway-carriages to the *palkis* (some of which are of silver), and, unseen by the eye of man, the ladies slip in and are carried after their lords and masters. Off we go ourselves at last, across plain and river, till in the evening we reach Delhi.

## CHAPTER III.

### DELHI.

I HAD telegraphed from Allahabad to Colonel Davies, the Commissioner of Delhi, to whom I was to report myself, to ask what I was to do on arrival; and he most kindly sent a *chuprassee* (which is the north-country word for *puttewallah*, mentioned before) to the railway, with a letter asking me to come to stay with him. So here I am at Ludlow Castle, Delhi!

The Colonel and his wife are charming hosts. Everything here is the camp and of the camp: I have seen and heard of nothing else. It is situated beyond the celebrated ridge held by our troops during the siege, and even yet in the midst of the camp are the ruins of bungalows destroyed by the war, asserting our empire more surely than all the preparations for the proclamation.

Far away on the plain are the encampments of the different rajahs. Never has there been such a gathering before. Mrs. Davies kindly drove me through the camp on the morning of Saturday, and in the afternoon I went up on my own account. This morning I have been up again, and went on to the place of assembly. Oh, horror! what have I to paint? A kind of thing that outdoes the Crystal Palace in "hideosity." It has been designed by an engineer, and is all iron, gold, red, blue, and white. The daïs for the chiefs is 200 yards across, and the Viceroy's daïs is right in the middle, and is a kind of scarlet temple 80 feet high. Never was there such Brummagem ornament, or more atrocious taste. Everything is designed by the Royal

Engineers, and you may fancy what they have done. In another hundred years, unless we can arrest their hands, there will not be a good thing in India. They have nothing to do but to employ themselves on Government works, and having no artistic training nor an atom of taste, they spoil everything. But of this more anon in my report on the Art of India.

I shall move up to camp to-morrow, and have had a tent pitched next to my brother's. He is Deputy-Assistant-Quarter-master-General, and has a certain number of rajahs to look after. I am to have a *shamiâna* to paint in, and shall be as comfortable as possible, no doubt.

*The Camp, Delhi.*

I moved up from the Commissioner's on Monday, and here I am, getting quite comfortable. I am in a private camp of my brother's, a little off the road, which is fortunate, for the dust is awful, and the soil absorbs moisture so fast that watering is of hardly any use. In some camps they lay down rushes to keep the dust down. It is not sand, but red clay, and penetrates everywhere. The camp itself is a surprising piece of tent-pitching. Tents of all kinds, from the noble tents of the Viceroy and other swells, with broad *shamiânas*, or canvas houses with flat roofs held up by poles like the columns of a temple, to every kind of lean-to, inhabited by *mahouts* and servants. You hear the natives all night long coughing, and their teeth rattling with cold. Poor devils! The frost lies on the ground every morning. Even I in a double tent have to muster up all my courage to get out of bed at 6 a.m. "The owl (or kite), for all his feathers, is a-cold." The cold does not last, however, and at nine it is quite hot.

Everything is wonderfully fascinating for an artist here. Irregular troopers with wonderful *pugrees*, fellows on camels with bright trappings, elephants, vultures, coolies,—all sorts of wild odd-looking beasts. Strange noises too: guns, bands, shrieks, cries, yells,—everything to excite the imagination, and this, too, morning, noon, and night. There is a camp of elephants near us, and these enormous beasts are continually giving forth the most ridiculous squeaks. It is odd that so majestic a quadruped should be so ridiculous at times. I have been out drawing them and the operation is worse than painting a child, as, notwithstanding their bulk, they are never for a moment quiet.

To-day we are to have a rehearsal of the viceregal processions and elephants "galore."

Of Delhi itself I have now seen something. The Jumma Musjid, or Mohammedan cathedral, has frequently been described; but no one in writing can convey the impressions it produces on the artistic mind. I say this advisedly, for the Anglo-Indian goes by general report, and never troubles himself with artistic impressions, nor does he see the beauties close under his Anglo-Indian nose. I am sore on the subject, and naturally so. Here these people could have chosen the front of the Jumma Musjid, about forty steps rising to a magnificent plateau, which overlooks a wide *maidán* or plain, backed by the ancient fort containing the palace of the old Mogul Emperors. From this position the Viceroy could indeed declare the commencement of the new "Raj"! But the Anglo-Indian has chosen a bare plain, and builds his Brummagem daïs with no surroundings or any historical associations. Well, perhaps it is a type of the new Raj—this daïs—cold, new, flaunting, and bare, without a rag of sentiment or beauty; but let us hope the Raj will prove stronger than that abominable erection, which nearly fell down the other day. But to return to the Musjid. Ascending by broad steps—of which there are three flights, one in front and one on each side—one climbs to the inside courtyard, rising high above bazaar and crowd, and open to the blue heaven above, as though lifted from the earth and things earthly. The architecture is not so fine, or rather, not of so fine a period, as (I am told) the Taj.* Yet the dirty red is just the colour to relieve against the sky, and the warm white of the marbles let in gives wonderful variety. I did not go into the mosque proper, which occupies one side of the

* Having seen the Taj, I venture to differ from the general opinion in this matter.

square, for people were praying. I saw it was only a shallow building, while the square is 150 yards across. The mosque proper is open to the air, of course, and the altar is a wonderful kind of mother-of-pearl colour. It is only alabaster, but this effect is produced by the friction of human bodies and the fall of the light. The people standing in rows before this were something to see.

I feel in writing home that my continual gush will perhaps bore. I write, however, my own impressions as an artist, and I wish rather to dwell on these things than to mention the horrors my countrymen have stuck up. Everything fine that I have seen has been so "rummy" and *bizarre*, and unlike anything else,—a continual surprise, in fact. Yet all this sense of beauty is to be found in this people even now; and we have left it unacknowledged, to almost die out. I know it exists, for the other day in a poky little lane out of the *Chandnee Choke*, or principal street, attracted by a fine door, I looked into an Indian house, and beheld a kind of small *taj*, all white marble, worked and carved into all kinds of traceries, and really fine; yet this has been done within the last forty years.

From the Jumma Musjid was preached the holy war against the English; and the sanctity of the mosque was so great, that after the Mutiny many were for entirely destroying it, as a warning. Happily Lord Lawrence was wise enough not to give way to the clamour of the many, and the advice of some high up in the service. The mosque was, however, used as a storehouse for years; and even now, though we have restored it to the Mohammedans, the great bronze central gate is never allowed to be opened, except by permission. The fort and all its beauties I must leave till next post.

*20th December.*

I left off without giving an account of the fort here. Seen from the Jumma Musjid, it presents a long red line of building, relieved at intervals by small cupolas; you see two gates also "becupola'd," and, in addition, a small row of tiny cupolas immediately above the gate proper. The red is not the red of brick, but a kind of hard red sandstone almost like marble, and a particularly happy colour. Through one of these gates we drove along a covered road of some length, where were formerly the bazaars of the palace, for the Moguls had not only all kinds of shops here, but every kind of workmen and of every trade, employed in large halls, each trade in one, according to Bernier, viz.: "Embroiderers, goldsmiths, picture drawers, workmen in lacca, joiners, tailors, shoemakers, workmen in silk and purpled gold, and in all kinds of those cloths of which they make turbans, girdles with golden flowers, and those drawers for ladies that are so fine and delicate as that sometimes they last but one night, though they cost them ten or twelve crowns."

Of all this nought remains, and the traveller only finds a kind of howling desert of barracks, hideous, British, and pretentious. Suddenly we come to a row of marble buildings containing the Dewan-i-Khas, the bath, and the Mooti, or Pearl, Musjid. The Dewan-i-Khas is the most beautiful building I have yet seen. All the inside, ceiling and all, is covered with a beautiful raised pattern, seemingly lacquered over gold; the lower panels are inlaid with wonderful semi-geometric renderings of flowers, mostly lilies and pinks. The bath at the left side looking towards the river is also inlaid, while on the right is a small suite of rooms quite covered with patterns painted. There are a few restorations in awful colours, made for the ball given here to the Prince of Wales, and, alas! many mutilations. The hand of time, however, has passed lightly over this beautiful work, and left it a perfect delight to the eye. The back of the building looks over what was once the bed of the river Jumna, and is still so when the rains are on. It must indeed be delicious on a hot day to sit in these rooms rising from the mighty river, with the noise of water to soothe one's dreams.

The Mooti Musjid forms part of these buildings, and is, as its name indicates, a small mosque of white marble, chaste and rather cold in style after the magnificence of the Dewan-i-Khas. In this Dewan-i-Khas the Mogul held his evening assemblies which sometimes ended in an orgie. There, however, much business was transacted.

The Dewan-i-Am, which was the place of public audience, formed originally a part of a large square, which has now been demolished, and only the *dewan* left. This is a stately portico, in the centre of which there is a raised kind of balcony, on which was placed the "peacock" throne, where, according to Bernier, "the King appears seated, having his sons by his side, and some eunuchs standing, some of which drive away flies with peacocks' tails; others fan him with great fans, others standing there ready with great respect and humility for several services. Thence he seeth beneath him all the omrahs, rajahs, and ambassadors, who are also all of them standing upon a raised ground, encompassed with silver rails, with their eyes downwards and their hands crossing their stomachs. Somewhat farther off he seeth the mansubdars or lesser omrahs, which are also standing in the same posture and respect as the omrahs do; and farther off in the remaining part of the hall, and in the court, he seeth a great crowd of all sorts of people, for there it is where the King every day about noon giveth a general audience to all, which is the reason this great hall is called Am Khas,—that is, place of audience."

Here is a description of "the King" on his throne, that will form a contrast to the ceremony I am going to paint. "His vest was of white 'sattin,' flowered, and raised with very fine embroidery of silk and gold. His turban was of gold, having a fowl wrought upon it like an heron, whose foot was covered with diamonds of extraordinary bigness and price, with a great ornamental topaz, which may be said to be matchless, shining like a little sun. A collar of big pearls hung about his neck down to his stomach, after the manner some heathens wear here their large beads. His throne was supported by six high pillars or feet, said to be of massy gold, and set with rubies, diamonds, and emeralds. I am not able to tell you aright neither the number nor the price of this heap of precious stones, because it is not permitted to come near enough to count them and to judge of their water and purity. Only this I can say, that the big diamonds are there in confusion, and that the throne is estimated to be worth four *kourours* (crores) of rupees (equal to £4,000,000), if I remember well. Shah Jehan, the father of Aurung-zebe, is said to have caused it to be made to show so many precious stones as successively had been amassed in the treasury of the spoils of those ancient patans and rajahs, and of the presents which the omrahs are obliged to make yearly on certain festivals. The art and workmanship of this throne are not equal to the matter; that which I find upon it best devised are two peacocks covered with precious stones and pearls, which are the work of a Frenchman that was an admirable workman, and after having circumvented many princes with his doublets, which he knew how to make admirably well, fled into this Court, where he made his fortune.

"Beneath this throne there appeared all the omrahs in splendid apparel upon a raised ground covered with a great canopy of purfled gold, with great golden fringes. The pillars of the hall were hung with tapestries of purfled gold, having the ground of gold, and for the roof of the hall there was nothing but great canopies of flowered sattin, fastened with red silken cords that had big tufts of silk mixed with threads of gold hanging on them. Below there was nothing to be seen but great silken tapestries, very rich, of an extraordinary length and breadth. In the court was set a certain tent they call the *aspek*, as long and as large as the hall and more. It was joined to the hall by the upper part, and reached almost as far as the middle of the court: meantime it was all enclosed by a great *balutre* covered with plates of silver. It was supported by three pillars of the thickness and height of a barge mast, and by some lesser ones, and they were all covered with plates of silver. It was red, without a line, with those fine *chites*, or cloth painted with the pencil of Maslipatam, purposely wrought and contrived with such vivid colours and flowers, so naturally drawn, of a hundred several fashions and shapes, that one would have said it was a hanging parterre."

This, too, was Aurungzebe, the most bigoted of the Mogul kings. Sir T. Roe, who visited as Ambassador the Court of Jehanghire, thus describes a day of the "Great Mogul."

"The Mogul every morning shows himself to the common people, at a window that looks on to the plain. At noon he is there again, to see elephants and wild beasts fight, the men of rank being under him within a rail. Hence he retires to sleep among his women. At noon he comes to the *durbar.* After supper at eight o'clock he comes to the Guzalchan, a fair court in the midst whereof is a throne of freestone, on which he sits, or sometimes below on a chair, where none are admitted but of the first quality, and few of them without leave. Here he discourses of indifferent things very affably. No business of the state is done anywhere but at one of these two last places, where it is publicly convened and so registered; which register might be seen for two shillings; and the common people know as much as the council; so that every day the King's resolutions are the public news, and exposed to the censure of every scoundrel.

"This method is never altered, unless sickness or drink obstruct it; and this must be known, for if he is unseen one day, without reason assigned, the people would mutiny; and for two days no excuse will serve, but the doors must be opened and some admitted to see him, to satisfy others. On Tuesday he sits in judgment at the Jarruco, and hears the meanest persons' complaints, examines both parties, and often sees execution done by his elephants." So strict is this custom of showing the person of the sovereign, at least once a day, that Aurungzebe, when sick "nigh unto death" of a fever, showed himself every day, and "what is almost incredible, the thirteenth day after he had re-collected himself from a fit of swooning, he called for two or three of the greatest omrahs and the Raja Jesseyne (Jey Sing), to let them see that he was alive, made himself to be raised in bed, called for ink and paper to write to Et-bar-Khan."

Nowadays, if a petition has to reach head-quarters, it must go through the district officer to the commissioner, through him to the secretary's secretary, then to the secretary, and so through a member of council to the viceroy. Yet in the end I fancy the petitioner is likely to receive more justice than he did in the old time, when he appealed directly "to Cæsar."

I have bought some rather handsome gold work here, and keep my eyes well open for all kinds of "finds." The native, however, is very suspicious, and all my inquiries are unavailing to find out the names of the men who have done the good work here. I have talked to several persons in authority, and more to their wives, on my project of reforming the arts of India, and find many of them agree with me; but of this more anon.

The entry of the Viceroy took place on the 23rd December. A truly magnificent spectacle it was, not so much from the procession of the Viceroy himself, as from native surroundings. I saw it from the Jumma Musjid, sitting between the Ambassador from Siam, who had on a kind of Quaker's hat, and was accompanied by his wife and granddaughter, and the envoy from Kashgar, a magnificent gentleman, in gold and green, with a belt of metalwork round his somewhat bulky waist that filled my heart with envy. The Siamese women were frightful to behold: like monkeys, and ugly monkeys. Before us lay the plain I have described, bounded by the fort. Round the edge of the plain wound the procession, through rows of troops, artillery and cavalry on the *maidán*, and infantry lining the streets. First came cavalry, then the Viceroy and Lady Lytton on a splendid elephant, with an abominable English silver *howdah* made for the Prince of Wales. Then the body-guard, a very fine body of natives, then the governors and swells on other elephants to the number of fifty; then more cavalry and artillery, &c. All this is very well, but might have been matched by Mr. Myers's circus and tinsel; but nothing I ever saw or have dreamed of could equal the rush of native chiefs' elephants that closed the procession. The chiefs themselves were not there, but their courtiers and retinue were, and they all jostled and pushed together in a most glorious confusion of dress, drapery, and umbrella. I stayed at the Musjid to make a sketch, and two hours afterwards set off for the camp to catch up the procession on the Ridge. *The* Ridge was the place held by our troops during the Mutiny, and from which we bombarded the city; now it was held by natives in force. A double line of elephants lined the way, swaying backwards and forwards, for the elephant, like some huge men I know of, never keeps a moment quiet. On their backs magnificent and sometimes magnificently grotesque *howdahs*, and in the *howdahs* a motley crew,—men in armour, men with shields and large swords, men with trumpets 8 feet long, all sorts of wild men shouting and scuffling; and behind all the golden sunset. If my head were not full of other work I should have a try at this. Alas! I have got more than I can get through as it is, and can hardly dare to make a sketch on the sly.

All our party dined with the Viceroy on Christmas Day. Lady Lytton is as charming as ever, and very popular, and the entertainment good. It is very easy for those in authority to be popular. They have only to give themselves the trouble to look pleased and smile, and the world finds them charming. Some are born with this talent to please, like our Princess of Wales, whose gracious manner has won the love of all, and for whom the world is ready to do and say anything, so that I have seen people wait hours in the park for the chance of a passing smile. Lady Lytton has much of this charm of manner.

On Tuesday, by-the-bye, I went with the Viceroy to the Place of Assemblage, as it is called, and further acquaintance does not tend to change in any way my first opinion. They have been heaping ornament on ornament, colour on colour, on the central or Viceregal daïs, till the whole is like the top of a Twelfth cake. They have stuck pieces of needlework into stone panels, and in shields and battleaxes all over the place. The size—which, by the way, will make painting it impossible—gives it a vast appearance, like a gigantic circus, and the decorations are in keeping.

On our return from the daïs we saw poor Clayton on the ground virtually dead, for he died at midnight. It was through an accident at polo, but no one seems to have actually seen him fall. The game had been played most jealously, and Clayton himself remarked that some accident would happen. As the iVceroy passed, two ponies cannoned, and when people turned round from seeing the viceregal cavalcade, there lay the poor fellow with a broken neck. No one could be more missed; he was most deservedly popular, and the type of a cavalry officer—handsome, well mannered, and excelling in all games, especially polo, of which game he was said to be the champion. He was buried in the old burial-ground of his regiment (the 9th), just behind the viceregal tent, where many another brave fellow who fell at the siege of Delhi lies asleep waiting for the grand "reveillé."

On Wednesday I went for the first time to paint a rajah. I was to have begun with Sindia, but he begged to be excused, so Holkar was my first victim. Of course it was ridiculous to begin making studies before my design was made, but the committee were anxious for me to begin work, so off I went with Captain Barr, the political officer attached to Holkar. We were half an hour late, through no fault of mine, and when we arrived Maharajah Holkar was having his bath. We were received in his absence by the Prime Minister, a fat little tub of a man, with a silly manner, but who talked English well. Holkar's elder brother also came to join us. Holkar is the child of the late Maharajah by adoption only. Hindoos always adopt a younger son, leaving the eldest to perform the rites of his father's family. Hence it happens, as in this case, that the elder brother has to do homage to the younger. Barr, while we were waiting, observed Sindia's carriage waiting also; so he asked whether the rival Maharajah was there. He was. "What is he doing?" "I cannot tell you," said the Prime Minister; but when Holkar *frère* left us he told us in confidence that Sindia had come over to cook Holkar's curry that morning! Some one had said Maharajah Sindia makes the best curry in India. So Sindia, in his delight at the compliment, had come to show Holkar what he could do. Holkar, after keeping me waiting an hour, at last made his appearance. Rather a fine-looking man, 6 feet high, with a dreamy, tired look. They say he suffers from bad health. After an introduction, I set to work. Barr said he behaved badly; but without breakfast, and a Maharajah, what could you expect? He made some jokes, at which, of course, all the world laughed, and lolled lazily in a chair, as if the world were not worth looking at. People brought bracelets and necklaces, and placed them on him, he hardly moving his arms the while. Then a Bombay merchant brought more jewels to show him, strings of pearls were spread on the floor, for which the jeweller asked £20,000, for one diamond he asked £40,000, &c. The Maharajah looked on sleepily and yawned, whereupon all the Court standing around snapped their fingers to keep the devil from jumping down his Highness's throat.

I never saw a man so bored, and should have felt more for the breakfastless potentate, but that I was equally bored. Painting in a tent in this climate with a shining and blazing sun is next to impossible, even when you have a good sitter; and as I could not the least see what I was doing, I did not make a good beginning. After I had been painting half an hour, the Maharajah requested me to show him what I had done. "Ah!" said I, in excuse for saying no, "the great God himself took at least five and twenty years to make your Highness as beautiful as you are, how then can you expect me to reproduce you in half an hour?" Holkar smiled, and was, I flatter myself, "tickled."

I went straight from Holkar to see the receptions of the Viceroy. He was mostly polite to the princes of India, and to each he presented a large banner, worked by the order of the Queen, to be carried to the daïs. I saw all the chiefs of Central India, including the Begum of Bhopal; only she had her veil down, and looked like a ball of clothes. She used to show her face pretty freely; but lately she has married, and her husband objects to her showing herself.

In the afternoon I went with the Viceroy to see all the Rajpoot rajahs, and here again a species of artistic *delirium tremens* supervened. One beautiful sight succeeded the other with such rapidity, that after three rajahs all was a-blaze in my brain. Five minutes was all allowed to the smaller fry, and we topped up with twenty minutes with Kashmir. Oodeypore was most interesting to me: I am going to paint him at home. We were covered with golden garlands, and smothered with stinking attar, or some other horrible stuff, each rajah giving a garland and "attar and *pân*." In some places, at the reception of the Bundelcund Rajahs, we were dabbed between the eyes with sandal-wood, which implies an acknowledgment of fraternal affection. Then again the costumes varied in an extraordinary way. Jodhpore was all in petticoats in the old Rajpoot dress, with an enormous head-dress of yellow. Bhawalpore had a diamond head-dress with wings and a top-knot; Kashmir a small turban, an aigrette, and so on. In some camps there were men in full armour; in some, those of Dholepore and Chamba, the Rajah was a small boy, and looked very funny in the place of honour among so many and such exceeding hairy men. The Viceroy was particularly civil to the little fellows, and as they all have English tutors, and are all supposed to be out of reach of the Zenana, perhaps they will turn out well. There is something very nice about the native child: he is very graceful, and often pretty and engaging. Rajahs, however, get very fat; I suppose it is *de regle*. Almost every one I've seen (a pretty good lot, I can tell you) has a portentous swelling below the girdle. They "go" in the legs too, and even when quite young have an awkward gait. Some had a regular store of all kinds of rubbish displayed on tables, a jumble of china birds, lamp-shades, dressing-glasses, all kinds of cheap stuff. One venerable gentleman, Nâbha, I believe, had a man grinding "God save the Queen" on a hand organ, when we entered his tent. Jheend had a band of bagpipes, and gave us "God bless the Prince of Wales," played by pipers as black as soot, but with pink leggings on their knees to make them like their Highland originals. We got back to camp only at half-past seven. On Thursday I went to Sindhia, or Scindhia, or Sindia—it is spelt here "promiscuous." Maharajah Sindia of Gwalior, who has an income of £3,000,000, and is perhaps the most powerful man in India, next to the Nizam, is a, fat black-looking fellow with very curly whiskers, like an old-fashioned hussar. He had behaved very badly the day before to the Viceroy, who made him Chancellor of the Empire, an English general, and gave him the title of Sword of the Empire, and twenty-one guns; for all which Master Sindia forgot to say "thank you." The fact is he has an awful temper, and moreover stutters, and on that morning had been kept waiting an hour and a half in the sun, with the people crowding "betwixt the wind and his nobility." When "the black dog" is on him, I am told, he is awful to behold, and cannot say a word. His Ministers and Court stand round with their hands clasped, speechless the while.

This morning he was friendly enough. I buttered him up finely, and put him where he could see his picture as it went on. I did not do a good day's work, for all that. A tent is not the place to paint a life-size head in. In the afternoon I went round again with the Viceroy, who this time presented me to all the swells as his friend and a great artist from England. This is as it should be; not that I am overwhelmed with pride, but that these rajahs have many of them paid and subscribed money for my picture, and would otherwise perhaps give themselves airs.

*Thursday.* I had Holkar sitting again; he was gorged this time, having had his breakfast, and could hardly keep awake. I had but a short sitting, and left him with the promise of going to Indore, to paint him and his son. The Maharajah kept me waiting again, so I had only just time to start to meet the Viceroy at the Baroda camp for another series of visits. Alas! owing to ignorance of the language, I found myself left at the wrong camp! I wandered about helpless till I stopped a man driving his wife in a buggy. I asked him the way. "Jump up," he said; "I will take you." And so he did, and he turned out to be one of my father's old nominations for the service, so, you see, he repaid the debt of gratitude to the name of Prinsep unwittingly. I was, however, too late for Baroda, and picked up the Viceroy at the Mysore camp. The Mysore Rajah is a boy. It is curious that the three great swells (the Nizam, Baroda, and Mysore) should be all minors. Mysore is the eldest of the three, being a heavy-looking lad of sixteen. This reception was much like the rest, except that a herald came forward with raised arms, and chanted a couple of verses in praise of his Rajah. His voice was good, and the whole had a pleasant Homeric effect. I went afterwards to the Khan of Khelat, who is a wild hill man, with long hair. His suite were very wild fellows too, who advanced to be introduced to the Viceroy with a fine swing, and a *salaam* very different from the salutation of the cringing Hindoo. He is under the charge of Major Bradford, who on his arrival sent him up a dinner ready cooked. The Khan, or rather his friends, appropriated all the spoons, and all they could lay their hands on. The story goes that they ate all the soap prepared for their use. They certainly do not look as if they had ever used that article, except as food; and if shown the way it ought to be applied externally, their civilization may be commenced here.

All these visits made me late for my letters, and this journal was not written up till a week afterwards. Luckily my memory is pretty good, and my head clear. I will never let my journal run down again, however, for it is very hard work writing up arrears, besides one's other work.

*Saturday.* I worked at Sindia again, with an equally unsatisfactory result. I am told, however, that his Highness of Gwalior is not to be got at at home. I have wasted many days through my dependence on other people, and that makes the task I have to do doubly difficult. We dined again with Lord Lytton—I beg his pardon, the Viceroy—on Sunday. There were very few people.

*Monday.*—The grand day has at last passed. A hurried, dusty, noisy, and to me very unsatisfactory day. Luckily it was not hot; in fact, it was thought by some that rain would be brought down by the salutes. I left camp early in a buggy, and soon got into the string of carriages, all hurrying to the place of assembly. All kinds and sorts of vehicles there were. They say an Irish race meeting presents the most singular collection of means of locomotion, but a grand *tomasha* in India, even putting elephants and camels out of the question, would beat even Donnybrook Fair. The dais I have previously described. On the central erection they have heaped enormity on enormity—the Ossa of bad taste on the Pelion of shrieking colour. The very ropes were clothed in red, white, and blue bannerets. Happily, I get out of painting it as it is, and find the Viceroy himself anxious that I should make rather a fancy picture of it, and introduce the Jumma Musjid into the background. Of necessity my picture must be a picture commemorative of the Assemblage rather than a faithful reproduction of the scene. Presently the banners began to arrive. They are the work of local men, and some are not so bad for the kind of thing. They form quite a circle round the rajahs, and will help me a bit, I think, in my difficult task. The Rajahs themselves arrive one by one, and as each has a separate entrance and a guard of honour to himself at the back of his place in the semicircle, all collision is avoided. I go round and make my *salaam* to those I know, and inspect and take down names. I also have the whole thing photographed, but as the figures are very small I fear the photograph will be of little use.

Presently, the few walking in the magic circle are cleared out, and the Viceroy is announced. On this grand occasion no one is to receive a salute but the Queen ; so, with no noise but the rustling of his blue silk mantle and the clank of his aide-de-camp's spurs (I acted as aide-de-camp on this occasion), preceded by his trumpeters, and followed by Lady Lytton and his children and suite, Lord Lytton appears on the daïs, then trumpets sound out, arms are presented, and all the princes and chiefs arise and *salaam.*

Lord Lytton *salaams*, so the rajahs are pleased, and sit again, on permission being given, as the Viceroy takes his seat on his throne.

Then Major Barnes, the biggest man in the army, in herald's tabard, takes off his hat and reads the proclamation, informing us that the Queen has assumed the title of Empress and will use it on all deeds, writs, &c., &c., "God save the Queen." All this was well heard. Then Thornton, who looked small in comparison with his enormous predecessor, read the same in Persian. Then trumpets sounded for the Empress, and thirty-five guns in salvoes of three at the time were fired from the right wing of the army drawn up in line. After this rather tedious banging, the infantry fired a *feu de joie*, commencing on the right of the front rank, running all along the front, then back along the rear rank. This was splendidly executed and with excellent effect, for it made the rajahs jump, and raised quite a stampede among the elephants, who "skedaddled" in all directions, and killed a few natives. After this another thirty-five guns more, then another *feu de joie*, and another stampede among the natives ; then thirty-one more, making the one hundred and one to salute the new Empress. After this came the Viceroy's speech, which was excellently written, but, if I might make a criticism, was much too long, especially as not a word could be heard by the rajahs around. He was quite half an hour praising everybody. After this was over, trumpets sounded again. Then, to everybody's surprise, Kashmir, Sindia, and Sir Salar Jung each addressed the meeting, the two first in their native language, and the last in excellent English. Then trumpets again, and the Viceroy bows and declares the meeting over. All this you will have read in the papers probably in choice language, if not so truthfully, and you will ask what I thought of the business. Well, candidly speaking, it was what is called a splendid sight, but so was Batty's hippodrome, and so is Myers's circus: of the really splendid and impressive there was an utter want.

People said the rajahs had no business to sit down while the Viceroy stood. No doubt this was so. To declare our empire properly we ought to have made them *salaam* to the ground before the flag. The new school, however, are all for the native, and the rajah has things made easy for him.* Pictorially, as I have already said, this thing cannot be rendered. I must try to put something into it which it had not—more dignity and distinction.

* I see by the official book by Talboys Wheeler, that a great point is made of the difference of the homage exacted by the Mogul, who forced every tributary prince to crawl up to the throne, and that which we in more enlightened times expect. The great question is, however, how this difference affects the natives' minds, and whether they are sufficiently civilized to attribute the change to our greater enlightenment and not to our greater weakness.

Alas! there is a frightful amount of detail to be got through, and how or when can I do it?

The jog back to camp was very amusing; but, oh! the time one had to wait for carriage and buggy, and the bliss of a b.-and-s. when back in the cool! And so finished the grand day.

In the evening there was a grand reception at the Viceroy's, after a dinner, at which the new honours were announced. There was much discontent, of course, as might be expected. The reception was very amusing, as all the great rajahs were there. They are trying to make Englishmen of them. It seems to me they are beginning at the wrong end. The small fry take to receptions and champagne, but the big ones look awfully bored, and do not understand waiting in the cold for their carriages; and the crowding, both here and at the *levée*, was so great that at one time the poles of the *shamiâna* swayed in an ominous manner. Indeed, we were lucky in our escape, for had that weight of canvas fallen upon us and the lamps, we must have all been burnt alive. Then what promotion there would have been! I 'm afraid the whole thing was wanting in dignity. The *entrées* were very small, and the lucky individual, English or Hindoo, who was nearest the door, was often shot into the presence by the pressure of the crowd behind in a way calculated to ruffle the most dignified comportment. The exit through an opening in the *khanaut*, or wall, of the reception-tent, was, if anything, worse.

*2nd January.*

I find the discontent and dissatisfaction of the European community is much increased by the proceedings of the 1st. People here talk of the "Black Raj," where everything is sacrificed to the native. There have been no balls for the ladies, who have come with trunks full of new dresses, and indeed, no parties without dark gentlemen. I myself do not see much harm in all this attempt to civilize the native, but I fear it does not always succeed.

To see the great rajahs at a party is pitiable. Their dignity is offended, and they sit and sulk in corners. The smaller ones are much more gregarious. The whole lot, with few exceptions, are quite uneducated, and have no occupation but those of the Zenana and drinking. Some, like Sindia, have a hobby,—his being soldiering. Holkar is a kind of banker, and deals in money. My experience of the gentlemen is getting very extensive. I find the head men very civil, if taken properly, but their *dewans*, or prime ministers, are bad to deal with. These have to spend their whole time in keeping their rajah in good humour, and of course do it by flattering and pandering to his vanity generally. That such men, so surrounded from their earliest youth, should be unfit for European society, is not to be wondered at. Add to this the fact that they are constantly watched and necessarily snubbed by some political officer, who is often a fine fellow and a gentleman, but who from the nature of his office is viewed with mistrust and suspicion by the rajah, whom he in his turn is continually convicting of conduct not usual in an English gentleman but which a native thinks not unbecoming. It is not everybody who can deal with natives. You must have a presence, and be familiar but very firm.

There is no denying the fact that lately the distance between the races has been much increased, especially on the English side. Through the effort to exalt the native unduly, the unthinking part of the English community is up in arms against the "Black Raj." I hear all kinds of stories about the British subalterns. I myself was witness to their behaviour at the Viceroy's *levée*. They made loud remarks about the rajahs there present, and expressed a wish to cut their ears off to get their jewels, or bonnet them, &c. —quite forgetting that many of the rajahs understand English. This was, no doubt, mere silly chaff of a lot of young fellows who were hot and uncomfortable, and kept up their spirits by a running fire of *badinage*. But I doubt whether rajahs understand chaff. One cannot be surprised if they, like the worm, wish sometimes to turn.

At the races the other day, for the Viceroy's cup, we had an instance of a rajah's generosity, which, I think, is worth recording. The horse that won the cup was disqualified through some slight cause. The next horse was, of course, then entitled to the prize; but the Rajah of Jodhpore, to whom this horse belonged, at once went up to the other horse's owner, and said, "Your horse beat mine fairly, and I must beg you will accept the cup from me." They say he did the thing capitally, and it was a nice thing to have done, considering that he had brought his horse from England for this particular race. Rajahs are not all so generous.

My time from the first has been mostly spent in rajah society. I have begun, as I said, Sindia; but he once forgot all about my appointment, and once, after sitting a quarter of an hour, calmly announced that the Nizam was coming to see him, and that he must go and dress. I was obliged to say to him, "If you do not sit better, I shall have to represent you very poorly in my picture;" whereupon he invited me to Gwalior; and I shall have to go, bad luck to it!

My next sitter was Orcha, then came Dattia—both Maharajahs of Bundelcund, and living in parts of the country very difficult of access, as do all the Bundelcund *wallahs*. It would take three months' travelling to do them, I am told; so I had to content myself with such water-colour drawings as I could manage here at Delhi. Orcha is a decidedly handsome fellow—a great *chasseur*, they say. He wears his turban quite close to his right eye, and the consequence is that the corner of his eye is rather drawn up. This rajah sat beautifully, but alas! his coat is so elaborate that I could hardly do anything but the merest blot of it. And this applies equally to each of these fellows. I have been knocking them off in two sittings, which is perfectly absurd. I have got a tolerable likeness of head and *pugree;* the rest is quite hopeless, for to do each properly would take a month. Orcha's is one of the oldest families in India. It is said that the Rajahs of Orcha never did homage to any superior till the arrival of the Prince of Wales. They were once very powerful, and owned a great deal of territory; but their obstinate independence has been fatal to their power, and the family possessions are now driven back to the hilly and inaccessible parts of Bundelcund. The Orcha retinue was conspicuously splendid in different kinds of armour.

Dattia, the other Bundelcund Rajah, is not handsome. He has a largish nose, pig eyes, and an enormous stomach. He was very inquisitive, wished to see the whole process of painting, and examine the colours, &c. A rajah sitting is a wonderful sight. He has his ministers round, who speak to his Highness with clasped hands. Then he has sweetmeats brought him, or rather some beastly stuff in a leaf, which he chews.* Then he has a turn at his hookah. Meanwhile I curse inwardly. All round there are strange noises—tom-toms, flutes, or horns being practised on, till I get nearly distracted. Sometimes his Highness says, "I am hungry, and must eat." Away he goes. In fact, it is the privilege of the great to eat and sleep when and where they wish. You see mine is not a bed of roses.

I have lately taken three a day, beginning with Sampthar and Panna. Sampthar, another Bundelcunder, is a thin, consumptive-looking Rajah, and the only Rajah of his nation, viz., Gooja, or Herdsmen. When I arrived at his tents, his *dewan* declared his master must sit on his throne, which was an enormous erection with a hood. I said he should not, whereupon the Minister said it would never do for the Rajah to sit anywhere else. "Very well," I said, "then I will not do him at all;" and the Minister yielded. Sampthar himself made no bones about sitting in an ordinary chair; so I painted him. Then came Panna's turn. A sharp little fellow is Panna, stout and short, and, strange to say, intelligent. He has diamond mines of his own, and has a gorgeous collection of precious stones generally. Panna has an amusing stutter, and has to slap his leg to get out his words. He paints his eyes, and speaks English.

* This is *pân*, and consists in an assortment of nuts, aromatic and astringent, and a dab of lime, all wrapped in a leaf of the betel-tree. Some of the nuts are rather pleasant to chew in very hot weather, as they moisten the mouth, and render drinking unnecessary.

I ought next to have painted Bijawar; but he was away larking with Rewah, so Ajigurh sends for me and I draw a hasty sketch of him. He is a neat little chap, with a most elaborate dress, which it was madness to attempt in the time. My drawing was most slight, and will only serve for his head.

To-day I was to have done Bijawar, Chatterpore, and Chirkaree. The first was not up, and declared he was ill, so I have cut him off my list. Chatterpore is a little boy, with no nose to speak of, and is generally frightful. Fancy this youth of twelve demanding his hookah! It appears he used to smoke cheroots, but the political agent very properly stopped that. He was covered with jewels, yet for all that was a miserable object. Chirkaree has the reputation of being a little wanting. I went there an hour and a half too soon, in consequence of the failure of Bijawar. His Highness sent to ask me to lend him my watch to see the time, and, after keeping me a short while, turned up fully dressed and very polite. He was the only one of the whole lot that presented me, during my tour of sittings, with attar and *pân*, and a magnificent garland of tinsel or *harh.*

I have thus done six rajahs, and begin two more to-morrow. These Bundelcund chiefs were all kept in Delhi to enable me to paint them. Some of them had struck all their tents but one little one, in which it was almost impossible to work. All were anxious to know when I should have done, and showed as much joy at being let off as schoolboys going for their holidays. To-morrow I pause, before I begin her Highness of Bhopal.

I went out last Friday to see the march past of the native troops, which closed the *tomasha* for the swells. It was really a curious sight. Fancy Myers's circus, only the real thing. Elephants are here much painted both on trunk and body, and have their tusks completed with false ivory. They trumpeted and salaamed as they passed. One elephant waved a pocket-handkerchief; one had two rose-coloured bell-glasses on the end of his false tusks. There were squadrons of men in armour, bands playing impossible tunes, and finally one contingent who marched by with presented arms. The only drawback to all this was that it lasted two hours, and we went away, all of us, heartily tired, for the sun was very hot.

Delhi camp may now be said to have ended its troubled existence. Of many camps not a tent remains, and soon the whole plain will assume its usual monotonous appearance, and nought will remain to tell of all these great doings but chimneys built of mud, arranged in rows, and even now tumbling to ruin. There were at least four Delhis before our time. Three are in ruins: the one that exists (properly called Shah-Jehanabad) is the fourth. We have built a fifth, that has lasted a shorter time than any of its rivals; but a fortnight, butterfly-like, with many colours—making much noise with banging guns and martial music—and now nothing! And as if to wipe out all sight of it, last night the weather changed, and rain has set in. It blows great guns—the only great guns we hear—for all is over. "Long live the Empress and Empire of India!" and off go chiefs and officials to their homes far away. The curtain falls, for the great and imperial spectacle-drama is ended. Turn down the lights.

To-day, despite the wind, I drove out to the Kutub, or Minar of Kutub-ood-deen, as it ought to be called, eleven miles from Delhi. Along all the way from the present Delhi you see ruins of the former cities. Indian houses are mostly made of mud, easily effaced by the heavy rains of the country; so all these eleven miles are huge formless mounds of earth, on which great vultures perch, but where no grass grows. Only here and there are the tombs of the former owners of all this power. These are mostly in ruins too, but being built of stone, still rear their proud heads o'er the forgotten dead they were raised to immortalize. Some few of the principal ones alone have names. There are the tombs of Humayun and Sufter Jung; the former is the tomb of an emperor, but is better known among Europeans by being the place where Hodgson took the two sons of the King of Delhi. A grim story, that. Nothing is finer in history than that figure of a single Englishman among those three thousand courtiers of Delhi, who were all desperate from the failure of their plans, but yet surrendered their two leaders at his imperious demand without a struggle. So Hodgson rode off, and would that the gallant *sabreur* had ended there! But he who had not quailed at the tomb of Hamayun declared he was afraid of a rescue from the rabble of Delhi, and bid his royal prisoners alight. "Surely the bitterness of death is past!" they cried, with Agag. "Take off your coats!" was the stern reply; and he pistolled one, while his *sowar* killed the other, and their bodies were thrown before the *kotwal*, or police station, in the *Chandnee-chowk*, the principal street of Delhi.

I have never seen anything more impressive than these cities (for there are more than one) of the dead. The Kutub itself, built to assert the sway of Mahomet over India, stands in the middle of an Indian temple. By it was a magnificent mosque, but mosque and temple are alike ruins, and the Kutub alone remains perfect to assert the power of Mahomet over dust. Truly Delhi is a city of tombs!

As to the Minar itself, I can only say that I have seen most of the splendours of Italy, yet nowhere—not even in Florence, where they can boast of Giotto's Tower—have I seen so perfect a work. Ring or belt after belt of delicate tracery, interwoven with texts of the Koran, rises to the height of 250 feet, while the whole is a beautiful reddish colour, slightly mottled, not by time but intentionally. I have not seen the Taj: I go there next week; but if it equals what I have already seen, it must be a wonder indeed! The Jumma Musjid, the Dewan-i-Khas, and the Kutub have sunk deep into my imagination; why, then, am I to paint Cremorne and the Crystal Palace and Brummagem iron-work?

The night I dispatched my last, we had a tremendous down-pour and thunder-storm. It began while we were at dinner, and lasted all night. Before we had finished dinner the rain-water was streaming through the tent. I never saw such rain! Most of the tents were flooded, and some were a pitiable sight in the morning. Our neighbour, Major Bradford, had a *nullah* or stream 3 feet deep, formed through the middle of his child's sleeping-tent! Where the ladies of our camp had their tents there were

18 inches of water. Luckily, all our ladies had left or we should have been in a pretty state. This was on Thursday night, 11th January. On Friday we left camp, and are now living at the Northbrook Hotel.

I had my first sitting of the Begum of Bhopal on this day. I went down to see her with the "political" in charge, Captain C——. The Begum has taken a house in the city for a week. We entered through a dirty doorway in the Lalpure Road, and passed through one still dirtier courtyard into another, where we found a crowd of natives and a guard with presented arms to receive us. Here we alighted, and passing through another door, we came to a larger courtyard, in the middle of which there was the usual stone canal surrounded with trees. It was a pleasant place. Across it was drawn the *purdah*, behind which the Begum resides. To the left was an open verandah, where we found the Nawab, the Begum's Prince Consort. He is a stout, good-looking fellow, with a determined face, and eyes rather fiercely scowling from under his knitted brows. He has just been recognized by our Government and now receives seventeen guns. The Begum, like the Grand Duchess of Gerolstein, chose her Fritz from the lower classes. His Highness the Nawab was originally a schoolmaster and copier of books. Even now, report says, he drops the Prince Consort, returns to his pedagoguish habits, and corrects the Begum soundly. He is polite enough to us, and after a little delay and a thunder-storm, he finally announces her Highness.

Straightway the court is cleared of males. Poor C—— is placed behind a column, with his back turned, and I am left to receive the hitherto invisible lady. All this is nonsense, but the habit of the country. Before marriage the Begum was very visible, but since the advent of the Nawab she has become a *purdah* lady. I had seen her, as I have described, at the audience Lord Lytton gave her; and now the same little figure, like a blue ball with thin red supporters, or legs, comes waddling across the court. The Nawab gallantly advances, and conducts her to a chair placed on a carpet, and down she sits. I look aghast; she wears a veil. After a moment I call out to C—— that her Highness has forgotten an important ceremony. He explains to the Nawab, who advances and throws back the veil. Well, I am not

HER HIGHNESS SHAH JEHAN, BEGUM OF BHOPAL.

dazzled. The Begum is decidedly plain, and not young. Presently I perceive she has good eyes, but her mouth is pinched, and traces of age are on her cheek. She is only thirty, but natives of that age are somewhat *passé*. Her dress is not particularly becoming, and she has none of the jewellery and precious stones found on the ruling male, whether Moslem or Hindoo. Her Highness has a heavy, weary look. She keeps continually glancing towards the Nawab. I fancy she is awfully afraid of him; and I feel for the poor thing: even Begums are human, and dislike the stick. I have had several sittings since then, and she has always the same frightened, stolid look when he is by. To the second sitting C—— did not come, and the "Master Sahib" was called on to supply his place. This gentleman is a native, called to teach the Nawab's sons (by a former marriage) English. You may imagine his proficiency when I tell you what he said to me after the sitting. With enthusiasm he cried, seizing me by the arm, "Ah! you are a wonderful painter, I do not think." This man's pupils are a nuisance, as they keep chanting their lessons close by, swaying their bodies after the manner of all Eastern children at school. The Begum, like all natives, is fond of noise, and there are about twenty parrots immediately outside the verandah that serves me as a studio. You cannot conceive the effect all this has on the nerves when work is not turning out well.

I find, on a second visit to the Dewan-i-Khas, that the decorations are more knocked about than I thought at first. We have restored one of the ceilings, and the restoration is awful. The restoration of ruins is a very serious question. It always seems to me that it is much more difficult to repair than to design,—to enter into another man's plans, than to invent for oneself. A real artist would have retouched without repainting. Here, of course, the Engineers advise on the matter, and "fools rush in where angels fear to tread."

On Saturday, 13th January, we had some jugglers in our sitting-room at the hotel here. I have heard all my life of Indian jugglers, and was prepared to see marvels. These are the second I have seen; and the head man, apparently very well known, was furnished with innumerable *chits*, or letters of recommendation. Every native who comes near you asks for a *chit*. Some this man showed me, in his simplicity, were very amusing. One said, "Rumchund fleeced me out of thirteen rupees and half a bottle of brandy, after performing some indifferent tricks." His tricks were of the usual kind: he was certainly a clever prestidigitator; but as he had two women and one man accomplices, his tricks, to any one accustomed to conjuring, were not very wonderful. The basket trick he did not do. The mango trick he performed; but as the mango produced was anything but fresh, and could easily have been produced by one of the abovenamed accomplices, there was nothing astounding about it. Descriptions of such things never convey the right impression. After the conjuring we had some *Nuts*, or gipsies, to tumble. We had invited some people in the hotel to see the tricks, and among them Major and Mrs. C——. Mrs. C—— was rather disturbed by the announcement of the conjurors that ladies sometimes objected to this performance, and more so when both men and women began taking off their clothes. She stopped, however, to see the beginning. First, these two men, entirely nude except the thinnest cloth round the loins, threw somersaults through hoops in a really wonderful way; then came the woman's turn, and here Mrs. C—— fled. She might have stayed, however, for there was nothing the least shocking in the performance. The woman merely contorted herself very much in the way one sees on classical vases. Altogether she was very graceful, and well worth seeing.

To-day I have received visits from the artists of Delhi: they are three in number, and each appears to have an *atelier* of pupils. The best is one Ismael Khan. Their manual dexterity is most surprising. Of course, what they do is entirely traditional. They work from photographs, and never by any chance from nature. Ismael Khan showed me what his father had done before photographing came into vogue, and really a portrait of Sir C. Napier was wonderfully like, though without an atom of *chic*, or artistic rendering. I pointed out to the old man certain faults—and glaring ones—of perspective, and he has promised to do me a view of the Golden Temple without any faults.

"These," said he, pointing to his miniatures, "are done for the *sahibs* who do not understand. I know they are wrong, but what does it matter? No one cares. But I will show you that I can do better."*

It is a pity such wonderful dexterity should be thrown away. Some means of really educating these fellows might be hit upon. If only they could see better work, they would quickly improve. At present the talent seems to be hereditary, and father, son, and grandson are necessarily painters, and all with the same mechanical capacity and admirable patience. "Time is of no more value here than it is to a sitting hen," said my Yankee.

Some of this young fellow's sayings are very funny. One of our party who went to see the jugglers was a man who looked anything but 'cute. "Well," said G——, "that man is hardly capable of getting out of his own way."

Describing a shot he made at a quail to-day, he said, "I made the meanest shot ever made by a white man."

To-morrow we leave Delhi for Agra, and I confess I leave with great regret. I had calculated on two or three days' sketching, but, alas! it has taken to raining, so I have quite failed. Indian landscape under a cloudy sky does not do. I do not suppose I shall ever find time to return to do what I wanted, so my good intentions must go to —— that well-paved place below. I trust, however, to-morrow may be fine, and give me one chance.

It never rains long together in India at this time of the year, and I had a fine day, which I devoted to making a sketch of the Jumma Musjid. Jumma Musjid means general mosque, in fact cathedral. I have described the one at Delhi before. My sketch was necessarily slight, as Eastern architecture, and Indian in particular, goes into such minute detail, that it is impossible to give anything but the vaguest idea of its colour; but with the help of photos and my own sketches for figures, I think I shall be able to knock up a picture of the mosque.

* This better miniature I never received; perhaps my friend Ismael found it not so easy to do a perfect picture.

That afternoon I had to go and thank the Commissioner for his hospitality, and to pay a visit; and on the 16th January, in the evening, we left, and arrived at Agra by 7.30 a.m., Wednesday, 17th January.

## CHAPTER IV.

### AGRA.

YOU reach Agra by a bridge across the Jumna. Some few minutes before you get there, out of the left window of the carriage you see in the distance the celebrated Taj. The sun was rising when we first saw it, and the white domes told in faint lilac against the golden sky. The outline of the Taj, I frankly admit, I do not like: other domes or cupolas rise from a square or hexagonal base, but the dome of the Taj rises from a circle, and swells straight away. The view from the railway prepared me for disappointment on a closer inspection. Crossing the river, the railway takes you close to the fort. Like the Delhi fort, the fort at Agra is built of red sandstone, and the Red Sandstone Gate, close to which you find yourself upon leaving the station, is very imposing. We had little time, however, to inspect, for breakfast has great charms for the traveller who has sped all night long by rail, and our lodgings had to be secured. Off we went to the club, of which, owing to the foresight of my brother, we had previously been made honorary members. We drove past many comfortable-looking bungalows, whose inhabitants were many of them starting for their morning ride. Unfortunately the club bungalow was full, and we had to content ourselves with two rooms in an indifferent hotel called the "Agra Cantonment Hotel." There we breakfast, and by eleven o'clock are ready to start sight-seeing.

First we go to the fort. It is not so big as the Delhi fort, but more irregular in shape. As at Delhi, towards the river are the royal buildings, and, as at Delhi, the hand of the Englishman has done its best to destroy. At the summit of the rising ground on which the fort is built, the pious Mohammedan has erected to his deity a mosque of white marble, which is called, as usual, Mooti Musjid, from its white colour. It is much larger than the mosque in the fort in Delhi, and has been lately cleaned and repaired. This perhaps may account for a certain cold, chilly, unsympathetic look. From the mosque we went to the Dewan-i-Am, and found it entirely spoilt by the restorations. It looks something like a railway station ; but behind this outer abomination there is a series of courts which defy description. As this is not intended for a guide book, I will not attempt to describe in order the different things to be seen ; indeed, having been only once to the fort, it would be impossible for me to give such a description. I can only record my impression of the thing as a whole.

There is, then, an inner *dewan* built of marble, and sumptuously inlaid with cornelian and lapis, and from the back of this you come on a white marble balcony looking over the river, which is a perfect gem. Fit indeed is it for a king! One can imagine Shah Jehan gazing fondly at the Taj, seen some mile and a half distant, rising over the remains of his beloved Mumtaz-i-Mahal, the mother of his children. Behind this *dewan* you come to a series of splendid buildings. One of them was decorated with ornamental flowers painted on marble, like those in Dewan-i-Khas at Delhi, and which are still singularly beautiful in their faded colour. Alas! the hand of the English Engineer has been here also! One corner of the lovely room was repainted to show the Prince of Wales what it was when new. Ye gods! what a sight!—the most tinselly gold, the crudest reds and yellows, the coarsest possible work. If this is what it was when new, let us have no more like it ; let us at least leave what is picturesque and beautiful to delight the eye as long as there remains a trace of the pattern. Let us keep up the building and keep out the rain. But for Heaven's sake, O ye higher powers who direct such matters! spare us the decorations of the unartistic and the wild imaginings of the Engineer, which are not only horrible in themselves, but replace the traces, the beautiful traces, of former art.

Yet I heard a high official asking whether it was not very fine!

4—2

Thank Heaven, the experiment was so costly that, in the present state of Indian finance, it is not likely to be repeated for the next year or two, and by then I hope the authorities will have awakened to the necessity of having some responsible artistic advice in such matters.

In the tracery of the beauteous balcony I mentioned above are some great holes, torn by the cannon-shot of the victorious rebels during the Mutiny. Such random damage is easy to repair; it's only that inflicted at leisure by the hand of the skilled labourer that it is impossible to restore.

Beyond these chambers and courts, which are of the later Mogul period, there is a corner of the fort where are the ruins of a palace built in an early and more robust style, inspired, and no doubt carried out, by Hindoo workmen. Some of this is very fine, and I must say, in justice to the Engineers whom I have before roundly abused, that the portion already restored seems done in a good spirit, and with a feeling for the original work. It was time this was done, for there has been much wanton destruction, and the place was in absolute ruins. To restore a building stone for stone, when there is a pattern to go by, is much easier than to restore a decoration, for colour is more subtle than stone. Not only has this portion fallen into a dilapidated state, but some one has built a European house in one of the most prominent corners.

Behind this portion of the palace, which is built of red sandstone, there is a beautiful garden, and out of this opens the celebrated bath, decorated with talc and looking-glass, called the Shis-i-Mahal; it is curious, but to my mind somewhat childish in taste.

Agra is celebrated for its inlaid stonework, which art, they say, was introduced into India by Italian workmen. It is said that the Taj, and all the work of that date, was done by Italians. I don't think this can be so. At first, no doubt, the Mohammedan work was an adaptation of the Hindoo style, but finer and rather bolder in its original design. Then came the later style, which has much more delicacy of finish, and employs much more exquisite material—where everything looks like a precious gem, but which to my mind loses in grandeur and originality. Nevertheless it has a beauty of its own, very different from any Italian Renaissance work that I have seen; and I am convinced that, though some Italians may have been employed on it, an Oriental designed it—and a very clever fellow he must have been. The palace at Agra, and that of Delhi, in their fanciful decoration, give one quite a thrill of pleasure. They are all roses and lilies, Swinburne's poems, with melodious rhythm, meaning Heaven knows what, and no one cares what; but they have not the settled beauty that sinks into the mind and lasts.

The fort at Agra has been more spoilt than that at Delhi. At Delhi the ground upon which the buildings stand is flat. At Agra the ground rises till it reaches the Mooti Musjid, which the pious Emperor meant to stand as the crown of his work; and surely no more fitting crown to man's work could be found than this marble temple to the One God. The English Engineer has, however, thought otherwise, and the *ensemble* of this glorious building has been needlessly spoilt by the erection, on an equality with the Musjid, of two stupendous and horrible barracks.

The famous Taj-Mahal is the most perfect specimen I know of the "roses and lilies" art I mentioned above. Not only is it complete in itself, but all its surroundings, and even the approach from Agra, tend to increase its peculiar charms. You leave Agra, and drive under the red and frowning walls of the fort, called in Hindoo poetry the Lal-Kehlah, or Red Fort; then along the banks of the Jumna, with ruins and bare mud hillocks on your right-hand side, the river on your left, and the Taj glittering in the distance; then you turn round to the right and are amidst ruins. On you drive, till you pass under a ruined arch, into a spacious but ruined court; then you stop at a tall gate, mount some steps, and Taj is before you. No ruins there!—a beautiful garden, with a well, paved walks on either side, a long strip of water, flowers, bright-foliaged trees, and dark cypresses,—all that could render the wonderful white marble more white and dazzling by contrast; and above all the blue heaven, or glittering white clouds, that are positively out-glittered by the whiter marble of Shah Jehan.

It is all this that impresses the multitude, and causes them to exclaim, "See the Taj, and die!" It is idle to criticize: the thing is most beautiful, and far be it from me to exclaim, as the French critic makes Michael Angelo's Adam exclaim, "*À quoi bon?*" "Let us eat and drink, for to-morrow we die!" Did Shah Jehan forget Mumtaz-i-Mahal in the glories of the tomb he erected to her memory, even as Mr. Shandy forgot his grief for the death of his firstborn, in thinking of the many beautiful things that had been said, or could be said, on the subject? And Mumtaz-i-Mahal, whose very name has been forgotten by the multitude, who assert that the sepulchre raised by Shah Jehan was built for Noor Jehan, his mother (who they say was his wife), instead of Mumtaz-i-Mahal, the Exalted of the Palace!—did Shah Jehan think, when he was weeping for her, that one of his sons would wage bitter war against him, and imprison him? Roses and lilies! thorns and poisons! Let us enjoy the Taj and such things while we can.—By all this you will see that I am out of spirits, and have been reading my history.

Of the Taj itself there is no need of description. Every one has seen photos innumerable of its white domes: let guides and guide books give the number of rupees it cost, and enumerate the number of workmen employed on it during the seventeen years it was being built. Think not of the misery of the myriads forced to labour without pay, and starved meanwhile by wretched grasping contractors. All these things are for others. For me, the two or three days I spent in the gardens of the Taj were truly delightful. What a change! the smell of roses instead of betel-nut and frowzy rajahs; the wild shrieks of the kite, the cooing of doves, instead of the noise of tom-toms or the gurgle of hubble-bubbles. Nature, in fact, and art. Ah, me! in a day or two I must "rajahfy" again.

The Taj has certainly a wonderful effect on everybody. While painting in the gardens, hundreds of British soldiers tramped in to see "one of the wonders of the world," as I heard one say.

p. 54

THE GARDEN OF THE TAJ, WITH THE TAJ MAHAL IN THE DISTANCE.

"Tommy Atkins's" remarks were curious. One youth exclaimed, "Lor', Jim! what a lot I shall have to say when I next write home." I should like to see the boy's letter: he was young, and has, no doubt, dear ones at home who will wonder at all the things written by their scapegrace. And possibly the Taj will make him write the sooner. Blessings on Shah Jehan! not in vain have all those tears been shed!

Another youthful warrior said, pointing to some repairs that rendered scaffolding necessary on one of the minarets, "It reminds me, Bill, of Lichfield Cathedral: they was always a-doing some repairs to that, I remember." "Home, sweet home." The Taj and Staffordshire!

"I should like to have it in New York as a show, for fifty cents a head," said my matter-of-fact American; but then he is a citizen of the world.

Within the beauteous building side by side lie the royal pair, their tombs inlaid with precious stones. The Faithful even now place flowers on these tombs, and pray to Allah, and to the *burra sahib* for rupees. The English treat the Taj well, and spend much on keeping it in repair; and the grateful Mussulman shows with a shudder the gashes made by the Rajah of Bhurtpore as he forced out the cornelian and jasper flowers from the inlaid tomb with his heathen and ruthless dagger. Maharajah Sindia, or Maharajah Holkar, the cherished and well-hugged friends of His Excellency Lord Lytton, would probably follow the example of His Highness of Bhurtpore had they his chance of occupying Agra.

I am happy to see by the best authority that it was not an Italian that designed the Taj, but the Turk. There is, however, authentic record of one Italian who was employed on the decorations.

On Saturday, 20th January, we left Agra for a couple of days to see Futtehpore Sikree, which is twenty-four miles distant.

The drive thither is delicious; the roads are good, and trees on either side lend their grateful shade. The country, like all of Hindostan I have hitherto seen, is as flat as a pancake; but the plains are green, and Agra and its neighbourhood boast many beautiful trees, some of which are remarkable for their size, and picturesque with their gnarled and twisted trunks. Two hours and a half, and we see the city of Akbar before us. On we roll through the ruined gates, and as we go glance on the formidable walls, seven miles in circumference, which were made for a magnificent city, but where no city ever stood. Up, then, to the fort. On either hand we see two small villages: that to the right Futtehpore, on the other side Sikree, but neither of them covering a fifteenth part of the vast space within the walls. Then we reach the outer court of Akbar's palace, and alight at one of his pavilions, now the *dâk* bungalow.

Then I go round the sights. Akbar, be it remembered, was the contemporary of Queen Elizabeth. He was wedded to a Hindoo princess, who gave him the great Jehanghire. Probably this lady influenced his taste in architecture, for he of all the Moguls was the most ready to employ Hindoo architects and Hindoo forms. Do not think, however, that the great Akbar was a model husband. Far from it. All round his central palace are the small houses of his wives—Turks, Persians, and even, report says, one Christian. Only the largest palace was reserved for the mother of his boy, and goes by the name of the Hindoo Court. Perhaps there was more than one Hindoo princess. On the highest ground, as usual, rises the mosque, and a magnificent one it is, worthy of so great an Emperor. But first for the palace. Truly the ruins are superb. Red sandstone almost as good as marble is the material universally employed, and not a bit of wood for floor, rafter, or roof have I found. This red sandstone takes a wonderful finish, and seems very easy to work. Court after court, pavilion after pavilion have I seen, all wonderfully wrought over with ingenious and beautiful patterns, and all as fresh and sharp in detail as the day they were done; only here and there has it been found necessary to build a prop to support the great weight of all this stone on the roof; and so it all remains, almost as perfect as when the great Emperor left it in disgust. Yet it has been for years uninhabited—in fact, Akbar alone lived here.

> "Men say the lion and the lizard keep
> Their watch where Jamseed revelled and drank deep;"

So here, where the great Emperor feasted, there is no dread, and where the mighty voice gave judgment and the whole world trembled, nought is seen but the timid little grey squirrel, or heard but the cry of the green parrot or the coo of the innocent dove. Two reasons are recorded in history for this desertion. Some say that Akbar lost a favourite son at Futtehpore Sikree, and left the place in disgust. The more likely reason is the want of good water. There is a green and dirty tank, certainly, into which for a small sum certain natives plunge from the height of 80 feet; but I can well imagine, if that is the only water (and I saw none other), that it would not be either pure or wholesome.

They show a most curious *dewan,* in the centre of which rises a broad column, with swelling capital.* From this radiate four causeways leading to the four corners of the room. On the centre column sat Akbar, while the four ministers sat in the four corners. The column is about 12 feet high, and the room is by no means large, 25 feet square at most. This was the Dewan-i-Khas, or Cabinet of Akbar. The Dewan-i-Am, or Public Audience Place, is a large courtyard, particularly plain in its decoration—good enough for the public of his day, no doubt. The whole palace is of Hindoo architecture.

One cannot help wondering at the smallness of the rooms inhabited by this great people. Akbar's room, or rather the one shown as Akbar's room, is 12 feet square. In none of his wives' pavilions are the rooms larger, and the largest has only six such small rooms. I remember, however, when I went round the tents of the Jummoo Maharajah, which were magnificent in size, finding that his Highness of Kashmir himself slept in a tent 8 feet square. What astonished me most was the enormous wealth of ingenious design displayed all over the palace. There was hardly a chamber undecorated with carved work, yet rarely

* A cast of this column is in the South Kensington Museum.

a pattern repeated. Every fruit and flower was represented, and in one pavilion birds and beasts; but the bigoted Aurungzebe had, they say, with his own hand chopped off and obliterated all trace of their heads. *Àpropos* of Aurungzebe, in my historical reading I came across a curious protest against the religious persecutions of that monarch, addressed to him by one of his *sirdars*, the Maharana of Oodeypore, which I wish to record. It ends thus:

"Pagans and Moslems stand alike before the great God. In your mosques it is in His Name that the call to prayer is uttered. In the house of idols, where the bell is rung, it is still He that is the object of adoration. To vilify the religious customs of other men is to set at nought the will of the Almighty. When we deface a picture we necessarily incur the resentment of the painter."

The mosque here is one of the most famous in India, and is certainly one of the most beautiful. The courtyard is nearly as big as that of the Jumma Musjid at Delhi, but the great gate does not face the mosque proper, which is curious; the gate, however, was built fifty years after the rest of the mosque.

On the south side is the celebrated marble tomb of Selim Shisti, a saintly man, who was Akbar's parson. The traceries of his tomb are the most elaborate I have yet seen, and inside are what I imagine to be the earliest attempts at mural painting on white marble. I was very pleased to see these, as they are clumsier than either the decorations at the Dewan-i-Khas at Delhi or in the fort at Agra, and, though the same kind of thing, clearly the work of Hindoo artists. This proves to me that the later work was not, as some people suppose, inspired by Italians. The tomb proper of the saint is like a large four-post bedstead, and has been beautifully inlaid with mother-of-pearl. Alas! the upper part has been ruthlessly destroyed, and the legs alone remain perfect to show the beauty and delicacy of the design.

They tell a curious story of Selim Shisti. One day his infant son asked his father why he looked so sad. "Alas!" said the saint, "I have had a revelation that our lord and master, Akbar will never have a son unless some sinless being is willing to sacrifice his life." "That I will do," said the boy, and straightway died, and here he lies; and, after three hundred years, ladies who desire male heirs make pilgrimages to his tomb, and branches of a tree that grows thereby are, if plucked and taken away, sure preventives against fever and all the ills flesh is heir to. Even the traceries around the Saint Selim's tomb are covered with little bits of worsted, tied there by heirless ladies!

The mosque proper is on the west side of the courtyard, looking, therefore, east. It is of the usual shape, one large arch leading to an inner shrine. All the courtyard round is Hindoo in character, but this mosque has the pointed arch of the Moslem. The decorations inside are most beautiful,—not roses and lilies here. Every part of the walls, roof and all, is covered with designs, all of them most original and fine: some are geometric patterns, made of inlaid marble and painted pieces of vitreous tile; some are panels painted on the stone itself. But the richness and beauty of the whole has, so far as I have seen, never been surpassed. *Àpropos* of tiles, I have never seen a painted tile in India: all I have seen have been cut into shape, are of one colour, and are used as mosaic to make the pattern.

One thing I noticed in this mosque as differing from anything I have seen in India, and yet recalling an English tradition—the whole of the great gate, as far as a man can reach, is covered with horse-shoes nailed on the wood of the door, and making a curious decoration.

While I have been busy looking round the wonders of the place, my friend G—— has been out shooting. He was much excited on the way here by seeing a herd of antelopes.

"I am not going to look at ruins, while there is anything to shoot," said he; and off he started, with a *shikaree* from the village, and several coolies. Late in the evening he returned.

"Well, where is the black buck?"

"I haven't got any."

"What! not a shot?"

"Why, yes," he said; "I saw one herd, when all my coolies

shouted '*Harrin! harrin!*' as if they were all stark staring mad, and I hadn't got eyes to my head, and of course away they went. I let 'em have it, but missed 'em. I caught one of those coolies I beckoned to, and cuffed him round a ten-acre lot."

"Good gracious!" cried I; "recollect you are in India, and might have ruptured the man's spleen."

"I did not care," he said. "I was so riled, I 'booted' him, I can tell you."

He is a very good fellow, and most useful at a bargain, only sentiment is not his line.

For myself, I have made two sketches of the Taj, which I hope to finish to-morrow, when I return to Agra, and here one sketch. I have also drawn many of the patterns here, which will be very useful in many ways.

On Monday, the 22nd January, we returned to Agra, and I spent the afternoon again on the Taj. On Tuesday I went to the jail, which is one of the best places for the manufacture of carpets in India. I had never been in a prison before. Here they have 2,400 human beings, all dressed alike. They all squat down as you pass, smack their hands, and produce their prison number. One poor feeble old fellow was lying in the corner of one of the sleeping-huts. Dr. Tyler, the obliging superintendent of the jail, touched him with the end of his stick, and he raised his poor old hands and pitiful face, crying, "I am cold and ill." Dr. Tyler ordered him to be taken to the sun.

"He is an old prisoner," he said; "he has been here since eighteen thirty-seven."

Fancy, the year before I was born! He was a Thug, and consequently did not benefit by the declaration of the empire, when two hundred prisoners were released by the Empress's kindness.

The carpets here are very good—but too good. As specimens of manufacture they would hold their own against any carpets made. Dr. Tyler showed us by the backs how well every thread was brought home, &c.; but I was obliged to confess, artistically, they were a sad falling off from the carpets of other places, which as manufactures were much inferior. I saw some made for

R——, K——, and others, where the colours were rather crude, and the manufacture looked like drugget. This place is one of the instances of well-intentioned effort failing from want of artistic knowledge. I was informed that the men who were taught carpet-making here, when liberated invariably went back to their old pursuit, generally agriculture, although they could earn more than twice as much by making carpets.

In one court we passed a man condemned to death for the murder of a boy. He was shamming madness, and his gestures and cries as he squatted on the ground in the sun (watched by two warders and chained heavily) were very weird. He had committed an atrocious murder. One could not have much pity for such a wretch, but the sight of him continued to haunt me all day.

At twelve I was back again at the Taj, where, by the courtesy of the gentleman who looks after the garden, water had been run into the straight tanks leading up the central avenue, which have been lately dry, owing to their leaking. The long reflections of the white marble much improve the magic of the effect.

The gardens are particularly well managed. There are two rose gardens and lawns, quite English, with good turf. Perhaps they may be out of place here, but the green must be grateful even to the eye of the native, and to the Englishman recalls many pleasant places in the old country. Mr. Smith, the gardener, showed me one tree, a cotton-tree, which he says was four hundred years old, and consequently stood here before the Taj existed. Possibly this is so, and Akbar and Shah Jehan feasted and drank (they did drink, though Moslems) beneath its shade. Yet here it is, green and flowering. What a life! The tree is 45 feet in circumference.

By eleven o'clock on Tuesday evening we found ourselves in two *dâk gharries*, bumping along towards Gwalior. A *dâk gharry* is an extraordinary-looking vehicle, something between a four-wheel cab and a hearse. It is painted green, has a double roof, and solid blinds instead of glass windows. The centre between the seats is boarded up, and the traveller reclines at full length, and sleeps if he can. Into this strange vehicle two little horses are harnessed, one in the shafts and one on the near side, and off we go at a gallop, while the driver blows a horn to prepare the way. They change horses every six miles, and manage to get you along, including stoppages, about that distance every hour. On the roof your luggage is piled, and your servant with it. It is extraordinary how these fellows curl themselves up, and sleep anywhere, in balcony or passage. No one ever pays the slightest attention to them, and they look like bundles of clothes lying about. I am reminded, by finding my bearer in all sorts of corners, of the account in St. Simon, of the death of Monseigneur, eldest son of Louis XIV. He and some others were talking rather openly against the lately deceased man, thinking no one was by, when one of them touched a bed in the passage where they were, and out of it rose a half-dressed Swiss Guard. They all hurried away in great fear lest they had been overheard. Well, these fellows, if they understand the language, must hear funny things, for they sleep everywhere.

The road from Agra to Gwalior is not bad, luckily, yet even on these roads the jolting of the *gharry* was such as to "give me to think" of the many miles I have to travel thus during the next month or two. I slept notwithstanding, but in a fitful way, constantly awakened by the wretched too-tooing of the driver's horn. At 3.30 we crossed the famous river Chambal, and at eight sighted the still more famous port of Gwalior, about which so much has been written lately, and at half-past nine reached Gwalior itself, from which place I am writing.

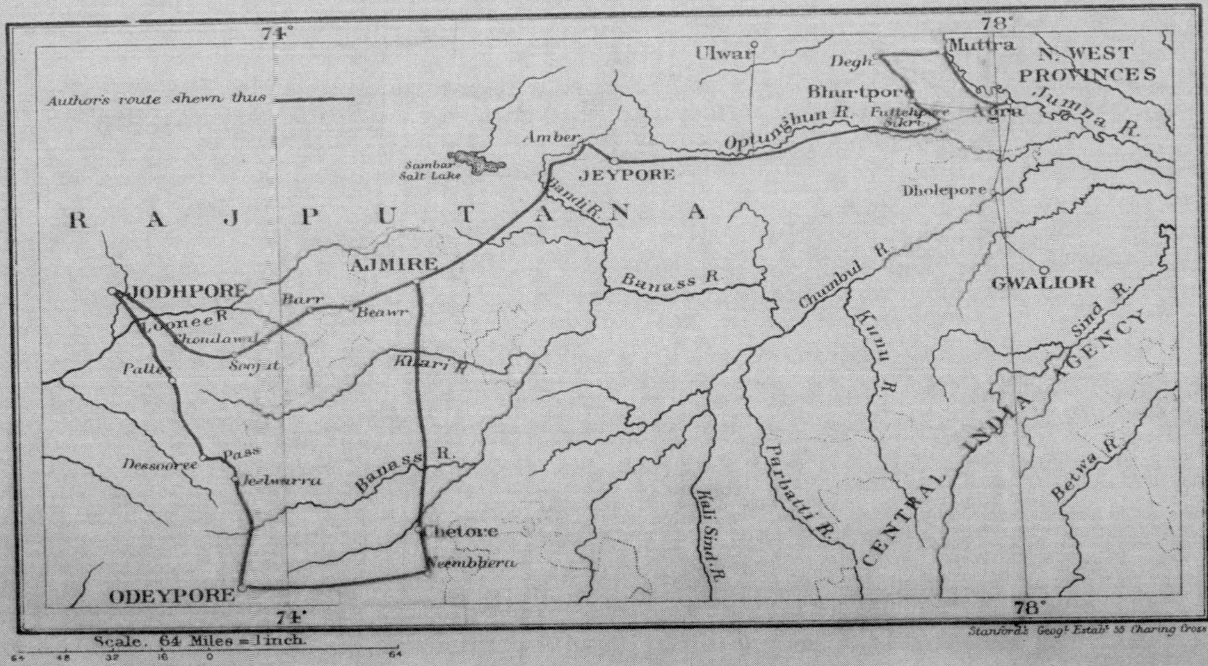
74°
78°
Author's route shewn thus
R A J P U T A N A
JODHPORE
Loonee R.
Choondawal
Soojat
Pallee
Barr
Beawr
AJMIRE
Sambar Salt Lake
Amber
JEYPORE
Bandi R.
Banass R.
Khari R.
Pass
Dessooree
Jeelwarra
Chetore
Neembhera
ODEYPORE
Ulwar
Degh
Bhurtpore
Muttra
N. WEST PROVINCES
Jumna R.
Agra
Futtehpore Sikri
Optunghun R.
Dholepore
GWALIOR
Chumbul R.
Kunu R.
Sind R.
CENTRAL INDIA AGENCY
Betwa R.
Parbatti R.
Kali Sind R.
Scale. 64 Miles = 1 inch.
64 48 32 16 0 64
Stanford's Geog! Estab! 55 Charing Cross

## CHAPTER V.

### GWALIOR AND DHOLEPORE.

*26th January.*

GWALIOR is the capital of Maharajah Sindia. It may be said to consist of three parts—modern Gwalior, which is called by the natives Luskar, or The Camp; the old fort and town; and the cantonments, or Morar. Coming in by *dâk*, we stopped at Old Gwalior, on the north of the fort. Here there is nothing but a *dâk* bungalow and a few houses. South rises the long line of sandstone on which is built the fort, and which is a mile and three-quarters in length. We quickly perceived that this would not do, had our things re-packed in the *gharries*, and drove to the cantonments, six miles off. Of Luskar, or Gwalior town, we saw nothing, except the glitter of Sindia's new palace in the distance. We stopped and breakfasted with Sir Henry Daly, who is Governor-General's Agent in Central India, and then drove to the *dâk* bungalow, in the cantonments. Sindia ought to have put me up at his own *dâk* bungalow, but he excused himself by saying that he had lately enclosed it with a wall, and that it was now in his women's garden. Altogether, the Maharajah has behaved very badly to me. The policy of the Government appears to humour him in all things, and I have been partly sacrificed, as the sequel shows.

Morar, where the Europeans live, is a pleasant place enough; the roads are broad and good, the trees shady, and the bungalows pleasant. Sir Henry, too, was personally most kind, and invited us to dinner. He said that Mohurrum was being celebrated (it took place yesterday and to-day), and that he had great difficulty in getting the Maharajah to give a sitting for the 25th, but that on the 26th it was impossible, as it was *Durwaza bund*,* and he could see no one during the Mohurrum. I amused myself during the day by painting a copy of the head I had begun at Delhi, and had got it into a good state to be worked upon the next day, Thursday, 25th January, when I was to go with Daly to the palace, by appointment, at one o'clock. I had brought a Parsee boy from Bombay, who came with a good character, but who turned out utterly useless. On Thursday I told him to pack up my new picture, and particularly not to take my old one. Off we started, and, after half an hour's drive, came to the new palace. This has been built by a European in the Maharajah's service. It is of considerable extent, and was got ready first for the Prince of Wales during his visit. Architecturally it is not a triumph, being a base sort of Renaissance; but it is considered something quite extraordinary here, where such things are rare. We drive into a courtyard, go up a staircase of marble, and are received by Sindia in person. Of all the rajahs, he is most powerful, but certainly, of all I have seen, has the least etiquette. He is very comic in his own palace, where he looks like a respectable *baboo*. The palace itself is an odd jumble of all kinds of funny decorations. Hanging from the stairs are lines of chandelier-drops. The principal room is a fine large place with white and gold decorations, and two enormous chandeliers, which cost, they say, £2,000 apiece; altogether, His Highness is great in cut glass. The room is lighted with semicircular windows, filled with the common coloured glass which one sees in lodging-houses at home. They say the decorations (white and gold) were all done here in Gwalior, and that it was a wonderful feat. Like Doctor Johnson, I felt inclined to say, "Sir, I wish it was not only wonderful, but impossible." Round this central room are several handsome apartments, in one of which down squats the Maharajah, the courtiers group around, and I am to begin. Imagine, then, my horror at finding that my brilliant Parsee had left my new picture, and only

* *Durwaza bund* means literally "door closed," or as we would say, "not at home."

brought the old one covered with dust, and sunk in! I confess I lost my temper as I have not done for a long time, and cursed him audibly. If the Maharajah had not been there, I believe I

HIS HIGHNESS JAIAJI RAO SINDIA, MAHARAJAH OF GWALIOR.

should have kicked him, and run the chance of rupturing his spleen. Here was I, after ten hours' *dâk* and several days' travel, with my only chance of painting the great Sindia, and utterly unprepared!

I was so angry that I could not work even at my old study. Meanwhile, Sir Henry Daly, one of the *burra sahibs* of the service, was doing his best to amuse Sindia, and talking of all sorts of things. It was too sad.

Sindia is the worst sitter I have yet had to contend with. He is not steady for a moment. "If Sir Henry were not here I wouldn't sit at all," he said; also, "This is worse than the hardest day's *pooja* (praying) I ever had; and after all, what is the use? I don't get anything by it." With all this, however, he was not in a bad humour, and laughed a great deal. Meanwhile here was I toiling away, I felt, to no purpose. I shall not forget that morning, I can tell you. I tried in vain to pull myself together, both for Daly's sake and my own, but it would not come. I was obliged to say at last, when I saw it was impossible to keep him any longer, "There, that will do," with the happy consciousness of having made a "mull."

In the room were two very comic full-length portraits of the Maharajah, one by a native, done from a photograph, extraordinarily worked up to look like a nightmare, and the other by Mr. M. W., which looked like a picture from the New Road.

If anybody in future tries to paint Sindia, let him do it from a photograph, for Jaiaji Rao Sindia will, I am convinced, never give an artist a chance of painting him from nature. The moment Daly said the sitting was over, up jumped the Maharajah and bolted from the room.

When talking and animated, Sindia has rather a pleasing face. He can be charming and do graceful things. At the Delhi Assembly he made a very good speech, which—as it was never, I believe, reported—I give from Sir Henry Daly's translation. After the Viceroy's address, Sindia had to speak.

"Are you ready?" said Daly, who was sitting next to him. Sindia nodded. "Let it be short, and with plenty in it."

Up jumped His Highness and said (and I heard every word, though, of course, I did not understand): "Shah-in-Shah, Padishah! the Princes of India greet you. May you enjoy long life and happiness, and may your Raj last for ever!"

Nevertheless His Highness does not know what is due to an artist who has come a hundred miles for a sitting. I am now to get a photograph of him in his jewels, and a coat and a hat, from which to paint him.

The first Sindia was slipper-bearer to the first Peishwa. One day, so goes the tale, the Peishwa coming out unexpectedly found Ranoji Sindia asleep, with his slippers firmly clutched in his arms. Conceiving a high opinion of one who was so faithful to a small trust, the Peishwa gave him a post in his body-guard; from which he rose. The Sindias, though so proud now, are descended from this slipper-bearer of this Peishwa, who was himself only Prime Minister or rather Mayor of the Palace to the descendants of Sivaji. Madaji Rao Sindia, whose genius first formed the power of the family, and who was at one time all-powerful from Delhi to the Nerbudda, always acknowledged the superiority of the Peishwa. On one occasion when the master had reason to be dissatisfied with the servant, Sindia suddenly appeared at Court. He approached the Peishwa with great humility, and said he had never forgotten he was but his slipper-bearer. He then stooped, drew off the Peishwa's slippers, and furnished him from beneath his clothing with a new pair. The old ones he carried away with him: they say they are still at Gwalior. It would be well if Jaiaji Rao, the present Sindia, could have them presented to him when he is in some of his haughtier moods, to remind him of what his ancestors were.

We were invited with Sir Henry to go with Sindia to see how the Mohurrum is kept in Gwalior. We drove to the palace, and there took elephant. I do not know what Gwalior, or rather Luskar, is by daylight; by torchlight it is the most picturesque thing I have seen. Sindia is a Maratha, and consequently a Hindoo by religion. But Marathas have made a compromise with Mohammedans, and keep all their feasts, the Mohammedans returning the compliment.

This compromise was made when Madaji Rao first made conquests in Hindostan. Sivaji, the first Maratha sovereign, was the starter of the great Hindoo revival that changed the state of

India; but his revival was essentially Hindoo, and none but Hindoos filled all the offices of trust and command in the new Maratha confederacy. Madaji Rao first somewhat broke through this rule. Finding so many Moslems, Patans, and Pindarrees joining his standard, he trimmed his religion to the breeze of fortune. He was always in search of popularity, and never gave himself any of the airs of a sovereign, though he was virtually much more powerful than the Peishwa he served. Both he and Holkar wished to be considered merely *potails* or head men of villages in the Maratha State; hence it is a common saying in Hindostan that "Madaji Sindia made himself the sovereign of an empire by calling himself a *potail* or head man of a village." When the Peishwa was going to war with the English, he wrote to Daolut Rao, Madaji's adopted son and real great-nephew, who was supposed to be friendly to the English, "Your father, Madaji Sindia, agreeably to the orders of the Sircar (the Peishwa), went to Delhi, was made a vizier, and acquired a high reputation. He served us with his heart and soul. When you became his successor you entered into an alliance with the English. Thus you govern in Hindostan, and thus you show your gratitude. In thus serving us it is befitting you to put bangles on your arms, and sit down like a woman. After my power is destroyed, is it possible yours should stand?"*

Daolut Rao, when he read the above, was in much distress for two hours; he then went to sleep. But he sent no answer. Daolut Rao had none of the great qualities of the son of the slipper-bearer. Jaiaji Rao, the present Sindia, is ever a seeker of popularity. Does he hope to rival Madaji Rao in greatness? Who knows?

Now all was gay in Gwalior. The Mohurrum is, I believe, instituted to commemorate the death and martyrdom of Hassan and Hosein, the sons of Ali and grandsons of Mahomet. Why everybody should be in a state of wild delight I do not know, or why the Hindoos and Moslems alike should build enormous

* This is from Malcolm's "Central India," a capital and most entertaining book.

temples of gold and silver tinsel, at great expense, to be afterwards buried or tossed into the river, I have failed to discover. Anyhow, everybody was shouting, "tom-toming," and excited, and the streets were full of these glittering temples. The Maharajah on an elephant, preceded by torchbearers, and followed by us also on elephant-back, with difficulty worked his way through the crowd. Up to the housetops, every place was crowded. Long rows of squatting men and women in all kinds of shining drapery are the best artistic decoration I know; the houses, too, are most picturesque, with many pierced windows and balconies. Besides the torchlight, ever and anon some one would fire Bengal lights, and show the houses and their many-coloured lines of squatting natives to great advantage. "Wah Maharajah Sahib!" cry the natives, and bow to the ground before Sindia. The *shroffs* or money-dealers of Gwalior are said to be the richest in India, and accordingly we had the usual barbaric display—coloured glasses and cheap pictures, to be found in every well-to-do native's house, and on occasions of this kind hung all over the walls outside. At the door of each house was its owner, to *salaam* to his Maharajah, and many received a greeting from his Highness in return. How different this would be in the English states, with their cold, unsympathetic rule!

At length we come to a kind of place where the elephants are wheeled round, and, at a sign from Sindia, a kind of march past of these miniature temples begins. How they manage to get through the crowd is a wonder, for the whole place, from our elephants to the elephants which lined the opposite side, was a sea of heads. The turbans were all kinds of colours and shapes, and looked, being packed close together, like a box of roses prepared for a journey. On passed temple after temple, some 20 feet high, and all turned round before the Maharajah. All too were accompanied with tom-toms, drums, horns, and a peculiar cymbal worked on a kind of stick with tremendous energy. Before some of these temples there went a devotee, who swayed himself backwards and forwards, continually crying in an agonized voice, "*Hassan, Hosein! Hassan, Hosein!*" He was always supported by two men, or he must have fallen. Once the procession stops for a curious display of sword dance, and once to show the contortions of some excellent tumblers; and there Sindia sat for hours,—the same Sindia who could not sit ten minutes for his picture,—and there we left him to make a night of it. I hear he was out again the next day. Verily there is no accounting for taste. The scene was one of the most striking sights I have ever seen, yet two hours of it and it became somewhat monotonous. Temples of tinsel are much alike; once only we had a variation in the shape of a wonderful animal, with the body of a bird and the head of a white woman; and once too a case with two figures, also white, which looked like women, but possibly might have been intended for Hassan and Hosein.

What the natives enjoyed in the business was the row and *tomasha*. Our servants went out to see it next day, but none of them knew what it was all about. One, a Mohammedan, knew that some one had died that day, but could not say who it was.

The architecture here is very curious; the patterns of the windows and balconies most original and beautiful. I asked Daly whether it would be possible to get any made like them. He said Jeypore was the place to see such things, and as everybody says the same thing, I must wait till I get to Jeypore. I was disappointed of my carriage on Friday, and spent the day trying to relieve my mishap of Thursday, and make something of a portrait from memory and from what I had already done. I think I have somehow painted something recognizable.

On Saturday again the carriage promised by Sindia did not come, which was too bad. Yesterday he sent to say that all the carriages had been out all night at the Mohurrum, but that excuse could not apply to to-day. There was to be a garrison meeting and sports in the afternoon, called the Sindia Sports, as Sindia had given the prizes, and this, with rage in my heart, I had resolved to attend. His Highness was there, and as it was the first time for five years that he had been into the cantonments, he was well received. I had determined to start that night for Dholepore, my next rajah; but as Sindia said he would certainly sit for his photo the next day, and promised also to send a carriage to take us to, and elephants to take us over, the fort, I relented.

The sports were but poor fun, the only good show being the tent-pegging and camel race. I had never seen tent-pegging before. It is a fine sport, and well worth seeing, though I believe the fellows here do not do it so well as the Punjaubees. The race of the day for Sindia's cup was a mile race, open to Europeans and natives. To the surprise of all, natives were first and second; the third was an artilleryman. He was much done on reaching the post, and could only gasp and point to the winner. It turned out that No. 1 had quietly sat down half-way, and joined the runners on their return journey, and that there were great doubts as to whether No. 2 had been round the post. Verily the native is a slippery and artful being.

*28th.*—At 7 a.m. the promised carriage arrived, and off we started. At the foot of the hill we took elephant. Gwalior fort is approached by a very steep incline, with several gates. On the top is a very fine old palace, with curious decorations, consisting of bands of blue, green, and yellow tiles let into the stones; one band is composed of ducks and geese, and one has occasional elephants. The whole is much out of repair. The perpendicular sides of the great rock on which is the fort (for fortifications proper there are none) are much carved. Many temples are hollowed out, and there are some colossal figures, showing, as one might expect from its situation, that it was a stronghold and place of residence in most remote ages. On the plateau, at the top, there are two temples very highly decorated and most interesting from the sculptures on them, which are full of "go." * There are also several tanks. The British have marred the whole by their abominable barracks.

This fortress of Gwalior was used as a state prison by the Moguls. It was here that the unsuccessful competitors for the

* There is a very full description of the temples and architecture of Gwalior in Rousselet's "Rajahs of India." He attributes all the buildings to the Jains, who were no doubt the great builders of India.

imperial throne were consigned to a lingering death. Bernier, who was an eye-witness, describes the interview between Soliman Chekouh, the son of Dara, Aurungzebe's elder brother, and the Emperor. It must be remembered that Dara had been defeated, hunted down, and killed shortly before.

"Aurungzebe, that nobody might doubt it was Soliman Chekouh himself, commanded him to be brought before him in the presence of all the grandees of the Court. At the entry of the gate the chains were taken from his feet, leaving those he had about his hands, which seemed gilt. When this proper young man, so handsome and gallant, was seen to enter, there were a good number of omrahs that could not hold their tears; and, as I was informed, all the great ladies of the Court that had leave to see him come in, fell a-weeping. Aurungzebe, who appeared himself to be touched at his misfortunes, began to speak very kindly to him and to comfort him; telling him, amongst other things, to fear nothing, that no hurt should be done to him; that he had caused his father to be put to death for no other reason than that he had turned *kafir*, and a man without religion. Whereupon this young prince returned him the *salaam* and blessed him, abasing his hands to the earth, and lifting them as well as he could up to his head, after the custom of his country; and told him, with resolution enough, that if he were to drink *poust*, he entreated him that he might die presently, being very willing to submit to his fate. But Aurungzebe promised him publicly that he should drink none of it, that he should rest satisfied of that, and not entertain any sad thoughts about it. This being said, he once more repeated the *salaam*, and was sent to Gwalior with the rest. This *poust* is nothing else than poppy expressed and infused a night in water. And it is that potion which those that are kept at Gwalior are commonly made to drink; I mean those princes whose heads they think not to cut off. This is the first thing that is brought them in the morning, and they have nothing given them to eat till they have drunk a great cupful of it; and they would rather let them starve. This emaciates them exceedingly, and maketh them die insensibly, they losing little by little their understanding, and growing torpid and senseless. And by this means it is said that Sepe Chekouh and the grandchild of Morad Baksh, and Soliman Chekouh, were dispatched. Morad Baksh," Bernier proceeds to say, "was thought so dangerous that his head was given to the family of a certain Syed, or descendant of Mahomet, who had himself suffered death by order of the unfortunate Morad, when Governor of 'Amadevat' (Ahmedabad). This retributive justice was carried out in Gwalior." What other tales of smaller victims to imperial policy these walls could tell! And if they were given up to Sindia, to what use would they be put? Surely the most innocent things ever imprisoned in Gwalior are those 45-pounders shut up in store, but ready for use, should occasion require it!

As a fortress against a civilized foe, Gwalior would be of little use, since it could be bombarded from at least two sides from adjacent hills, and there are, as I said above, no real fortifications. Its only strength is from its position, rising as it does from the plain, with only two possible ways of entering; also from the fact that neither Sindia nor any other rajah has artillery of sufficient calibre to silence the 40-pounders we have there. No wonder it is a sore thorn in the poor Maharajah's side, for it commands not only his palace, but the new town of Gwalior (Luskar), and it would be easy to destroy either in half an hour.

At 2 p.m. I was punctually at the palace, and found Bulwant Rao (Sindia's natural son, and a very good lad, who talks English), with his photographic machine ready.

While waiting for Sindia to put on his jewels, I had the honour of being photographed myself, and, judging from the negative, the result was pretty successful.

I have been anxious to get a turban, or *pugree*, of the Maharajah's, and a coat; but Bulwant Rao informed me that he thought there was a religious prejudice against giving any such things. Presently in comes Sindia; he was in a capital temper, and I had a long conversation with him, and finally, on my leaving, I received my turban from my friend Bulwant Rao, with an intimation that the Maharajah, as a special mark of favour, gave it to me to show the people of England how the Marathas were dressed.

I saw some of Sindia's jewels, diamonds, with very fine inlaid work at the back, which inlay is generally supposed to be the speciality of Jeypore. Sindia, however, assured me that it was all done here in Gwalior, but that the process was a secret. Altogether, I was more pleased with His Highness on this visit than I expected. He is very fond of children: one little chap of about five came up and saluted him, and the Maharajah's face quite lit up. It is a pity he came to the throne so soon, and had no education.

Some months after this I was painting the Rajah of Nabha Sikh. He sat beautifully, so well that I said, "You sit much better than Maharajah Sindia, who said sitting was harder than the hardest day's *pooja*."

Nabha laughed, and said, "It was not sitting Sindia found so unpleasant, it was being obliged to sit."

Nabha was no doubt right. In my experience of great rajahs, I always found my position, as accredited painter to the Government, led to my being viewed with suspicion. This, of course, should not be. But rajahs are but children.

To-morrow morning I go to Dholepore.

*29th January.*

Dholepore is a small strip of country about eighty miles by thirty, lying along the river Chambal, which divides it from Gwalior. Originally, the Rana of Dholepore possessed a large tract, called Gohad, on the farther side of the Chambal; but Madaji Rao Sindia and his descendants annexed it during the Maratha troubles. There is, therefore, no love lost between the Rana of Dholepore and Sindia, and this hereditary enmity has been increased by the fact that when the English took Gwalior Fort, they handed it over to the charge of the ancestor of the present Rana.

Dholepore is thirty miles from Gwalior on the Agra road. It

took us five hours to reach it, and we found a hearty welcome in Major Dennehy, the political agent, and his family, whose hospitality is proverbial through this part of India.

The Rana is a small boy of thirteen, who speaks English as well as an English boy, and runs about the Dennehys' house as if he were one of their children. He is not pretty, having a very retreating chin and rather projecting teeth, but he is very intelligent, with a great feeling for humour. Altogether, he is a very attractive boy, and we got on splendidly together.

Of Dholepore I have very little to say, as the town is poor and squalid, with no good buildings. There is a good tomb of one of Akbar's generals, Sadik Mohammed Khan; and a curious tank, supplied by a spring, which is said to have sprung up at the bidding of Krishna; it is consequently surrounded with temples, and is considered a very holy place.

The little Rana tried to give us some cheetah hunting, but it would not come off, as, when we found deer (and they were scarce enough), we could not get the cheetah, and of course *vice versâ*.

The Dennehys live in truly patriarchal style. Their home at present is the place which, when the Rana grows up and comes to his own, will be used as a *durbar* house. The house, therefore, is really one large room. In this room are found during the day all kinds of *sirdars* and officers waiting for an audience, and among all romps the little Rana.

Three years ago, when we undertook the management of Dholepore, he was a sickly lad, who required three men to hold him on horseback: now he is strong and healthy, rides to hounds which he hunts himself, plays polo, and is up to any fun. His mother, the ruling Ranee, is a sister of the late Rajah of Puttiala. At first she objected to the English education for her son, but being a reasonable woman (fancy that!), she has quite given in; and, except when eating and sleeping, the boy is always at the Dennehys'. The difficulty is to get him to go home at all. If he had been left to his mother and Indian ways, he would have been married, and quite ruined in health and mind; so in some things we English have done some good.

The Ranee has a curious history. She was married at twelve to the son of the then reigning Rana of Dholepore, a boy of the same age, and took an extreme dislike to her husband at first sight; indeed, the first interview between them resulted in a fight, and the high priest had to be called in to separate them. A marriage begun under such unfavourable auspices could not, of course, be expected to turn out well. Luckily, the father-in-law became very fond of the Ranee, and took her part. Now, the lady had brought from Puttiala thirteen ladies of honour, and on one of them the husband fixed his amorous eyes. The Ranee was furious, and such a row ensued that she was sent in disgrace to a fort, which was to be a prison, some distance off. From this she contrived to escape to Puttiala, and there the boy was born. The Rana (*père*) was naturally anxious to have the charge of his grandchild and heir, but the lady was resolute, and only consented to return when her woman (the favoured of her husband) should be given up to her. The husband yielded; the lady returned; and the favoured one was sent to the fort instead of the wife. She took the precaution of cooking her own food, poor woman; but, curiously enough, died three days afterwards. It is curious, too, that the present Rana succeeded his grandfather.

This is only one of the stories of the Zenana that I have heard. Fancy what a world of intrigue it must be, and a world into which no man able to record its life, with its passions, joys, and tears, has ever been able fairly to penetrate. Unhappily, most of these Indian ladies are too uneducated to write their experiences.

Early marriages are the curse of the country. Husband and wife are both children; they have, of course, never met before marriage, and are often weary of each other before either has arrived at the age when Europeans marry. I was pointed out a young fellow of seventeen who had been a father three years! Of course children of such marriages are far from strong. The lady's only anxiety is to keep the matrimonial couch from any lawful rival, and she encourages all other peccadilloes so long as she is not disturbed in her supremacy in the Zenana. The intrigues by which all this is kept up are wonderful. The following story is worth recording as *trait des mœurs*, even at the risk of offending not only the high and mighty persons therein concerned, but the Indian Government.

A great Maharajah, then, had once a favourite, of whom, in the course of time, he grew tired. To save expense, she was allowed to return to her relatives, with a small pension. There she attracted the attentions of a worthy *baboo*,* who married her. The husband was a sharp fellow, and rose in the Government service. Meanwhile the Maharajah heard that his quondam favourite was married, and being worked on by his courtiers to consider himself insulted, he started, with a small retinue, and *incog.*, for the city where the fair one resided with her *baboo* husband, in order to bring her back. The lady, however, heard of his coming, and received him with shut doors. In vain His Highness tried to persuade her, by promises, to return to him; probably she knew what would be her fate, and she remained firm. He then tried threats, and proceeded to batter down the door. But the husband was by, and had taken the precaution to have some police handy, and the Maharajah was actually taken prisoner to the police station. He was of course recognized, and escaped in disgrace, after having been soundly rated by the representative of the English Government.

These princes are all like boys, and spend their whole time in trying to aggrandize themselves and improve their position, not in an open way, but by intrigues. Of course there are honourable exceptions.

One of these was Puttiala, and this is how he was said to have ended his days:—He was very popular, and was thought to be quite above all his fellows,—in fact, quite English at heart. Well, he had one European fault, a weakness for brandy. He invented a drink, which goes by the name of the Puttiala Peg,† consisting of half champagne, half brandy; and this you may imagine had

* Hindoo gentleman of the middle class.

† A Peg is in India ordinarily composed of brandy and soda-water. The

very rapid action in this country; and if the Maharajah had not *delirium tremens*, he had something so very like it that he may be said to have lost all control over his actions. He imprisoned a number of people without any reason; he is said to have killed his wife, the mother of his children,—but of this I have no proof,—and finally he died from some disease brought on, as the English doctors say, by drink, but the natives firmly believe by poison. It is curious how very seasonably many chief swells die here. Probably toxicology is practiced in other places than Baroda.* At Dholepore much native prejudice has been broken down by the open style of living practised by Major Dennehy. Not only is the Rana always there, but even the high priest is constantly to be seen playing at Indian backgammon, and otherwise making himself at home. It would have done some fox-hunting parsons good to have seen the reverend gentleman on a strong nag out cheetah hunting; and I have even seen him playing at lawn tennis. The Rajah's constant attendant is a high-classed Brahmin called Gôpi, who acts as his Master of the Horse, and not only goes out hunting, but looks after the hounds, and "whips." He is, moreover, a most merry and obliging person. The day we went out cheetah hunting, owing to the stupidity of my servant, I had not been called before sunrise, and while I was at my early toilet, who should appear but His Highness and Gôpi, and the Brahmin actually buttoned my braces for me! Yet the Ranee, when asked why she did not show herself to the world, said, "I have no objection myself, but I am afraid. My brother (Puttiala) would probably kill me."

We had an audience with her in the palace, if palace it can be called. We were taken to a small verandah, opening into which

name is supposed to imply that every time it is imbibed a peg is driven into your coffin.

* Every compound or garden has growing in it the *datura*, a most deadly poison, whose effects depend on the quantity used. Many people are drugged with this, and, losing all command over themselves, are robbed with impunity. One case I heard of where several men had been robbed; it was being investigated while I was at Ulwar. The men recovered from the effects of the poison after a time, but were quite out of their minds for some days.

HIS HIGHNESS THE RANA OF DHOLEPORE.

were two pierced windows, and a door on which hung a thick wadded silk *purdah* or hanging. On each side of one of the windows were placed chairs; inside the window was quite dark; probably there, too, was a *purdah*. Major Dennehy talked through the window, and presently a voice answered. It sounded like a sweet voice; but even Ranees suffer from cold, and a "snuffle" would destroy the voice of a Grisi.

Mrs. Dennehy says she is very handsome and regal in her manner, and also full of talent. Fancy such a woman spending her whole life behind a thick curtain!

Native women are, amongst themselves, tremendous gamblers, and spend most of their time at backgammon or cards.

I painted a tolerable study of the little Rana, of which even the Ranee expressed her approval, and on 1st February left Dholepore with great regret. It has been quite a contrast from the difficulties I had with Sindia, to find here a Rajah who asked me to fix my own time, and sat well. The Dennehys, too, were most civil and hospitable, and seemed to have brought the customs of Ould Ireland to the wilds of Rajpootana.

# CHAPTER VI.

## BHURTPORE AND JEYPORE.

*3rd February.*

ON arriving at Agra I found a telegram from the Maharajah of Bhurtpore, asking me to come to Deeg to paint him. As Deeg is one of the curiosities of this part of India, and only twenty-one miles from Bhurtpore Station, I was not sorry to have the chance of seeing it. We left Agra by the 6 a.m. train, and travelled by the Rajpootana Railway, which is one of the new-fashioned narrow-gauge lines said to be singularly adapted for India. If slowness forms a qualification, surely the narrow gauge is well qualified, for we were really three hours going thirty-two miles!

At Bhurtpore we were met by a *vakeel* of the Maharajah's, who took us to his *dâk* bungalow to breakfast. A *dâk* bungalow is one of the institutions of India. It is generally a well-built house, with tolerably clean rooms, each room having an outer room for washing, &c., and as furniture, a table, two arm-chairs, always of the same cane-bottomed pattern, and a *charpoy* or Indian bed—a frame of webbing on four short legs. None of the *dâk* bungalows I have seen have more furniture. To one just arrived from England all this is desolate in the extreme, but one gets used to it, and in this climate what more do you want?

A *gharry* was quickly produced, and, followed by an escort of two *sowars*, as became the guest of a maharajah, off we started.

I regret that I have not been able to examine Bhurtpore more at my ease. We passed the celebrated mud walls from which alone in all India British troops were repulsed, drove through some well-to-do and well-attended bazaars, and that is all I saw of the town. Then out we went into the usual plain. All this part of Hindostan is the same parched arid plain, interspersed with patches of green, where corn is already in ear, or where the ground has been artificially irrigated. Here in Bhurtpore the monotony is pleasantly relieved by the size of some of the trees near the road, and by the villages being raised, artificially I fancy, and surrounded by mud walls. The inhabitants of this part of the country are Jâts, and have always been husbandmen. They are of the same caste as the Sikhs. A short, truculent, sturdy race they have always proved, and seem so still. Much trouble have they caused both to Mogul and British in times gone by. Increasing in might during the confusion of the later Mogul empire, under Suraj Mul Bhurtpore was a most formidable state. But the paramount Power has been too much for them: their territory has been curtailed, and however much they might wish it, Agra is safe against their malice. For some years, however, it was in their hands; and I have told you before how one of their rajahs treated the tomb of poor Mumtaz-i-Mahal in the Taj.

With the Maharajah's horses, and amidst the *salaams* of the Jâts, the twenty-one miles from Bhurtpore to Deeg were soon passed, and three hours brought us to historic ground. There have been two battles at Deeg or Digh, and both have been decisive in the history of India. Once the conquering Jâts were overthrown by the last general the Mohammedan empire produced; and again, Lord Lake, in what he thought his hardest battle, vanquished the ancestor of my friend Holkar, and checked the tide of Maratha victory. There is still a considerable fortress with mud walls, which must have been very formidable before the science of artillery was developed; and I could see on the ramparts some odd-looking guns, which have probably been there since the time of Nujuf Khan. Past these we drove, and stopped at the palace gate.

The Palace of Deeg is a collection of pavilions, like all native palaces; but these are scattered about in spacious gardens, bounded on two sides by considerable tanks. One of these the Maharajah sets apart for his guests, and here we are now. The

Maharajah is most hospitable; he readily receives here any officers from Muttra, where there is an English cavalry regiment, and provides them with sport in his preserves, which are full of wild boar and deer. Neilghau (wild blue bulls) and peacocks are sacred, and must be spared. Pigs are, of course, sacred to the cavalry officer under ordinary circumstances; but at Bhurtpore the woods are so thick that pig-sticking is impossible.

In front of us is the pavilion, where his Highness holds his *durbar;* on our right is his Zenana. Both these are built of the sandstone of the country—not, alas! the beautiful red sandstone of Futtehpore Sikree, but a pale pink, which is rather sickly in tone. The pavilion we live in is of white marble.

Deeg is a summer palace. In the summer heats white marble floors and walls, and doors impossible to shut, would be nice enough; and there are pavilions hanging over the placid tanks, which must be cool and delightful in the hot season.

To-day has been grey and decidedly cold, and whilst I am writing, the well-known splash of rain reminds me of "other climes," and I feel marble out of place. The rooms are very low, and surrounded with funny little passages, through which my bulky frame can with difficulty pass. There is, however, a sense of "rummyness," not unmixed with romance, about it all, that is delightful; and after the shabby treatment I experienced from Sindia, I feel thankful to His Highness of Bhurtpore.

The Maharajah announced his intention of coming himself to see me on the very evening of my arrival, and, notwithstanding the rain, was as good as his word. Wrapped up in a thick policeman's coat, with a common sword sticking out behind, the Maharajah does not present a very distinguished appearance. He is a young man, I believe, but he looks much older than he is, and has a worn-out appearance. If report speaks true, he is a very naughty boy, and much given to debauchery. He is also accused of being unfriendly to the English, and, like Sindia, too fond of soldiering. I can only say he was most polite and friendly, and offered me as many sittings as I wished. We shall see how he will redeem his promise.

Next morning was fine, and I had another opportunity of seeing the gardens. There are, as I said, four pavilions, Gopal Bawhun, where the Maharajah transacts his business; Sudra Bawhun, where we live; Krishna Bawhun, where the ladies are cooped up; and Nuno Bawhun, of the inhabitants of which I know nothing. There is also a kind of open summer-house, called Sāwun Bawhun, looking over the sacred tank. The whole thing

TANK AT DEEG.

was built by Suraj Mal, one of the earliest Rajahs of Bhurtpore, and the first to take that title. I have begun two sketches, one looking down the principal walk (which is a kind of imitation of the Taj), towards the Sāwun Bawhun, and the other of the largest tank: the latter is really a wonderful place, frequented by innumerable blue pigeons, which here, as in Venice, are sacred. There are also many peacocks strutting about: they are sacred to Khrishna, as indeed are all blue things; Khrishna himself being represented as a blue man.

I had a good sitting from His Highness. He was very polite,

and, as he talked English, I could keep him amused. I had hard work, however, for it was after breakfast, and he was very dozy at first.

The learned say that these Jâts are relations of ours, being the same as the Getæ and Massagetæ of the ancients, and Jutes of Europe, who settled, many of them, in England in early Saxon times. It may be so; but I am inclined to say, as Spurgeon said when lecturing on the gorilla, "Some say you are my cousin, but I say, 'between you and me there is a great gulf fixed.'" Anyhow, Deeg is a delightful place, and I wish his English cousins had as pleasant a palace as the Maharajah of Bhurtpore.

I have but little to add to the above, and this must be but a small batch of journal. It has to close two days before the usual time, and as I get farther from the great highways of India my time will get shorter and shorter.

My Maharajah here is done as far as I require him. On the whole, he has behaved very well. He has bothered me a great deal to know what the Government are going to give him for sitting, whether he is to have a copy (great Heavens!) of the picture, or an engraving. Most of these gentlemen have subscribed, and it is rather hard that I should have to explain to them that they get nothing for their money.

We left Deeg, as we came, with the Maharajah's horses, and escorted by his Highness's *sowars*. This season appears to be the season for marriages. All day the singing-women are chanting about, and, preceded by tom-toms, conduct the well-veiled bride to the—let us hope—impatient bridegroom. It was very pleasant as we drove along, both here and at Bhurtpore, to come upon a flash of crimson and scarlet, a kind of flame of singing-women, whose monotonous chant in itself had something in character with the scene. Thus we sped on to Bhurtpore, changing horses at Koombhere, a considerable place, conveniently half-way; where, too, the Maharajah has a palace, which towers over the town.

We had an opportunity of seeing more at our leisure the town of Bhurtpore. It seems well-to-do and flourishing, with broad streets, and good stone-built houses the whole length of its crowded bazaar. There was nothing, however, to tempt me in the shops, and I had not time to devote to searching. Hindoo shopkeepers, like all Easterns—except Jews, by-the-bye—and unlike European tradesmen, seem to have a great dislike to show any of their best things. You have to go into the shop, talk of the weather, &c., and by degrees things are brought to you. Everything takes time here, as I know to my cost in travelling.

At Bhurtpore, too, we saw the Rajah's palace, which consists of a large courtyard with buildings on two sides. Facing you, as you enter, is the open *dewan*, where the Maharajah holds his Court on grand occasions. On the left is a staircase conducting you to the show-rooms, which are on the first floor of the left block as you come into the courtyard.

The principal room is a long gallery, with windows looking into the court. Behind this are many smaller rooms—dining, drawing, and billiard-rooms—all darkened and having few windows on account of the heat, but profusely furnished with European carpets and knick-knacks of the most tawdry kind. In the long gallery there are lots of pictures and prints; a colossal daub of the late Highness, done like "Carver in oils" by a native, and several others of the same Highness in many attitudes—in *durbar*, on horseback, &c.—all equally monstrous. One of the present Rajah, by Mr. M. W., I believe, is better (owing to the invention of photography, I fancy), but still pretty bad. There are four large prints—all the same—of Mr. Batty driving his sixteen horses to his circus, and many other pictures of that kind.

These people, directly they touch European tastes, seem to lose their inherent feeling for the right thing. The worst "shoddy" is not so bad as the masses of objects heaped together in their palaces; yet they have beautiful things, and dress themselves with some feeling for colour, barring a taste for aniline dyes which I see growing all over the country. Is it, perchance, that they see so little good taste among the Europeans out here, whom of course they copy? If so, the Europeans have much to answer for.

Leaving Bhurtpore by the 10 p.m. train, you arrive at Jeypore at 8 a.m. The morning of the 8th broke with unusual splendour; for lately there has been cloudy weather, and to make either a good sunrise or sunset you must have clouds. "Towards six o'clock in the evening or morning chrome yellow thrusts itself into nature," lectured the French landscape painter. On the 8th there was both chrome and madder mapped out on the blue sky; and, moreover, such hills as I have not seen for a long time. A solitary ridge there is at Delhi, and at Gwalior the fort and a few low hills have more pretension. These at Jeypore are the beginning of the range which I shall find again at Ajmere, and farther on between Jodhpore and Oodeypore, and which form the backbone of the plains of India.

The acting political agent, a certain Captain B——y, was on the eve of his departure for England on sick leave. He had never answered my letter, and I did not know whether the Rajah of Jeypore was here till I arrived. At the station, however, I found a carriage, and drove to breakfast with B——. I heard that the Bundi Maharajah was here, and that he of Jeypore could not sit that day. Rajahs have been much stirred up by the Delhi business, and are on the trot all over the country. Like muddy water, they require time to settle. Jeypore is very religious, and takes all the morning to say his prayers: he can only be seen at 4 p.m., said the agent. I had found the last two mail-letters here, so I was content to wait and digest the home news, which proved not very good, and I was therefore not in the cheeriest mood.

I spent the afternoon in reading and making arrangements for future journeys. The Oodeypore agent is away travelling through the Bheel country, in Mewar. Jodhpore must therefore be done first, and has to be written to to prepare *dâk*, &c. While writing my letters I hear the most extraordinary sounds, which I find proceed from a man who has the next room to mine. Once he appeared in the verandah in his shirt-sleeves, and quickly disappeared. These roarings continued, and by-and-by I find they are principally demands for brandy-and-soda. By the evening Mr. —— is in a state of complete inebriation; but alas! his drunkenness is not speechless: I wish it had been, for all night long the roaring continued, and at 6 a.m. the noise was awful. Thank Heaven! it was Mr. —— preparing to depart, and demanding more "Pegs;" and so he remains in my memory as a kind of "hideous noise."

Such are the trials the traveller is subjected to here, where brandy pawnee and D. T. are anything but uncommon among the lower class of Europeans.

On Friday, 9th February, I went to see the sights of Jeypore. The political agent had applied for a carriage for me, and last night a common *palki gharry* appeared from the Maharajah. I returned my thanks to His Highness, and told him I could get a better one here, and preferred to pay. This morning, however, a better trap with two horses turned up. Rajahs have fine carriages for swell occasions, but those they lend are of the shabbiest description, nor have they any idea of turning out either carriages or servants. This one was like the flies one sometimes sees at country towns, which are traps bought second or third-hand, but which have once been handsome and probably belonged to some neighbouring squire. In this "has-been" off we go.

Jeypore* was built early last century by the then Rajah Jey Sing. It is, I believe, the only Indian town built on a settled plan, for Jey Sing was not only a rajah, but a mathematician and a scientific man. The city was planned actually by a certain Vidhyadhur, a Jain, who also assisted the Rajah in his astronomical pursuits. It has, then, two broad straight streets, crossing each other at right angles. They have pavements on either side, and gas (!) which the present ruler has introduced and manufactures from castor oil. The houses have a curious appearance, the fronts being all plastered, and painted pink with white patterns. This gives a rather trumpery and toylike appearance to the whole town, which from its size and regularity lacks the charm and picturesqueness of many Indian places I have described. When the eye gets used to the colour it is not unpleasing;

* The foundation was laid by Jey Sing, A.D. 1728.

and, after all, I do not know but that the Rajah Jey Sing was right; for in this climate, had all the houses been white, the effect would have been too dazzling. The lime from which this plaster is made is the same employed for the roads all over Northern India, known as *kunkur*, and is singularly fine. The plaster has almost the look of marble, and is used for making all kinds of pierced windows of geometric patterns. I have not, however, seen any that equalled those of Gwalior for beauty and intricacy of design, and regret much that I believed those who told me Jeypore was the place to find such things, and dissuaded me from ordering a whole balcony from Sindia's city.

Jeypore has a school of art, and being of course much interested therein, I stopped there, and was shown over by the principal—a worthy and well-to-do *baboo*.* It turned out to be a kind of general school for trades; and turning, watchmaking, carpentry, pottery, electrotyping, and many others are taught there. So far, no doubt, it does good, but there is also a school of drawing, and over this I should wish to cast a veil. Of all the feeble institutions here, it is the feeblest. The master is an Indian; the things turned out, so many nightmares: large copies of photographs of the Prince of Wales, Lord Northbrook and other Governors-General, with the ghastly stare such things have when done by beginners; drawings done from nature without an atom of art: in fact, a perfect artistic Bedlam. The *baboo*, however, seemed satisfied, which is a great point. He showed us with considerable triumph some small heads copied in needle-work from photographs. Poor Lord Northbrook! if he could

* It may be indiscreet to give the history of this gentleman's appointment: I may give offence to some of his relatives, who are high up in the public service of Jeypore; but the appointment is so characteristic of the way such things are done in India that I cannot refrain from recording it. Our excellent friend, then, was sent to Calcutta to study medicine; but for medicine he had no turn, and time after time was plucked in his examinations. At last he returned to Jeypore as a failure, and by the interest of his relatives was put in charge of the newly-started art school. "*T'es propre a rien, fais toi artiste,*" exclaims the exasperated mother in Gavarni's inimitable caricature.

only see himself, he would not, in his recent speech at a distribution of prizes in England, have been so laudatory of Indian schools of design.

The only good thing in the place was a silver goblet, unfinished, which G—— has bought, and of which I have ordered a replica.* In encouraging individuals who are good workmen to take pupils, as is done here, the Maharajah has done the right thing. It is what I should propose in my report on the influence of English art on natives. Art schools as we have them in England are of no real use to the native. Government should look out the best workmen in different art manufactories, and spend the money now spent in making indifferent artists in paying premiums to such workmen, and creating thereby a good school of ornamental art.

I was disappointed of my sitting again to-day, and, owing to the dilatoriness of my friend at the Residency, who is a good deal exercised on the great salt question, which at present agitates all this portion of Rajpootana, I was not given timely notice, so that another day has passed *sine lineâ*, or nearly so. I went, however, to the Residency, and was introduced to the Maharajah, who was paying a visit there. Ram Sing of Jeypore is about forty-five, and wears spectacles. He seems a cheery old fellow, and was very civil, fixing a sitting at 2.30 p.m. to-morrow, when I shall have an opportunity of seeing him more at my leisure.

*10th February.*

This morning I went over Jeypore again. It is certainly a very interesting place, and the busiest Indian town I have yet been in. Behind our hotel, which is outside the town, are a number of poor wretches encamped. These I find to be the sweepers of the city, who have all struck on account of some ill usage alleged to have been received from the authorities. They all crowded round me, and humbly begged me to do something for them.

* Which, of course, I have never received.

Such is the belief in the *sahib* justice. They are now lying in miserable bundles round the walls of our compound. The Prime Minister was for imprisoning the whole lot, but the Maharajah said "No, that will cost money: better to imprison the leaders only." And so trades unions and strikes exist, you see, in Jeypore, and I fear will avail but little. Meanwhile the streets have been unswept for three days.

In the afternoon I went by appointment to paint the Maharajah. Jeypore Palace is a vast pile, said to contain three thousand persons. The late Maharajah and his predecessor left twenty-seven widows between them, each of whom is attended by many women: the present man has seven wives; and the result is all this swarm of human beings living unproductively. Ram Sing, the present Rajah, has no children. He is, as I said above, very religious, and spends regularly from ten to four at *pooja* or prayers. He had appointed half-past two with me, and about that time I appeared. I had great difficulty in getting in, as all the attendants said the Maharajah was still at *pooja.* Finally I was ushered through many dark passages into a courtyard, where there were a dozen fellows with hawks; from that again to another court, and then up some steps, when I found myself in a comfortable room, where the Maharajah spends his leisure time photographing. Praying during the lightest hours of the day, he can have but little time for anything that demands light. He has, however, several Europeans in his service, and with them I had to spend an hour and a half waiting. I do not like this sort of thing, and if it happens again I shall make a row. The windows of this photographic-room look over a charming garden, beyond which rise the hills that encircle Jeypore, on whose precipitous sides I can yet trace in gigantic letters the "Welcome to Jeypore" placed there for the visit of the Prince of Wales. This garden contains fountains and tanks. One of the latter I see covered with a net, which I am told is to protect the goldfish from kites and hawks. These fish are much esteemed in some parts of India. Sailors bring quantities of them from China, and even from England, to Bombay, where they are eagerly bought by rich natives, who on grand occasions are fond of serving up a curry made of them, and swagger about their having cost a shilling or eighteenpence apiece.

The garden has also a green and pleasant-looking croquet and Badminton lawn; and the whole thing is kept in a way very creditable to His Highness, and would be worthy of a Scotch gardener, were it not for the Maharajah's dogs, which every afternoon are let loose here, and career over beds and flowers after the manner of dogs all the world over. They are a motley pack—English spaniels and greyhounds, mixed with Rampore and other native breeds noted for their excellence. With these the Maharajah tells me he hunts boar, and deer, and leopards, and even tigers, as they fear nothing. It is amusing to see His Highness—who, notwithstanding his prayings, is a keen sportsman—standing on his balcony and calling each dog by name. This, however, happened on another occasion, as you shall hear.

Presently the Maharajah is announced, and in he comes. A funny little fellow is Ram Sing, short and frail-looking, with a very hooked nose and spectacles. As I have painted him, I had of course time to study his expression. A sharp, shrewd man he seems,—and is, by all accounts,—with a brisk bright eye, notwithstanding his spectacles; withal a very unhappy look. As he sits the first time, all merriment fades from his face, an ascetic pinched look contracts the upper nose, and his eyebrows are raised with an anxious expression. This is heightened by the *pooja*-marks across his forehead, and the two round spots in the centre; moreover, there is a black line indicating his having finished *pooja*, and the space between his eyebrows and his eye is whitened to a sickly hue. The first day I could not get a word from him, but I heard afterwards that this Saturday, 10th February, was the eve of a festival, and that even while sitting to me, the Rajah was at his prayers and religious meditation.

Ram Sing is a curious instance of a man who is strict, even bigoted, in his religious observances, but who is singularly tolerant to other creeds. I hear, however, to those of his own way of thinking he is not so tolerant. The Maharajah worships Siva;

many of his subjects follow Vishnu. The other day he confiscated some land belonging to the opposite sect. They protested in vain, and finally, instigated by their priest, left the town, to the number of 30,000. Amongst these were most of the merchants of the town. Ram Sing was firm, and, like the strike of the sweepers I mentioned before as now camped near us, this strike was all in vain. Finding they could not get any satisfaction here, the whole band went off to the Rajah of Bikaneer, a neighbouring Rajah of very old family, but whose country is principally desert. Here, again, they were met with coldness, and sent away, as his Highness of Bikaneer was afraid of being eaten out of house and home; so they returned to Jeypore, and the merchants gradually saw the error of their ways, the thirst for gain getting the better of their religion. The priests were soon left alone, and having sworn they would never go back to Jeypore till their property was restored, are living now miserably a few miles off.

Ram Sing prides himself, and with reason, on his enlightenment. Jeypore town, when he came to the *guddee*, had its streets —wide though they were—much obstructed by small shrines, sacred to different deities. These the Rajah has gradually cleared away, and but a few of those most esteemed by the vulgar herd remain. Yet this is a man who prays six hours a day!

After a good sitting, I left him till Monday, as Sunday was the great feast of the Hindoos, and the Maharajah would be busy all day "feeding Brahmins," all this caste receiving gratuitous meals on the 11th February. Ram Sing has to feed 50,000, they say. Arrangements were, however, made to take us to Amber, and I had a most charming day at the ancient capital of Jeypore. Amber is six miles away: you drive through a delightful valley, and pass half-way a lake, where Jey Sing built his first city. The space, however, was found too small, and he moved to the larger plains of the present Jeypore. Of this first town nothing now remains but a palace in the midst of the lake, and one or two houses. Presently we came to a steepish ascent, and as Indian coachmen (and I suppose horses too, as olive-eating and alpine climbing are matters of education) object to hills, we had to mount elephants.

At the top of the first hill we sight Amber, built on the other side of the valley, on the banks of a small lake. The town is very picturesque, but mostly in ruins, and one sees that Jey Sing had reason on his side in wishing to forsake the mountain home of his ancestors, for the hills crowd close in on the town, and prevent any possible expansion on any side. The site is, however, admirably adapted for the stronghold of a mountain chief, and all these Rajpoot Rajahs were no more than heads of clans at the commencement of their history. The palace is well kept up, and the Rajah twice every year visits the cradle of his race.

Built on the spur of the hill, Amber Palace hangs nearly precipitously over the lake on its south-eastern side; towards the north and north-west is a large fort on the top of the hill, the celebrated Nahrgurh, which towers over both palace and town, and commands the whole country. In architecture the palace is much as such places usually are in India. There is a fine *dewan* built by Jey Sing, which was so magnificent that his suzerain of Delhi was jealous, and sent down ambassadors to find out if report spoke the truth. The shrewd Jey Sing, however, had timely notice, and managed to cover up his beautifully carved columns with plaster before the Emperor's messengers arrived, and so they are to the present day; that is, all but two, which have been uncovered, to show the truth of the tale. The ceiling of the *dewan* is decorated with talc and looking-glass, and is to my mind better done than the celebrated bath, the Shis Mahal, at Agra. I made a sketch of the palace from the lake below.

*Monday.*—I had another sitting from his Highness, who, notwithstanding his night-long praying, was quite brisk and talkative. We became great friends, and finished the afternoon playing billiards together. Among the curiosities of Rajpoot Courts are the *nautch* girls, who are a kind of privileged people, and wander through the palaces unveiled and unmolested. I had noticed a number of them here, and, presuming on my intimacy, got the Rajah to order one of the girls, whose photograph

I saw, to sit. On Tuesday, then, I had a sitting from her. She is not young, but has a remarkably fine head. Her costume is very handsome, though, of course, rather *bizarre.* She wears a long flowing robe, and winds her drapery round her with the air of a queen. Never did I regret more my want of knowledge of the Hindoostani language than here. The Rajah, as I have said before, is surrounded by a lot of English of not the highest education, and to them I have to leave the translation of my most polite speeches. I cannot help feeling that these lose much when expressed by those vulgar fellows, who give themselves most odious airs. Ram Sukee, this *nautch* girl, is a great friend of the Rajah, and soon he came to see how I was getting on, and pottered around me, arranging drapery and fancying he was of great assistance, whereas he generally spoilt everything. My model is not only a *danseuse,* but a singer. She is from Marwar, generally called Jodhpore, from its capital, as this State is called Jeypore, instead of Dhoonder, and Mewar is called Oodeypore from its capital. The Indian airs are some of them very wild and pleasant, though of course all sung through the nose. I do not know that they have ever been written down for the English public. Like the Arab airs, they ought to be collected, and would, I am sure, give some ideas to our musicians, as the Hungarian music has already done.

On my return home I found a card: "Thakoor Futteh Sing requests the honour of Mr. Prinsep's company to dinner." This being the Rajah's Prime Minister, and hearing that the dinner was given to the Resident, I wrote back "Mr. P. would be delighted." At seven I started, and after a long drive through the town arrived at the Minister's house, in a narrow lane off the principal road. All the nobles have their houses off the main road, the palace alone being permitted to face the street. The host, smoking a cigarette, politely received me at the door and ushered me in. Futteh Sing's house has just been rebuilt. The part we saw consisted of three large rooms, of which the first served as anteroom, being the largest; the second, smaller, as dining-room; and the third as drawing-room. They were all lighted, though not very brilliantly, with gas which is made from castor oil. On the assembly of the guests we sit down, to the number of twenty. Dinner is served in the European style. It is cooked, I believe, by the political agent's cook, and is pretty good. The natives, of course, do not eat with us, as thereby they would lose their caste. Our hosts, father and son, sit outside the circle of the guests and converse over the backs of the chairs on which the *convives* sit. Other native swells drop in, and presently the room is full. After the dinner is over, the Maharajah comes in, and he and some of the greater men have champagne and drink the health of the company, after which they smoke cheroots much like Christians.

This is an awful blow to the old ideas of caste—the greatest, indeed, since this very Rajah's ancestor, a Rajpoot of Rajpoots, gave his daughter to the great Akbar in marriage. This was thought at the time such a disgrace, that the Rajahs of Oodeypore have always refused to eat with either this Rajah or him of Jodhpore. We were told yesterday that the Rajah of Bhoondi, who is here, would not eat in a room in which a European had been, and regularly washed his hands after shaking hands with one. He is an old man of sixty-six.

Jeypore is, however, nearer to Delhi, and much more accessible, than Oodeypore or Bhoondi; so perhaps the Maharajah Bhagwandas was right to sacrifice his prejudices to his worldly prosperity.

We English cannot understand the character of the native, nor enter into his prejudices, and his ideal is quite incomprehensible to us. That the marriage of a daughter should lower a man's caste is astonishing; but what can we say to the tenet that if a Brahmin allows his daughter to come to the age of puberty unmarried, he and his family are consigned to the lowest hell for ever!

This Ram Sing, the most enlightened Rajah in India, according to the Indian officials, is very strict in secluding the women of his *rawala* or Zenana. No one has ever seen any of his wives. Even English ladies are not allowed within the sacred precincts, and a doctor told me he had to prescribe without seeing his patient, and was informed he might, if he liked, feel the pulse of one of the servant women, but not the pulse of the Ranee. The *nautch* girls I have mentioned above do all the shopping and commissions for the Zenana.

After dinner at Thakoor Futteh Sing's, we had a *nautch*, which was the first I had seen. It is generally supposed that a *nautch* is an improper sight, and in England such things are talked of with bated breath. There were ladies present during this *nautch*, and I can assure you, on my honour, that it was eminently respectable. The women, too, were not pretty; but the monotonous chant they kept up and the movements of their hips were curious; and although I should no doubt get heartily tired if I saw more of it, I confess I was amused. This monotonous slow movement is adapted for a hot climate, where the whirls and bounds of more active dances would be out of place, impossible or at least irksome to the dancer, and disagreeable to the looker-on, who could not fail to feel hotter from seeing such violent exercise.

The party broke up at half-past ten. The Rajah, however, slept at Futteh Sing's, as I found out to my cost, for he never turned up at the palace for his sitting. I contented myself with his *nautch* girl, and, if I can only get drapery made like hers, shall paint a picture from my sketch on my return home.

My American friend leaves me to-day, and I shall miss him much. He is of a practical turn of mind, without much poetry; but in matters of business has been of great use. He continues his "globe trotting" *viâ* Calcutta, Madras, and Ceylon, and will eventually reach home *viâ* somewhere.

I have here made the acquaintance of Tod's "Rajasthan," a book full of information of these parts, and, though published nearly fifty years ago, still the great authority on Rajpoot affairs.

The Rajpoots are all divided into clans: the four greatest divisions remaining are—the Sesodias, who rule at Oodeypore; the Rahtors, of Jodhpore; the Cuchwahas, of Jeypore; and the Haras, of Boondhi and Kota.

The Cuchwaha, the ruling clan of Dhoonder or Jeypore, take their name from *cuchwa* (a tortoise), came originally from Lahore, and were the sons of Cush, the second son of Rama, King of Koshula, who emigrated from Ayodea, or Oude, to the Punjaub. Several generations afterwards Rajah Nal, his descendant, migrated west, A.D. 295, and settled at Nurwar. The thirty-third in descent from him was Sora Sing, on whose death his brother usurped the throne, depriving his son Dhola Rae of his inheritance. Dhola Rae was an infant, and his mother, fearing the usurper, placed her child in a basket and carried him on her head till she reached Khogong (a place five miles from Jeypore), then inhabited by the Meenas. Overcome with hunger and fatigue, she placed her precious burden on the ground, and was plucking some wild berries, when she observed a hooded serpent rearing its form over the basket. She uttered a shriek, which attracted an itinerant Brahmin, who bade her be in no alarm, but rather rejoice at this certain indication of future greatness in the boy. "What may be in futurity I heed not while I am sinking with hunger," replied the mother of the future founder of Amber. The Brahmin directed her to Khogong. Taking up her basket, she reached the town, where, accosting a woman, who turned out to be the slave of the Meena Rajah, she begged for any menial employment. By direction of the Ranee she was entertained with the slaves. One day she was ordered to prepare dinner, of which Ralunsi, the Rajah, partook, and he found it so superior to his usual fare that he sent for the cook, who related her story; and as soon as the Rajah discovered her rank, he adopted her as his sister, and Dhola Rae as his nephew. When the boy attained the age of fourteen (which is the age of majority among the Rajpoots), the Meena Rajah sent him to Delhi with the Khogong tribute. After a residence of five years there, Dhola Rae determined to kill his benefactor and usurp his power. But first he consulted the Meena *dhati*, or bard, as to the best means and time for carrying out his project; and this worthy recommended the Festival of the Dewali, when it is customary to perform ablutions *en masse* in a tank. He accordingly brought a few of his Rajpoot brethren from Delhi, and accomplished his object, filling the reservoirs in which the Meenas bathed with their dead bodies. It is a satisfaction to know that "the treacherous bard" did not escape: Dhola Rae with his own hand put him to death, observing, "He that has proved unfaithful to one master could not be trusted by another." The grandson of this gentleman founded Amber. After all, most empires begin in the same way.

Fifth in descent, again, we come to a rajah of the name of Pugoon, who was well known in Rajpoot chivalry, and was immortalized by Chund in the poetic history of the Emperor Pirthi Raj, the last of the Hindoo Emperors of Delhi. Pugoon, however, was killed before the final struggle. The story, as far as I can make it out, bears a considerable resemblance to the Homeric legends. The lovely Princess of Canooj has to choose a husband; her father, Jeichund, Emperor of Canooj, accordingly summons all the great of Hindostan; but Pirthi Raj, of Delhi, deeming himself the equal of the Emperor of Canooj, treats the summons with disdain. The insulted Emperor thereupon has an image made of gold to represent Pirthi Raj, and at the great feast, when all the chiefs are assembled, and when to each is assigned some office (for, in the rite of Leonir, every office must be performed by royal persons), to the Emperor of Delhi, or rather to his image, is assigned the post of porter, being that last in rank, by the door of the hall. The princess enters, bearing in her hand a garland which she is to give to the man of her choice. She passes by all the chiefs, and presents her garland to the image of Pirthi Raj. In duty bound, the Chohan prince accepts the "quest;" in open daylight he bears off the princess from Canooj, and a desperate fight of five days' duration takes place. To use the words of the bard, "he preserved his prize; he gained immortal honour; but he lost the sinews of Delhi;" and Pugoon was one of the sixty-four chiefs chosen to help in the rape of this Rajpoot Helen. With him was Govind, a chief of the Newar house; and thus sings Chund:

"When Govind fell, the foe danced with joy. Then did

Pugoon thunder on the curtain of fight, with both hands did he ply the *karg* (sword) on the heads of the barbarians. Four hundred rushed upon him; but five brothers, Kehuri, Peepa, and Boho, with Barsung and Cuchra, supported him. Spears and daggers are plied—heads roll on the plain—blood flows in streams. Pugoon assails Itimād; but, as his head rolls on the plain, he receives the Khan's lance in his breast. The Coorma (or Cuchwaha) fell in the field, and the Apsaras* disputed for the hero. Whole lines of Northmen strew the plain: many a head did Mahadeo add to his chaplet. When Pugoon and Govind fell, one watch of the day remained. To rescue his kin came Pallan, like a tiger loosed from his chain. The army of Canooj fell back; the cloud-like host of Jeichund turned its head. The brother of Pugoon, with his son, performed deeds like Carna; but both fell in the field, and gained the secret of the Sun, whose chariot advanced to conduct them to his mansion.

"Ganga shrank with affright, the moon quivered, the Digpah howled at their posts; checked was the advance of Canooj; and in the pause the Coorma performed the last rites to his sire (Pugoon), who broke in pieces the shields of Yeichund. Pugoon was a buckler to his lord, and numerous his gifts of steel to the heroes of Canooj. Not even by the bard can his deeds be described. He placed his feet on the head of Shesnag; he made a waste of the forests of men; nor dared the sons of the mighty approach him! As Pugoon fell, he exclaimed, 'One hundred years are the limit of a man's life, of which fifty are lost in night, and half this in childhood; but the Almighty taught me to wield the brand!' As he spoke, even in the arms of Yama, he beheld the sword of his boy playing on the head of the foemen. His parting soul was satisfied."

And well it might be. After all this "losing of the sinews of Delhi," Pirthi Raj could not wonder at his defeat by Shabudin of Ghoree.

The most powerful Rajahs that succeeded the above-mentioned Pugoon were Maun Singh, who was a great general in the time

* Evidently akin to the "Valkyra" maidens of the Northern *Sagas*.

of Akbar, being brother to the wife of Jehanghire, and after him Jey Sing, commonly called the Mirza Rajah, who, in the days of Aurungzebe, took prisoner the great Sivaji, the originator of the great Maratha revival. He was said to have been poisoned by his son at the instigation of Aurungzebe, in consequence of an idle boast. He sat in *durbar* with two glass globes, one in each hand. The one he called Delhi, the other Sattara (the capital of Sivaji): the latter he dashed to the ground, crying, "There goes Sattara! The fate of Delhi is in my right hand, and this, with equal ease, I can cast away."

It is pleasant to turn from the Homeric, or rather Ossianic, butchery described above to the deeds of Jey Sing II., better known as Sevai Jey Sing. This Rajah built Jeypore, and was the astronomer of India. He erected observatories at Delhi, Jeypore, Oojein, Benares, and Mathura. Great buildings they are, but alas! now in ruins. In these places his observations were so accurate, that he detected errors in the calculations of all the astronomers of Europe. He caused to be translated into Sanskrit "Euclid" and Napier's "Logarithms," and by his book all almanacks are still constructed—at all events, in India. Hear the preface of the learned Jey Sing, and recollect it is a Hindoo who writes:

"Praise be to God!—such that the minutely discerning genius of the most profound geometers, in uttering the smallest particle of it, may open the mouth in confession of inability; and such adoration that the study and accuracy of astronomers, who measure the heavens, may acknowledge their astonishment and utter insufficiency. Let us devote ourselves to the altar of the King of kings, hallowed be His Name! in the book of the register of whose power the lofty orbs of heaven are only a few leaves, and the stars and that heavenly courser, the sun, small pieces of money in the treasury of the empire of the Most High! From inability to comprehend the all-encompassing beneficence of His power, Hipparchus is an ignorant clown, who wrings the hands of vexation; and in the contemplation of His exalted majesty, Ptolemy is a bat, who can never arrive at the Sun of Truth. The demonstrations of Euclid are but an imperfect sketch of the forms of His contrivance! But since the well-wisher of the works of creation, and the admiring spectator of the works of Infinite Wisdom, Sevai Jey Sing, from the first dawning of reason to his mind, and during its progress to maturity, was entirely devoted to the mathematical science, and the bent of his mind was constantly directed to the solution of the most difficult problems, by the aid of the Supreme Artificer he acquired a thorough knowledge of its principles and rules."

Besides his mathematical knowledge, Jey Sing had a considerable knowledge of the world, and managed to preserve his state in the midst of Jât uprisings and Maratha invasions; and I think, if what I hear is true, his descendant Ram Sing has inherited with the state some of the "canniness" we find in several of his predecessors.

The great question of the day in these parts is salt. This necessary article of consumption is manufactured all over this part of Rajpootana. On the borders of Jeypore and Jodhpore there is a salt lake called the Sambhur Lake, from which our friend Ram Sing makes a good sum annually. Now, salt is a Government monopoly in British India, and one of the great sources of revenue; so the English have actually put a fence of prickly pear round Rajpootana. We passed it on the way from Agra to Bhurtpore. It is I don't know how many hundred miles in length, and I suspect about as effective as its great prototype, the Great Wall of China.

The Government have been trying to come to an agreement with Ram Sing in the matter of his salt. Last year he was invited up to Simla to discuss this business; and the Viceroy, with his usual extreme friendliness for Orientals, said, taking his hand in both his:

"Maharajah, if there is anything I can do for you, please mention it."

"There is one thing," answered Ram Sing: "please not to mention the word salt,"—by which reply, I think, the Rajah got the better of the Viceroy, albeit a quondam diplomat.

I am writing this in a Rajpoot State where I find a railway and an hotel. Surely the prejudice of the Hindoo can never resist these two levellers! It is true they use the railway, but never the hotel. Oh, Caste! Caste! how long wilt thou resist the so-called civilization of the nineteenth century?

HIS HIGHNESS RAM SING, MAHARAJAH OF JEYPORE.

# CHAPTER VII.

## AJMERE—ROAD TO JODHPORE.

*Beaur, 33 miles on the way from Ajmere to Jodhpore.*

I LEFT Jeypore with anger and vexation of spirit, and view the old Rajah as a "pious fraud;" for I delayed my departure a day to have one sitting from him in his robes, and when I went to the palace, I was told the old man was ill, and could not sit. Perhaps it may be said that this was not his fault. Certainly it wasn't, but then I had been a week at Jeypore, and he might have given me another sitting. *Pooja* and his Highness of Bhoondi were against me; indeed, I fear that the former is much used by the Jeypore *wallah* as an excuse when he is wanted for important business. Somehow, too, either from a chill, or what is more likely, from exposing myself too much to the sun, I had a touch of fever, so that when I arrived at Ajmere I felt "all over like." As this was my first experience of fever, and as such attacks are very common in India, though happily rare in England, let me bear witness to the unpleasantness of the sensation. A couple of quinine pills and a day's rest quite set me up again, only my stay at Ajmere was not as profitable as it might have been had I been in my usual robust state of health.

I arrived at 2.30 a.m., and had difficulty enough in waking the sleepy inmates of the only and indifferent hotel of the place, where I threw myself on a *charpoy*, and finished my night's rest. I had not been dressed an hour before I received a visit from the Commissioner, Mr. Saunders, with whom I had been at Haileybury, who kindly asked me up to his house, or rather to a tent in his garden, as his house was under repair. Gladly did I accept, and as I felt rather seedy, as gladly did I defer my departure for a day.

Ajmere is most picturesquely situated at the foot of a high hill, with other beautifully shaped hills all round. The clearness and blueness of the air make the colour of these truly delightful. The city was an early Moslem conquest, and was for a long time the summer residence of the Emperors of Delhi. The Commissioner's house was formerly a palace built by Jehanghire, and yet contains two rooms, inlaid with marble, and a *dewan*, built for that monarch. It is on the *bund*, which encloses a good-sized lake, on two sides of which rise hills of 1,000 feet, so that the view from the windows is most lovely. Although I was not in a very bright state, or fit for much artistic enjoyment, I was glad to be taken out for a drive through the town, the streets of which have not been spoilt by British improvement, though we have been in possession over fifty years. Many of the houses are very beautiful, rising with pierced windows and balconies several storeys high, and some having the pierced work painted with excellent effect. There is a very holy Mohammedan shrine here, to which pilgrimages are made from all parts of Hindostan; and deep down in the rock, with irregular steps leading thereto, is a curious tank, also sacred. I did not go into the shrine, as even Europeans have to take off their shoes, and I felt feverish and unwell.

The Mosque of Ajmere is the oldest in India, being of the time of the Kutub of Delhi. It is formed, as was that at the Kutub, from a Jain temple, having a *façade* of early Moslem work, with five arches, two on each side of equal size, and a large one in the middle, all carved with intricate patterns, over which is an elaborate inscription—I suppose quotations from the Koran. At the Kutub but one arch remains, and as the Jain temple is unconnected with the Moslem *façade*, you cannot understand the mixture of architectural styles till you have seen the mosque here. This mosque commonly goes by the name *Arhai din ka Jhompra*, which means "built in two days and a half." This title evidently applies to the Jain temple, which was probably cleared out and prepared for a Moslem place of worship by decapitation of all representations of living things. The screen of five arches, built by Altumsh (*vide* Fergusson's "Indian and Eastern Architecture") A.D. 1211—1236, must have taken a long time to carve and place *in situ*. The mosque is being very carefully restored under the eye of my friend Saunders, who is most anxious lest too much should be done. The centre arch is still down, but all will shortly be finished, and be a great credit, both to the Government who pay the expenses, and to the Commissioner and those employed on the work. It is a great pleasure to me to have to record these rare occasions where good work has been carefully and well done. Fergusson notices the state of decay and filth in which the mosque remained till very recently. He also tells a story of a zealous officer at the time of the arrival of Lord Mayo at Ajmere. To make a triumphal entrance for the Viceroy, this gentleman utilized one of the beautiful arches, but it was put together so carelessly that the Viceroy was not allowed to pass under it! It is probably owing to the expostulations of Mr. Fergusson that the Government undertook the necessary repairs.

My *dâks* having been laid by the Marwar Rajah, and my quinine pills having worked my cure, I started on the morning of the 19th February for Jodhpore. His Highness sent his own coachman, one Roopjee, and six horses. These were good enough, but I trust his Highness does not travel in the carriage he sent for me, which is like an open hearse, and has no blinds to keep out the sun. However, one is told not to look a gift horse in the mouth, so why a gift carriage? And here I am resting in midday, as jolly as possible, and looking forward with keenest expectation for the next two days to take me to Jodhpore, and out of civilization.

The route this morning has been an agreeable change from the landscapes hitherto seen by me while *dâking*. There was no lack of variety in this landscape, for on all sides rose beautifully shaped ranges of hills, round whose jagged peaks were all kinds of lovely blues and pinks in the morning sun. No wonder the

Rajpoots have a vein of romance and poetry in their disposition, not found on the flat plains of Hindostan. Like the Britons, the Welsh, the Scotch, the Norsemen, they have their bards and poets, who are held in high estimation amongst them, though of course the deeds they extol and the examples they cite for imitation are principally murder, rapine, and revenge; and if anything tender does find its way into their heroic lays, it takes the terrible form of *suttee* for a dead husband, or the yet more terrible *jogir*, where the whole of the women of a city go forth to cheerful immolation, while their male relatives don "their saffron robes and rush on their foes." After all, the beginning of all poetry was this, and old Homer's "Siege of Troy" might find an echo in the sack of Chitore, the capital of Mewar or Oodeypore.

The spirit of clanship still exists here, I am told, the chiefs still holding their lands in feudal tenure from the rana or rajah. They live like the Highland chiefs of old, and want but a magician like Sir Walter Scott to clothe their feuds and legends with a mantle of romance. Are such people capable of what we call civilization? I should almost doubt it. From what I hear, the Rajpoot pure and simple, like the Highland chief, is a gentleman according to his lights, one who would rather do anything than work. They are, of course, the owners of the soil; how long will they keep it against enterprising capital and the steam plough of improvement?

I left Beaur (where the above was written) at 3 p.m., in the same carriage, with five horses, four harnessed as usual, and the fifth with a postillion in front. About three miles out the road begins to ascend, and for the rest of the way winds through a kind of pass. In many places it is very bad, and the jolting considerable.

These twelve miles were most curious. The hills here can hadly be called mountains, but yet are very jagged and abrupt. I know nothing of geology, I wish I did, but though I have travelled among mountains before, never have I seen such formations of rock. Right up to the summits are all kinds of wonderful squirms and holes, and steep hill-sides are marked like the beds of torrents in Scotland and other mountainous countries. Some great Gulf Stream must have rolled over all this for ages, to have caused the effects I have seen to-day. Geologists have, no doubt, noted all this before. I can only record my impression of astonishment at the effects left everywhere by the waters of the great deep. This is the backbone of the great Indian plain, and 2,000 feet high at least. The balcony of Saunders's house at Ajmere was 1,700 feet above the sea, and we must have risen considerably since then. At the top of a high hill I could see a great squirm hollowed out 20 feet deep in the solid rock, evidently by water, and as if done yesterday. I wish I was learned enough to know what it all meant.

At six we arrived here at Burr, a very small village on the frontier of Marwar (capital Jodhpore), where there is a very comfortable *dâk* bungalow, from which I am writing.

The sun sets with its usual beautiful pink and gold, and tom-toms and gongs send forth their hideous discords; for this is the time for the Hindoo marriages, and the great Hindoo Festival of the Full Moon approaches. I am the only white man within a radius of thirty miles. Truly the British Raj is a wonderful thing: if we have not won the native love, we have gained his respect or inspired him with a wholesome fear. The numerical inferiority of the ruling race must always strike the traveller in India. It is true I have not been to many garrison towns, where English troops may form a good per-centage of the population. In this state of Marwar, with its 1,700,000 inhabitants, there are two white people, one a doctor at Jodhpore, and the other an artist at Burr, the extreme frontier town, distant from each other sixty miles; yet we are both as safe as if we were in London, and safer, for no native would think of garotting or offering violence to a *sahib*.

*20th February.*

An early start was my order last night, so the sun had not shown his red face over the squirmy pass of yesterday ere the things were packed on my carriage (which, by-the-bye, from my last night's sad experience, I might call "the buggy," though not the shape of that vehicle), and off we trundled over a flat plain again. There are mountains still to be seen, and high ones, to the south; but for sketching purposes the landscape has no capabilities, from an absence of foreground.

Villages are scarce and hidden away, I suppose, to escape the notice of marauders, who overran the country as late as the early part of this century. In some places there are great signs of prosperity, wells being worked and crops well forward; but the country is not only flat, but covered with most characterless little trees, dotted about in a most tiresome way. At the only large village we passed I saw the first signs of the cultivation of opium, and very beautiful did my old friend the poppy look, spread, all white and red, like a gorgeous carpet, two or three acres in extent, and blazing under an Indian sun. The Rajpoot is a great opium-eater, and can do nothing without his little dose, which accounts for his contempt of death, and possibly for his love of poetry.

I do not know who fixed on the spots for the *dâk* bungalows of India. I have observed many beautiful landscapes near these establishments, but the houses themselves are all placed where nothing can be painted. They generally stand some way from the village. This one at Chondāwal, where I am resting my horses and now writing, is in the usual dull situation, surrounded by frightful pepul-trees, with only an occasional glimpse of blue mountain to be obtained through their uninteresting foliage, and no sight at all of the village. We make a short *dâk* to-day of only thirty miles. Having done sixteen by 11 a.m. I shall stay here four hours, and would have sketched had there been anything to do.

I had not been here ten minutes when the *thakoor* of the village, a feudal tenant of the Maharajah's, came to pay his respects to his Highness's guest, and present his gift of milk and butter. He is a fine-looking fellow, nearly 6 feet high, with an aristocratic aquiline nose, and a pair of piercing black eyes; his whiskers and beard are brushed at right angles to his face to give him the appearance of a tiger; and with plenty of opium in his stomach, and a *tulwar* in his hand, I dare say he would be capable of deeds to be recorded by the bards of Rajasthan. Of what these fellows were capable, take this, culled from the pages of the gifted but somewhat redundant Tod, who relates it in his account of Mewar or Oodeypore.

"The *herole*, or right of leading an assault, was held to be a great honour by the braves of Mewar. The right belongs to the tribe of Chondāwat, whose chief lives at Saloombra, and this is how they got it. The Rana was besieging a town, and decreed the assault: the head of the Chondāwats claimed the right to lead the way, but his right was disputed by the Saktawat clan. Now, the Chondāwats were very numerous, but of the Saktawats there were only sixteen, but all men of approved valour, sons and grandsons of Sakta, a relation of the Rana. Neither party would give way, and it seemed likely at one time that, instead of taking the town, the Rajpoots would turn their swords on each other. At last out spoke the Rana:

"'To that clan shall belong the *herole* for evermore whose first man is first over yonder wall.'

"To this both parties agreed. At an hour before sunrise the great drum was beaten, and each clan under its leader rushed to the town. The Chondāwats, in the dark, got into a marsh, and lost the way to the gate, but rushed to the walls themselves. The Saktawats, more lucky, reached the gate. Alas! in their haste they had forgotten to bring ladders, and the gates were spiked outside, so that elephants were no use. Delay was dishonour. The chief of the Saktawats slid down from his elephant and placed himself with his back against the spikes, calling on the *mahout* to bring the elephant against his chest. The gates yielded, and over the dead mangled body of their chief the sons of Sakta rushed to glory. At that moment a shout from the wall proclaimed their defeat. The Chondāwats, arrived at the wall, placed their ladder, and up rushed the chief: at the top of the wall he was shot, and fell back. The next to ascend was a mighty hunter, and called from his feats in the chase the Tiger Thakoor. Grimly smiling, he seized his chief's body in his muscular arms, and reached the top of the wall: 'The *herole* to the Chondāwats!' he cried, with a voice of thunder, as he pitched the body of the dead chief inside the wall of the town, and the clan shouting their war-cry, 'The Portal of Mewar!' followed the Tiger chief. So the Chondāwats gained the *herole* by a second.

"When the town was being sacked, two Moslems were found so intent on a game of chess as to be unconscious of the noise of the assault. Being told to prepare for death, they begged to be allowed to finish the game. The chivalrous Rajpoots delayed their vengeance, and the game being finished, the Moslems cheerfully submitted to their fate. The Saktawats were very angry at the granting of the above war-cry, saying nothing was left for them, till a bard gave them their war-cry, 'The Bar that closes the Portal.' These clans exist now."*

These waitings during the heat of the day are very tiresome. There are no *chics*† to the doors—or windows, for they do duty for both—and flies are innumerable; the intolerable tickling makes it difficult to collect one's ideas. The hum of noises out of doors lulls one's senses, and invites sleep. Alas! drat the flies!—on the hands and face alike they settle and bite. I wander out, hoping to find something to do: no, nothing I could do with profit; so I sit down to my journal again.

Have I ever introduced you to my man Noor Khan? He is a Moslem, and a very strict one too. Nothing will he eat that has not been killed in the orthodox way. On arrival here, he asked me to shoot some pigeons for him,—there were a quantity on a tree. As it's for the pot, I let fly into the middle, and down flop four. "Cut their throats!" cries Noor Khan; and he and the *khansamah* here, another Mohammedan, fly about to make the necessary sacrifice. "See," cries Noor Khan in triumph, holding

* This story I find in Rousselet's book, but having taken it from Tod's "Rajasthan," the Frenchman puts it into the mouth of a wandering *charun*, or bard.

† *Chics;* thin rush blinds costing four rupees each; hence, in slang, a *chic* means R. 4.

up the bloody spoils of the chase to Roopjee, the Rahtor coachman, "see what a good *shikar* my *sahib* has made!"

The Hindoo turned away without a word, and with evident disgust. He wouldn't touch one were he starving, such are the different prejudices of these people. I found out afterwards I had done a very shocking thing. All blue things are sacred to the Hindoo, and these pigeons were "blue rocks"!

At Jeypore I had to blow up Noor Khan for being out all day in the bazaars, leaving my traps unguarded, while I was away painting the Rajah. Coming back at 6.30 the next day, I find him on guard.

"May I go get something to eat?" he cried faintly.

"What do you mean?" I asked.

"I not eaten since yesterday afternoon, and master say no go to bazaar."

"Good gracious! cannot you get anything to eat here? my other bearer can."

"He and G—— Sahib's servant eat anything; they Christians; eat what master leave. I cannot."

So to provide himself on the journey here, he procured at Ajmere half a sheep, of which he has cooked curious-looking joints for his *sahib* each day. Last night, to my astonishment, he produced a very tolerable pudding, and as I chipped off the brown round the dish, I thought of home, and how as a child I had been fond of such things years ago, and I blessed Noor Khan.

He has his weaknesses,—a tremendous love of finery, especially in *pugrees;* a great love of buying things, in which, as he generally succeeds in anticipating one's most confirmed dislikes in the way of Manchester abominations, he has to be checked. He has also a wild delight in illuminations, and has produced and broken more lamps than it is possible to conceive. Even now, when I have restricted his luggage to a minimum, he not only brings out my usual hurricane lantern, but two or three bottles with candles stuck in them. These are amiable weaknesses, you will say. His worst weakness is his fearful jealousy of my other servant, the Madrassee Manuel. He hates the sight of him, and his eyes glitter with rage whenever Manuel approaches me. Poor Manuel, being a Christian (?), is a mild specimen of an elderly man on whom all contrive to trample. Even G——'s Bombay "boy," who was really a boy, ordered him about with great *hauteur*. He is very slow: not so Noor Khan, who is always rushing about, a most comic figure, with his head, on which is folded an enormous and resplendent *pugree* or turban, thrown up, and his elbows brought back. So enormous is his *pugree*, that he looks like a large ninepin.

With these two I shall have to spend my time for the next three weeks, and speak to none others, intelligibly at least; so it's right you should make their acquaintance. Noor Khan I got at Bombay; he comes from Cawnpore. Manuel, or "boy," as all Madrassee and Bombay servants, notwithstanding their age, are called, is a "treasure" recommended by my brother from Calcutta. Manuel has gone with my heavy luggage to Jodhpore by camel-carriage; and for the time Noor Khan is delighted. As a rule the latter looks after my clothes and person, and the former cleans my palette and waits at table. Prestongee, my Parsee boy, I have sent back home, as he was a great expense and a useless incumbrance; being neither man nor master, neither fish, flesh, fowl, nor good red herring. I should have retained the little man, who was a useful slave, but for his extreme *insouciance*. The fact is, he bored me to extinction.

At 3 p.m. we started from Chondāwat for our second stage that day. Again we sped along a sandy plain stretching on our left towards the south, far away to the mountains on the borders of Mewar, across which I must pass on my way to Oodeypore. On our right were several villages, with tanks or ponds, and of course rich vegetation. The whole country wants but water to be a Paradise. So I have heard that the Suez Canal has done wonders in Egypt: that you have only to upset a cup of water, and the next day you have grass.

On this plain were quantities of black buck, at which I popped away, but without success. An accident had bulged my Purdy, and with a smooth bore it is hopeless to try to hit at more than

70 yards, and these shy creatures never let me get within 120 or 200. However, the excitement of trying to hit relieved the monotony of the journey, and the afternoon passed pleasantly enough. At six we arrived at Soojut, where we were to pass the night. The secretary to the *hakim*, or principal man of the town, was waiting for me, and I had barely time to wash myself before the *hakim* himself came to offer his *salaam* and two trays of almonds, sugar-candy, and fresh vegetables. Having dismissed him with honour, I strolled out to a camp of people on their way from Delhi back to Baroda, hoping to find some British with whom to fraternize. The British were not such fools as to come so long a journey, and I found the "colonel *sahib*" decidedly black. He told me they had been five months going to Delhi and back. This gives an idea of the size of India, and how long it took in the olden days to do your travelling: people were three months doing what we now do in thirty hours by rail!

Soojut has a fort and two funny-shaped rocky mounds, which have formerly been fortified, but which are now covered with ruins. I suppose it is an important place, since the *hakim* seems to be a swell. Don't confuse this gentleman with a *hākim* or physician. He is the Maharajah's officer in charge.

To-morrow we are to start at six, and I am promised relays enough to take me to Jodhpore by three. I must to bed and prepare for my forty miles' jolt through the sand. We have had at present what is called in India a *puckah* road, that is, a made road; but to-morrow we have only *cucha*, so I must steel my bones to many a bang. It has got very hot to-day. I keep wonderfully well, and am quite set up from my Jeypore cold.

*Jodhpore*, 21*st February*.

Up to Soojut, the travelling had been pleasant enough; but from Soojut here the roads were said to be bad, and they did not belie their reputation. I think I explained in my last the difference between *puckah* and *cucha*. These roads were *cucha* with a vengeance! My old hearse of a carriage swayed and lurched like a small boat in a storm. The timbers of its old frame shivered and trembled, and I thought every minute they would part company and leave me flop on the sand. The shaking I got was a sensation, I can assure you; and when I finally sailed into Jodhpore, I offered up a prayer to the divinity to be invoked by *dâk* travellers for my safe arrival. The distance from Soojut to Jodhpore is fifty-six miles. We had four relays of six horses to do the journey.

The last half of the time a hot wind arose, and with it a storm of dust; so I had my first view of the city of Jodha as if through a thick London fog. Jodhpore is a considerable city of some 100,000 inhabitants, over which towers the palace and fort. The streets are very narrow, and my hearse, albeit a narrow carriage, had great difficulty in forcing a passage along the crowded thoroughfares. Ever and anon we had to wait till an unlucky bullock-cart was shunted, with screams, shouts, and imprecations, out of the way of the Maharajah's guest. The architecture, as usual with purely Hindoo cities, is most picturesquè, with endless varieties of pierced window and balcony. Many very splendid temples we passed, all which I hope to see more at my leisure; and then, going out of the farther gate, we went up a terribly steep hill, and finally stopped at the Residency.

## CHAPTER VIII.

### JODHPORE.

HERE I found the Maharajah's servants waiting for me with many *salaams*. The Residency has been one of the old palaces, and is surrounded by a high wall. Within are two large buildings: the largest, in which I now reside, being inhabited by the political agent, who is at present absent, and the other by the doctor.

I was received with all courtesy by the latter, who is himself going on furlough next month, and, so to speak, camping in his house. Soon the Maharajah sends a deputation with the usual *dholle*—a number of trays with vegetables, sweetmeats, flour, rose-water, &c., which I graciously receive; and shortly His Highness's private secretary follows to offer his *salaam*. Pundit Sheo Narain talks English, and we get on beautifully. He informs me that the Maharajah holds his race meeting the next day, so cannot sit then. He invites me to the Jodhpore Races, and with many compliments we part. It is no use being in a hurry with these people, and I must kick my heels, happy if I can book his Highness for the day after.

I here received three mails from England. Those who have never been out of the way of posts can little imagine the avidity with which home news is devoured, and how the longest letters seem all too short. This morning I have been inspecting my new home. The pavilion in which I live is large, and strongly built of stone. A long room, running the whole length of the house, is lined with marble; this forms a handsome sitting-room. The bed-rooms, of which there are two, are large and cool; in fact, for a native-built house, this is most comfortable. The garden, which lies between this house and the doctor's, is well kept, the paths being raised masonry, with little water-courses running by their side. The Indian gardener's work consists entirely of watering. He constructs little water-courses and earthen dams all over his beds, and you see him squatting all day long on the ground changing the course of the water, so that each tree and plant may have its share. The water has to be drawn from the well. Two bullocks and their driver work here, and contrive, by primitive machinery, to supply the main water-course from which the supplementary ones are fed.

This gardener has many enemies to contend with in the monkeys. There are swarms of them here, of the huge grey and black kind. The walls round the gardens are high, but nothing is too high for them. They swing from the tops of the trees on to the roof of my present abode, on which they drop with a heavy thud. They climb down into my balcony, and fill me with dread lest they should find their way to my paints and canvases, when, indeed, they would play what my Yankee friend would call "merry hell." My friend the doctor here told me that they got into his room one day after his servant had laid out his clothes for dinner, and ran off with the whole lot. One old monkey was seen on the top of a tree trying on the Medico's best inexpressibles, while many portions of raiment were found scattered about the country for a mile round the house. Monkeys being sacred, one is not allowed to revenge himself as human nature would suggest.

At 2.30 we were bound to go to the Maharajah's race meeting, and off we (the doctor and myself) started, in a carriage and four. There are certainly wonderful things to be seen here. The city does not, like Jeypore, lack picturesqueness through its regularity. Every turn in the street gave you a fresh picture, and every picture would be worth painting. The houses are built of the red stone of the place, which is whitewashed over. The fort and palace were newly whitewashed for Lord Northbrook, who was here about a year ago. The white is still on the walls, for whitewash holds well here, since there is so little rain—only 4 inches a year.

Right through the town we drive, past palace, temple, and tank. The *syces* shout and distribute their blows on obstinate bullocks, inattentive drivers, or innocent passers-by alike; we jostle the corners of the streets, but happily the carriage is strong, and we survive; and finally, passing through the opposite gate of the city, we reach the race-ground on the farther side of the town. The first thing I perceive is a placard with "Jodhpore Race-ground" written in English thereon. Everything is done in English style, and all the directions and names written in English; and yet I have reason to know that in all the crowd there were but two who could read the directions on the boards. This is one of the many instances of the extraordinary desire of the native to imitate the European. I wish this would lead them to sacrifice any of their prejudices; but, I fear, as yet the desire is only to conform outwardly. The Maharajah has built a grand stand of solid stone, for which five rupees admittance is charged; we, happily, are admitted free. Most of the Maharajah's jockeys are the Maharajah's brothers, and the horses belong to them or to the chief. It is a pleasant sight to see the enthusiasm they display in riding a race; and as riding is a manly exercise, and these brothers are fine young fellows, all this is very well. I only trust the want of communication will preserve Jodhpore from the professional ring man, who is the scum of the population.

The Maharajah receives us with great cordiality, and conducts us to his grand stand, seating us to his right and left in places of honour. His delight in his new amusement is too strong for his politeness, and he soon leaves us and joins the crowd of amateur jocks and others by the weighing-house. We are, however, plied with cheroots and brandy-and-soda by his orders, and, as it is impolite to refuse, are forced to take more than we want. He also sends from time to time to apologize for his absence.

Jeswant Sing, head of the Rahtors, and Maharajah of Marwār,

is a good-looking man of, I should say, forty; probably he is not so old. His father, Tukt Sing, succeeded the famous, or rather infamous, Maund Sing in 1843. He was chief of the Rahtors of Amednugger, and was invited to give up that principality for Marwār, on the death of Maund Sing without children. Jeswant Sing was born in Amednugger. Now, the next brother was born here, and has caused much trouble both during his father's life-time and at his death, by claiming the *guddee* on that plea. The father, too, was an unsatisfactory rajah, difficult of access, and full of strange quips. It was he who caused all the row at Lord Mayo's *durbar* at Ajmere, in 1867, by refusing to sit below Jeypore, though the matter had been settled by treaty years ago. The *durbar* was held with Jodhpore's place vacant, and the old gentleman was packed off, bag and baggage, the very next day, and had two guns taken from his salute—a terrible punishment for a rajah. The real reason for his absence I heard from his "political:" Tukt Sing was too drunk to appear. In truth, he was a truculent and absurd old thing, and played "ducks and drakes" with his property. He gave most of the crown jewels to a lady whom he delighted to honour, and who has them still, and sticks to them. He left ten legitimate sons, and of the baser kind five times as many. There were many of these of both kinds at the races, some quite lads.

Jeswant Sing succeeded to the *guddee* only a few years since, and found a considerable amount of debt, and much discon-tent, left as a legacy by the truculent Tukt. He had to com-mence by exiling his brother, Suroor Sing, who claimed the throne. He is, however, a very good fellow himself, and very popular: you can always see whether a rajah is a good fellow by his treatment of his brothers. Now, these here, except the before-named Suroor, are very good friends: the only fault I have to find with Jeswant Sing is, that he has, as usual, no idea of time, and I have been kept waiting two days for a sitting. I wrote a most touching and "high-faluting" letter to his secre-tary, saying "that I could only stop a certain time here, and during that time my services and talents were at the Maharajah's service, but that I could not lengthen my stay, since other rajahs were waiting for me;" that "I was particularly anxious that the head of the Rahtors, of whom I had read such glorious things, should be well represented in the picture to be hung up for ever in the palace of the Empress; and that, although it might be irksome to sit, it was a small price to pay for the immortality I should confer!" and suchlike. As Wigan used to say when he played the Frenchman in "The First Night," "I think that will tickle him."

I had a visit from Bigi Sing, the Prime Minister, yesterday, and made a sketch of the old man. It is the first drawing I have tried here, and the discomfort of such efforts is great. The heat was tremendous, and the bread dried between one's fingers, so that it was impossible to pick out high lights in the way one can in England. The dryness of the atmosphere is wonderful. You may slop on your oil colours with pure oil to any extent, and, of course with the exception of the lakes, all is dry the next day: even lakes only take two days. The curse is the dust, which penetrates everywhere. Flies, too, are very annoying. At Ajmere the wind blew at night off the lake, on the *bund* of which Saunders's house is situate. The plague of midges set in, and I assure you it is no exaggeration to say that lamps were put out by them. Their mangled little corpses strewed the table two inches thick, and there was quite a smell of burnt midge!

The feud between Jodhpore and Oodeypore dates back from the time of Akbar, in the sixteenth century. Jodhpore early succumbed to the blandishments of Delhi, and gave its princesses to the arms of the Emperor. Not so Oodeypore; and on one occasion, when Jodhpore went to Oodeypore after his loss of caste, the Rana refused to eat from the same platter as the Rajah. Wars innumerable succeeded, but the final split occurred as late as 1804 (*vide* Colonel Tod, who was then at Oodeypore). Bhim Sing, the reigning Rana, had a daughter Krishna Komari, "the virgin Krishna," whose fame for beauty went forth throughout Rajpootana. She was the daughter of a princess of the Chawara race, the ancient Kings of Annulwara of Southern India. In infancy she was betrothed to the Rajah of Jodhpore; but the bridegroom died, and his brother and successor claimed the bride. Meanwhile Jujgut Sing, the dissolute Rajah of Jeypore, sent to demand her hand, and was secretly favoured by the Rana. But neither Rajah would give way, and with the help of a certain Amir Khan, who alternately sided with one or the other, the whole of the Rajpootana, including Oodeypore, was laid waste. Amir Khan, a kind of Mohammedan freebooter, finally laid siege to Oodeypore, and through his agent, a certain Agit (on whose head the curses of the Rajpoots will for ever rest), persuaded the Rana that the only way to heal the wounds of his country was to sacrifice his daughter. The Rana, a weak man, consented. Daulut Sing, a relation, was sent for, and told to "save the honour of Oodeypore." "Accursed be the tongue that commands it! Dust on my allegiance, if to be preserved at such a sacrifice!" he cried, and rushed from the presence. Jowanda, an illegitimate brother, was then called on. The dire necessity was explained, and it was urged, for the honour of the family, that no strange hand could be permitted to perform the sacrifice. Unwillingly he accepted; but at the sight of Krishna Komari, her beauty so overcame him that the dagger dropped from his hand. His emotion betrayed the purpose for which he had come, and soon the cries and lamentations of the mother resounded through the palace. But the danger was not past: poison, prepared by female hands, was presented in the name of the father. Krishna bowed and drank, sending up prayers for his prosperity; and to the imprecations poured on the head of her father by her frantic mother, sweetly replied, "Why afflict yourself, my mother, at this shortening of the sorrows of life? I fear not to die: am I not your daughter? Why should I fear death? We are marked for sacrifice from our birth.* We scarcely enter the world, but

* It was usual for the Ranas of Oodeypore to kill their female children. When a child is born, his or her birth is notified to the Rana. If it proves a girl, the Rana, by turning down his thumb, silently decides the poor thing's fate. The nurse presses her finger on the top of the poor infant's skull, which at birth is little thicker than skin, and the child ceases to exist.

we leave it. To my father I owe my life; let me thank him that I have lived so long." But Mata, the preserving goddess, watched o'er her life, and the poison refused to assimilate with her pure blood. Twice more was the bitter potion prepared, and three times the goddess averted the decrees of fate. One would have thought that even the enemies of the Rajpoots would have been appeased. But no! Amir Khan insisted, and Agit, said to have been a most pious man, still urged the necessity of the sacrifice on the reluctant parent. This time opium, against which neither gods nor men can contend, was the poison tried, and it was mixed with *kasumba*, a soothing draught. With a smile, the poor girl drank again, wishing all was over. She slept, never to wake, as pure a victim as ever fate demanded or poetry has recorded; and her mother, overcome by her anguish, followed her daughter to her funeral pyre.

Agit, who had worked all this desolation, when he reported the sacrifice, was spurned from the presence of the freebooter Amir Khan. "Is this Rajpoot valour?" cried the Moslem. Four days after, Sangram, of the clan of Sakttawat, the rival of Agit, arrived at Court. A true Rajpoot, he feared neither the swords of his enemies nor the wrath of his sovereign. Forcing his way into the presence of the Rana, he found Agit there, seated. "O coward," cried Sangram, "who hast thrown dust on the race of Sesodia! the blood which has flowed in purity through a hundred ages has now been defiled, its course is now checked! Alas for the blot so foul that no Sesodian can again hold up his head, for the sin no punishment can wipe out! the godlike race of Bappu Rawal is at an end! The gods have decreed this for our destruction!" The conscience-stricken Rana covered his face. "And thou, Agit, impure of Rajpoot blood! dust be on the head that brought this shame on us all! Mayest thou die childless, and thy name die with thee! Why this haste to consummate the foul sacrifice? Had the Moslem stormed the city and violated the sanctity of the Zenana? If he had, you could have died as your ancestors the Rajpoots have ever died. Was it thus they gained a name among heroes? Was it thus they opposed the might of kings? Have you forgotten the *sakas* (sackings) of Chitore? You are no Rajpoots. Had the honour of your females been in danger, had you sacrificed them all, and, putting on your saffron robes, found death in the ranks of the enemy, the Almighty would have found means to continue the divine race of Bappu Rawal, and you would have gained immortal honour. You did not wait the threatened danger, you owed your safety to an unhallowed deed! Alas, the end of our race approaches!"

Strange to say, the curse was nearly fulfilled. Of ninety-five sons and daughters, but one lived to succeed his father as Rana of Oodeypore, and he died childless; and the line of Bappu has had to be perpetuated by two adoptions in the last fifty years.

The fate of Agit was still more dramatic. Within a month his wife and two sons were numbered with the dead. For years he wandered a mendicant through the shrines of India, with "Rama! Rama!" constantly on his tongue, and the hatred of all true Rajpoots on his head. Not all the waters of the sacred Ganges can wipe off the blood of the virgin Krishna, and for ever will he live the execrated and loathed theme of Rajpoot poetry.

The story reminds one of Iphigenia; and if it does not yield in poetic interest to the Greek tale, it has one additional merit: it is true, and happened in this very century, attested by an Englishman on the spot.

Since then Jodhpore and Oodeypore have not been friends, and I have told how the late Rajah behaved when he met the Rana at Ajmere. At Delhi, however, they became reconciled, and now, I believe, consider each other "friends of the stomach."

*25th February.*

To my pathetic letter of yesterday I received an answer that the Maharajah would sit at four to-day, and being freed, I went out and made a sketch of the palace and citadel, that rise high over the town. Jodha, the founder of the town, was very wise in the selection of the site. From the plain or plateau between this and Soojat, the ground falls, and, after two or three miles, rises again in several respectable hills, on the highest of which is the palace and fort. It was, of course, a place of immense strength in olden times, before men had digged "villanous saltpetre out of the bowels of the harmless earth." During the troubles produced by the Rajpoot Helen, mentioned above, Amir Khan besieged this place, and, planting his guns on a hill near this house, sent several shots plump into the palace. Such ungentlemanly conduct had not been foreseen by Rajah Jodha, who planted his palace on a precipice, and trusted to its height for its protection. Probably the tough old Rajpoots of that date would have resisted even at the expense of the destruction of the palace. Not so Maund Sing, who surrendered at once. The havoc made by Marathas at the beginning of this century (Amir Khan was nominally the commander-in-chief of Jeswant Rao Holkar) is still to be traced throughout Rajpootana. Villages are only just starting up and ground being re-cultivated; for now the seventy years of peace given by the paramount Power, and secured by its firmness, have begun to produce their natural effects. And the Rajpoots are grateful too; for in the Mutiny, when the troops throughout Rajpootana mutinied, the Rajpoot princes stood firm, and even the truculent Tukt Sing, father of the present Rajah, protected all European refugees, and gave his assistance in every way.

I have been to my first sitting since writing the above. A picturesque but decidedly hot drive round the outside of the town took me to the Rae-ka Bagh, a palace built for himself by Jeswant Sing, the present Rajah. Pundit Sheo Narain, his private secretary, informs me that his Highness did not like the old palace in the fort of Jodha, because the rooms are small and confined, and so he set to work to build a palace of his own, after European style. It is not finished even now, so I ought not to criticize.

Like most Indian palaces, the Rae-ka Bagh is a collection of pavilions in a garden, round which there is a high wall. After being kept waiting some time in the hot sun, I was shown into a pavilion of two storeys. The lower one, open to all the winds that blow, was littered with bundles of linen; so I thought "The Rajah is having covers made for his furniture." What was my astonishment at finding these heaps of linen were all recumbent Rahtors, probably suffering from the effects of opium! Above this open *loggia* was a largish room, fitted up with European articles according to the habit of rajahs. On the table in the centre were two large clocks, endless cases for photographs, and knick-knacks of all kinds; on other tables similar ornaments. To the ceiling hung three chandeliers and about twenty-five lamps; in the four corners of the room were four large photos of the Prince of Wales, all the same, in the uniform of the 10th Hussars. Soon I was joined by Pundit Sheo Narain, the private secretary, &c. We cleared out a small room at the side, where the window was somewhat larger, and thus made a rough sort of studio. The Maharajah uses this room for a bedroom sometimes, and it was nearly filled with an iron bedstead. These people are full of caprice, and will sleep anywhere if the fancy seizes them. A *charpoy* and a *rezai*, a rough four-legged bedstead and a counterpane, are enough for the greatest rajah. They have no love of home or *chez soi*—no household gods—no comforts. How can they understand England and English literature, where these things occupy such a prominent place?

I have to wait for the Rajah. Alas! one has always to wait. Presently in he comes, in his undress—spotless linen and muslin, so that you can see the colour of the brown skin underneath; bare legs and a common-looking *pugree:* such is the get-up of the chief of Marwār, the head of the Rahtors! He is a good-looking man, but very shy, I should think. He won't talk much, and to me only remarks that he would like to be taken the other way round, as then the jewels of Marwar would show. To humour him, I turn him so that he will look out of the picture. Most of these fellows—like Henry VIII., by-the-bye—dislike to be taken in profile. All around, on the floor, squat, as usual, the Rajah's courtiers; and as ever fresh numbers join the throng, they *salaam* to the ground. The Maharajah takes no notice of the *salaams*, and, enlightened prince though he is, according to his private secretary, and good fellow as he is reported to be by all who know him, he looks heartily tired of everything, and has the usual ineffably bored look that all such people acquire.

Merry laughter comes from outside; I hear shouts of "Wah! wah!" and am aware of the fact that the brothers are playing at Badminton on a piece of green sward I had noticed. The Rajah does not care for Badminton. Perchance he thinks it is *infra dig.* for a Rajah to rush about and get warm. I should like to work him up and amuse him. I make feeble starts in conversations; I try all kinds of subjects. No, there he sits, bored and placid, a Rajah all over.

His Highness having been late, the sitting is soon over, as it gets dark.

The next day I have another sitting. As usual, the Rajah is late again, later than ever, and I am in despair! He sends a swell *thakoor* to make his excuse, and with him I try to converse. My Hindoostani is very feeble. I wish to say I hear the Rajah is very fond of dogs. The *thakoor* looks confused. What have I said? I am afraid of having committed myself, and stated the Rajah is a beautiful dog. I'd better hold my tongue. I look from the window. All about me are pigeons, some with silver bangles round their red legs. What am I to say? The *thakoor* is as bored as I—as the Rajah. What a nuisance that I cannot communicate my ideas! I gaze from the windows again. On the opposite window I see an inscription; it looks in a strange character; but, no surely, though half worn out, that must be an "A" and that an "L." Yes! I have it! "Ladies' superfine cloth,"—that is what I read on the Rajah's blinds, in rather worn golden letters. It is twenty minutes past five, and I cannot see beyond six. Confound all Rajahs!—Ah! here he comes! I must smile and be happy, with black rage at my heart. These are my suffering, O my friends! and should anybody wish to paint rajahs, I should say, "Don't!" Yet the man does not appear to be rude. Verily rajahs have no more idea of the value of time than sitting hens. G—— is right.

p. 126

H.H. JESWANT SING, MAHARAJAH OF JODHPORE.

"Hooli," the great festival of the Hindoos, being now on, and there being an eclipse of the full moon, the Rajah has asked to be excused sitting for two days. More delays! However, it can't be helped, and I must employ my time sketching.

These Rahtors are descended from Seoji, a grandson of Jeichund, the Emperor of Canooj mentioned before. By the sword, like every other empire, was the State of Marwar gained, and if any one reads the pages of Tod, he must own it was plentifully cemented with the best Chohan blood. The Rahtor is essentially a man of the sword. One Rahtor is equal to ten Cuchwahas, and the Rao and Rajahs of Marwar are mighty warriors rather than statesmen, like the Jey Sings of Dhoonder. If the feudal system is prevalent in Rajpootana, it is all-powerful in Marwar. From Jodha the land was divided among eight great clans, called in the language of the poet "the Eight Pillars of Maroo;" and although in the main the chiefs of these clans were faithful to the crown, the Rahtor blood was easily fired, and many a time the throne itself has been shaken for a sarcasm or imagined slight to heads of the Champāwats or Koompāwats. Moreover, these chiefs seem always to have reserved the right of deposing their liege lord if he should prove unfit for the "cushion of Jodha." This right was exercised in the choice of a successor to Rajah Guj, who left two sons, Amra and Jeswant. Amra was of a most violent and impracticable disposition, and at a solemn convocation of the feudal chiefs of Marwar, he was solemnly deposed. "This ceremony, which was marked as a day of mourning, was performed with funereal pomp. As soon as the sentence was pronounced, that his birthright was forfeited and assigned to his younger brother, the *khelat* of banishment, consisting of sable garments, was brought forth. In these he was clad; a sable shield was hung on his back, and a sword of the same hue girded round him; then, being mounted on a black horse, he was commanded, but not in anger, to depart whither he listed beyond the limits of Maroo."

Jeswant Sing, the other brother, was the great Rajah of Marwar. "Jeswant," says the bard, "was unequalled amongst the princes of his time. Stupidity and ignorance were banished, and science flourished, when he ruled; many books were composed under his auspices." He was much employed under the Emperors Shah Jehan and Aurungzebe, but his policy was that of Jey Sing, viz., to ruin the power of Delhi as much as he could without actually breaking with the Emperor. Gallantly was the *pānch runga* * carried through many a hard-fought field; as many times did the Rajah treacherously deceive his sovereign, and fail at the last moment. Yet the vassal was too powerful to be punished by the cunning Aurungzebe, and if any monarch deserved to be outwitted, surely it was the cruel persecutor of the Hindoo. That Aurungzebe duly appreciated the power of Marwar, and hated the ruling house, is shown by the cruel way he tried to massacre the family of Jeswant Sing, who had died in his service amidst the snows of Cabul. But first let us glance at the fate of Amra, which at least justified the preference given by the chiefs of Marwar to his younger brother. These tales are not given as history, for this is not a history: I only recount or quote from Tod such stories as I think are good traits of the Rajpoots among whom I am staying; and let me add that at each of the Rajpoot agencies I have found Col. Tod's volumes, which are indeed the great authority on the affairs and history of Rajpootana.

Amra, then, with a considerable following, went to Delhi, and was well received by the Emperor Shah Jehan, who gave him the Munsoob of 3,000, with the grant of Nagore. But Amra was of an independent turn of mind, and once, while the Court was at Agra, absented himself a whole fortnight from his duties, hunting the boar and tiger—his only recreation. Shah Jehan reprimanded him for his absence, and threatened him with a fine. Amra proudly replied, putting his hand to his sword, that that was his sole wealth, and left the presence. Shah Jehan then sent Sallabut Khan, his paymaster, to Amra's quarters to enforce a fine. This was refused, and the observation of the Syud not suiting the temper of Amra, he unceremoniously told

* The five-coloured flag of Marwār.

him to depart. The Emperor, thus insulted in the person of his officer, issued a mandate for Amra's instant appearance. He obeyed, and having reached the Am Khas, beheld the King, "whose eyes were red with anger," with Sallabut in the act of addressing him.

Inflamed with rage, Amra then passed the *omrahs*, or lords of five and seven thousand, who stood between him and the throne, as though to address the King (or Emperor); then with a dagger which he had concealed in his sleeve he stabbed Sallabut to the heart. Drawing his sword, he made a blow at the King, which, descending on a pillar, shivered the weapon to pieces. The King abandoned his throne, and fled to the inner apartments. All was uproar and confusion. Amra continued the work of death, indifferent upon whom his blows fell, and five Mogul chiefs of eminence had fallen, when his brot er-in-law, Mjoon Gore, under pretence of cajoling him, inflicted a mortal wound. Nevertheless he continued to ply his dagger till he died. To avenge his death his retainers, headed by Bulloo Champāwat and Bhao Khoompāwat, put on their saffron garments, and fresh carnage ensued in the Lal Kelah (red fort at Agra). "The pillars of Agra bear testimony to their deeds, nor shall they ever be obliterated from the record of time; they made their obeisance to Amra in the mansions of the sun." So sang the bard. The faithful band died to a man; and Amra's wife, a Princess of Bhoondi, came in person and carried away the body of her husband, with which she committed herself to the flames. The Bokhara Gate, through which they gained admittance, was closed, and called Amra-Sing's Gateway; neither was it opened till the English came to Agra.

This "running a-muck" was not an uncommon thing with the Rajpoot, whose undaunted spirit was sustained by plentiful doses of opium, which rendered them insensible to pain, and I fear sometimes to reason.

Agit, the son of Jeswant, was born amid the snows of Cabul after the death of his father. The faithful Rahtors bore him towards their home. On their arrival at Delhi, Aurungzebe offered to divide the state of Marwar among the feudal chiefs who attended their infant sovereign, if they would deliver up their charge. Now, land has irresistible charms for the Rajpoot, and many are the deeds of what seems to us the basest treachery, that have been perpetrated to gain landed property. But the Rahtors were true to their trust. "Our country," they replied, "is with our sinews, and these can defend both it and our lord." With eyes red with rage they left the Am-Khas. In a basket of sweetmeats they sent away their young prince, and then prepared to defend their honour against the hosts of the Emperor; they made an oblation to their gods, took a double portion of opium, and mounted their steeds. "Let us swim," they cried in the song of the poet, "in the ocean of fight; let us root up the Azures, and be carried by the Apsaras to the mansions of the sun!" Then Soojah, the poet, took up the word. "For a day like this," said he, "you enjoy your fiefs, to give in your lord's cause your bodies to the sword. As for me, who enjoyed his" (the deceased Jeswant Sing's) "friendship and his gifts, to-day will I make his salt resplendent. My father's fame will I uphold, and lead the death in this day's fight, that future bards may hymn my praise!" Then spoke Doorga, son of Assoh. "The teeth of the Yavans is whetted, but by the lightning of our swords shall Delhi witness our deeds, and the flame of our anger shall consume the troops of the Shah!"

They thereupon set fire to a train of gunpowder, and the *raja loca*, or their wives and children, were sent to inhabit *swerga*, or heaven. Lance in hand, with faces resembling Yama,* the Rahtors rushed on their foe. Then the music of swords and shields commenced; wave followed wave on the field of blood; and Sankra completed his chaplet in Rajpoot history, as he had many occasions of doing.

Most of these faithful Rahtors fell that day. Some few, with the faithful Doorga, succeeded in cutting their way through the Moslems, and escaped to their infant chief, whom Doorga, a great name in Rahtor history, conveyed to Mount Aboo, into a

* The Hindoo Pluto.

place of safety known to him alone; and for years the country, overrun with invading Moslems, was content to know that "Dhunni," their lord, was living. Doorga was a constant thorn in the side of Aurungzebe; so much so, that upon one occasion "rage so got the better of his religion, that he threw the Koran at the head of the Almighty." Six years the Pillars of Maroo sighed for their chief, till they could resist no longer; "without the sight of our lord bread and water have no flavour." At length they had their wish; then, "as the lotus expands at the sunbeam, so did the heart of each Rahtor at the sight of his infant sovereign. They drank in his looks, even as the *pipaya* in the month of Asoj sips drops of *im ritsu* (ambrosia) from the blossoms of the *champa*."* Verily—

> "I had a dream of chivalry,
> And large white plumes are dancing in my eye."

Yet this is in 1687!

Through his long reign of forty-three years Agit was the beloved ruler of his people. Fearless in war, his strength was only equalled by his courtesy. At the age of eleven he dared to present himself at his enemy's palace, and in the most ceremonious of courts behaved with the dignity worthy of the head of the Rahtors. Yet was he foully murdered, and by his eldest son and declared heir. From that day the chivalry of Marwar declined. The bard from whom I have quoted was the celebrated Karna, who played a great part in the deeds he recounts. His "Surya Prakas" consists of 7,500 stanzas; but in it he merely says, "At this time Agit went to heaven." Abhye Sing, his successor, and Bukhta Sing, his brother, but for that foul murder, would have been worthy of their father and grandfather. But their children, Ram Sing and Behem Sing, ruined their country; and their successors, Beyz Sing and Maun Sing, finally succeeded in reducing Marwar to the level of the other native states of India. Alas for feudal chivalry! Three gene-

* There is a tradition that the peacock (*pipaya*) gets quite inebriated from sipping the blossoms of the mango-tree when it is in full bloom!

rations of tyrants or fools will reduce it by natural selection to nothing. As yet nothing has taken its place, but a nation with such traditions, which has produced men like Doorjadas and Agit, may yet bring forth heroes in a better cause.

The wonderful circumstance to me is that this should have happened in the last century. Agit was killed in 1728! Fancy Richard Cœur de Lion, Bayard, or Lancelot in the eighteenth century!

Yesterday morning, 29th February, we went to see the fort. I was conveyed up the steep incline in a *palki* by several old fellows, who must have found a considerable difference between my 18 stone and the weight they generally have to carry.

The fort is perched on a high rock. From it you get a most extensive view of the plains of Marwar stretching far away, as far as the eye can reach, as flat as a pancake. At the foot lies the town of Jodhpore, a dense mass of small houses, with no trace of streets and open places except where you can trace the large square of the Maharajah's stables and the occasional green splash of a tank. On the top of the cliffs are many guns, the worn-out relics of what must have been formerly good artillery. I should be sorry now to fire the old things in wrath, though I suppose the sight of their honeycombed old muzzles may inspire awe in the town which they seem to command.

In the steepest part of the fort is the palace and Zenana. Most picturesque and old are they, and built up many storeys, with beautiful old windows of pierced stonework. Many a funny story could those walls tell, since they were fixed by Rajah Jodha in the fifteenth century. At the entrance to the fort I noticed on each side of the gate rough impressions of many hands. Small were they, and evidently feminine, and silvered over with great care. On my questioning the obliging old commander of the fort (who is also Master of the Horse to his Highness), he told me they were records of former *satis* performed by ladies of the ruling family. Poor little silvered hands! belonging to wretched creatures who possibly had never been out of the walls of that Zenana for years, till they made that sad journey to the Chatries of Mundore, and their horrible deaths. The tom-toms are sounding now, for it is Hooli, the Saturnalia of the Hindoos,—the same tom-toms which beat loud to stifle the screams of the victims to Brahminical tradition. No more little hands will be added to that ghastly record; never more will a rajah be carried out with all his robes and jewels, to be burnt with those he loved. Make up the number, finish the tally, and turn over a new leaf.

Listen to the description my friend Karna, the bard, gives of the *sati* performed after the death of Agit.

"On Asár the 13th, the dark half-moon of 1780 (A.D. 1728), 1,700 warriors of the eight ranks of Maroo for the last time marched before their lord. They placed his body in a boat,* and carried him to the pyre made of sandal-wood and perfumes, with heaps of cotton, oil, and camphor. But this is a subject of grief: how can a bard enlarge on such a theme? The *Nazir*† went to the *rawala*, and as he pronounced the words, '*Rao Siddoe*,' the Chohani Queen, with sixteen damsels in her suite, came forth. 'This day,' said she, 'is one of joy. My race shall be illustrious. Our lives have been passed together: how, then can I leave him?'

"Of a noble race was the Bhattiani Queen, a scion of Jessul, a daughter of Berjung. She put up a prayer to the Lord who wields the discus.‡ 'With joy I accompany my lord: that my fealty (*sati*)§ may be accepted rests with thee, O Krishna!' In like manner did the gazelle of Derawal and the Tuar Queen of pure blood, the Chaori Ranee, and she of Shekhawati, invoke the name of Heri, as they, too, determined to join their lord. For these six Queens death had no terrors; but they were the affianced wives of their lord. The curtain wives of affection, to the number of fifty-eight, also determined to offer themselves as a sacrifice to Agni (fire). 'Such another opportunity,' they cried, 'can never occur if we survive our lord. Disease will seize and make us a prey in our apartments. Then why quit the society

* A vehicle shaped like a boat—perhaps figurative of the sail across Voiturna, or the Styx of the Hindoo.

† *Nazir*, the officer in charge of the *rawali* or chief Zenana.

‡ Krishna. § Or "*suttee*" as it is pronounced.

of our lord when, hap what may, we must fall into the hands of Yama, for whom the human race is but a mouthful? Let us leave the iron age behind us.' 'Without our lord even life is death,' said the Bhattiani, as she bound the beads of *toolsi* round her neck, and made the *tilac* with earth from the Ganges. While thus each spoke, Rahoo, the Nazir, thus addressed them: 'This is no amusement. The sandal-wood you now anoint with is cool; but will your resolution abide when you receive it with the flame of Agni? When this scorches your tender frames your hearts may fail, and the desire to recede will disgrace your lord's memory. Reflect, and remain where you are. You have lived like Indrani,* nursed in softness amidst flowers and perfumes; the winds of heaven never offended you, far less the flames of fire.' But to all he said they replied, 'The world we will abandon, but never our lord.' They performed their ablutions, decked themselves in their gayest attire, and for the last time made obeisance to their lord in his car. The ministers, the bards, the family priests (*purohets*) in turn expostulated with them. The chief Queen, the Chohani, they told to indulge in affection for her sons, Abhye and Bakhta, to feed the poor, the needy, the holy, and lead a life of religious devotion. The Queen replied: 'Koonti, the wife of Pandu, did not follow her lord; she lived to see the greatness of the five brothers, her sons: but was she to be envied? This life is a vain shadow; this dwelling one of sorrow; let us accompany our lord to that of fire, and there close it.'

"The drums sounded, the funeral train moved on. All invoked the name of Heri†. Charity was dispensed like falling rain, whilst the faces of the Queens were radiant as the sun. From heaven Umia‡ looked down; in recompense for such devotion she promised they should enjoy the society of Agit in each successive transmigration. As the smoke emitted from the house of flame rose to the skies, the assembled multitudes shouted, '*Khaman! khaman!*' (well done! well done!) The pile flamed

* The Queens of Heaven. † Khrishna, the Interceder.
‡ The Hindoo Juno.

like a volcano. The faithful Queens laved their bodies in the flames, as do the Celestials in the Lake of Mansurwar. They sacrificed their bodies to their lord, and rendered illustrious the races whence they sprang. The gods above exclaimed, '*Dhun, dhun,** Agit! who maintained the faith and overwhelmed the Asures!' Savitri, Gouri, Saravasti, Gunga, and Goomti† united in doing honour to these faithful Queens. Forty-five years, three months, and twenty-two days was the space of Agit's existence when he went to Amrapoora, an immortal abode."

The poet forgot to give the dying speech of the Chohani Queen, who, as she ascended the pile, exclaimed, "May the bones of the murderer be consumed out of Maroo!"—the direst curse a Rahtor could utter. Bukhta, the actual murderer, the son of Agit and brother of his successor, remembered it when his day came, and the curse was fulfilled.

Having given a description of a *sati* taken from the poem of an Indian and therefore prejudiced writer, let me here quote again Bernier:—"When I was passing from Amadevat to Agra, over the land of the rajahs that are in these parts (Rajpootana), there came news to me that a certain woman was upon the point of burning herself with the body of her husband. I presently rose, and ran to the place where it was to be done, which was a great pit, with a pile of wood raised in it, whereon I saw laid a dead corpse, and a woman, that at a distance seemed to me pretty fair, sitting near it, on the same pile, besides four or five Brahmins, putting fire to it on all sides, five women of a middle age, and well enough dressed, holding one another by the hand, and dancing about the pit, men and women looking on. The pile of wood was presently all on fire, because stores of oil and butter had been thrown upon it; and I saw at the same time, through the flames, that the fire took hold of the clothes of the woman, that were imbued with well-scented oils, mingled with powder of santan and saffron. All this I saw, but observed not that the woman was at all disturbed; yea, it was said that she

* *Dhun* means riches, but in this sense glory, which is, according to Hindoo ideas, associated with riches.

† The five celestial Queens.

had been heard to pronounce with great force the words, 'Five, two,' to signify, according to the opinion of those that hold the transmigration of souls, that this was the fifth time she had burnt herself with the same husband, and that there remained but two times for perfection, as if she had at that time this remembrance, or some prophetic spirit. But here ended not this infernal tragedy. I thought it was only by way of ceremony that these five women sang and danced about the pit; but I was altogether surprised when I saw that the flames, having taken hold of the clothes of one of them, she cast herself with her head foremost, into the pit, and that after her another, being overcome by the flame and smoke, did the like; and my astonishment redoubled afterwards, when I saw that the other three took one another again by the hand, continued their dance without any apparent fear, and that at length they precipitated themselves one after another into the fire, as their companions had done. It troubled me sufficiently that I knew not what that meant, but I learnt shortly after that these had been five slaves, who, having seen their mistress extremely afflicted at the death of their master, and heard her promise not to survive him, but burn herself with him, were so touched with compassion and tenderness towards this their mistress, that they engaged themselves in a promise to follow her in her resolution, and to burn themselves with her. Many persons whom I consulted about this custom would persuade me that what they did was from excess of affection, but I afterwards understood that it was only an effect of opinion, prepossession, and custom, and that mothers, from their youth, besotted with this superstition, as of a most virtuous and most laudable action, such as was unavoidable to a woman of honour, did so infatuate the spirit of their daughters from their infancy; although at the bottom it was nothing else but an art of the men, the more to enslave their wives, and thereby make them have more care to their health, and to prevent poisoning them.

"She that I saw burn herself at Surat, in the presence of many Dutch and English, was of a middle age, and not unhandsome.

To represent to you the undaunted cheerfulness that appeared in her countenance, the resolution with which she marched, washed herself, and spoke to the people, the confidence with which she looked upon us, viewed her little cabin made of very dry millet straw and smallwood, went into this cabin and sat down upon the pile, and took her husband's head in her lap and a torch into her own hand, and kindled the cabin, whilst I know not how many Brahmins were busy in kindling the fire round them; to represent to you, I say, all this as I ought, is not possible for me; I can at present scarce believe it myself, though it be but a few days since I saw it.

"'T is true that I have seen some of them which at the sight of the pile and fire appeared to have some apprehension, and that would perhaps have gone back, but 't is often too late. Those demons of Brahmins that are there with their great sticks astonish them, and hearten them up, or even thrust them in, as I have seen it done to a young woman that retreated five or six paces from the pile, and to another that was much disturbed when she saw the fire take hold of her clothes, these executioners thrusting her in with their poles. I remember amongst others that at Lahore I saw a very handsome and very young woman burnt; I believe she was not above twelve years of age. This poor creature appeared more dead than alive: when she came near the pile she shook and wept bitterly. Meanwhile three or four of those executioners, the Brahmins, together with an old hag that held her under the arm, thrust her on, and made her sit down on the wood; and, lest she should run away, they tied her legs and hands, and so burnt her alive. I had enough to do to contain my indignation," said worthy M. Bernier, and I hope my readers sympathize with his feelings.

It was not an uncommon thing for other persons besides wives to sacrifice themselves with the great. When Rajah Maund was burnt, in 1843, seventy-eight persons committed *sati* with him, —not only his wives, but aged and infirm persons, who thought thereby to secure their salvation, and sneak up to heaven in the train of the great Rajah!

Yet the doing away of this custom has its inconveniences. Each wife has, on marriage, a certain number of villages given to her as a portion. In olden times these, on her death, reverted to the reigning rajah, so that a clean sweep of all the wives of his predecessor, sometimes fifteen or sixteen in number, was decidedly useful, as it naturally swelled his Highness's income.

Into the Zenana I did not of course penetrate, but the palace I saw. Here is the marble platform on which the Rajah receives his *teeka* or mask of succession: that marble seat is the cushion of Jodha, where the sword is girt about the Rajah, and the *toora* bound round his head. Here is the chamber where old Tukt Sing breathed his last; here is the hall he decorated, and there is his picture, and those of many of his sons, with their whiskers black and well turned up, after the manner of the Rajpoots. A curious room this, and a good specimen of late Hindoo work. Barbarous in its aspect, with rather raw colours, but still with a character of its own, infinitely preferable to what Jeswant Sing, the present Rajah, is now doing at Rae-ka-Bagh, some of the work in this room is really good. The ceiling is an elaborate gold carved pattern over glass, and I have no doubt in the evening lights up well. The whole has an odd look from the walls being built at all kinds of angles to suit the exigencies of the ground. As I said before, the traceries of the windows in the palace are particularly good. I hope to get some carved here, as Sheo Narain, private secretary, tells me he has made my wish known to the Maharajah, and his Highness says he will help me to carry out my wishes.*

Jodhpore is a very hot place, and already the heat in the middle of the day is getting very great. I don't go sketching then, but sketch in the evenings. Even then the heat seems to rise from the ground. I shall take very good care and keep out of the sun as much as possible.

I leave here on the evening of the 2nd, having deferred my departure one day, to enable me to attend an entertainment given in my honour by the Rajah. I shall travel as much as

* Vain hope! rajahs never perform promises of this kind.

possible by night, by bullock-cart, and I shall take four days to get to Oodeypore.

*3rd March.*

I am still lingering at Jodhpore. On the 1st I went out at 6.30 a.m. to Mundor, the old capital of Marwar. The road, if road it can be called, was awful. Imagine the stony bed of a Highland stream, and then fancy yourself dragged over such stones by six horses. Nature around, as old travellers used to say before Sir Walter Scott introduced a feeling for romantic scenery, was horrible and shocking, and melancholy in the extreme. At Burr, as I remarked in my letter from that place, all looks as if a great Gulf Stream had rolled over it for ages. Here the hills appear burnt up, as though scorched by some mighty fire. They are quite bare, except where here and there a most impassable prickly abomination, of which I don't know the name, rears itself up, like an array of green serpents, from the ungenerous rock. Through these hills we plunged and bumped for four miles, when we emerged on the plain, which reaches right up to the confines of Oodeypore, and of which I shall have something to say when I cross it. After some tough dragging for the six horses, we arrive at last at Mundor. A pleasant little green nook in the barren hills it seems. There is but little town left, and it could never have been much of a place, as the space is limited. A few houses and the celebrated *chatris*, or burial memorials of former rajahs, are all that remain. When a rajah dies at Jodhpore, he is placed, with all his splendour, in his state chair—formerly, surrounded by his wives—and carried to Mundor, and there burnt. His ashes are taken by his heir, and deposited in the sacred Jumna. His people, the males at least, show their sorrow and respect by shaving their heads, beards, and whiskers, only the successor being allowed to retain his prized locks. Over the place where his body was burnt is built a *chatri*, or half tomb half temple. And here they are, sacred to the memory of many rajahs, some small and poor, some really fine and beautiful; the two best are those of Jeswant Sing and Abhye Sing. Gradually, however, the sacredness of the edifice seems to be forgotten, and many of the *chatris* are used for different domestic purposes; only those of the two last rajahs had altars. At the tomb of my friend Tukt Sing I had to offer a rupee, according to custom, they said. The Maharajah has a summer residence and a very pleasant garden at the upper end of the valley, over which I was shown. Attached to this residence is a curious temple and arcade, in which are arranged colossal figures of the gods. Brahma, the God-father; Suraj, the Sun-god; Siva, the Avenger, with his wife, the convivial Sati; Rama and Krishna, the two incarnations of Vishnu, the latter with the wives of Gopio, or Herdsman, with whom he is said to have behaved in a most compromising way, entirely destroying those ladies' reputation for all time; and a *guru* or saint whose name I could not catch. In another gallery are the effigies of many rajahs, all alike, mounted on their steeds, and turning round to stare at you.

I 've let my journal run down two days, and now, while waiting for my breakfast at a wretched *dâk* bungalow, must see whether I cannot write it up.

I was to have had a sitting from the "Jodhpore Wallah," as he is sometimes called, on the afternoon of the first; but on my return from my expedition to Mundore, I found a message, saying that the Rajah did not feel well, and hoped I 'd excuse him. The fact is, Hooli is a kind of Saturnalia, when it is considered the right thing to commit any folly, and his Highness had probably what is vulgarly called "coppers." I again gave vent to my feelings, and cursed all rajahs. The whole day was wasted, and I consequently felt in a rage. In the evening we were to dine with the Rajah ("we" means here self and the doctor, with another doctor, Inspector-General of Hospitals, who had arrived the day before). I did not see that there was much the matter with our august friend when we arrived at the palace. He received us with great friendliness, and after a little ceremonious "talkee-talkee," conducted us to the upper room of the pavilion I have previously described. Of course he could not dine with us, but he sat behind us and talked convivially all the time, producing his guns, &c., for us to examine. Guns are always produced, and afford subject for endless talk, as sport is what most excites the enthusiasm of the Englishman and native alike. I was waiting for him to say something about the sitting, but it was not till much later in the evening that he expressed his regrets; and he behaved so well on the two subsequent days, that I have forgiven him.

The dinner, after one or two mishaps, such as rum being served round as sherry, &c., comes to an end, and already we hear sounds of singing and music below, for we are to have a grand *nautch.* Then we follow the Rajah downstairs, and sit in state. The *nautch* is arranged on the Badminton ground and the walk at the side, both covered with red cloth for the occasion.

First comes the *prima donna*, who chants an interminable love song, with an occasional slow wave of the hands.

But Jodhpore is celebrated for its dances, and we, not understanding the words of the song, which is the best love poetry of Rajpootana, grow impatient. Meanwile a quantity of dark squatting figures are dimly seen on the lawn. The Rajah gives the order. Torches are lit all round; a big drum sounds; the women stand in a circle, and the dance begins. It is called the *gummer*, and was instituted in memory of a former Rajah, one Rao Rinmul, who headed an expedition, and came decidedly to grief. This the Pundit would not allow, saying it was another Rao Rinmul. The character of the dance was quite enough to prove to me that I was right, and I shall refer to the pages of Tod as soon as I can lay hands on his bulky volumes for confirmation.* One hundred women dance round in a kind of stately measure, with "woven paces and with waving hands." They keep beautiful time, and in the strong light and shade of torchlight, with the glitter of many a bangle, armlet, and anklet, the effect is most striking. Ever and anon the great drum in the centre gives a boom, when the women all throw up their arms together, and behind all, the great moon rises over the dark trees. I never was more "fetched." To the *gummer* succeeds

* I can only find one Rao Rinmul, and he is the one I alluded to.

the *darower*, danced in threes by about thirty women, which is also very pretty. In this the women veil their faces. Then we have the *pugree* dance, danced to the tune of "Pinnee Minnee," which I had seen before; and then, refreshed with "brandy pawnees" and much be-attared and be-panned, and with garlands round our necks, we take our leave. The two doctors go off to Ajmere straight away, and I return to my "Residency" through the moonlight, with the *gummer* still ringing in my ears and filling my imagination. I should like to paint it very much.

On the 2nd I go to the Rajah at 3 p.m., and a very hot drive it is. Yesterday the thermometer was 84° in the cool of the house. The Rajah is punctual, and appears in the state dress of the Rajpoots. A kind of bishop's mitre is on his head and a wonderful stiff kilt round his waist. The latter he gave me, and I shall take it home to astonish the Scotch, and to prove that my study of Jeswant Sing is not pure invention, as wicked people might suppose.

GUMMER NAUTCH, JODHPORE.

p. 142

## CHAPTER IX.

### JODHPORE TO OODEYPORE.

ON the morning of the 3rd I got my long-wished-for telegram from the political agent at Oodeypore. To-day all the *dâks* are ready laid, and I determine to start to-night and bump through the cool. I had a good sitting, and I have bumped, and here I am, much shaken and terribly hungry. The worst is that I have outstripped my servant and my luggage, and am solitary, famished, and dumb, for I cannot explain to these fellows what I want.

The last six hours I have travelled by bullock-cart—a new experience, and one I do not relish. I must go on, however, in the same vehicle, which is a coffin, as usual, but on two wheels instead of four, and consequently bumps and jumps in a way to break limbs less sturdily constructed than mine. My next stage is Dessoori, the border town of the states of Marwar and Mewar, and in the mountains.

I manage to get a fowl from the old man at the bungalow, and I sit and write and growl many hours. Round goes the sun, and down he finally sinks, and still no luggage. I wander forth disconsolate, for I want to get on to the next stage—Dessoori—this night, and the time is passing. Finally I hear shouts in the distance. I shout too, and find my servant, Noor Khan, with a native and a bullock harnessed together, and himself pushing behind. "Couldn't get bullocks," says he. "Rajah's letter only to the *hakim* of Palli and Dessoori, and an intervening *hakim* says it doesn't apply to him." Red-tapeism in the state of Marwar! I am determined this shall not happen again, and when we start, as we do finally at 10 p.m., I mount my man on a camel, with strict injunctions that if he can't keep up he is to stop my bullock-hearse and get in with me. Alas! *L'homme propose et Dieu dispose.* By-the-bye, why do people always say this when things turn out "contrairy"? I arrive, after much bumping, at Dessoori, to find no servant again! I had seen him cheerily trotting after me half-way, and he had said he had been getting on well. He passed me and disappeared. He had, indeed.

Dessoori is a small fortified place, with a wall much like that of a town in North Italy. Through the streets I wandered, inquiring for luggage and servant. In vain I went to the fort. Nothing had been heard of him, but I catch the words "Oodeypore! *Tasvere sahib!*" * and make out that there are men waiting for me at a certain gate. I get there to find two *sowars* and eleven *palki wallahs*, with *palki*, who say they have been waiting three days, and propose starting off at once. I explain (?) that without servant or luggage this is impossible. We sit and stare at each other. They ask whether they may prepare their midday meal. "Certainly." They eat. I am famished. This is worse than Palli. There at least was a bungalow and a tough fowl: here nothing. Mustering my best Hindostani, I ask for milk, and get it. Emboldened by this refreshing draught, I determined to go to see the *hakim* or head man. It's awfully hot, but I won't starve. Off I start, wandering through the streets of the little town to my friend the fort. Here they tell me the *hakim* is at *catchery;* so there I go too, and find *catchery* a broken-down shed. I wish any one could have been by and seen the *hakim* and me, both very polite, and both incomprehensible. I ask for my "*noka*," well-remembered name! The *hakim* doesn't know. I essay all kinds of conversation, which is anything but Hindostani, for the *hakim* looks puzzled. Finally I *salaam* and go, but he sends after me to ask what he can do for me. "A fowl," I cry, "and *chapattis.*" So a live fowl is brought, and *chapattis*, covered with some beastly green stuff that makes them uneatable. However

* Literally "picture gentleman," or painter.

I eat and smoke, and wait for my luggage, and hope for Noor Khan. Still the sun revolves; I try to sleep in a temple, and in vain; I long for the flesh-pots I know to be in my luggage; alas! in vain. Towards evening I make up my mind to slaughter my fowl and cook him myself. But how? I have no saucepan, no plate, nothing. I go to the *palki wallahs*, who are reclining, full and happy, under the shade of some neighbouring trees, and ask them, with much politeness, whether anybody can cook a fowl. They look shocked. Have I offended their caste? Will they leave me and go? No matter. I must try myself. Here one of the *sowars* comes up; and seeing my fell purpose, for I am looking murder at the poor fowl, which the kind Hindoos have been feeding up, and which is clucking about unconscious of its fate, the *palki*-bearers gather round. I determine to do the deed, and dread failure. I seize the neck of the fowl and give a pull. Oh, horror! the head comes off, and the headless carcass goes, still fluttering, amongst the *palki*-bearers, who fly shrieking in all directions. I then proceed to pluck my evening's meal, but one of the *sowars* brings a low-caste native, who performs this task for me. Fire is made; the fowl, indifferently plucked, and with a stick stuck through him, is placed on the fire and actually roasted! They say anything will taste well to the person who cooks it, but this fowl was an exception. Never did I taste anything less appetizing! I had cooked it, and was eating it with my pocket-knife, holding it with the stick or spit resting on my knees, but it was disgusting. I ate pieces from the breast from a sense of duty, and then threw the rest to the crows.

Will my luggage never come? Some accident has probably happened to Noor Khan. The sun goes down. I pace about in the dark, thinking my luggage will come as yesterday. But no! I retire to my *palki*, bar the door with my shut-up chair, the only thing I have with me except a travelling-bag with my money, and I go to sleep. At two a noise. Oh, joy! it is my luggage. I decree a start at half-past five, and turn in again. Presently I am roused by the most diabolical row all round, and I jump up crying "All right." No; the moon shines clear; it is

3.30. Around are the recumbent figures of my native auxiliaries, each sleeping peacefully, wrapped head and all in the folds of his drapery; and the noise is only the peacocks amusing themselves. There are hundreds roosting in the trees beneath which I am lying, and the devil seems to have entered into them. "How I should like to eat them," I think to myself; but they are sacred. I gaze fondly at my long-lost luggage lying there in its bullock-cart, and determining never to leave it again, turn in.

At dawn we start, but I leave a letter to be forwarded to the Maharajah, asking him to set on foot inquiries for my missing servant. A bullock-cart and one *sowar* are told off to luggage, and eleven *palki wallahs* essay and actually do carry me through the Dessoori Pass into Mewar. The Pass itself has no particular beauties. It is mildly mountainous and very well wooded. Neither is it very steep; but ten miles with 18 stone must take it out of their brown backs. They trot along, however; but their joy is, I feel, sincere when they clap their hands as they finally land me under a large banyan-tree at Jeelwarra, on the Oodeypore side of the Pass, shouting as they place me on the ground, "*Ram! Ram! Ram!*" When I tipped them afterwards, they declared they thought nothing of the weight.

At Jeelwarra I find an elephant waiting for me, and I hear there are three more at ten miles apart, and then a carriage to take me to Oodeypore. I determine to travel during the night, leaving at 6 p.m. Meanwhile I demand milk, and breakfast off milk and bread, of which my luggage contains a store. I think dolefully of the day I have to pass, and the cooking I must do; neither are my spirits raised by seeing on the trunk of the tree a slice of bark cut off, and the sad inscription: "Under this tree died Dr. John Hunter, 1872." But joy! three *sowars* appear, under a *duffadar*, who hands me a letter from the political agent at Oodeypore, saying he hears the arrangements of the *durbar* are very bad, and I shall find it difficult to get my servants and baggage through, so that he sends three camels to help.

The *duffadar* is evidently a man in authority. He orders people about; coolies, milk, fowls, butter, everything comes pouring in;

and he insists on cooking my dinner himself. It is tough, but I eat it, with my grizzly friend gazing at me like a father. I am so relieved that I am emboldened to make a sketch, and feel quite happy. Presently, while sketching, I hear a noise of blows and shouting, and behold the missing Noor Khan belabouring a prostrate native.

"Come, come!" I shout, "what's this?"

"Sir, he takes me thirty-six hours about the country; he breaks the rein of a camel," &c., &c.

Well, the camel-driver got a sound thrashing, and may have deserved it, but I was so glad to regain some one who could interpret, that I thought it better not to inquire into the merits of the case.

After a visit from the *hakim* of Jeelwarra, and a good deal of noise and bustle with coolies who are to carry some of the luggage, off we go. A goodly procession! First come sundry coolies, two carrying my canvases on their heads, the said canvases having been strapped on a *charpoy* or bedstead requisitioned from the village; next a boy with a lantern; then the *sahib* on his elephant, followed by two *sowars;* then his retinue on three camels; and, finally, two more *sowars.* Violet lights lie on the mountains as we start, for the sun has just gone down, and it is six o'clock. The night gradually sets in, and the stars sparkle with unwonted brilliancy. Shall I forget that night in March upon the plains of Mewar? No, I don't think I shall. The *howdah* is a square box, with iron bars round, well stuffed with mattresses. It is constructed to carry a gent who can sit cross-legged, or rather on his heels. Now, I cannot do so, and am gifted with an abundant supply of lower limb; consequently after a time my legs go over the end. "That's better," think I, and I am beginning to enjoy the solitude and the changes in what ought to be a beautiful country if seen, and to look at the stars and think of home (who has not done all this?), when I become aware that the *howdah* is slipping. I observe the same to the *mahout,* who gets up, giving the elephant's head a kick as he does so, and then hangs over the side to right the *howdah.* It's no use. What good is 8 stone against 18? I am obliged to hang over myself, and gradually get things straight. I try cross legs again, and begin to enjoy, or think I begin to enjoy, the motion. There is something tremendous in the power of the great brute whose quarters you can feel heaving beneath you through many a pad and mattress. But oh! how cramped my legs become! Then my second elephant was a long-legged devil, who would not go. He had a swing that would have made some people sea-sick; but never mind if he would only go on.

We have passed the land of romance—of *nullah* and tiny lake, of trees that look hobgoblin against the sky, and of little pool reflecting sky and tree in strips, where the stars look double their natural size in the midst of the dark—and are now crossing a great plain, dotted with scrubby bushes. The moon is shining, and in the distance there appears a large lake, made from famine labour, and which is, I believe, 14 miles long. Strange noises one hears. "What's that?" I ask, to a shout of many voices in the distance, and a roar. "Tiger!" says the *mahout*. I should like to see him, and so strain my eyes, and think every bush a tiger. But the elephant won't move on: he trumpets so that you can feel the vibration through his mighty frame, through pads and all; he strikes the ground with his trunk; then he stops. The *mahout* hits him on the head, to no purpose, with his iron hook; he goes on awhile, then stops again; then more hitting, more shouting "*Hut! hut!*" and much abuse in choice Hindostani, till at last, after many a struggle, we reach the second halting-place at 4 a.m. instead of 2. The third elephant is a first-rate beast, and puts on the steam, and nearly does his five miles an hour; but the faster he goes, the more he jolts; my cushions tumble off, everything goes, and when I arrive here (Duspore) I am in a pulp. "*Ram! ram!*" say I with joy, and strive to jump from the ladder: my legs are all gone, and I fall flat. My back is as though beaten, and my neck stiff. I sink on a bed, and try to sleep. Alas! no. However, the very lying down is a relief, and after all, now, two or three hours after, I am, but for the flies, writing in comparative comfort. Can I forget? I thank thee,

Aide; but no, decidedly no, I shall never forget that night. I am off to Oodeypore by carriage at three o'clock this afternoon, so away with romance, and I hope discomfort too.

I may here remark that in travelling through India the unit by which they measure distances is a variable quantity. It is generally a *koss*. Now, a *koss* is supposed to be two miles, and from Jeelwarra to Duspore was said to be fifteen *koss*, or thirty miles, yet was I from 5.30 p.m. to nearly 10 a.m. doing the distance, and during the latter part going at least five miles an hour.

OODEYPORE TOWN AND CASTLE.

After bumping four hours more in a carriage, I arrive at Oodeypore. I don't mind jolting, if I know I am progressing; and these Oodeypore coachmen get along well. The carriage has been once a lady's pony phaeton. It has now four horses; on the off leader is a postillion, the driver sits sideways on the front seat, and we go at full gallop. I am not timid, luckily, for I see that the coachman, as often as not, has his reins under his horses' tails. Bang, bang! thump, bump! over a *cucha* road for three hours, then one hour over *pucka*, and we arrive. Here all is delightful, my host Impey most hospitable, my bed soft and clean (and did not I enjoy it!), and I am just writing for the post; while Noor Khan is snoring in well-deserved sleep outside my room.

# CHAPTER X.

## OODEYPORE.

*10th March.*

OODEYPORE resembles all the old capitals of Rajpootana in this, that it has a citadel and palace towering far above the town. But Oodeypore is surrounded by mountains, and, moreover, palace and town rise from the bed of a considerable lake, which is artificial, the town being built on the *bund* that encloses the waters.

Mewar generally is very fertile. Round here the corn—and a splendid crop too—is quickly ripening. Water is plentiful, and in India, where water is, there are always good crops. I have seldom seen a more picturesque place. From the lake the palace rises abrupt and vast. Every rana is expected to add something to this palace, so that it is really a very considerable pile. All along the east shore of the lake stretch the houses of the town, while above them appear some large temples, one of which is really very fine. On the lake itself are several islands, of which two contain palaces of the Maharana. The enthusiastic Tod describes these palaces as built of the purest white marble, "whose arched piazzas are seen through the foliage of orange groves, plantain, and tamarind." Alas! the white marble is but plaster! But Tod is not the first that has taken imitation for the real. "All is not gold that glitters," even in the wilds of Rajpootana. Though it is not marble, it is still very beautiful, being a kind of plaster called *chunam*, made of pounded shells and white of eggs, which takes a beautiful polish and looks like the finest marble. To the west of the lake rise some really high mountains, and hills surround the happy valley of Oodeypore on all sides. I shall, I trust, be able to do a good deal of sketching here; but the weather is getting very hot, and I keep from exposing myself to the sun, having received divers warnings from the faculty not to sketch outside of the house during the heat of the day.

The family of the Rana is descended from Rama, who had two sons, Loh and Cush. The eldest, Loh, was the ancestor of the Sesodians, while the Cuchwahas of Jeypore are descended from Cush, the second son. Tod has a large sheet of genealogy, giving the names of all the Rana's progenitors up to B.C. 2200. No Sesodian would doubt one of these names, but the mist of time has passed over all their deeds, and has left nothing but the name. From Vishnu sixty-three names bring one to Ramchunder; from him to Bappu Rawal there are eighty more, and this carries us to A.D. 714. This Bappu first seized on Chitore, and was the founder of the Sesodian house. His loin-cloth (*dhoti*) was 500 cubits in length, his sword (*khanda*) weighed 64 pounds, and he was himself 20 feet high! In early life, his father having been killed, he was adopted and brought up by the Brahmins of Eklinga, where is worshipped Mahadeva under the form of the sacred bull. This brazen bull is supposed to be the one still in existence whose flank shows the blow inflicted by the terrible mace of Mahmood of Ghuznee, who himself broke the brass of the image to discover whether there was any treasure inside.

At this moment India is preparing to invade Afghanistan: will any Hindoo dare to avenge his country's gods on the temples of Ghuznee?

Bappu, like many conquerors down to the time of Barbarossa, is said still to be alive. After founding the power of Mewar, he overcame the kings of the west, married their daughters, and left them one hundred and thirty grandsons. Well done, Bappu!

The power of the family continued to increase, though not without some interludes of misfortune and defeat, till we come to Samarsi, who was a contemporary of our friend the Pirthi Raj, A.D. 1193. On the invasion of India by Shabudin, an embassy was sent to Samarsi, asking for aid. Chund, the poet, gives a description of Samarsi, who, a worthy son of Bappu, had not laid aside the office of "Regent of Mahadeva." A simple necklace of the seeds of the lotus adorned his neck; his hair was braided, and he was addressed as "Jogindra," or Chief of Ascetics. He is represented as the Nestor of the host assembled to defend India. Nevertheless, in that fatal battle where Pirthi Raj was defeated and killed, Samarsi fell "asleep on the banks of the Caggar, in the wave of the steel." Then came confusion. Many victories were claimed over the Moslem, and much blood shed in domestic warfare. Six out of nine ranas perished in the field, and we may be assured that they did not perish alone. Then came Lakumsi and the sacking of Chitore, A.D. 1275. Hamir, A.D. 1301, restored the fortunes of the family, and we are told that though his reign lasted sixty-four years, his sword was never sheathed. He also regained Chitore. For two hundred years the princes of Mewar ruled over not only Jeypore and Marwar, but Boondhi, Gwalior, and many other places, and were by far the most powerful princes in India, repelling all the invasions of the Moslem, and even carrying war into the enemy's country. Their glory culminated in the defeat and capture of Mahmood Sutan of Malwa, an event which led to the building of the Tower of Victory at Chitore, so dear to the hearts of Sesodians.

The murder of Khumboo, the conqueror of Mahmood and the builder of the Tower of Victory, by his son, may be placed with the murder of Agit, narrated in the account of Jodhpore. Ooda, this parricide, is always known in history by the name of "Hatiaro," the Murderer.

The heavens revenged the death of Khumboo, his murderer being slain by lightning as he was quitting the royal presence at Delhi, where he was seeking aid to recover his own provinces. Raemul, the next Rana, was the father of Pirthi Raj, who is the Orlando of Sesodian poetry; and if any one would wish to form an idea of what the Hindoo esteems true chivalry, let him read in Tod the deeds of this maniac. Incited by his uncle, Sooraj-mull, he attempted to kill his elder brother Sanga, to whom a prophet had predicted the throne would descend; neither did Sanga escape without the loss of an eye. Then Soorajmull, becoming too powerful, was attacked. Uncle and nephew met in fight. The uncle was covered with wounds, but both being worn out, they mutually retired to repose. Soon Pirthi Raj quietly goes to see his uncle, and he finds him having his wounds sewn up by a barber.

PIRTHI RAJ. Uncle, how are your wounds?

SOORAJMULL. Quite healed, my child, since I have the pleasure of seeing you.

PIRTHI RAJ. But, uncle, I have not yet seen the *dewanji* (his father, to whose rescue Pirthi Raj had come). I first ran to see you, and I am very hungry: have you anything to eat?

Dinner is brought, and the two eat off the same platter, nor does the nephew refuse the *pân* at parting.

PIRTHI RAJ. You and I will end our battle in the morning.

SOORAJMULL. Very well, child, but come early.

The uncle is defeated, and flies to the wilds of Balurro, where he and his party form a stockade of trees. One night the neighing of horses is heard. "That is my nephew," observes Soorajmull. In dashes the nephew, and an indiscriminate slaughter commences. Soorajmull at last calls a parley. "If I am killed it matters not. My children are Rajpoots; they will run the country to find support; but if you are slain, what will come to Chitore? My face will be blackened, and my name everlastingly reprobated." The sword was sheathed in a moment, and uncle and nephew embraced. Nevertheless, next morning, at a temple hard by, during sacrifice, the impetuous Pirthi Raj attacked and finally killed Sarangdeo, his uncle's adviser, and offered his head at the shrine of the goddess Kali. Soorajmull fled, and founded the state of Pertabgurh.

Pirthi Raj was poisoned by his brother-in-law, whom he had punished for cruelty to his sister; and Raemul dying soon after, Sanga, who had been quietly living in seclusion, succeeded to the throne (A.D. 1565). Eighty thousand horse, seven rajahs of the highest rank, nine Rao, and one hundred and four chiefs bearing the title of *Rawal* and *Rawat*, and five hundred elephants followed him to the field. He defeated the King of Delhi, but in A.D. 1528 he met a greater foe, the Emperor Baber, who had just established his power in Hindostan. The success of the Rana was great at first. The van of the Moslems was cut to pieces, and Baber was compelled to throw up entrenchments and chain together his cannon. Yet was the mind of the conqueror uneasy as to the result of the fight. "On Monday," he says in his memoirs, "I mounted to survey my posts, and in the course of my ride was seriously struck with the reflection that I had always resolved to make an effectual repentance, and that some traces of a hankering of forbidden works had ever remained in my heart. I said to myself, 'Oh, my soul,

> "'How long wilt thou continue to take pleasure in sin?
> Repentance is not unpalatable—taste it.'

Having withdrawn myself from such temptations, I vowed never more to drink wine." The wine-cups were broken up, and given to dervishes and the poor. The army was sworn on the Koran to conquer or die. Nevertheless, for a month the battle did not take place, and the delay was fatal to the Rajpoots. A Tuar Rajpoot was bribed, and deserted to the enemy during the battle; and Sanga, when victory seemed to incline to his side, was forced to retire with the loss of most of his bravest chiefs. He died shortly afterwards. During the reign of his son, Bikramajit, who succeeded his brother, but was a bad ruler, Chitore was again sacked by Bahadur of Guzerat, and again were all the women killed. The Rana, however, recovered his capital by the help of Hamayun. Bunbeer, the bastard son of Pirthi Raj, succeeded to the throne by the murder of the Rana, but the real heir, Oody Sing, was saved by his nurse. "He had gone to sleep after his rice and milk, when his nurse was alarmed by screams in the *rawalla*, and the *bari* (barber), coming in to take away the remains of the dinner, informed her of the assassination of the Rana. The faithful nurse put her charge into a basket, covered it with leaves, and placed her own son in its place. Scarcely had she done so when Bunbeer, entering, inquired for the son of the Rana. Her lips refused their office ; she pointed to the cradle, and beheld the murderer's steel buried in the breast of her babe. So was the life of Oody Sing saved, that he might ruin Mewar, and give a name to its future capital." In his reign Cheetor was again sacked—this time by Akbar. The Rana shirked the responsibilities of a campaign ; indeed, unless history deceives, we must confess that the capital of Mewar takes its name from a coward. Oody Sing's own son said, "Had Oody Sing never been, or none intervened between me and Sanga Rana, no Toork would have given laws in Rajasthan." From this time the history of Mewar is one long series of struggles with the Moguls. One story more. Pertap Sing defended Mewar against Akbar, but his allies fell off, and he was left alone. Maund Sing, the Rajah of Amber (Jeypore) and brother-in-law to Akbar, was mortally offended by the refusal of the Rana to eat with him. "He could not eat with a Rajpoot who had given his sister to a Toork, and probably eaten with him," said the Rana. "It was for the preservation of your honour that we sacrificed our daughter," cried Maund Sing. "Abide in peril if such be your resolve, for this country shall not hold you. If I do not humble your pride, my name is not Maund Sing." So the forces of Delhi and the north bore down on Pertap, and bravely he faced them. In vain through the battle he sought Maund Sing, but he made good his passage to where Selim (Jehanghire, the son of Akbar) commanded. His guards fell before Pertap, and, but for the steel plates which defended his *howdah*, the heir of Akbar would have fallen by the spear of the Rana. The *mahout* was slain, and Selim was only saved by the flight of his elephant. Conspicuous by his red umbrella, which distinguishing mark he would not (like Lord Nelson) put aside, Pertap was thrice with difficulty rescued from amid his foes. Finally Manah seized the insignia of royalty and drew off the battle, whilst his prince, who had received seven wounds, was forced from the field. With all his followers this brave vassal fell, and from that day his descendants have borne the royal insignia, and enjoyed the right hand of their sovereign. It was artillery alone that won for the Moguls the battle of Huldighat.

Pertap fled on the gallant Chytur, the steed that had borne him all the day, pursued by two horsemen. But Chytur was wounded, and the pursuers gained on Pertap; already the sound of the hoofs on the hard flints sounded in his ears, when he heard, in the broad accents of his native tongue, the salutation, "Ho, rider of the blue horse!" He turned: there was but one pursuer, and he his brother.

Sukta, whose enmity to Pertap had made him a traitor to Mewar, had beheld the blue horse flying unattended. "Blood is thicker than water!" He joined in the pursuit, but only to stay the pursuer, who fell beneath his lance. For the first time the brothers embraced in friendship. Here Chytur fell to the ground, and as the Rana was mounting Unkarro, presented by his brother, the noble steed breathed his last. An altar was afterwards erected, which still marks the spot where Chytur fell. Sukta was attached to Selim's body-guard, and had great difficulty in explaining his absence. At last, on that prince's assurance of forgiveness, he owned "the burthen of the kingdom is on my brother's shoulders, nor could I witness his danger without defending him from it." Selim kept his word, but dismissed the future head of the Suktawats. Thus were the resources of the Sesodians wasted in constant struggles against the Moslem, until at last even the energies of the Rajpoots gave way. It is not my intention to give a history of the country; I only give extracts, which are illustrative of Rajpoot character, showing the mixture of staunch fidelity under all trials, mixed with fickleness and childish inconsistency. For an imagined insult many a rana has been killed, while the very name of the descendant of Bappu has called back many a Rajpoot to his allegiance. This name is not without its power nowadays, though the ranas are sadly shorn of their power. The bright light of Maratha usurpation has dulled the lustre of the sun of Mewar, but I fancy any one would prefer dealing with a Rajpoot, even at this date, than with a Maratha. The one is a gentleman, and the other a *parvenu*. But let any one in treating with natives remember that their code of honour is not the same as ours. Even Colonel Tod, whose book on Rajasthan I have so freely quoted, and who is a firm and enthusiastic believer in Rajpoots, in his private letters to the Government, which I have seen, has no term of abuse too great for the conduct of the Rana and his son. Surely, the native is a difficult study!

The first day of my stay here the Maharana came to see my host, Colonel Impey, his political agent. Sujjan Sing, Maharana of Oodeypore, and the representative of the oldest dynasty in India, dating from the sun (who dare go farther back?), is eighteen years old. He is a large, stout, heavy-looking lad, with a curious face, having the long almond eyes one sees in old native pictures, said to be the characteristic of the Sesodian race, of which he is the head. He has, unfortunately, suffered much from small-pox, and his face is considerably disfigured.* He is decidedly amiable-looking, and not devoid of intelligence. I had met him at Delhi; so that he received me as an old friend, and willingly undertook to sit, though he seemed somewhat to dread the operation. He has just come into "his own;" the state has been handed over to his charge, and he is very anxious to do the right thing.

In the afternoon, on our way to row on the lake, we drove through the town. I should say that Oodeypore is smaller and its streets much less crowded than Jodhpore, neither is there so much to see in the town. The tracery windows do not here exist, for easily-worked stone cannot be had on the spot, as at Jodhpore. There are many handsome ornaments, however, made of *chunam*.

The evening on the lake was delightful; we were rowed about by four men in a broad flat-bottomed boat; and finally we landed at Jugnawas, one of the islands mentioned above, and were shown round the palace, or rather villa. Here there are several very

* Many rajahs are much disfigured by this disease. On my first interview with the Maharana, he told me that he had been many months ill and suffered greatly. I took the opportunity of urging the advisability of enforcing vaccination.

original decorations, of which I have also since seen specimens in the palace. They are made in panels, the patterns being filled in with pieces of coloured glass cut into shapes. The effect is really very good, where, as is frequently the case, the pattern is composed of flowers or trees; but it is very comic when figures are introduced, the faces being drawn and then covered with coloured glass. There was also a series of scenes of hunting done in bas-relief, and coloured with very harmonious effect. The gardens on the island are very well kept, and are celebrated for their oranges.

The other island is the one where Shah Jehan, when flying from the wrath of his father Jehanghire, was entertained by the rana of the day. The palace there I have not yet seen, but I am told it is in bad condition.

The keeper of the Jugnawas said the lake was very deep: "Put one elephant on another, and a third on the top, and you would not reach the surface." Yet was this lake quite dry during the great drought of '67, when thousands of people all through Rajpootana died of starvation, and no one heard a word. Two years ago the lake overflowed, and caused much damage both to the decorations of the palace and to the town generally.

Yesterday we (Col. Impey and self) paid a return visit to the Maharana. We were received at the door by a crowd of courtiers, and led with much ceremony along several passages, up steep stairs, and through courts, to the presence. There is a curious feature to be remarked in all really Indian palaces, viz., that the doors are ridiculously small and the stairs terribly steep. There was not a door in this palace of Oodeypore through which a moderately-sized man could pass without stooping. Why, I wonder? Is it to force people to bow when they come into a room?

We are led finally into a pleasantly shaded courtyard, where we find the Rana seated with his Court. He rises to receive us, but does not leave his place. I notice also that he has his shoes on. Both he and his Court are all in white, and he wears but few jewels on such occasions, as he says gems are not in good taste!

I observe he has thick gold bangles on his feet. In the morning I had been looking at some jewellery here, and asked for such bangles; but I was told that no one out of the palace is allowed to wear gold on his feet.

One great characteristic of all these Sesodians is their hatred of anything Moslem. They say that no rana will use a Persian word if he can help it, and certain it is that many of them took, amongst other titles, that of King of the Hindoos and Enemy of the King of Delhi. The last Rana died young, "of nothing to do, and too much time to do it in," the usual complaint of these people, which leads to the use of stimulants, opium, or even worse. One great chief was heard to declare that it was waste of time to get drunk on anything weaker than cherry brandy! A celebrated drink called the "Puttiala Peg," which I have already described as consisting of half brandy and half champagne, effectually did for its princely inventor in four years.

The present Rana was chosen by the Court here, on the death of his cousin, his father, who was a man of turbulent disposition, and had been in disgrace, being passed over. The father is yet alive, and lives at some distance from Oodeypore, being forbidden to see or in any way influence his son. The uncle of the present Rana also put in his claim to the *guddee*, and had it not been for the influence exercised by the paramount Power, there would have been a nice row in Mewar.

A sitting was fixed for this afternoon in the Jugnawas, on the island, and we were invited to dine afterwards with the Maharana in the new English palace, built by his predecessor, and newly furnished by His Highness. By-the-bye, this palace is a sad eyesore on the otherwise beautiful line of the other buildings, being of Indian classic, surely the most debased style of all architecture.

I was then shown over the palace. There were innumerable small rooms, all highly decorated, with pictures let into the wall, and elaborate patterns made of coloured glass all over wall and ceiling. Several apartments had pigeonholes of looking-glass, in each of which was placed some small glass box, or jug, or vase. The effect was savage; but the light being, of course, admitted only through the smallest possible windows, and these very often covered with patterns (done in *chunam*), the effect, somehow, was very rich. There were two rooms done with blue tiles, imported, I should say, from Holland; and one covered all over, ceiling and all, with the old familiar willow-pattern plate! It really looked very cool and pleasant. It is strange what materials these men will use for decorative purposes. I remember seeing, at one of the camps at Delhi, a looking-glass brought for sale, of inlaid ivory-work, flowers, &c. "Dear me!" said I to myself, "that looks very pretty!" On examining it, I found the flowers were made from shirt buttons, the holes being filled with metal rivets. In this palace I saw two portraits of one of the later ranas, with very elaborate frames made of glass and plaster, in which were solid glass bosses composed of those well-known paper weights, with flowers and views of Brighton, found at all sea-side bazaars.

There were many life-sized figures on the walls, sculptured in alto relievo, and coloured; most of them of ladies ministering to the sacred sun—the royal crest of Mewar.

Altogether the decorations were the most truly original I have seen in India, and certainly had one of the great elements of beauty discovered by Ruskin, namely, "Surprise."

My first sitting went off very well, as Impey accompanied me and talked the whole time with the Maharana. I don't think his Highness will be pleased with his portrait, for his complexion is very dark, and I have been truthful in rendering the chocolate tinge of his skin. What am I to do? Must I sacrifice fact to please my sitters? There is not one of them that does not wish to be made white skinned like a European!

It is extraordinary how quick the mind of man is to take prejudices, and how soon a chief acquires a knowledge of the forms and ceremonies incumbent on his position. This boy, three years ago, was running about in his paternal village, with his father in disgrace, and with no notion of the honour in store for him. He is now quite the Rana. At Bombay, when the Prince arrived, he got into a great scrape for refusing to walk after the Guicowar; and to-day, while sitting, he said, "There are but few real dynasties of good caste left in India." "There are Sattara, and Nepal, and

Kolhapore," said Impey. "Kolhapore was good caste," said our young friend; "but they are nothing now, for they have given a daughter to the Guicowar, a mere herdsman."

After the sitting we bundle off home to dress for dinner. We are driven at 7 p.m. to the palace and up a narrow lane, with barely six inches on each side of the wheels of the carriage, and then still up, amidst the well-known strains of "God Save the Queen," to the English palace. All around are coloured lanterns and bowing officials, who conduct us to our feeding-chamber. The palace is not badly done. It is neither worse nor better than a first-class Indian-European house, and except, perhaps, that there is as usual an over-abundance of musical box, the whole thing is in very good taste. The dinner table is laid out in high European style, with candelabra and fountain, silver elephant and golden calf, and such things as one might see on the table of Mr. Jones of Manchester. Presently the Maharana arrives, and we sit down to an excellent dinner (cooked by Impey's cook) and first-rate wines provided by the Maharana. Lord Northbrook was lodged here on his visit to Oodeypore last year, and so the service is more complete than any I have seen.

When the eating is over, the Maharana joins us, and we duly drink the health of first the Empress, and then his Highness, the band playing variations on "God Save the Queen" meanwhile. Then we go up to the first floor, where there is only one room, a very handsome one, leading on to a large terrace, which extends over all the suite we have dined in. Here we are shown fireworks on the lake, with which, of course, we were delighted, but which were no great shakes, and afterwards a *nautch*. They dance the *gummer* here, but only with eight women, and with none of the swing of Jodhpore. A dance with sticks was rather pretty. At half-past ten we retire, with garlands and *attar* and *pân*, amidst a shower of rockets and fizz of catherine-wheels.

Yesterday (11th March) I had another sitting, and moreover made a sketch from the Jugnawas before the Maharana arrived. His Highness sat in his *durbar* dress, all in white, with no ornaments, but some pearls round *pugree* and neck.* After the sitting the Maharana took us out for a row on the lake. The more I see of him the more convinced I am of his good-nature and good intentions; and if he can only have the sense to keep clear of the evil advisers who must necessarily be around his throne, and who constantly strive to make him foolishly puffed up with pride, he will make a very good ruler. Alas! ranas have always been good-natured, but weak. In Tod's time the Rana was constantly giving away village after village to favourites, men and women; and when expostulated with, and told that soon there would be nothing left, he said, "Well, never mind my *sunuds* (orders), let them go for nothing." Again, when ill, they have a distressingly extravagant way of having themselves weighed, bed and bedding included, against gold, and then flinging an equivalent sum amongst the crowd. One-third of the provinces belongs to the Brahmins and "charitable institutions," which means here the support of such idle vagabonds; one-third belongs to the *thakoors*, or nobles, and one-third to the Rana; yet with all that he has to carry on the state, and pay his tribute, &c. The feudal system holds good here as in all Rajpootana. Each *thakoor* is independent, and rules his state, administering the laws as though he were king. He owns allegiance and military service to his chief, the head of the state. Only recently we have introduced a Court of Appeal, in which cases decided by the *thakoors* can be re-heard at head-quarters.

Some of the *thakoors* are rich, and have titles—Rajah or Rao—with £20,000 a year, and they want constantly keeping in order. I heard that Jodhpore was preparing to carry war and desolation into the country of two disobedient *thakoors* while I was at his capital. I wish I had time to go to see the fun. The army of Jodhpore mobilized would be a queer sight.

There are sixteen great *thakoors* of the highest class in Mewar, of whom the Rao of Baedla is now the head. He is a very pleasant old gentleman, very sharp, having vast influence with

* This simple attire reminded me of the description given before of Samarsi, who liked to be called "Jogindra, or chief of the Ascetics."

the Rana, and happily very well disposed towards the English Raj. At Delhi he was given the title of Rajah, but he did not seem very pleased; "For," said he, "the same title was given to a *seth*, a mere merchant, at Ajmere." Natives cannot quite understand the levelling tendency of English law.

On one day of the year, "the 3rd of the month Cheyt," the Baedla Rao is conducted to Court with all the royal symbols of Mewar, and the Rana, advancing to the *Ganesa Deori*, or Hall of Ganesh, the elephant-headed God of Wisdom, conducts him by the hand to the hall of audience, only the Rao's hand is above that of his sovereign. These honours date from 1569, when the ancestor of Rao did good service at the battle of Huldi Ghat. The Baedla Rao is of the Chohan class of Rajpoots.

Another of the sixteen whom I saw was the Rawat of Saloombra. As the head of the Chondāwats, the descendants of Chonda, whom I have mentioned, he has the right of placing his sign—a lance—before the Rana's, which is the palm of a hand, on all treaties. This dates from A.D. 1389, when Chonda surrendered the throne to his younger brother.

This story is a very remarkable instance of the generosity of a Rajpoot. Lakha Rana was advanced in years, his sons and grandsons established in suitable domains, when the cocoa-nut came from Rinmul, Prince of Marwar, to affiance his daughter with Chonda, the heir of Mewar. Chonda was absent when Lakha received the embassy. "My son," said the Rana, "will shortly return and take up the gage, for you would hardly send such a plaything to an old grey-beard like me." Here the Rana twisted his moustachios, and the courtiers laughed. Chonda heard of the jest, "and, offended at delicacy being sacrificed to wit, refused the symbol which his father had even in jest supposed might be intended for him." Now, as it could not be returned without gross insult to the Rajah of Marwar, the old Rana agreed to accept it, provided Chonda would agree to renounce his birthright in the event of his having a son by this new wife, and to be to the child but "the first of his Rajpoots." Chonda swore by Eklinga to fulfil his father's wishes. A son was born; but when he had attained the age of five, Lakha Rana, finding age creeping on him, wished to end his days at the sacred city, Gya. Before he left, however, he wished to settle the succession, and asked Chonda what estates were to be settled on the youthful Mokulji. "The throne of Chitore," was Chonda's reply; and at the installation he was the first to swear fealty, reserving to himself the right of signing as I have mentioned. His life was one of devotion to his younger brother, whom he saved from the usurpation of his grandfather Rinmul, whose departure from Mundore was celebrated in the *gummer* dance I described above.

The present Rawat is a pleasant gentlemanly man of about thirty-five. Alas! he has a most fearful eye, and will not be operated on. Saloombra, his castle, is a beautiful place, and well worth a visit, but I fear I cannot get there, though he was warm in his offers of hospitality. Others of the sixteen I saw. They are all distinguished by having a gold band round the turban, and sit on the right of the Maharajah on state occasions in a regular order. Below these sixteen sits the eldest son and heir to the throne, and then the rest of the royal family. This law was made when the Rana was obliged to sue for peace from Jehanghire. He was excused personal attendance at Delhi, but the heir-apparent was made to serve in the Imperial Court. A sad blow this to the pride of the King of the Hindoos and Enemy of the King of Delhi, and to mark their sense of the degradation they then underwent, their sons are even yet degraded below the sixteen.

When we made our treaty, and they acknowledged our suzerainty, they stipulated that they were not to be bound by the treaty should our Raj ever be transferred to the Moslem. On Lord W. Bentinck's visit to Ajmere, the Rana was made to go to see him, but before starting he sent in a list of stipulations, and one was that on this occasion he was willing to go to the G.-G., but that it must not be taken as a precedent, for in future the G.-G. must come to him!

Things are changed now: our young friend the Rana has been to Bombay to meet the Prince of Wales, and to Delhi to acknowledge the Empress of India. There are those about him who would still urge the absurdities of the olden time; and I have no doubt that, if left to themselves, they would, as in bygone days they undoubtedly did, make the sacrifice of a Bheel when the Maharana crosses the Matic river. Within the last forty years this sacrifice was certainly made; the man had his throat cut, and his body was thrown into the river.

Meanwhile my sittings have gone on well, and I am on the most friendly terms with the Maharana and Court. One of my friends is the *charun*, or Court Bard. The other day, while the Rana was talking business, this man and the favourite *thakoor*, Manoa Sing, came to me and said, "We wish you to stop here, for you do not seem as melancholy as the rest of the English." I told them they were only complimenting my digestive organs, which happened to be better than those of most Anglo-Indians. From that our talk fell on poetry, and I was asked to write some for them. I composed that night a doggerel rhyme, which I sent the Maharana, to draw out my friend the *charun*.

At the next sitting my lines were produced and read aloud by one of the Court who understands English. Then, line by line, it was translated into Hindoostani, the Court and Maharana marking their approval by nodding their heads. When the reading and translation were over, the *charun*, as if inspired, called for paper and pencil, and after having collected his ideas, pencil in mouth, produced his reply. This was written in the Court language of Oodeypore, which contains a number of Hindoo and Sanscrit words, and proved a hard nut for the staff of the Residency to crack. However, by laying their heads together, they evolved the following very literal translation.

> "We have heard Prinsep *sahib*, most excellent and priceless;
> If we too knew English, then would we speak with open heart.
> Men wish to remain near you, Prinsep *sahib;*
> But this causes them to hesitate, that he returns to his country.
> Keep your favours on us like the shadow of an afternoon,
> Remember us ever in your native land, and forget us not."

The *charun* or poet was particularly pleased with the simile of the afternoon sun. "The morning shade is not good," he explained; "since, however great it is, as the sun rises it gets ever smaller; but the afternoon shade, though it begins small, ever increases, till thousands can sit in it!"

You see I am on pretty good terms with the Court here; indeed, one of the sixteen, Manoa Sing, invited me to stay with him for good and teach him to paint. Oodeypore has been altogether a very pleasant place for me. The political agent, my cousin, and his wife were most hospitable, and the comfort of their house after the roughing I went through on the journey was most acceptable. And here let me bear witness to the universal politeness that I have received from all natives in Rajpootana, from the highest to the lowest. The cordiality with which they greet you in street and market-place is very different from the surly indifference you meet in our own states. No doubt, there things are better administered, and the people ought to be happy, but they do not look so, nor is the amusement and fun of a purely Indian town to be found in our provinces. Perchance they have caught the melancholy of the European, from which happily I am exempt.

Thursday, the 15th, was a busy day. First my letters had to be finished for the mail, then I had to go to the palace to see the Hooli played. The proper day for the Hooli was a fortnight ago, on the day on which it was kept at Jodhpore; but the Maharana, for some reason of his own, postponed it till this day, for the Maharana is above all considerations of time, and, like an admiral who "makes it eight bells" by firing a gun, can make it Hooli when it suits him. The Hooli is, as I said before, the Saturnalia of the Hindoos—a feast to the Bona Dea, in which Priapic worship mingles. "Great people play the fool and feast," said my servant Noor Khan, who is a Mohammedan. At 9.30, then, Col. Impey and myself go to the palace, where a state place is prepared for us in the great square. On the north side rise the towers of the palace, the east is formed by the picturesque gate, the south by a line of low buildings, which are crowded, roof and all, with the vulgar crowd; on the western side, in a kind of pavilion, we sit in state. There are some thirty elephants, on which are mounted all the *thakoors* and the *élite* of Oodeypore society, for it is the Court alone that keeps the feast to-day. The great game is to pelt everybody with red powder made of cinara nuts, and called *abira*, and coloured a rich crimson. The Maharana, when we took our places, was playing the Hooli in the Zenana. Presently out he comes already much ruddled. Down goes his elephant: he mounts, and the Hooli begins. The Maharana is in white as usual, but covered, as I have said, with red dust; he wears the *jama* or large old-fashioned Rajpoot petticoat, and on his head a high tinselly aigrette. The *thakoors* are similarly attired. The elephants, already in a line, advance, and each man throws a handkerchief of red powder towards the chief, who advances and returns the compliment. The powder is thrown by means of a handkerchief tied round the wrist at one end, while the fingers hold the other, thus making a kind of sling. The scrimmage now begins: everybody pelts his neighbour. Anon the elephants form a circle and career round; again they form two lines and engage in mimic fight, till great clouds of red dust arise, and the air is thick with powder. The effect was very extraordinary under the fierce sun, with the blue atmosphere and white buildings around. The Maharana sent us a tray of balls about the size of pomegranates, which were made of some thin brittle substance, and filled with red powder. With these I made some good practice at the Chief and his friends on the elephants, and as the balls fell and popped on the backs of the huge beasts, the crowd below applauded, shouting "Wah! wah!" The whole scene reminded me of a carnival at Rome in the old days.

After an hour a procession is formed, and, all alike as red as blood, follow the Maharana through the town. Passing an enormous elephant who is kept in a corner of the palace yard, the Maharana does not forget to salute him with a shower of *abira*. Of this elephant more anon. Having let them clear off, we return to the Residency, and in the afternoon I go to sketch at Jugnawas, where the Maharana has also a gathering of swells. I discreetly keep to a corner of the island, so as not to disturb the festivities, which are sometimes wild and fast. In some places every one gets drunk; here, however, they keep within bounds, as we had an opportunity of knowing, for the Maharana later on came into our boat and went with us to the palace to show us an elephant fight. He is most simple and cordial in his manners, and I should think astonishes people here with his friendliness to us, coming and going with us alone, without any ceremony or fuss.

It is dark by the time we get to our destination, which is a gallery overlooking the great square, in which the Hooli was held. We are in a corner, and just below us, by help of torches, we discover the great "*must*" elephant, whose acquaintance I had the honour of making before. He is enclosed by a wall some 5 feet high and 4 feet broad, and as he moves we hear the jangling of the mighty chains round his legs. His *mahout* is quietly sitting on his back, and making himself comfortable for the fray. Presently more jangling is heard, and another magnificent beast appears dragging his chains after him, and surrounded by men with torches and spears. His chains weigh some 10 maunds, a maund being 80 pounds. The name of the new arrival is "Ganesh," and he is called after the God of Wisdom, the son of Siva. The story is that Siva, in a drunken fit, cut off his son's head, and when expostulated with by his wife, in grim jest put on the head of an elephant, and so Ganesh, the God of Wisdom, is always represented. The first elephant's name is "Manuk Gudge," or the Ruby elephant, "*gudge*" being Persian for elephant. The Maharana would never use such a word, but *mahouts* are all Moslems.

"Ganesh" quickly sights his rival, and approaches the wall, where old "Manuk" rushes at him. Smash go their heads; their tusks clash, for "Ganesh" receives "Manuk," with trunk up and mouth open, on his tusks. Backwards and forwards they sway, sometimes lifted off their front legs, sometimes with their hind legs quite flat on the ground. Sometimes they remain locked as though carved in black marble, and it is only by the clank of their chains that one realizes that they are alive. Then they separate and breathe. Then bang goes "Manuk" again. and "Ganesh" is ready to receive him on his tusks as before.

Sometimes they get pushed round, and had there been no wall mischief would have ensued.

With varying results the combat lasts full an hour, and all the time the rival *mahouts* encourage their mighty beasts by clapping them on the head with their hands, and shouting. Finally we express ourselves satisfied; but they have great difficulty in persuading "Ganesh" he has had enough. Thus is the battle drawn; and surlily, surrounded as before by a company of spearmen, he jangles off to his home, and we have to wait till he is well chained before we can venture forth.

Elephants, when "must," are most dangerous, and, although they can be cured after some months' physicking, they are never quite safe afterwards. The *mahout* can always tell when the fit is coming on from a curious exudation from a hole just above the eye. With all that I should not like to be a *mahout*. They are all Mohammedans, and never live long, the motion of driving an elephant being most injurious.

I had a sitting next day, to finish the Maharana's portrait. It is the best I have yet done, as he has given me a better chance than any of the others, sitting both better and longer. He was evidently pleased with my work, and said, "At first I did not think I should like it, but now I like it too well."

I had arranged to set out on the 17th, but the 18th was the Gungore, or women's festival, and by the especial invitation of the Maharana I graciously consented to stay and witness the *tomasha*, which is celebrated with special splendour in Oodeypore. The 17th I spent in sketching. I went also to see the Jugmunda, the farther island, where I had not yet landed. Here is the home built by Rana Kurna for Shah Jehan. This prince, the son of Jehanghire, was the first who subdued the Sesodian pride, and to whom a Rana surrendered. He was then the second son of Jehanghire, and went by his name, Khurm. He was so kind, and softened the disgrace he brought on the Rana with so much consideration, that, when he revolted against his father, Mewar sided with him, and in his subsequent disgrace he found a home in Oodeypore. To avoid the scandal daily brought about by the conduct of his followers in slaughtering sacred animals, it was found convenient to lodge him in an island, and the Palace of Jugmunda was built. A pleasant place this island, with a most lovely view of the blue hills and glistening towers of Oodeypore. Here is the chair of state, prepared by the care of the Rana, for the future Emperor of the hated Moslems; and here, too, is a mosque for him to worship in according to

THE ISLAND OF JUGMUNDA, FROM JUGNAWAS, OODEYPORE.

his belief. Pleasant courts and gardens there are, with rich decorations, and some of the best figure work I have seen in India. Alas! the floods two years ago have destroyed much that was good, as in the neighbouring island of Jugnawas, and the gardens have not yet recovered their pristine splendour.

It was reserved for the Rana to hail Shah Jehan Emperor of Hindostan, and he was crowned in the palace hard by. Emperor and Rana, in sign of brotherly affection, changed *pugrees*, and Shah Jehan's is still to be seen in the treasury of Oodeypore; while on the island is still kept trimmed the light that burnt before the shrine at which he worshipped; a curious instance of the tolerance of the Hindoo. Fancy a Moslem doing the same for anybody else's gods!

On the afternoon of the 18th I drove to the Gungore *ghât*, where we have usually taken boat for our excursions on the lake. I found the streets full of people, mostly women, who squatted close together on parapet, corner, and housetop, in many-coloured *sari* and petticoat, looking like wonderfully arranged bouquets of flowers. I was taken to a room over the archway leading to the *ghât*, from which there was a good view on the one side of the steep street leading from the upper town to the lake, and on the other of the *ghât*, or landing-place, with the lake itself. The Gungore, I must explain, is the Feast of Mata, the wife of Siva, the goddess-mother, under her name, Gouri, she being the particular deity of Oodeypore.* On this one day she is brought from the precincts of her shrine in each Zenana to the lake, by the brink of which her image, clad in yellow, is placed, and 'midst song and solemn dance the goddess drinks and bathes. Formerly no men were allowed to profane the procession with their presence, and the Rana himself, from his state barge, *salaamed* to the sacred images. The festival became so popular that it was found convenient to increase the number of the days, and the Gungore at Oodeypore now lasts a week.

Down the narrow street image after image is borne, surrounded by singing women, for there is no quarter of the town so poor but it subscribes for its figure; and down, too, on capering and dancing steeds (such as are dear to the heart of rich Hindoos), or on mighty elephants, come the *thakoors* and swells to wait the coming of the Maharana. By the side of the *ghât* is moored the state barge of Oodeypore, a large vessel with stem and stern turned up, and rising some 10 feet from the lake. On the bows is the place of the Maharana, and on the steps forming the incline, according to their rank, are reserved the places of the sixteen great *thakoors*. These take their places as they arrive. Presently the chief appears on horseback, with about twenty richly-caparisoned steeds led before him, as becomes a rajah. He bows to me as he passes under the arch over which I am sitting, and, led by two chamberlains, takes his place on the bows. His suite stand in the body of the boat, and about forty gaily-clad *nautch* girls squat in the stern, forming a most extraordinary combination of gaudy colours, which seem somehow to blend into a

* *Gouri* means yellow, and although celebrated in the spring, Mata, Isa, Parvati, or Kali—for by all these names is this goddess known—is at this season the Ceres of the Rajpoots.

harmonious whole. The boat is pushed from the side, and, slowly paddled by sixteen rowers (eight a side) in crimson and pink, glides over the calm bosom of the lake. It is a ravishing sight. The old *Bucentoro* might have beaten it for rich harmony, but for originality never was there anything like the state barge of Oodeypore.

I too get into a rowing-boat, and quickly overtake the more ponderous barge, to have a good look at it by the twilight. Alas! too short a time does the Indian twilight last. By the time the Maharana in all his splendour has paraded himself past the lake palaces, where, carefully hidden by thick *purdahs*, the queens can gaze on their lord and master, it is dark. Then by the torches on the *ghât* we know that the palace Gungore has arrived, and we hasten back. The steps are covered with white linen, and to the edge are brought three highly-dressed dolls. Close by lies the state barge, with its freight, *thakoors*, with their voluminous white petticoats and nodding gold and silver plumes, Rajah, *nautch* girls, and all. The women chaunt a solemn hymn, and occasionally bow to the figures, while ever and anon, in time to the air, many silver *chowries* flash in the light. Imagine all this by torchlight, and you have a scene not to be forgotten.

The Rana gets up and bows to the figures, and the women, bearing them aloft, troop back home to their solitude, for the Gungore is the only day they are allowed to leave the Zenana.

The Maharana then sends for me to his barge, where, advancing through the ranks of the assembled *thakoors*, I receive *attar* and *pân*, and a *har* or garland, from his Highness's hands. Many civil words are exchanged between us through an interpreter. I don't know whether the Maharana is sincere in his words of regret, but I can vouch for the fact that I am, and that I never was more sorry to leave any place than Oodeypore. The Maharana wishes me "God speed;" I shake hands with him and with several of the *thakoors* with whom I have made acquaintance, say good bye to my friend the *charun* or bard, and rush off to dine with my hospitable friends the Impeys.

# CHAPTER XI.

## CHITORE, AGRA, MUTTRA, AND ULWAR.

At nine I left Oodeypore in a coach and four. I travelled all night, and, as the roads were good, made considerable way during the hours of darkness. At daybreak I turned round to catch a last look of the Aravalli, but alas! the mountains had disappeared. Farewell Oodeypore! farewell Lake Pechola and its fairy islands! farewell to the land of romance. Good bye! I shall have to say to thee, O Tod! but once more I must turn to thy bulky quarto, for I am to be at Chitore to-night; and then I return to Agra and civilization. I am writing still in the land of Mewar, at Nembhera, sixty-three miles from Oodeypore. Towards the north-east and east these lands have been sadly curtailed. Towards the north, between Mewar and Marwar, the vegetable limits of Mewar are very exact, they say. It was Chonda who first fixed the boundary with Jodha, the founder of Jodhpore. Hence the Rajpoot distich—

> "Aonla, aonla, Mewar;
> Bawal, bawal, Marwar."

Wherever the *aonla* puts forth its yellow blossoms, there is Mewar; where the *babool* begins, there begins Marwar. This division held good for years. I fear, however, the fanciful limit of Chonda does not now hold good to the north. To the south and east, neighbours like Sindia and Holkar have not spared the King of the Hindoos. Many a village and district has been seized by these Maratha robbers, and are still held by their agents, in the midst of the plains of Mewar.

Pleasant enough it was to drive over these plains in the early morning, with the ripening corn all ablaze against the rising sun, and the trees throwing long shadows across the green fields of poppy and maize. The poppies have lost their glory, for of the masses of blossom I saw three weeks ago, but one or two remain, blushing unseen, like the last rose of summer; but to make amends, the fields are full of country-folk—man, woman, and child—all scraping the slit pods for the precious juice which, when dry, is sold as opium, and the bright *saries* and *dhotis* of red, blue, yellow and white, form, as they glitter in the level sun, a study indeed. So I roll along in the Rana's carriage. Too soon, however, does the sun assert himself, and oh! how hot it gets! Under sketching umbrella (double best) and hood of carriage I recline, and drink in artistic effects till I reach here (Nembhera) at 10.30. At four I take carriage again, and drive on to Chitore, the ancient capital of Mewar, where I propose stopping the night, that I may inspect the wonders of that city in the morning.

While changing horses at a small village, I saw a curious custom of the cultivators of the soil. A group of these, either Bheels, Menas, or Jats, I am not learned enough to decide which, was squatting under a tree by the roadside. Then comes a man, evidently a traveller, but well known. They all stand up, and the newly-arrived goes round to each, placing his right hand under the knee, while the man so saluted places his hand under the armpit. They all cry "*Ram! Ram!*" The land of Mewar belongs of course, to Rajpoots, but it is cultivated by these Bheels, Jats, or Menas, who were the original possessors of the soil. They are, in fact, serfs of no caste. All natives have a pretty way of putting flowers behind their ears or in their *pugrees.* They have, of course, no button-holes. I once saw a Rajpoot go up to a Bheel who had so stuck a yellow flower, and tear it from his ear. For the ancient treatment of these aboriginal tribes by the dominant Rajpoot I refer you to Tod. Oaths and promises were never kept by the latter, and even when a Mena or a chief of that tribe protected and fed one of these Rajpoot heroes, on the first favourable occasion the guest turned on his host, who was often his father-in-law, and slew him, and took his land. It is pleasant, however, to find some exception to this ingratitude. Bappu, the founder of the Sesodian race, and the first Sesodian of Chitore, had to fly from Nagda, about A.D. 720, to escape vengeance for some youthful freak. He was accompanied in his flight by two Bheels, Ballo and Dewa. These faithful companions assisted at the drawing the *teeka* of sovereignty on the brow of their master; and to the present day the descendant of Ballo draws the *teeka* on the forehead of the sovereign of Mewar, and places him on his throne, while the descendant of Dewa holds the tray containing the rice and spice mixed with blood, to make the sacred mark. The blood comes from the thumb of the Bheel.

The road to-day has been along a plain; only towards evening do I see hills, and when I arrive at the Chitore bungalow I am aware of a height looming through the darkness. To my horror, when I wake in the morning, I see the ruins of Chitore on a lofty hill some way off! On inquiry, I find Chitoregurh, the modern town, at the foot of the hill, is a *koss* (two miles) off; and that the old town (alas! don't I see it?) is on a cliff above the modern one. I see, however, the ascent is all in shadow; so, after a frugal breakfast, I start to explore. Half-way to Chitoregurh I meet an official sent by the *hakim* of that town, to see my wants supplied. This young man accompanies me back to the town, and sends a *cicerone* with me to explain. Chitore proper, the Old Chitore, is on the top of a high hill that reminds me somewhat of the fort of Gwalior. I saw the fortifications meandering away in the distance, but in the hot sun and on foot I could not explore sufficiently to ascertain the dimensions of the old city. It was evidently big, from the ground I walked over, like Falstaff, "larding the lean earth" as I went.

Here was the bazaar; alas! now a desert, with a palm-tree growing "where merchants most did congregate." Here the palace, here the temple—in good preservation—and here the Tower of Victory. This last is really very fine, not quite so high as the Kootub, perhaps, and not of so precious a material as Giotto's Tower at Florence, but quite as original as the first, and even more wrought than the second. It is built of yellow-looking stone, which must be very hard, for the carving is as sharp as ever. But I hear it was struck by lightning some years ago, and some of the upper stones are displaced. I see also a tree beginning to grow, which is sure before long to bring the building to the ground. I trust either the Government of the Rana or the paramount Power will do something for it.

It was Rana Khoombho who built this "aigrette on the brow of Chitore, which makes her look down upon Meru with derision." The foundation was laid, according to Tod, in A.D. 1451, eleven years after the victory over the Sultan of Guzerat, which it was intended to immortalize, "when shaking the earth the lords of Goojurkund (Guzerat) and Malwa, with armies overwhelming as an ocean, invaded Medpat (Mewar)." Nearly one million was spent on this tower, round whose summit is a vainglorious description of the glories of Khoombho. Alas for the vanity of man! Khoombho himself was murdered by his son, and the Moslems have three times sacked Chitore, and even tried to obliterate the inscription of the Hindoo Rana; and this, like the Kootub at Delhi, remains an empty boast, a priceless work of art surrounded by ruins. By the tower is a cool and refreshing spring gushing from the rock in three places, and beyond this, again, is a wall concealing a subterranean chamber, where lie the remains of all the women of Chitore who were immolated the day the sacred city was taken.

The last time Chitore was sacked was in the time of Akbar, when the degenerate Rana, Oody Sing, forsook the capital of his fathers. Then the tutelary deity of the Ranas left the sacred city never to return. A cruel deity was Māta, the goddess of Mewar, as evil a bogey as was ever conjured up by the human imagination, ever more easily influenced by fear than love. From that time no rana has entered the sacred precincts, and whenever they have sought to do so, an invisible arm has barred the passage. Yet is Chitore the revered home of Rajpoot tradition, and if a Rajpoot wishes to swear by an oath that must be inviolable, he swears by the sacking of Chitore.

Before bidding adieu to my constant companion, Colonel Tod,

let me give the grim story of the siege of Chitore, by Ala-oodeen, abridged from his pages.

When Lakumsi was Rana of Oodeypore, being but twelve years old, his uncle Bheemsi acted as Regent. Bheemsi had to wife Patmani, a daughter of a chief of Ceylon. She was so beautiful that Ala-oodeen, the Pathan Emperor of Delhi, demanded her for himself, and on refusal marched to Mewar and stormed the town of Chitore. The gallants of Mewar rushed to oppose him and after a terrific struggle he was repulsed, but at the cost of three thousand lives of Sesodians. Badul, the nephew of Patmani, a boy of twelve, returns wounded and weary to the palace.

"And what did Bheemsi?" asks Patmani.

"He was the reaper of the harvest of battle," replies the young chief, who had himself done wonders. "I followed his steps as the humble gleaner of his sword. On the gory bed of honour he spread a carpet of the slain. A barbarian prince his pillow, he laid him down and sleeps, surrounded by the foe!"

Again the lovely Queen asks, "Tell me, Badul, how did my love bear himself?"

"O my mother," replied the youth; "how further describe his deeds, when he left no foe to dread or admire him?"

"Farewell, then!" cried the wife with a smile; "*salaam*, Badul! My lord will chide my delay!" and she sprang into the funeral pile lighted for the slain.

Thirteen years afterwards the Pathan Ala-oodeen returned to Chitore. Then Māta, the goddess of the race and city, appeared to the Rana, fatigued with battle, and cried aloud, "I am hungry."

"What! after eight thousand of my race have lately been offered thee?"

"I must have kings!" said the terrible deity. "Unless twelve who have worn the royal diadem bleed for Chitore, the land will pass from thy line."

So the Rana called a council, and each day a fresh son was crowned, and devoted his life for his country. Only his favourite son remained, when the Rana cried, "Now I, the twelfth, devote my life for Chitore!" and, sending his son away from the ill-fated city to perpetuate his line, he rushed to his fate. In vain! The Moslem conquered. Then the *johur* is proclaimed, the funeral pile burned high in a vast subterranean cave, and the Queens lead the way; and when Ala-oodeen entered the city, he found nothing but smoking corpses to satisfy his lust.

A hot walk I had of two hours and a half, and glad enough I was to get back and wash and breakfast. I then dispatched my luggage and made a sketch. A hot wind sprang up in the afternoon, to my no small discomfort, but at 4 p.m. I started in a *palki*, and was carried thirty miles; and in this journey I doubt which suffered most, the carriers or the carried. I can only say I was profoundly miserable at 2.30, when I arrived at Bheelwarra; neither did a further eleven hours into Nusirabad improve my temper or ease the cramp in my legs. Anyhow, here I am in Ajmere, in the land of railways and hotels, and I start by the 2.40 a.m. train for Agra.

*Muttra.*

Agra was a great rest after the fatigues of my last journey. I had here to re-fill my exhausted colour-box and re-stretch canvases for another campaign. I wanted also to see two tombs that I left unvisited during my last stay here. On Thursday morning I made my first expedition to the tomb of "It-mud-ud-Doulah," which lies in a pleasant garden on the farther side of the Jumna.

There is never any unpleasant reminder of death in these Moslem tombs: all smacks of houris and certain Paradise.

This one is of marble, beautifully inlaid, the work being of the best period, "Early Jehanghire." It is being repaired by Government, who I pray may be induced not to do too much. There are four rooms painted in the four centres, where the ruins of former decorations are splendid indeed. Were they equally beautiful when new? Perhaps not; but if the hand of the Englishman is put to them, they will be spoilt for ever, and we shall incur additional claim to the curses of posterity.

Akbar's tomb at Secundra I next visited. This, too, is in a spacious garden, the beauty of which is being restored. Here, as at Futtehpore Sikri, the boldness of the pattern and originality of design strikes one very forcibly. Hindoo architecture has a wealth of detail almost distracting. This seems to have been continued by the early Moguls, who had a much greater idea of the fitness of things and grandeur of general design than the Hindoos ; I must, however, make an exception in favour of the Tower of Chitore. Later work is much tamer ; the celebrated Taj Mahal contains but few patterns of originality of detail, while you may find hundreds here at Secundra and Futtehpore. The later men seem to have felt this want of invention, and strove to make up by costliness of material for absence of imagination. Modern Moslem work is utterly without originality, a mere dry echo of what once was.

I am writing this at Muttra, a city sacred beyond all cities, for it is declared that one day in Muttra is worth a year in Benares. Here Krishna was born, and here the wrath of the pious Aurung-zebe descended, destroying temple, shrine, and idol. Yet have temple and shrine risen again, displaying the same exuberance of design as before ; only the modern sculpture is not up to the old. It seems as though the first designers of the gods had been obliged to study from nature ; consequently there is a sign of humanity and beauty in their work. Those who followed were content to take nature and divinity second-hand, and have necessarily gone on getting more and more conventional.

The same beauties and the same faults are to be seen at Bindra-bun, a very holy place near Muttra, in temples built three hundred years ago and those now building, which are very numerous. The vitality of the Hindoo religion is most surprising, and vast indeed the amount of money lavished on the temples of that religion. The money-makers of India are mostly Hindoos, and perchance they wish to make their *salut* when old, by spending the money they have saved on their gods. One of the institutions of Muttra is Seth Govend Das. He has innumerable carriages and horses, which he is always ready to lend (one of them brought me here); he does everything in Muttra ; yet he has retired to Bindrabun, and lives the life of a *fakir* in a temple he has built after the Madras style. A sly-looking man is the Seth, with a suspicious cast in his eye; he is grey-bearded now and pious, yet in the Mutiny he was "suspect," and was made to build the magistrate's house in which I am now writing, to save his neck; so goes the tale. Meanwhile, his temple at Bindrabun is said to have cost 40 lacs (£400,000)! It covers an enormous space of ground, and through the door of its holy of holies, itself a vast pile, I saw a tall column covered with thick plaques of gold. What a wicked man the Seth must have been once to require so much religious whitewashing!

I came over here for two days, hoping then to get on to Ulwar; but I found a letter to say that the Maharajah had left for a week, to pray; so I must needs stay here a whole week doing nothing to forward my *magnum opus.*

Muttra itself is a snare and a delusion, curious enough to deserve an afternoon visit, but after what I have seen, stale, flat, and unprofitable. It is *very* flat, lying on the Jumna, and from no place can you get a good sketch save from the *ghâts*, which are small, and beset by crowds of greasy Brahmins and dirty pilgrims. Perhaps the rest will do me good. Meanwhile, the hospitality of the English community is unbounded, and were I not in a place where such an act is considered an impiety, I should say that the fatted calf is daily slaughtered for me. This state of things is perhaps a foretaste of Simla, and my journal will suffer therefrom, for it is not my intention to record the stale amenities of civilized life.

As there is but little to be seen in Muttra, I have devoted some of my time to sports. Yesterday we had the native wrestlers of the town to this house. Wrestling must be thought a noble pastime here, since all the professors of the art were Brahmins. Some—the great masters—were very fat, their corpulence oozing over their tight loin-cloths. The wrestling itself was somewhat like the French, the object being to put a man clean on his back. The wrestlers begin by trying for the catch, and then they get locked, and over they go rolling on the ground, twisted in and in—writhing masses of brown flesh, out of which emerges from time to time a foot or a hand, coming from the most improbable places. The exhibition was curious, but somewhat monotonous.

I don't think the men were really trying, but making show. Their muscles were well developed, and the young men were fine-looking fellows, who would have made their fortune as models in London. They seem to be made of a different material from us, as, though they were undoubtedly strong and active, their flesh was quite soft and pulpy, like a woman's. The taste for the sport seems to be very general. We had a great crowd looking on, who followed the movements of the wrestlers with much interest.

This morning we went out to see a buffalo fight on the racecourse. The great stupid brutes were brought out, each with his attendant cows. When they saw each other they trotted together, locked horns, and pushed and struggled for some time, when all of a sudden one would give way, and run as hard as he could, pressed by the victor. Somehow fear is a greater incentive than rage, for the pursuer never caught the vanquished. One old bull was evidently the champion. On three occasions they brought him opponents, who no sooner saw him trotting towards them than they bolted, and a most exciting chase through the crowd invariably ensued. It was dull work, however, and as the sun was very hot, I was glad to get home to breakfast.

This afternoon I go to Ulwar, and hope from there to write something more amusing than I have found for this week's budget. I have tried to find some legends of the place, some deeds of Krishna, who was born and brought up here, to record; but I fear it would interest no one to know how the godlike child allowed himself to be swallowed by a demon in the shape of a snake, and then swelling himself prodigiously, burst his living prison and came forth smiling. And the loves of Krishna! Oh, fie! Surely the *chronique scandaleuse* of no country could furnish such a list! But these are the favourite and most sacred legends of the people; and the god is always represented either playing his flute, standing cross-legged, to the amorous Radha, or dancing with the wives of the Gopis. It is curious that the sacred legends of a clever people should be so improper; and apparently without any poetical interpretation, like the Greek legends. Amongst the Rajpoots, whose stories I have plentifully stolen from Tod, you find chivalry and poetry, but Rajpoots are both soldiers and opium-eaters. At Muttra (or Mathera), sacred to Krishna, the people are fat Brahmins, and their legends prodigious rubbish, without poetry or charm; but then this country is flat and monotonous, and the other full of mountains.

I left Muttra on Thursday, 29th March, and drove to Bhurtpore, twenty four miles over the usual flat. One gets used to the sights of an Indian high-road somehow. Habit is everything, and even those who have to put up with the heat here get used to it, or succumb at last, they hardly know why. Yet as the heat is surprising, so are the sights that meet you at each town. The little children of both sexes, whose dress consists of only a thin thread or a bead (literally), with their stomachs distended in the most frightful manner with rice or *chapatti*, or some such nastiness; the men almost as naked, but presenting torsos of the most classical form, with the legs of scarecrows or monkeys; the women coming up from well or tank with two enormous *chattis* or earthenware pots balanced on the head, their movement and draperies worthy of Phidias;—these are seen at every village. Then, having cleared the village or town, you pass through a belt of cultivation, amid the creaking of the busy water-wheels, worked by oxen, with circular machinery invented in the year one, or more often having a rope drawn over a drum, by bullocks walking down an incline. Then on again into the arid plain, where, the sun being hot, you doze off, till awakened by the shouts of *syce* and coachman, "*Aie gharry wallah!*" or "*Barega hatte wallah!*" and bullock-cart or elephant are shoved on one side to allow the *sahib* to pass. No wonder in this country bullocks and cows are worshipped, for by them everything is worked, and worshipping them does not prevent their being ill used. It is a curious sight to see the bullock-waggons and *ekhas*, or carriages, getting out of the way. The driver, who has the beasts with a rope by the nose, seizes their tails, and screws them the way they are to turn and bang go the bullocks into the ditch or against a tree,—no matter, so long as they are out of the way of the *sahib*.

Thus I passed the twenty-four miles to Bhurtpore, where I took rail, and arrived at 6.30 a.m. at Ulwar.

The obliging political agent, Major Cadell, received me with unbounded hospitality, and, owing to his kindness, I have seen all that is worth seeing here.

Ulwar is a modern state; it was formed by a certain Pertap Sing, the head of the Naruka clan of Jeypore Rajpoots, on the general break-up of the Mogul power, and was declared independent in 1776. Pertap Sing, having no son, adopted a child of the Thakoor of Thanna, and the way he fixed on the fortunate youth was characteristic. He summoned to his Court the infant sons of all his nobles, and assembled them in a large room, which he had previously strewn with all kinds of toys and sweetmeats; and the children were told to take what pleased them. Bakhtāwat Sing chose a sword and shield, and running to the Rana, sat down by his side, and he was forthwith hailed heir to the Raj.

The right of adoption brings about strange changes in the lot of natives. Sindia (the great Sindia!) ran about the palace as a youth, happy with twelve rupees a month. Sujjan Sing, Rana of Oodeypore, albeit the nephew of the late Rana, little thought he would be called to the *guddee*, over the head of his father. The father and predecessor of Jeswant Sing was a *vakeel*, and stood with hands crossed before the *sahib*, until he was adopted by the Rajah of Ahmednugger, from which place he was called to Jodhpore. Holkar, who puts on more "side" than any rajah I have yet seen, was an adopted son; so are the Rajah of Mysore and the Guicowar of Baroda. This little Rajah was chosen two years ago from the same Thanna family as Bukhtāwat Sing, quite unexpectedly, on the decease of the late Rajah at the early age of twenty-six, through strong drink and excess. The father of the Rajah was alive when he succeeded, and his elder brother has a patrimony of £1,000 a year, while the lucky No. 2 is a Maharajah, and comes into £240,000 a year next November!

The state of Ulwar, having been administered by Major Cadell for seven years, is quite a model state. Money has been spent with wise profusion on profitable works, roads, *bunds*, wells, and such things; the stud of horses, elephants, and bullocks is really worth seeing; and the city is clean, well kept, and well to do. And all this will be handed over next November to this young gentleman of eighteen, with free power to spend and squander. When the last Rajah succeeded, in 1863, my cousin Impey (now at Oodeypore), who had been managing for him in the same way, handed over a treasury in which there were 20½ lacs (£205,000). In 1870 the Rajah was deprived of his property for mismanagement: he had spent his income, and the 20½ lacs, and was 18 lacs in debt. Pretty well for seven years!

The city of Ulwar is prettily nestled into a nook of the hills. Below lies a green and fruitful plain, plentifully irrigated by the waters of a lake formed up in the mountains at Silleser, ten miles away, and which is the work of Bunnee Sing, who reigned from 1815 to 1857. Even now there is a saying expressive of great happiness: "As in the day of Bunnee Sing."

Between the mountains and the city lies the palace, and between it and the mountains, again, is a tank. I have seen larger and more splendid buildings, but this little nook, with palace, temple, and tank, and the bare hill behind, is as characteristic a bit of India as I could imagine. There is no bastard classic or ridiculous Gothic here; all is true Indian; and although, of course, full of absurd inconsistencies—the squalid jostling the splendid, as is usual in the East—the whole is somehow picturesque and original. Yet was all this done within the last thirty years!

Mangol Sing, the present Rajah, is a young man of seventeen. Although only called to his throne two years ago, he plays the Rajah to the life. He seems to have dropped into it without any trouble. He talks English very well, yet nothing will make him learn to read or write; while the two hours a day he spends in study utterly exhaust him. Sitting he thinks a nuisance. But he is a good-natured, good-looking little chap, and delights in riding, driving, and shooting, playing at racquets and such amusements. The other day he was married. He doesn't think much of the society of ladies, however; for, to my certain knowledge, he was

HIS HIGHNESS MANGOL SING, RAJAH OF ULWAR.

two days without even seeing his wife. I hear, when he goes down to the palace in the city, his adopted mother and grand-mother make him *pooja* or pray, and he doesn't like it.

Life in a Zenana must be dull indeed. Each wife has her settlement, and manages the villages forming that settlement through a *vakeel*, and very good managers some of them are. Beyond this they have no connection with the out-door world, never even leaving the walls of the Zenana, except on rare occasions when they are allowed to perform a pilgrimage. The Zenana itself is ruled by the principal wife, or more generally by the mother. This lady is supreme; and I am told by ladies who have penetrated into the Zenanas of the great, that when the rajah comes into the room all the wives rise and veil themselves, the head ranee alone remaining seated and uncovered. The other wives, however, in some courts are allowed to receive visits (from ladies, of course) in their own rooms, which open generally out of a courtyard common to all. I hear the principal amusement of the ladies is gambling, both at cards and backgammon; and this is the cause of their eagerness for money, which one would think they could not possibly want, or find occasion to spend. The allowance given to a wife here and also at Oodeypore is £2,000 a year, and quite enough, too, I should say.

Yesterday, the 4th March, we were promised an elephant fight. Major Cadell had never seen one, and indeed had always discouraged them, but I persuaded him there was no danger, so he gave way. The grand space of the Hatti Khanah was to be the scene of the entertainment, and there ought to have been a wall for the beasts to fight over; but the Rajah either forgot to order this wall to be prepared, or thought there would be greater fun without. When we arrived one of the elephants was already in the square, and the Rajah's people were teazing him with scarves, like the *torreadors* in Spain. He wanted but little teazing, being very "must," and the "*hattiadors*," if I might coin a word, would have stood but a poor chance had not the huge beast had vast chains round his hind legs, which dragged well behind. As it was, he swung round his trunk with fury when any of his enemies approached him, and it required all their nimbleness to escape his charge.

Presently the other elephant was seen approaching. This one was only "must" enough to be dangerous to any one foolish enough to go near him. He was larger than his adversary, but not so furious. No. 1 is "weaving" his trunk, having had a cloth lowered over his eyes by his *mahout*. No. 2 is now in the middle of the square. Up goes the cloth, and No. 1 furiously charges.

Though No. 2 is the larger, he is borne backward, and there was real danger to the *mahouts*, &c. Major Cadell immediately gave the order: a Catherine-wheel was fired and thrown between the combatants; and both elephants, lately so furious, turned tail and skedaddled, each to his own corner. It was a curious sight.

I wonder how this Rajah will succeed when he comes into his own? He is obedient enough now, but I see, or imagine I see, some impatience for the time to arrive when he will be independent.* The last Rajah, Sheodan Sing, was a very bad lot. He was a very small man. There was very little of him, but all that was, was vicious. Here is a little story of Rajpoot manners.

Ulwar, the state, was carved partly from Bhurtpore, partly from Jeypore. The Rajahs of Ulwar and Jeypore had never met till my cousin Impey brought about an exchange of civilities between them. Now, it appears that Ram Sing of Jeypore had a beautiful *nautch* girl, whom he delighted to honour, devout though he is. Her name was Ganga. Sheodan Sing hearing of her beauty, offered her vast sums of rupees to leave Jeypore and come to Ulwar. The frail one yielded. All was arranged, and a *dâk* of quick-trotting bullocks conveyed Ganga in an incredibly short space of time from Jeypore to Ulwar and its amorous Rajah. Perhaps Sheodan Sing would soon have tired of his expensive conquest, but the Duke of Edinburgh arrived not long after, and the Rajah was obliged to go to receive him. He was determined that Ganga should not return to Jeypore in his absence; so he married her in a kind of left-handed fashion—that is, she had gold bangles fastened on her feet and was taken into the Zenana. The idea of being a Ranee was too much for the poor *nautch* girl; her head was turned, and she consented. Once in the Zenana, and there was no escape. Now, *nautch* girls are brought up with singular ideas of freedom; alone of all Indian women, they wear no veils; and they are treated with respect wherever they go. I have written how, even at Oodeypore, they form a part of the

* I am happy to see that he is doing well. By the last mail came the news that the Maharajah of Ulwar has offered to fit out a camel corps at his own expense to help the Government in the Afghan campaign. Well done, Mangol Sing!

pageant of the state. Imagine, then, poor Ganga imprisoned in the Zenana, frowned down by rival queens, who, being *pucka* wives of noble families, looked on the *nautch* girl as the dirt of the earth. And Sheodan Sing? The miserable little man's sole idea was revenge on Jeypore. He swaggered past Ram Sing in *durbar*, saying, "I have cut off the whiskers of the Jeypore Rajah;" but he never thought of the poor *nautch* girl, and never saw her again. The political agent here told me he had many touching epistles and messages from the prisoner, begging him to liberate her, brought by her old mother, who threw herself on her knees, imploring him to save her child. But what could he do? The Zenana was sacred. At last she escaped by the only road of escape from the tyranny of custom—*she starved herself to death!* This is a true story, told me by the political agent to whom the mother applied.

Another story of Ulwar deserves here to be recorded. Two rajahs ago the ruling chief married, or was said to have married, a *nautch* girl. Rajahs of Ulwar seem ever to have had a passion for the stage! This lády had a son presumably by the Rajah. Now, at the Rajah's death, as the wife was a Mohammedan, this marriage was declared illegal, and the child illegitimate. But the mother maintained she was legally married, and, to prove the legitimacy of her child, actually performed *suttee* with the Rajah! Yet she was a Mohammedan, not believing, of course, that Paradise was to be attained by self-cremation! I don't know that history or romance contains a story of more touching maternal sacrifice. The English Government insisted on the acknowledgment of the son's legitimacy, and the division of the state of Ulwar, which has only lately become united by the want of heirs of the son, for whose royal line such an awful price had been paid!

This is my last Rajpoot state. To-morrow I shall be well on my way to Jummo and the Sikhs. I only trust they will behave as well as the Rajpootana rajahs have done on the whole. Some of them have been quite friendly. From Muttra I sent Oodeypore a long letter on Indian art, which I trust may do him good.

# CHAPTER XII.

## LAHORE.

*5th to 12th April.*

I LEFT Ulwar, with great regret, on Thursday, 5th April, and arrived at Delhi at 3 a.m. on the 6th. I had determined to pass the hours of the early morning, usually spent in bed, in quietly snoozing in my railway carriage. But I reckoned without my host. The carriage was shunted and re-shunted, and each time I was banged about as though the engine-driver took a delight in preventing a sleep which he by his duties was debarred from enjoying; so at 4.30 I rose and went to the Northbrook Hotel, which I had left full of guests of the *durbar*. Now all was desolate, and when I went to breakfast at the table I had seen thronged with notables, I was alone.

I had various businesses to attend to during the day, but at 4.50 p.m. started again for Lahore, where I arrived at 4.35 a.m. on Saturday, 7th April. Here I am now, the guest of the Government Advocate, and very comfortable.

There is a mighty difference between an English station, the centre of an administration like Lahore, and the house of the political agent at a native court. There are no picturesque horsemen waiting in the yard or "compound," no prisoners clanking about the garden, preparing your vegetables and watering your flowers, no suitors with eager look awaiting the pleasure of the agent *sahib*, no visits from friendly nobles or *thakoors*. All is respectabie, humdrum, unpicturesque, and comfortable. And, above all, there is but little to write about, unless it be personal criticisms and remarks, that might wound the feelings of hospitable Englishmen and kind friends. I came here to have my future movements settled for me. I wish myself to do Kashmir at once, and then retire to the cool of Simla; but I find that the Nawab of Bhawalpore is expected, and that he will probably not be allowed to go to Simla, so that I must do his Nawabship here.

It is much cooler here than it was at Ulwar or Jodhpore a month ago; not that Lahore is a cool place, for I believe it may give points to a place nameless in polite circles but well known for its high temperature; only the heat does not begin so soon as in places more south. We have had moreover two thunderstorms; one on the 6th I caught between Delhi and here; and there was another on the 10th, which was quite dramatic in its fury, great wind and heavy rain accompanying the incessant thunder and lightning. People here wonder what has come to the weather, as storms at this time of year are almost unknown. I can only be thankful that it keeps cool a little longer than usual.

Lahore city lies about a mile from the English station at Anarkali. This journal is not intended as a guide book (there is an excellent one of Lahore), so I will not give you all the places worth seeing in the capital of Punjab, but only the things that strike me personally. It is to be noted, in the first place, that the English town derives its name from a slave girl of the Emperor Akbar—Sharif-ul-Nissar—who had the title or name of Anarkali (meaning "pomegranate blossom") given her; but because she was supposed to have smiled on Jehanghire, Akbar's son, she was here buried alive. There was evidently some cause for Akbar's jealousy, since Jehanghire, when he came to his own, erected a tomb to the poor victim, on which he says—

> "Ah, could I behold the face of my beloved once more,
> I would give thanks to my God till the day of resurrection!"

The tomb is now the English church, and the white man prays where Jehanghire shed tears and recorded his not very creditable passion.

Akbar seems generally to have been rather hard upon the loves of his son Jehanghire, who, before he ascended the throne, was known by the name of Selim. The unfortunate youth formed a violent attachment for a certain Mher-ul-Nissah, the daughter of a Tatar chief of the name of Mirza-Ghayas-Beg, who was steward of the household of the Emperor Akbar. The lady was already affianced to an officer named Sher Afghan, and Akbar would not have the engagement broken off to please his son. And most unlucky was Sher Afghan. Jehanghire not only remembered the slave girl, but the wife. He built a tomb for one and he killed the husband of the other! The lady, however, was taken into the royal Zenana, and became the favourite wife, being first called *Nur Mahal* (Light of the Palace), and then *Nur Jehan* (Light of the World). Under the latter title she is best known. She exercised great influence over her husband, who promoted both her father and brother to high places at Court. Her father was It-mud-ud-Doulah, whose tomb I have described at Agra; her brother, Alif Jah, was well known in history. Nur Jehan we shall meet again, I dare say.

The fort of Lahore has some decorations in large mosaic on its outer face, built by Jehanghire, that are very good in their general effect. Several panels of elephants, their fightings and general goings-on (and off), are very good indeed in colour—the elephants being bright blue, and the ground brimstone, or white, or green. This coarse mosaic is very common in this part of the country, where stone exists not. A mosque (Wazir Khan's Musjid) is richly decorated in this way, and so are many towers in the neighbourhood. Nevertheless, Lahore, as a town, has not many attractions; for, although tracing the date of its foundation to the mythical ages of Rama and his son L'oh, there are not many traces of age in the present city. From the top of the minaret of the Wazir Khan's Musjid you get a good view of the town, which looks like an enlarged village, of which the houses have the same monotonous look we know so well in London, only that they are mud colour, and not smoke-begrimed. The absence of stone probably caused the gradual destruction of what was old.

Lahore boasts a school of art and a museum. The first is, I am told, and I can readily believe it, in a state of infancy. Let us hope it may develop into something if allowed to continue. The museum contains many interesting objects; among them a quantity of fragments of sculpture dug up near Peshawur, that are remarkably curious, as displaying more plastic power than any sculpture I have yet seen, and even, it is supposed, a Greek influence. These remains are Buddhistic, as are all the finest remains in India. Of course I talk of sculpture.

The printed cottons are here remarkably good. Some of the finest patterns are printed in tak and all kinds of dyes, not *pucka*. They are used for marriage ceremonies, and not being *pucka* implies they will not wash.

There are too many things brought here by the Central Asian Trading Company, which has its depôt at Lahore. The best of these are silks printed in the strangest colours, with the wildest harmonies and discords, which I confess tickle my artistic sense exceedingly.

The whole talk of Lahore is of the frontier and its policy. I don't know much about it, I confess; and as this journal is not intended to be political, will not treat you to any of the gossip and stories told of the soldier who is conducting the negotiations at Peshawur. He must be either a very great man or a very weak one. I, for one, will give him the benefit of the doubt; at all events, he is a well abused one.

I have come back from my first sitting of the Nawab of Bhawalpore. As his title implies, he is a Mohammedan. His family were originally tributary to the Afghans, and though they set up for themselves some three generations back, with difficulty succeeded in keeping their independence. They also had to knock under to Runjeet Sing. Luckily for them, during the Sikh troubles, their hatred to that nation proved greater than their dislike of the English; so that they helped us, and were rewarded by increased estate; though, of course, they had to acknowledge the paramount Power.

The present Nawab is a young fellow of sixteen, good looking, though of somewhat weak cast of feature. He was to have met me at Simla, and there sat; but, on arriving here, I found that there is some doubt about his being allowed to go to the English Capua. There is a great feeling against permitting native chiefs to congregate at our sanitarium, as they bring up a quantity of followers, who have to be huddled together in close quarters, and are apt to bring cholera and all kinds of sickness with them. However, the Nawab, and especially his white following, are very eager to get there, and make my painting an excuse for their journey. It is natural enough they should wish to escape from the heat of Bhawalpore, one of the hottest places of this oven, to the cool breezes of Simla; and, although I shall make a study of his head, in case leave be refused, I shall say that I cannot possibly finish here what I want, for the dress and get-up of his Nawabship is fearfully elaborate.

The Maharajah of Kashmir desires to be painted at Sreenuggur, and telegraphs to that effect. This will necessitate a fortnight's more travelling; but, on the other hand, will enable me to see the far-famed Valley of Kashmir. Well, I must grin and bear it, and hope that the good will counterbalance the delay.

At Ulwar I had a curious insight into the superstition of the country. The political agent wished to build for the young Rajah a new grand staircase to his Dewan-i-Am. My friends in England will hardly consider me competent to act as architect even to an Indian rajah; and I am modest enough to think, and indeed to be certain, that I know little about the noble art; yet I know more than my worthy friend the political agent, and I gave him what I thought rather a good scheme, which he submitted to the intelligent Hindoo engineer who looks after that department in the state. A model in wood of my plan was made, but the number of steps had to be altered to suit the prejudices of the country. I had noticed before that Hindoo stairs were prodigiously steep, and I now found the reason. It appears that going up and down you must count thus, as the foot comes down on each step:—"Indra" (heaven), first step; "Jan" (hell), second; "Raj" (earth), third: and as you must begin always with "heaven," so must your foot, both going up and coming down, come on "Jan" (hell) on the last step. Unless this is so, no pious Hindoo will ascend or descend, as it would be eminently unlucky to do so.

Another odd superstition is this:—at Muttra and at Ulwar the authorities were building new bazaars, and proposed planting the square with pepul-trees. At both places the *banyas* or merchants protested; "for if you plant such trees, we shall not be able to deal there."

"Why?"

"Because the pepul (*ficus religiosa*) is sacred, and under it we must tell only the truth!"

If this feeling existed in England, how the moral tone of the City might be improved by a few pepul-trees!

The following is a true story of Ulwar. It appears that there is a law there that no man is allowed to marry a girl who is only a third of his age. The reason of this law is that old men constantly married girls of ten or eleven, and left them widows, and they had to pass the rest of their lives in forced celibacy, looked down on by their relatives. In the old time *suttee* put an end to their troubles; now the laws are changed, and life-long misery takes the place of a glorious death. What wonder, then, if young widows frequently change their ignominious fate for a career of vice? This law can only be evaded by order of the Council of State. Well, there was a wealthy contractor, who had made his fortune in the British territory, but he was childless. Always hoping to have a son to light his funeral pile, he came to Ulwar, and quickly found a parent who was willing to sell his child of ten; but the bridegroom was more than three times the age of the bride,—indeed he was sixty,—and permission was refused. The case came before the political agent while I was at Ulwar. He refused to interfere.

"Let the law, which is a good law, be enforced. If this man likes to marry, let him marry a woman of suitable age."

"But," urged the worthy *baboos* who appeared for the eager bridegroom, "there are none of suitable age. It is a disgrace to have an unmarried daughter, and so all our daughters are married at ten."

"There are widows."

"Yes, but to marry a widow is a sin. What is a poor man to do?"

"You ought to let widows marry," cried the sensible agent.

"Religious prejudice, *sahib*," urged the *baboo* with clasped hands.

The man was in earnest, and the next day there appeared an English advocate from Agra to plead his cause. He had no *locus standi*, and was told so; but he urged that the bride's father should at least be allowed to leave the country, and take up his residence in British territory, where you can marry your child to Methuselah, if he is rich enough.

"What prevents him?"

"He is not allowed to leave," said the advocate.

The agent said, "I will see to it, only if he comes back to Ulwar, he must abide by the laws of Ulwar."

It was quickly found why papa-in-law could not leave the country; he was in prison for breach of promise, having already sold his daughter to and received the money from another man, to whom, however, he refused his child on the appearance of a richer suitor!

The question of marriages is perhaps the most serious of all the knotty questions we English have to deal with here. The above case is one of many curious cases constantly cropping up and bewildering the courts and judges. From an educational point of view, it is most fatal to allow marriages with girls of ten or even eight years of age, as is common here. In each family there may be seen one or two poor women, who are looked on as lepers, and are, to native ideas, a disgrace and a shame. And why? Because they are widows. No doubt every aspect of this question has been canvassed and talked over hundreds of times. Nothing can be done in a hurry; and after all, the prejudice against marrying your deceased wife's sister, which is so strong in England, is quite as stupid, or perhaps more narrow-minded than the prejudices of the poor Hindoo against widow marriage. Out here one sees the harm all such prejudices work to the good of the community at large, so is the mind enlarged by travel, and the traveller encouraged to make priggish and sententious observations!

I was much amused at finding in the handbook of this place (from which I have freely borrowed) a translation of a Punjabee song in the vernacular, which was very popular some ten years ago. It is a complaint against the laws and regulations of the English, which I can well imagine the Indian fails to appreciate or indeed to understand. The following is one verse as a specimen:

> "In the Raj of the Rajahs there were holes, there were hills;
> In the Raj of the English level highways appear.
> We die, oh! we die, and the worst of our ills
> Is the hard law, Punjabees! the English bring here."

*17th April.*

For the first time in India I find I have but little to write about. I hope I am not getting *blasé* to the sights around me. I don't think so, for each figure I see in the streets would be a reproach to me. One seems to live among statues here; each man or woman with his or her drapery around him (or her) is a sight for the Greeks; and yet I have drawn none of them, and am continually gnawing the file of repentance on the subject. My picture, however, sits like an Old Man of the Sea on me, and takes all the energy for other work out of me. I can only see, mark, learn, and inwardly digest, with the hope that my gazing may have some effect by-and-bye.

The Punjabees wear much more flowing robes than the Rajpoots. The men dress all in white, wear enormous *pugrees*, and very loose and curious trousers, nearly to the ankle. The women wear the same trousers, only coloured, and the *saree* over the head. I have not yet penetrated the mystery of the trouser. I rather fancy it is made of one piece of voluminous stuff, ingeniously twisted so as to form a nether garment. As the twisting begins from the outside, and the folds lap round inside the leg, the whole population appear bandy.

We have had most unusual weather. There has been a thunder storm every day for a week, and quantities of rain. This has, of course, cooled the air, but already the heat has re-begun, and general limpness asserts itself. There is a bird here called the köel, which has the reputation of being a sort of St. John to the summer, appearing always as hot weather sets in. This wretched bird has been singing most lustily for the last two days, the rain having kept him quiet before. A most unpleasant noise he makes, like a mason striking a flagstone with a metal hammer. This noise continuing for hours is apt to get on the nerves.

Meanwhile I have been getting on with Bhawalpore, and have finished his head. His coat is not here, so I must defer painting it till I meet his Highness at Simla. Like most rajah's coats, it is fearfully elaborate, covered with *kincaub* pearls and jewellery. He has a *pugree* of enormous size, that was originally wound round a sort of wide-awake, and now displays two curious ears. Altogether he has a kind of theatrical look, and reminds one of Astley's. He is an odd lad, very impulsive, but without any strong affection ; not stupid, but with a stupid, loutish look, the result of his shyness. I have seen a good deal of him, and have come to the conclusion that his surroundings are oppressive, and that the life of a young rajah under tutors appointed by Government, who may be good fellows, but who are dull and not amusing, must be very very tedious. Of course people who apply for such places are not *pucka* civilians. There is a young *sirdar*, Nizam O-Deen, of Mum Dhote, of the same age, who is being educated with the Nawab. This young lad is one of the handsomest boys I ever saw. He and the Nawab are great friends, riding, playing lawn tennis and racquets, and, I hope, studying together.

Since writing the above I have been again to Bhawalpore, for the last time, and I got him to show me a pair of his inexpressibles, which are about six yards across, and gathered up with a string round the waist. As the foot and ankle pass through a hole in the extreme corner of this bag, the drapery between the legs is very voluminous, and getting twisted round the ankle, gives the bandy look I mentioned before.

To-day I am expecting to leave this for Jhelum, *en route* for Kashmir. I have telegraphed for a *dâk gharry* to take me thence to Rawal Pindee, and am now waiting an answer.

My life here has been singularly placid. I rise at 7 a.m., or thereabout, have my *chota hazree*—a cup of tea and some toast—and read, write, and work till breakfast at ten; after that meal I go to Bhawalpore, and work at him till *tiffin*, which meal I generally take with his Highness. I sometimes go on painting there till four; then home, and more work till 5.30, when, weather permitting, I go to lawn tennis, which lasts as long as we can see; then more letters till dinner—and so the days go on. This, putting office instead of work, is the life of a civilian out here. Quiet, monotonous, but not unprofitable. A very good set of fellows they are; wonderfully kind and affectionate to each other when in sickness or trouble, and ever ready, with advice and hospitality, to aid the traveller on his way.

I had an instance of the extreme kindness of the English community to each other in the case of a poor fellow whom I knew very slightly. The devotion shown to him by his friends—for his wife and belongings were in England—was most touching. Alas! the best of nursing was of no avail. The stroke of death is swift in India. You hear a man is "down" in the morning, and next morning he is "'gone,' poor fellow!" and you frequently follow him to his grave the same day. The English cemetery of Lahore is, like all such places in India, a sad memorial of hopes blighted and promises unfulfilled. Here rest none who have passed long and happy lives, and finally been gathered to their fathers in the fulness of time. Few of these simple graves have been placed by weeping children over silver heads that time alone has laid low. Here are records of widows' tears and husbands' despair, of strong men and loving women, taken in their prime, full of hope, full of love. More touching still are the multitudes of small mounds where so many blossoms lie, that under a cooler sun might have ripened to cheer a parent's home. Poor little children! one sees them living, pale, thin, and fretful. When the prime of life and strength are no security against the insidious foe, what chance have these frail ones? Happily the hills are close, and communication with hill stations getting easier every day. Let us hope each year the dread Reaper will have a less heavy crop. Who knows whose turn may come next? Strength is as nothing, for who so strong as —— was two days ago, yet now——!

Thank Heaven my life is so busy that I have but little time to think of such things, or perchance mere anticipation of sickness might produce the dreaded evil. Yet such events grow so familiar that they are soon forgotten, except by the sorrowing few. The sober festivities of the station are only interrupted for a day, to, perhaps wisely, recommence on the morrow with steady vigour.

But English life is not what I want to record here, and the excitement of a flower show or amateur concert does not inspire me to write. I am *blasé* to such things, I own, and have a horror of recording the *menu* of the last dinner I have eaten, or giving a minute description of the company I have met, like a correspondent of "Vanity Fair." Therefore will this week's journal be a very short one; and if I miss the next post, do not be surprised, as I am journeying somewhat away from the regions of post; and as travellers going east have to put on their watches, so shall I have to push on my post-day, till, like the said travellers when they get right round the world, I may find I have missed a post as they miss a day.

## CHAPTER XIII.

### RAWAL PINDEE—MURREE.

*On the Banks of the Jhelum, 22nd April.*

ALTHOUGH I had been very comfortable at Lahore, and reposing in the lap of luxury and civilization, yet I confess to an ungrateful eagerness to depart on my further journey to Kashmir and the backbone of the world. It is not so easy, however, to get there at this time of the year. On the 15th April begins the leave season for the officers of the army, and the subalterns of India swarm to all places where sport is to be had; and where are they promised such sport as in the Happy Valley? Moreover, by reputation these sports are those peculiarly dear to the British subaltern, though condemned, and rightly, by Mrs. Grundy. I found, then, on applying for conveyance from Jhelum (where the railway ends) to Rawal Pindee, that I could not get a *gharry* for two days; and there was another delay in prospect between Rawal Pindee and Murree, my next station. It was only on the 20th that I started by the evening train, and safely reached Jhelum at 4 a.m. on the 21st. There I took *dâk gharry*, and after much talking and delay, started at five. As I drove out of the *dâk* bungalow, the east was just beginning to show signs of coming day. It was a limpid barley-sugary effect, but wonderfully striking, for I saw the sun rise behind the Himālaya (a long A, if you please) for the first time. There they were, the famous mountains—blue against the early dawn—sharp cut, as though all those jagged peaks were equally distant, while the foot hills (considerable mountains anywhere else) showed a darker blue, and the foreground was a sea of yellowing corn, with here and

*The Figures denote the height above the Sea in thousands thus 21 means 21,000 feet, and 9·7 means 9,700 feet.*
*The Figures in small type refer to Summits those in larger type to Valleys; those in brackets (18·5) to Passes.*
*The positions of Mountain Summits and Passes are shown by dots ∴.*

Scale $\frac{1}{2{,}027{,}520}$ (32 Miles to 1 Inch)

English Statute Miles

10 5 0 10 20 30 40 50

there a dark tree in the distance. It was a simple harmony of colour, one of those things that every artist has essayed; but for delicacy of tone and wonderful limpidity, I never saw anything to match it. Meanwhile, the sunrise quickening, one or two thin streaks of cloud shine golden on the delicate yellow. The distant snow-peaks are gradually fused in the glowing sky, becoming an extraordinary tender yellow lilac; and then, bright and hot, up leaps the sun! Gradually, before the car of Suraj, the abode of the Gods disappears. He is not to be trifled with, this Sun-god of latter April, and the visible presence of him fills all his portion of the sky. But as he rises higher and gilds each peak by turns, one perceives the enormous space between the mountains themselves. Range behind range show themselves touched by his golden ray, blushing into rosier tones as he passes, and when he has passed and risen much higher, the distant ranges reappear with their snowy peaks now shining in mid-sky, while the lower parts of them are lost in aërial blue. I had seen them during my journey from Delhi to Lahore, like a line of surprising clouds. I have seen, too, the Alps something in the same light; but the Alps are nothing to these, for are not these peaks part of the Kailas, and not one of them under 20,000 feet high? while those hills in front vary from 6,000 to 8,000 feet:—*Kailas*, abode of the gods, where the great Brahma passes his time in godlike contemplation; and Siva, in active malignity; and Vishnu, in abstraction, only to be roused occasionally to throw his spirit into some fresh incarnation for the good of mankind in general and Brahmins in particular: the Kailas, from which flow the holy rivers, symbols of divine grace, and whence, too, according to modern ideas, has flowed the religion of the whole world; for is not the Teuton word for "heaven" derived from Himālaya, and is not Kaila the same as *cœlum?* So say the philologists; and, gazing at those lofty peaks glistening there a hundred and fifty miles off, as they have shone for ages past, unchangeable because not to be approached, like the high gods themselves, passionless and sublime, far be it from me to say that it is not so.

Meanwhile the foreground of waving corn has been passed,

and we go uphill. The surface of the earth is broken up into seams and deep ravines,—shadow and light flecked about in a most indescribable way, telling of mighty rains and much disturbance from those far-off masses of snow; but through this cut and scarred surface English civilization has made a straight level road; and here, amidst all that is sublime in nature, I rattle along at the rate of eight miles an hour, including stoppages, and as I gaze full of artistic fervour at those distant hills, am constantly brought back to this world by the objurgations of the driver and *syces* and the yells of passers-by, who all join together to urge forward the jibbing horse. Every horse seems to jib, and innumerable are the dodgings employed to get them on: sometimes the *syces* run in front, with a thong through the bits, and lug them on; sometimes they are pushed on by passers-by; and sometimes the trace of one is passed round the trace of the other, and the non-jibber pulls along his timid companion; but always is there shouting and thrashing, and as Bishop Heber says,—

> "Every prospect pleases,
> And only man (and horse) is vile."

And so I travel, with the wondrous mountains on my right hand, and the noise of wheels and natives around, till after eight hours I perceive hideous barracks before me, and arrive at my destination—Rawal Pindee.

Rawal Pindee is a very strong military station; not strong in fortifications, but from the number of soldiers here assembled. There is a general and a brigadier-general and an English cavalry regiment, the 4th Hussars (with whom I am stopping), and two English infantry regiments, three batteries of artillery (one horse), a native cavalry regiment, and two of native infantry. It is a pretty station, with mountains close by. Murree, the hill station, is but four hours off, on the foot hills, and I was shown how you could, with flashing-signals, telegraph with ease to the sanitarium of the garrison, forty miles away.

Thunder and rain seem to be my portion at present. As at Lahore, so at Pindee, it thundered constantly. However, seizing an auspicious moment on Monday, 23rd April, I left in a hill-cart for Murree. This cart is an extraordinary vehicle, on the principle of a dog-cart, but hung low so as to make it easy to jump in and out. One horse is harnessed into the shafts, and one to each side, and off they start at full gallop, at a fearful pace. We did on the flat a mile in four minutes, and the whole distance, thirty-eight miles, in four hours and a half; and recollect Murree is 7,435 feet high! No bad going.

Of the way up there is nothing much to tell. The foot hills are much like all hills, and the road itself might be Mont Cenis, or any other pass. We are caught in a thunderstorm, but that again has become so common an occurrence lately, that we take no notice of the lengthened boom of the thunder among the hills. We pass many a bullock-carriage filled with luggage, and many an English family, on the road to the hills and Kashmir. Sportsmen have left some time ago; for first come first served, and once occupy a *nullah*, and no one can shoot there without permission; but families go to Kashmir for cheapness, as houses can be had for next to nothing, if you do not mind roughing it, and sheep cost two rupees and fowls two annas.

At length Murree is reached—a long line of houses at the top of a hill, which I believe is a description of most of the sanitaria of India. The prospect from the hotel is very fine and varied, as you have views on all sides. To the north and north-west you look over an endless sea of plain, then the foot hills advance like tiny waves, and, getting bigger as they get towards you, pass on in solemn succession till they seem to beat against a noble range of peaks, the Pir Punjal, which rises 16,000 feet high, and forms the bulk of the mountains I passed on my way to Jhelum. The highest points are on the other side of the Kashmir valley. It was very cold, and a roaring fire quite acceptable. This, after the heat I have suffered, is most extraordinary. At Pindee it is so hot, you find it a labour to move about, and at Murree you are shivering at 4 p.m.

Alas! I find no news from Sreenuggur, and next morning I get a letter from the resident there, to say that the Maharajah is not expected for a month. This, after his telegram, is too bad. However, the weather has been so exceptionally cold that he may have changed his mind, as even maharajahs do so occasionally. Here have I come to the confines of Kashmir, and must I turn back and go off to Jummo in the plains? That is the question. After some consideration, and a consultation with the Deputy Commissioner here, I determine not to go back, but to scamper through Kashmir, just to say I have seen it. Meanwhile, the Maharajah has been telegraphed to to provide every facility, and I hope to get from here to Sreenuggur in six or seven days, by doing double marches, and, after staying two or three days there, to go down to Jummo by the Maharajah's private road. Another week! At Jummo I shall paint the chief, and then get to Simla as quick as I can. This is the first expedition I have made for my own pleasure, but I think I am entitled to it, having got thus far, and I trust to make it pay by the sketches I shall bring back.* There is one thing certain, and that is, by no possibility can I get a letter by the next post, and I shall be lucky if I catch the one after, at Sreenuggur. I have just received the mail of the 28th March, and I shall get no more letters till I arrive at Simla, which if I am fortunate will be about the 26th May. What I am to do at Simla to get through my work there I do not know.

## ON THE BANKS OF THE JHELUM.

*27th—30th April, 1st, 2nd May.*

Having heard nothing of the Maharajah, and having to my disgust wasted four days at Murree, I determined to start for Sreenuggur, and make my way as well as I could on my own account. Not that I was left helpless, for the Deputy-Commissioner of Murree was most obliging, and not only helped me to make my arrangements, but sent a *chuprassee* with me to the

* This shows how little a traveller can lay out his route beforehand when his movements depend on rajahs.

borders of British territory. More, of course, he could not do. Well, on the morning of the 27th I sent my baggage off as early as possible—not very early, however, as the row and talk delayed the departure considerably. At 9.30, after breakfast, I started for Kashmir. I was almost ashamed to mount my pony (*tat* or *tattoo* in Indian lingo), as I was the larger animal of the two; yet the little beast bore me nobly throughout a march of twelve miles.

Sreenuggur is by the new route 160 miles from Murree; the last forty are by boat. The distance is, therefore, really nothing and several active young military men have cantered the whole in one day to save their leave; but for the convenience of travellers it is divided into eleven marches, and it is well this is so, for even the martial youths above mentioned would find it hard at present to do the distance in anything like good time. This year there has been an exceptionally hard winter. At Murree there was 17 feet of snow; and the melting of this snow has proved a sad trial to the road. At first, however, we found everything rosy. The day was splendid, although as usual a thunderstorm seemed coming up from the plains. The road was good, being freshly put in repair, and it wound through the most beautiful trees, reminding one of the glens (carefully kept and much esteemed) of some Scotch houses, only the trees were if anything finer, and certainly more varied. Through this enchanting scenery we trudged, my pony and I, along the brow of a descending ridge, the road being now on one side, now on the other, each side showing a deep valley and a stream far away below. But I was not to escape. I had expected at starting a storm from the plains; and now it came rolling down from the hills. Down poured the rain and hail in torrents—thunder and lightning; but I had lately seen so much of the kind of thing that I found the truth of the proverb, "Familiarity breeds contempt," and I unconcernedly continued my journey, till at last my *syce* begged to be allowed to take shelter, and we stayed under a thick tree. Anywhere else this might have been dangerous; here, however, there were so many trees that I felt the odds were in my favour as to the striking of my particular shelter. I saw after a time that the storm was very partial, and insisted on going on, and in a quarter of an hour we were out of it. A couple of miles farther on there had been no rain at all! But the downfall while it lasted was very severe, and we were quickly shown what water can do to a road. Splashing and slipping, on we went. Thanks to a good waterproof, however, I was mostly dry, and after walking for the last three miles to dry my boots, I arrived at Dewal, the first stage. Here I stayed for the heat of the day, and made a sketch of another storm that seemed working its way up the valley, but which happily did not reach me, and starting at 4 p.m., I made my second stage in the cool of the afternoon, with great satisfaction to myself and beast. I reached Kohala and my new friend the Jhelum, after dusk, and rode up to the bungalow to find two fellow-travellers finishing their dinner by moonlight. An enchanting scene! A little lawn, with small trees, through which the moon shone aslant, and two travellers seated at a table, *al fresco*—a scene for the theatre. But no scene painter could have given the distant roar of the Jhelum, a clay-coloured and much-swollen stream, not more than fifty yards wide at most, roaring and tossing among the rocks with a mighty noise, like a tempest among fir-trees, not in gusts, however, but steady and loud.

This roar we have had ever since, for our way winds along the banks of the Jhelum for miles. Mountains rise on each side, and the bed is, as I said, narrow; but there is a sense of power in this mass of water so confined, that fills the mind with awe; and its roar grows quite familiar to my ears, for it seems to talk far more intelligibly than the dusky fellows around. And so each morning before daybreak I am up, and having dispatched my luggage on the backs of coolies after much noise and bustle, without which no natives can work, I mount my *tat* as the sun begins to touch the higher hills, and start on my morning's ride of twelve miles. I do a like amount in the afternoon; indeed, my days' journeys have averaged over twenty-five miles. Delightful rides have they been; uphill and down dale, following the winding of my friend the river. Sometimes the way (road it cannot be called) would take me far up a gully, till the noise of Jhelum would fall faintly on the ear, and I came on some mountain torrent falling in lofty cascade, or dashing wildly through large boulders, and making a sharper noise than the mighty river I had just left, like the voice of a child to that of a man. Sometimes, from lofty tree-top to tree-top below the road, a flock of green parroquets would flash out like a flight of fairy rockets, their yellow tails gleaming fire, and their sharp cry forming the treble to the bass of the falling waters.

From Murree to Kohala the ground falls rapidly, so that the latter place is nearly as low as the plains of Pindee; but from Kohala to Baramula the level of the Jhelum rises considerably, and as you approach Kashmir proper, all kinds of well-known flowers greet the Britisher. I do not know anything of botany; like the Irishman, I can say, "God has denied me that knowledge;" but still I recognized much here that recalled the native wilds of Kensington. Clematis of the large white kind was in full blossom; wild roses, both white and pink, twinkled here and there among the more robust shrubs. On one day's march (a two days' march in guide books), between Chakooti and Ramnugger, the air was quite laden with the well-known odour of hawthorn, while under the trees grew great hyacinths, and beneath the bushes the ground was spotted with wild strawberries in full blossom. Here, too, I saw some wondrous birds, some blue* as turquoise, some with bright golden tails, and some with white. Magnificent butterflies—dark purple, with crimson tails—floated over the trees. In fact it was Paradise itself, and reminded me, as the cockney says in Bret Harte, of Greenwich.

Every medal has its reverse. The landscape was lovely,—so bright, so wondrous in its fantastic variety; but amidst all this fairy blossom, yet seeming to come from the ground itself, so like do they look, and so earthly, you find the inhabitants of these enchanting valleys. Fine tall-looking men, with the look of slaves, beasts of burden, and worse; for beasts of burden at least have

* This blue bird is the nearest approach to the humming-bird that is to be found in India. The long-tailed birds were, I believe, orioles, who change the colour of their tail-feathers according to their age.

some one to rub them down, and keep them moderately clean, but these have no one. I have seen gipsies, I have seen Irish, and I thought I had seen the worst; but no, these people beat them all in filth, and the traveller finds it, to his cost! Happy is the man who gets quit of the flitting flea, with which trifling though active inconvenience all the Maharajah's bungalows literally swarm. Recollect that these men bear everything one has on their dirty backs, or dirtier heads, and imagine what comes to bed and bedding, which every Indian traveller carries with him!

Between Chakooti and Ramnuggur I passed through my first grove of *deodars*. They are not so big as those I have seen described in books of travels; still they were mighty trees, and not only formed a grateful shade, but gave out an aroma, that was not the least pleasing of the delicious scents of the day. From the river the groves rise over a considerable height; while above the bungalow at Ramnuggur tower lofty cliffs of 600 to 700 feet high. Alas! here the hand of man has been doing its worst to deface the beauteous work of the Creator. Whole hill-sides have been charred and blackened by fire; magnificent trees destroyed by wanton carelessness. It appears that the *goojas*, or herdsmen, in winter are in the habit of chopping their firewood from the stems of these splendid fellows; and, not content with that, when the hole has become sufficiently deep, actually light their fires in the heart of the tree! Hence you constantly see trees quite dead, with the hearts of them completely burnt out. Sometimes you pass whole forests of black and charred skeletons, instead of beautiful living forms to delight the eye.

All along this route I found and passed at every bungalow parties of people hurrying from the hot plains to the cool valleys of Kashmir; whole families, suffering every possible inconvenience from travel and parasite; sometimes the parent (male) bird, and sometimes even a delicate lady, accompanied by unruly brats (all Indian children are unruly); to whom Sreenuggur was a veritable Promised Land, but to whom the daily stage could not have been a pleasure, and whose household gods were constantly falling down *cuds* and being lost in the rivers.

Finally, after five days' riding, about nine o'clock a.m. on the sixth day, I ascended the sharp incline of the Baramula Pass, and from the top I saw extended before me the real Valley of Kashmir; a flat rich green-looking plain, with snow-clad hills all round, through which wound our old friend the Jhelum, no longer the roaring, tossing torrent I had ridden by so many days, but slow, sleek, and prosperous, double its former size, and much like other rivers I had seen in Europe. Baramula is the one outlet of the valley, and of course there is a tradition that the whole valley was once filled with water: an immense lake, in fact, inhabited by a fiend in the shape of a dragon. A convenient deity cleft the mountains at Baramula and let out the Jhelum, and the dragon died, &c., &c. The road, unfortunately, does not pass the spot where the Jhelum pierces its mountain barrier, but I am told the cliffs are really very fine; and I can well believe it, for the fall must be considerable, and the wear and tear of ages will probably have made splendid precipices. In some parts of its course farther down there are tremendous rapids; particularly at Tinali, where I saw a plucky hill man descend the torrent on a *mussock*, a skin filled with air. He came down at a terrific pace, bobbing round like a cork amid the foam of the water. There seemed to be no difficulty in the operation, and I confess I had a great longing to try it myself.

The degradation of the inhabitants both of the valley of the Jhelum and the Valley of Kashmir proper is the more remarkable, inasmuch as they really seem prosperous. It is true I bought a sheep for R. 1 8*a*. (three shillings), and that a coolie gets sixpence for carrying a heavy load ten, twelve, or fifteen miles; but the land is well cultivated where it is possible for cultivation to exist, and pleasant great terraces of corn, in giant steps, ascend many of the hills to a considerable distance. Indeed, high up on the mountain you can see patches of green and occasional wreaths of blue smoke, telling of the presence of man and his works. Even there corn seems to thrive, and in some places is ripening fast. The crops appear, too, to be quite independent of season, for by the side of fast-ripening corn you see tender plants, hardly struggling into existence.* That these people—industrious, healthy, and prosperous—should be the veriest curs, is a curious instance for Darwin of inherited defects, and can only be explained by the fact that from ages immemorial they have always been kicked and trampled on by invaders innumerable. We added the last straw when we handed them over to the present Maharajah for 75 lacs—which, by-the-bye, have never been paid—and thereby lost the finest sanitarium for our troops, and earned the curses of Kashmirians, who, being Mohammedans, were turned over to a Hindoo and a bigot, with whom they have no sympathy, and who grinds them down in every possible way. Not only is beef forbidden in the country, but everybody is taxed in all kinds of vexatious ways, and even the miserable coolie has to give a quarter of his hardly-earned sixpence to swell this alien Maharajah's hoard. All this has been talked over and discussed by dozens of travellers lately, for writing of this part of the world has become the fashion, and we have had all kinds of sentimental names given to the Himalaya—"the abode of snow," "above the snow," "the backbone of the world," "the roof of the ditto;" all these and many more phrases are constantly in the mouths of British excursionists, who also quote freely from "Lalla Rookh," or rather from "Lalla Rookh" second-hand, through the guide book.

Descending from Baramula Pass, you quickly find yourself on a plain, and by a row of poplar-trees, which trees are found planted together in avenues all over the valley. I was much reminded of Switzerland by the general look of the country, but there were many things to tell one that Europe was far away. Baramula town was on the opposite side of the river. Its houses—indeed most of the houses hereabouts—are flat roofed, or with very slight incline, and covered over with thick grass. On many of them there were thick beds of blue iris, which appears to grow here like buttercups at home. The whole meadow at Baramula was carpeted with them. The bungalow was on the banks of the Jhelum, which is about as broad as the Thames at Maidenhead,

* This was rice.

and here you take boat for Sreenugger, and of course come in for the usual noise and bustle. Landing or embarking, there is always the same row, whether it be Dover or Calais, Leghorn or Venice Alexandria, Bombay, or Baramula. Here the row was increased by the number of shawl merchants, jewellers, and other tradesmen, who all requested you to put down your name in their books. Natives have a passion for *chits* or certificates; not a sweeper or *chuprassee* but wants a piece of paper with something written thereon, and as of course they cannot read English, some times their much-prized certificates are not what they imagine them to be.

Kashmir boats are long flat-bottomed concerns, of most primitive construction, made of long planks of *deodar*. They are pointed at the end, and turned up somewhat like a gondola, but they are paddled with a short paddle, the rower of course sitting or squatting down. There are two sizes, the smaller ones being called *shikarees*, the larger ones *dongas*. I embarked in a *shikaree*, sending my luggage in a *donga*. The boat was towed as far as Sopor (ten miles), where the Walla Lake begins. From this point we have to take to rowing, and many anxious glances are cast to windward, to watch for the coming squall; for these boats, having grass roofs and flat bottoms, are apt to turn "up-so-down" with the least wind. Not that it would have made any difference; our wary watermen kept so close in to the bank that we frequently ran aground, and seldom were in water deep enough to cause the least danger. At about nine, however, the wind sprang up, and my boatmen refused to go on; so I rolled myself up in my rug, and slept the best way I could, though it was mighty cold. Long before daylight I woke, to find the moon well up and the weather calm, so routing out my lazy rowers I insisted on their starting again. Thus the hours slid by, till a number of poplars and a fort on the summit of a hill told us we were approaching Sreenugger. Soon we were gliding up the river between dilapidated-looking houses and tumbled-down temples, and had arrived at our destination.

## CHAPTER XIV.

### KASHMIR—SREENUGGER.

SREENUGGER, the capital of Kashmir, is a long straggling city, lying along both banks of the Jhelum, which here is a broad, stately stream, spanned by seven bridges made of logs of *deodar*. Besides these bridges there are one or two mosques, which, being built of wood and covered with vegetation, do not come up to one's ideas of a public building; one or two bright-looking temples also appear, built by the piety of the present Maharajah and his son, but they are small and unimportant. The palace, too, is a most tawdry edifice, with painted blinds and verandahs of the gaudiest colours, without an atom of real splendour or artistic merit. The houses are mostly built of wood or small tile, like bricks uncemented. Many of them have a decided twist, and look as if the least breath would bring them down. Altogether the town has a tumbledown, "has been" sort of look, as though its best days were over, and so I fear they are. There are 120,000 inhabitants in the town, of whom 90,000 are Mohammedans, and only 30,000 Hindoos, the ruling class here.

History, they say, repeats itself; rather, I think, events swing like a pendulum. Thus the Moslems, who for many years were the ruling race in India, and ruled with a rod of iron over the Hindoo, have been ousted by us; and here in Kashmir, where the rebound of our power did not quite reach, we handed them over to a Hindoo, who avenges the wrongs suffered by his forefathers with interest.

It is a mild form of Islamism here practised, but such as it is it is trampled on in every possible way. The Government is a tyranny of the worst kind, tempered by the character of the

Maharajah, who is a good sort of a man, but weak. Every trade practised by Moslems is taxed fearfully. Each shawl-weaver, for example, has to pay 20 rupees a year for the right to weave. The tax used to be much more in the flourishing days of shawl-weaving. Alas! the fashion has changed. The middlemen failed, the workmen could not pay their tax, and the Rajah found himself with the whole trade in his hands, and everybody bankrupt to him. He, poor man, has been trying to resuscitate the trade, but it is easy to pull Humpty Dumpty down, and all the maharajahs and all their men cannot put him up again. The shawls, too, have themselves gone off considerably. Europeans have interfered, and, directly they do that, a purely Asiatic manufacture seems to fall to pieces.

No inhabitant of Kashmir can leave the country without the direct sanction of the chief, neither is he allowed to follow any trade but that of his forefathers; so these miserable weavers subsist as well as they can on the poor rations served out to them by the Government.

Our Government seems to give its support to this one-horse sort of policy, for no officer is allowed to go into Kashmir without signing a paper binding himself not to bring away with him any subject of the Maharajah's. Many instances have been known of love-sick subalterns who have tried to evade the law. Kashmiree women have been conveyed out of that territory in *kiltas* (large leather boxes) on the backs of coolies. The very idea of breaking so stupid a law adds a pleasure to the risk, and after all, from what one hears, there is a brisk trade with the plain in Kashmiree houris, and it is certainly true that hardly ever can one meet a decent-looking young woman in Sreenugger.

The people themselves are a fine tall race, and are certainly clever. At Murree I broke my watch, and found it such a nuisance to be without the means of knowing the time, that I sent for the native watchmaker here, and ran the risk of having my English works destroyed. The man came, squatted on the floor, took my watch to pieces, cleaned the works with the end of his turban, and prcceeded to put them together. He asked me whether I had any gun oil, and finding I had none, sent his man out, who brought some back on the end of his thumb, with which the machinery was well greased. Strange to say, my watch has gone well ever since, and, without any further regulating, has kept most excellent time.

What plays the devil with the country is the terrible tyranny of the alien *dogras*. Once a weaver, you must still weave, even if you have to starve ; once a cultivator of the soil, and you must go on : you pay no rent, but half the produce of your land belongs to the Government, and of the other half much is seized by middlemen. A carpenter thinks himself well off with two rupees a month, but can hardly be expected to take much pride in his work when it only brings in one shilling a week.

I have not yet been in the back part of the town, or seen the Dall Lake, on which are the celebrated floating gardens. I am told the filth is perfectly astounding, and I can well believe it. It is the fashion of well-to-do Kashmirees to leave their drainage before their front door. *Verbum sap.*

The English quarter is a mile or two from the town, in some pleasant gardens. There, amid apple, mulberry, and pear-trees, the Maharajah has built some bungalows, of which he reserves a few, and the others are at the service of any English that may come. There is a great scramble for these bungalows. First come first served, is the law, and many squabbles arise when people arrive at the same time. However, there are many more people than bungalows, and all about are to be seen the tents of the English. I, being a guest of the Maharajah, have one of the reserved bungalows, close to the river. From my windows I have a splendid view of the Pir Punjal mountains, rising from 11,000 to 16,000 feet, with eternal snow on their summits. The weather having been much like an English May, I have an endless variety of effects before me. Heavy clouds, gleams of sunshine, snow glistening through the mist or far above the thunder-clouds, form a never-ending source of study and delight, and if I were inclined to be lazy, I could spend hours sitting at my window gazing with open mouth. From the river to the foot hills is a flat and rich plain, with rows of poplars and splendid *chenars* or Oriental plane-trees, while immediately under my windows rolls the Jhelum, with many boats floating on its calm waters, and in each boat a number of statues, looking as though they had been ages buried and had not yet had the earth cleaned off them, but superb in fold and limb. In such a place, and amid such surroundings, the delay of a Maharajah may be excused, and although I am much put out by the upsetting of all my plans, I am trying to make the best of a bad bargain. The worst is that I do not know if the Maharajah has yet left Jummo; and he is so superstitious that he may stop half-way for a month, if only his cunning astrologers say it is not lucky to enter his capital. He wrote to the resident here to say that if I was in a great hurry I could meet him half-way, and he would stay a day for me to make a sketch of him. This would be impossible, for not only is he a most elaborately-dressed potentate, but I have moreover to make a sketch of his little son, who was page to Lord Lytton on the grand occasion, and consequently occupied a prominent place in the ceremony. So I must e'en wait for His Highness here, and I have therefore set to work making studies of the inhabitants of the Happy Valley, and have already got well on with two *nautch* girls, with whose much-bespangled heads I hope to turn an honest penny by-and-bye. I lead a most healthy life,—up by half-past six, when I go out for a ride on a pony provided for my bulky requirements by the obliging Vizier. When I come in, I work or write till half-past ten, and then breakfast. My model comes at eleven, and sits till half-past four or five, when I go out and read the papers and potter about till dinner; and so to bed early. There is a large English colony here; and there is a reading-room, and polo, cricket, badminton, and lawn-tennis,—everything the world can desire. Added to this, it's cool, although we have thunder and rain pretty well every afternoon; so I shall do very well, only, as I said before, drat all rajahs! With all this English element about, there is a lack of picturesque Orientalism, and I find but little to record. Let me hope by next mail the Rajah may be in. Alas! it is almost hopeless to expect him.

*20th May.*

"If woman can make the worst wilderness dear,
Think, think what a heaven she must make of Cashmere."

So writes, or rather gurgles, Thomas Moore, and as he is quoted in the guide book, that part of "Lalla Rookh" is at least read I doubt whether "woman's affection" can exist here, and to me such thoughts have no attraction. My eyes are fixed in the direction of Jummo, and I look eagerly for the boats of the Maharajah. There is no doubt, however, that the Vale of Kashmir is a very pleasant place in May. In the early morning there is a keen bracing feeling in the air, which is truly delightful. Far away you see clear cut against the sky a snowy range of mountains, with fantastic and ever-varied form of Gothic spire or Saracen dome, stretching so far that the farther peaks seem like ghosts in the sky, and around you as you ride (and I do ride) you pass many a most picturesque object, human or otherwise. Along the mountain track finely-draped figures of men trudge by you, with brawny chest and arms of a splendid brown showing through their sad-coloured *puttoo* clothes, which you hope are the natural colours of the wool, and not filthy; or women with strongly-marked but handsome features, balancing heavy loads on their heads. These are the Kashmirees proper, the slaves of the soil and its Maharajah, going to work or market. Sometimes you meet a Punditanee or Hindoo lady, with clothes of a rich red (most acceptable to the artist), or men with red or blue *pugrees*; and in every *pugree*—red, blue, or white—do these people stick great clusters of yellow flowers or crimson poppies, which shine like jewels against *pugree* and skin. Then, as the ground gently rises, you pass over the shoulder of the Tukt-i-Suleiman, and see stretched below you the Dall (or town) Lake, turquoise, and purple as it takes reflection or ripple amidst the greenest meadows; and, as if the earth were not enough to bear the fruits of teeming nature, the very lake itself is covered with floating islands, on which are grown cucumbers and melons, now only in their first fresh greenery; while all around tower the lower hills, respectable mountains anywhere else, but here only hills. Or you leave the broader track called a road here, and branch off along a path through the fields, where the corn is well up and shining with dewy diamonds from beard and leaf, or where there are patches quite ablaze with poppies; and when the corn ceases, you ride through whole beds of irises, white and blue. Below you see the green valley, and in the blue distance the snowy peaks of the Pir, already, at seven, gathering clouds which at midday will quite obscure their lovely outline. Quite a heaven indeed is Kashmir, you think, till you come to a tumbledown house, filthy and miserable, round which are one or two squalid children deep in muck, but no homestead or farmyard. This is where the people live who till this Paradise, and have to pay three-quarters of their produce to the Maharajah and overseer for the questionable privilege.

N.B.—An agriculturist would no doubt say that the flowers that delighted me showed either poor land or indifferent cultivation.

The ride I have attempted to describe above is the one I have taken for the last four mornings, while I have been employed in making a sketch. I can imagine nothing pleasanter than the whole scene, temperature and all, at 5.30 a.m. One morning I rode along the embankment that separates the lower town from the Jhelum. A treacherous friend is the now peacefully-flowing river. In the months of June and July, when the snows melt on the hills, and there happens to come on one of those frequent thunderstorms, the river rises with wonderful rapidity. Three years ago, all the English who live on its banks had to take to boat, or camp as best they could on the Tukt-i-Sulieman, the hill overlooking the English quarter; and the *bund* that enclosed the Dall Lake and the lower part of the town was nearly washed away. Now everything is green and pleasant. The *chenar*-trees, which give the name of Chenar Bagh ("garden of chenars") to the low-lying land on the river side of the *bund*, are magnificent in foliage and shade, and form a pleasant camping-ground for bachelors. But my road farther on led through a part of the town, and truly I may say that in filth Sreenugger has few equals and no superiors. It has this year been partially cleaned, for last year there was a terrible visitation of cholera. Now, Sreenugger is over 5,000 feet above the sea, and ought to be exempt, especially as draining is comparatively easy, there being a deep and quick-flowing river handy. In India, however, the cholera comes where-ever there is the least encouragement, and here they meet it half-way. Even in Murree, an English sanitarium, the ravages were fearful; which was hard on those people who sought its pleasant heights to escape the perils of the plains, like the lassies in the old Scotch song:

> "Jenny Lee and Bessie Bell,
> They were twa bonnie lassies;
> They bigged a bower on yonder hill-top,
> And theaked it o'er with rashes.
>
> "They bigged a bower on yonder hill-side,
> And theaked it o'er with heather;
> But the pest came up fra yonder toun,
> And killed them baith tagither."

So the people of Murree had a great scare, and the Government at Simla shook in its shoes, for the cholera was there too; and I am partially affected by the fright of last year, for Lord Lytton will have no Rajah there this summer, as it is supposed they (the rajahs) bring the cholera with them, or at all events produce it by the filthy habits of their over-crowded followers.

Another morning I went to the Jumma Musjid, which is a vast quadrangle, with four square mosques in the centre of the four sides, built entirely of *deodar* wood. The pillars supporting the roof are made of single stems, and being very tall, have an exceedingly simple and grand appearance. Alas! all is now in ruin. There is a goodly crop of hay on the roof, interspersed with beautiful irises, which flower grows plentifully on most of the roofs of Sreenugger. But here, besides hay and iris, there are bushes, and almost trees, and of course the roof is quickly giving way, though the building was only built by Shah Jehan, in sixteen hundred and something.

Beyond these morning rides and excursions I have nothing to

record of Sreenuggur. I work all day long; in the morning at landscape, and in the day from people I have got to sit, generally of that class whose sayings and doings are not to be recorded. They are not very pretty, but lend themselves to picturesque treatment from the richness of their dress and multitude of their ornaments.

Time goes by rapidly and not unpleasantly, and consequently monotonously. To-day I heard that the Maharajah had really started three days ago, so that if he has not a stomach-ache, or anything to delay him, I may next mail record his entry into his capital, which I hear is worth seeing.

I believe the resident and I are the only English persons in Sreenugger who have anything to do. The others are come simply to kill time, and spend their six months' leave in a state of vegetation. Of the visitors here three-quarters at least are Irish. The rich brogue of the West of Ireland is heard everywhere, and if it were not for the mountains, you might think yourself on the banks of the Shannon instead of the Jhelum. Professionally, doctors and artillerymen form the most numerous class; civilians are rarely seen, I being the only un-military man among the hundred visitors now assembled. Of course picnics, &c., are the order of the day, but I keep away from them, as they are a great waste of time. There are several "spins" here, by which elegant name the unmarried and bachelor-hunting young lady goes in India. Some of them are pretty, or at least look pretty here.

I am, however, quite safe. It does not require woman to make the wilderness of Kashmir attractive to me.

*30th May.*

Still at Sreenugger. Happily I have at last got my sailing orders, and leave on the 3rd June to meet the Maharajah at Islamabad, or rather at Acchabul, a place six miles from that town. It appears that the stars are not propitious, and that His Highness is forbidden by their decree to enter his capital during this month. Now we are only at the 18th of the month, according to the Indian calendar, and I can't afford to wait so much longer; so I am to meet him half-way, and he has consented to give me the necessary sittings there.

Meanwhile I have made several expeditions to the neighbourhood. On Sunday last I started at 6 a.m. for a tour round the Dall Lake. It was truly delightful; everything was calm and delicious, without a ripple to disturb the reflection, so that you were quite unconscious of where the mountains ended or the water began, only here and there were little patches of water-lilies to give the necessary green note amid the blue reflection of the hills. Here is the place where Lalla Rookh lived and spooned. Alas! the water-lilies are not in blossom, and the famous gardens show signs of neglect and decay.

When Baber first won Hindostan for the Mohammedan Moguls, he lamented that through the length and breadth of the land there were no fountains or pleasant gardens. Both he and his descendants worked hard to introduce a Persian love of flowers and birds, and wherever they visited there are traces of green delight. The Nishat Bagh, celebrated for its cherries and its delicious view across the lake, owes its formation to the Mogul; and Shallimar, famous throughout the world, full of pleasant pavilions and shady groves, was built as a present from the amorous Jehanghire to his Noor Jehan. Both are full of magnificent trees,—mostly *chenars* or plane-trees,—and 'tis pleasant to recline in their shade, and think of the mighty monarchs of the past, who here forgot the cares of state amid the beauties of nature and the smiles of their loved ones. Bigoted Moslems though they were, they did not disdain to pledge their favourites in wine-filled bowls; great kings, but with a true feeling for art and beauty. The present ruler of Kashmir has no such feeling. He cares for nothing but making money, and the sordid and terrible gods of the Hindoos. To him nature smiles not; swift river and blue lake for him have no charm, and are only tolerable as a means of taxation. From the hard-working cultivator of floating garden and from the toiling fisherman alike is exacted the half of the produce of his labour; only before the palace no nets must be spread or lines laid, for the great Maharajah believes that the soul of his revered father inhabits the body of a fish which now haunts the banks of the river whence rises his former home.

Shallimar must have cost a pretty penny. Its pavilions are pillared with black marble, which must have been brought a great way, and, with no roads and plenty of mountains, they must have been costly indeed. But what was that to Jehanghire, when a smile of Noor Jehan was at stake? She was a superior person, no doubt, and fond of power, and on the death of her husband gave his successor a deal of bother. Well, she lies near Lahore in another garden, quiet enough now, or, maybe, filling wine-cups for her beloved in Mohammed's Paradise. Who knows? And will Jehanghire remain faithful there, or will the smile of innumerable *houris* win him from his earthly love?

A rollicking, wine-bibbing, lovesick monarch was this Jehanghire, of whom we have a curious account by Sir T. Roe, who was sent "Ambassador from James I. to Jehan Guire, the mighty Emperor of India, commonly called the Great Mogul." Take this account of an evening with the Great Mogul.

On the 2nd of September was the King's birthday, and Sir T. Roe found him "sitting cross-legged on a little throne, all covered with diamonds, pearls, and rubies; before him a table of gold, and on it about fifty pieces of gold plate, all set with jewels, some very great and extremely rich. His nobility were about him, in their best equipage, whom he commanded to drink merrily, several sorts of wine standing by in great flagons. He asked whether I would drink with them. I answered that I would do whatever his Majesty commanded, but hoped that it would not be too much or too strong. I drank a little, but it was stronger than any I had ever tasted, insomuch that it made me sneeze, which made him laugh. Then he made merry, and sent me word that he esteemed me more than he had ever done. . . . . Then he threw about, to those who stood below, two chargers of new rupees, and to us who stood around, two chargers of hollow almonds of gold and silver, mixed. But I would not scramble as his great men did, for I saw his son take up none. Then he gave sashes of gold and girdles to all the musicians and waiters, and to many others. So, drinking and commanding others to do the same, his Majesty and all his lords became the finest men that ever I saw, and of a thousand humours. But his son, Asaph Khan*, two old men, the late King of Candahar, and myself, forbore. When he could hold up his head no longer, he laid down to sleep, and we all departed." On another occasion the worthy knight records how "the Mogul fell to drinking of Alicante wine I had presented him" with a like result, for presently "he turned to sleep, the candles were popped out, and I groped my way out in the dark." Fancy Jehanghire sleeping "in his boots," like a good gentleman as he was!

Sometimes, however, the mornings were not so pleasant. It appears that when Jehanghire permitted any of his nobles to drink in his presence, their names were taken down by an individual of the name of the *bakshi*, and they were obliged to drink, whether they wished or no. One morning one of these unfortunate topers remarked what a fine drink they had had the night before. The King, being out of sorts, called the *bakshi*, and had the names of his last night's guests read over. "Some he fined; some that were nearer his person he caused to be whipped before him, they receiving one hundred and thirty stripes with a terrible instrument, having at the ends of four cords irons like spur-rowels, so that every stroke made four wounds. When they lay for dead on the ground, he commanded the standers-by to spurn them, and after that the porters to break their staves on them. Then, most cruelly mangled and bruised, they were carried out. One of them died on the spot." And no wonder, I should say! Who would not wish to live at an Eastern emperor's Court?

This, too, is a good picture of the Court of Jehanghire at his daily court of justice at the Jarruco window. "Two eunuchs stood on two trestles, with long poles and feather fans at the end of them, fanning him. He bestowed his favours and received

* Asaph Khan was brother of Noor Jehan the Queen, and Prime Minister. The son was Prince Khurm, who affected to be a strict Mohammedan. He was afterwards King under the name of Shah Jehan (King of the World).

presents. What he bestowed he let down by a silk string rolled on a turning instrument; what was given to him, a venerable, fat, deformed old matron, wrinkled and hung round with gimbels like an image, pulled up at a hole with such another clue. At one side of the window were his principal wives, whose curiosity made them break little holes in a grate of reeds that hung before it to gaze on me. I first saw their fingers, and then they laying their faces close, first the one and then the other, I could sometimes discern their full proportion. They were indifferent white, with black hair smoothed up; but if there had been no other light, their diamonds and pearls had sufficed to show them. When I looked up they retired, and were so merry that I suppose they laughed at me . . ." Then the King starts on a journey thus: "He came downstairs with such an acclamation of 'Health to the King!' as would have out-roared cannon. At the foot of the stair, where I met him, and shuffled to be next, one brought a mighty carp, another a dish of white stuff like starch, into which he put his finger, and touched the fish, and so rubbed it on his forehead, a ceremony used presaging good fortune. Then another came and girt on his sword and hung on his buckler, set all over with diamonds and rubies, the belts of gold suitable. Another hung on his quiver, with thirty arrows, and his bow in its case. On his head he wore a rich turban, with a plume of heron's feathers; not many, but long. On one side hung a ruby, unset, as big as a walnut; on the other a diamond as large; in the middle an emerald like a heart, much bigger. His staff was wound about with a chain of great pearls, rubies, and diamonds drilled. About his neck he wore a chain of three strings of most excellent pearl, the largest I ever saw; above his elbows armlets set with diamonds; and on his wrist three rows of several sorts; his hands bare, but almost on every finger a ring; his gloves, which were English, stuck under his girdle; his coat of cloth of gold, without sleeves, upon a white semain as thin as lawn; on his feet a pair of buskins, embroidered with pearl, the toes sharp and turning up. Thus armed and accoutred, he went to the coach that attended him, with his new English servant, who, clothed as rich as any player, and more gaudy, had broke four horses, which were trapped and harnessed in gold velvet. This was the first coach he ever sat in, made by that sent out of England, so like that I knew it not but by the cover, which was a Persian gold velvet. He sat at the end, and on each side went two eunuchs, who carried small maces of gold, set all over with rubies, with a long bunch of horsetail to flap away the flies. Before him went drums, bass trumpets, and loud music, many canopies, umbrellas, and other strange ensigns of majesty, made of cloth of gold, set in many places with rubies. Nine led horses, the furniture some garnished with rubies, some with pearls and emeralds, some only with studs enamelled, &c." Yet I do not envy the Great Mogul in his coach, for I know what the roads were, and can imagine that his dignity was much ruffled by the jolts that I too have experienced.

This place is getting unpleasantly full; there are as many as two hundred families here, and the encampments begin to be disagreeable. The weather is getting hot too, and soon will everybody flit to the Valley of Gulmerg, a place full of flowers, about 4,000 feet higher up the mountains, as its name implies—*gul* ("rose"), and *merg* ("a valley between hills"). There is a curious collection here of humdrum married people and wild subalterns. In the next bungalow to me there are four of these roysterers, and the well-known sound of many an English ditty mingles with the gurgle of the Jhelum and the sigh of the wind through the poplars. The other day, the mirth having got particularly furious, one of the youths seized a friend and proceeded to throw him out of the window, and was stayed in his intention of dropping him thence by the remark of an Irishman there, "Arrah, now! don't waste him: wait till some one is coming by!"*

Another expedition I made with the resident here, or rather Officer on Special Duty at the Court of the Maharajah, as his title runs. It was to see an old and rich merchant named Billih Shah. We went by boat through a number of small canals, winding

* The Irishman in question had heard, no doubt, of the same speech made at the Dublin theatre, where the flinger was asked to wait for a fiddler.

among many pollard poplars and willows, and unspeakable stinks. The merchant's house was built, like most of the houses of Sreenugger, of small bricks, and had the windows prettily fitted up with pierced woodwork, which made the whole place look like a toy house. Old Sreenugger (the City of the Sun—*sree* being *suraj*) was built of stone. All about one sees huge blocks, the remains of the old, but now used as foundations to the modern city, amongst which you may trace much carving destroyed by the iconoclastic Mohammedans years ago. To excuse their laziness, the modern Sreenuggerians say that they cannot build with stone—which is, by-the-bye, close at hand—because of the earthquakes. My notion is that it would require a devil of an earthquake to rouse them from their degraded apathy.

Billih Shah, being an old man, had his beard dyed a bright purple. He was evidently rather a dandy, and was neatly got up in white. A thin, dapper little man, with a sly little eye, hardly perceptible, so much is it screwed up with a cunning look—and a man must be sly to make his fortune in this benighted country. He treated us sumptuously with tea and innumerable cakes and sweets. Amongst the luxuries he brought for our approval was the brick tea drunk universally in the interior, which I have no hesitation in saying is by far the nastiest stuff I ever put into my mouth, and worse than the worst physic. It is prepared, I believe, with bullocks' blood, or something even more horrible.

One evening I went to a wedding. I was not allowed to join in the ceremony, but viewed the proceedings from an upper window. Seven days the *tomasha* had lasted, and day and night were women howling congratulatory verses to the bridegroom who sat feasting with his intimates the while. On a certain day rings are put into the bride's ears and nose; on another her hands are marked with henna, and so on. She lived in a house hard by, where the happy man was allowed to see her for a short time each day, being conducted to and fro with much ceremony and many torches stinking and reeking, as I found to my cost. I have taken down many of the distiches sung on the occasion, and am trying to get them translated, when, if they are worth it, I will add them to my diary. The continued howling of the women becomes very irksome after a time, and although the sight was curious, I was glad to get away after a couple of hours. The bride was nine years old.

The following is a translation of the songs sung at a Kashmiree wedding:—

THE BRIDEGROOM'S MOTHER TO HER SON.

What savoury dish shall I cook thee? Fishes of Shallimar?
On thy earring I will string pearls.
Thou art green grass, or if not, a red pearl.
O Parrot,* thy body is resplendent!
Why dost thou sit leaning thy elbow on the window?
Descend, and I will spread gold for thee.
When thou leavest this, sit in a plastered room,†
And thou must take a doll‡ with thee.

BRIDEGROOM'S MOTHER TO THE BRIDE.

O Mainah! Mainah! thou art a scornful Mainah!
Thou art the possessor of the riches of thy husband's house.
Thy vine§ clings on thee in spiral curves,
And round it pearls I will string.

MOTHER OF THE BRIDE TO THE BRIDEGROOM.

All thy companions are youthful,
Bearing rods of pearl in their hands!
All of them are wealthy—are great!
Which of them will be the bearer of thy *morchal?* ||
Thou didst emerge from beneath the mountains, resplendent as the sun!
I will string pearls on thy beardless chin.¶

MOTHER OF THE BRIDE TO THE BRIDEGROOM'S FATHER.

O youthful bridegroom's father, who was thy counsellor? **
Thy face is worthy of a pearl necklace!

MOTHER OF THE BRIDE TO THE BRIDEGROOM.

I have spread for thee the bed in the public sitting-room.
O cavalier! make thy heart happy!
Had I known thee to be of such distinguished rank,
We would have spread for thee a couch in the private apartment.††

MOTHER OF THE BRIDEGROOM TO THE BRIDEGROOM.

Urge on thy steed in every direction.
I will prepare thy seat in the garden pavilion:

* *i.e.*, Bridegroom. † The height of luxury in Kashmir.
‡ *i.e.*, The bride. § Curls of hair. || Emblem of rank.
¶ Rather a difficult operation, one would think, but meaning only kissing.
** Who chose this particular bride? †† Reserved for distinguished guests.

On thy right the Koran, on thy left the necklace.
Thou art worthy to be called Lalla Gopal !*

MOTHER OF THE BRIDEGROOM TO THE BRIDE.

Didst thou suffer any inconvenience in thy glass *jampan ?* †
Accept thy bridegroom's house as a *jogeer* ‡ to thyself.

SINGING WOMEN ENGAGED BY THE BRIDE'S FATHER.

O bridegroom's mother ! O kettle of *pilau !* ‖
Come forward, sprinkling rose-water !
Arouse her (the bride). Early give her to drink of tea.
Always consider her the beloved of the house.

SINGING WOMEN TO THE BRIDEGROOM'S FATHER.

Before God we have given her over to thee, O father !
What return shall we receive at thy hands ?

SINGING WOMEN TO THE BRIDE AND BRIDEGROOM.

The Parrot of Lahore and the Mainah of Kashmir !
How did you both become mutually acquainted ?

MOTHER OF THE BRIDEGROOM TO HER SON.

Why haltest thou in the warmth of the walnut-tree ?
Come and sit in the cool shade of the *chenar.*¶

MOTHER OF THE BRIDEGROOM TO ASSEMBLED WOMEN.

I spread a carpet for them on the stream's glossy bank,
Where Shirisi will be met by Farhad.

MOTHER OF THE BRIDEGROOM TO THE BRIDE.

O Mainah ! hast thou seated thyself on the green grass ?
Spare kneeling-room** for the Parrot !

SINGING WOMEN.

O bridegroom's father ! O black beard !
Roses have blossomed in thy garden !
Has the sound of our much singing reached thy ear?
O father ! it is for thee to give us the guerdon of our song !

I am indebted for the translation of the above to the courtesy of Major Henderson, C.S.I., who was political officer in Kashmir, and an excellent linguist.

The song is a good picture of the manners of the country, and the way that the Moslem and Hindoo customs have acted on

* Lalla Gopal, one of the names of Krishna, who was supposed to have been the type of loveliness. Curious, this, when sung by a Mohammedan !

† *Jampan* is the light palanquin used in the hills. ‡ *Jogeer*—grant.

‖ Term of praise. ¶ There is a tradition in Kashmir that the shade of a *chenar* is cooler than the shade of any other tree. ** The bridegroom performs his devotions on a coloured cloth on which the bride sits.

VIEW OF THE DALL LAKE, FROM THE NISHAT BAGH.

each other. Whilst at Sreenugger I have painted two or three *nautch* girls, and it was through them that I got to this wedding, as they were amongst the singers. Now these girls, like most *nautch* girls in India, were all Moslemehs, yet had they all the caste feeling of the Hindoo. Of moral sentiment they were entirely innocent, but they would never permit any one to drink out of their cup or smoke from their hookah, and they always went about with these two utensils, for smoke and tea are the two things necessary to a Kashmiree. So in this song a Kashmiree Moslem is made to say "beautiful as Krishna."

On the other hand, the Hindoos throughout India, and here especially, shut up their women, and never allow them to go out without the thickest veil; yet is the Zenana strictly Mohammedan. "Where females are honoured, there the deities are pleased; but when dishonoured, then all religious rites become useless;" "Strike not even with a blossom the wife guilty of a hundred faults," say Hindoo sages. Contrast this with the sentiments of Mohammed; yet Mohammed was a good husband to Cadija when young and poor.

p. 228

BEGOO, A KASHMIREE NAUTCH GIRL.

## CHAPTER XV.

### KASHMIR—ACCHABUL—THE LIDDAR VALLEY.

AT last I have left Sreenugger. The weather had become hottish, that is to say, 76° in the house: that is nothing, you will think, for India, but the thermometer is no criterion of the oppressiveness of heat. Sreenuggur at 76° was most oppressive, and, from the doctor's report, unhealthy. The atmosphere was quite thick and pea-soupy, the lovely range of mountains had faded from sight, and the river stank. So on Sunday afternoon (after church) I gladly got into my boat, and, with Major Henderson, the "political" here, was towed from the bungalow whence I had seen many wonderful effects, and the Moonshee Bagh, where I left many agreeable acquaintances. I don't know whether I shall see Sreenugger again; possibly not; but I am glad to have visited the Sun City, with its teeming, lying population, and its tumbledown, stinking buildings. In a short time the natives will have it to themselves, for the English part of the inhabitants will have fled to the upper valleys. Well, I do not grudge the wretched Kashmirees the rupees they got out of me by lying and cheating; I only wish them success in a better cause and more self-respect. Alas! how can they get it under the present reign? Such, maybe, are my thoughts as I recline in Henderson's barge, which, being the biggest, is used by me as well as by him and his friend; or maybe I think of England and friends far away, for there is much time to think, as at first we skim noiselessly along. I know this part of the river. By great bends the Jhelum manages to make very little progress in the direct line, and after a couple of hours' hard work you find yourself five minutes' ride from your bungalow. On we go, the water pleasantly gurgling against the slanting bows of the *donga*. We talk—we think—my companions are both married, so let me hope they thought of their better halves—we snooze—perchance we dream; until it is 5 p.m., and tea being wanted, shouts are raised for the boats with the *babacy khanah*, or cooking utensils. We each have one; and quickly, one on each side, up they glide to supply our wants. Then on again, the river getting broader and more sluggish, the mountains falling back on the left bank, and a sort of raised plateau appearing. This is the Pampor, celebrated for the saffron, which is grown on the plateau before mentioned, and is the best saffron in the world, they say; and, dear me! it is dinner-time, so up come the boats again, and we feed and drink and smoke, and pass a bridge, and lo! it is dark, and time to go to bed; so I get back into my own boat and turn in, in hopes of sleep. Alas! vain hope! Kashmirees can with difficulty be restrained from noise by daylight, but if they have to work by night they must shout. So all night long they shouted, and yelled, and squabbled, and the boats bumped together, or scrunched their rush-thatched roofs as they passed each other, and sleep, except at intervals (when I believe the devils left the boats altogether), was impossible. Kashmirees do not mind noise themselves; they roll themselves up in their *puttu* cloak, and the last trump would not wake them, nor would anything but a kick administered to a tender part of their persons. (N.B.—We all "cussed" in strange languages "some," that night.)

By 6 a.m. we were up, to find th. river narrowed considerably, and on we "glode," through lovely river scenery, reminding one of the Thames, or the Rhone, or any delightful river of our past; on by many a tumbledown collection of houses, and one considerable town, Bigbehara, with a holy temple, round which were congregated pilgrims from the plains, bright with a refreshing variety of coloured garments, in happy contrast with the universal dull mud-coloured raiment of the Kashmirees; till the river narrows and narrows, and branches appear, and finally, at a bridge over a now quite dwindled stream, we stop, and are at Islamabad.

At 10 a.m. we alight from our boats, and are received, as in duty bound, by the head man of the district, in the name of the Maharajah. Here we have more shouting, squabbling, and fighting, while coolies are loaded. I find, to my horror, that my saddle has been left behind. Henderson's *vakeel* kindly offers his "real English," as he assures me, and I am comforted; but when I come to mount, and with my usual lightness place my fairy foot in the stirrup, out comes the lower bar. Another is found, however, and though much inconvenienced by the want of powers of expansion at the base, I finally start. It is six miles to Acchabul, where we are to find the Maharajah. The road leads through Islamabad, which is neither dirtier nor cleaner than other towns of its kind in Kashmir; then it winds through vast paddy-fields, where the water is lying some three inches deep, and whence proceeds the hoarse croaking of innumerable frogs. Occasionally we come to a group of natives tilling their rice, and this is how they do it: every man and woman holds a long stick in each hand for support, and then has to work the rising rice-plant backwards and forwards with alternate foot in the rich slush. I should have thought they would have uprooted the tender green shoots, but they have the experience of past ages, and probably know best.*

Finally, about a mile and a half from Acchabul, we come to our camping-ground, a pleasant rising ground close to the main track. It was formerly a Moslem burying-ground, little round stones rising here and there to show where lie defunct believers, who are now possibly feasting with Mohammed and others, in a better place than even Kashmir. Close to the road is a small

* Alas! the rice was never reaped: a quarrel arose between the middlemen and the cultivators. The former would not let the latter reap their fields, when finally the snow came and the crops were lost! This last year a terrible famine has fallen on this fair province, whether from this cause I know not. The people have died by hundreds, I hear. The Government only recognized the danger of the situation when too late, and to introduce grain over the mountains was an impossibility. No English were admitted, and as the money spent by foreigners in a great measure supported the inhabitants of the country, the result was disastrous. Many have emigrated, I hear.

shrine sacred to the memory of some extra-pious man,—at least I suppose so, for many travellers have I seen *salaaming* to it as they passed on their way.

The Maharajah does not care about defunct Moslems, and does not suspect us of a fear of ghosts; so here are the tents prepared for me, under a magnificent *chenar*, and here too Henderson pitches, and we are told to consider ourselves guests of the chief.

Presently up rides a dandy-looking young gentleman of about twenty-four, with beautifully white nether garments of muslin, and neat little ornamented slippers, but with a military frock-coat on, and sword. This is Lachmansdass, Brigadier-General, and he comes from the Maharajah to know when we should like to pay our visit. We say five, and enter into a conversation with our friend, who, though I fear but a carpet knight, is intelligent and speaks English well. Nor does his dandified appearance belie his character. If he has not had a chance of succeeding in the field of Mars, in that of Venus scandal says much of his exploits. He was even found once with a guitar under the windows of an English lady, who, report says, did not frown on the dusky warrior. (N.B.—He is decidedly good-looking.)

At five we leave our encampment for Acchabul and the Maharajah. For about a mile our way lies between paddy-fields, then gently falls to a delightful valley, full of pleasant flowing waters, amid which, under some splendid *chenars*, rests the small village of Acchabul. Now the whole place swarms with His Highness's retainers, who have to be well shouted at and shoved about to allow our modest cavalcade to proceed. *Fakirs*, soldiers, coolies, Hindoos, and Moslems,—all are treated with like indifference when the *sahib*, and above all the *burra sahib*, passes. The scene is very striking with this crowd:—the rushing streams, the trees, and the winding road, with many simple bridges. At last the gate of the villa is reached, and we alight. Acchabul, or Achhabul (from *achha*, "good," and *bul*, "source" or "spring") is one of the three principal sources of the Jhelum; Vernag, about ten miles farther off, being another, and Bawan the third. It is no dribbling little spring, as you may imagine. The water gushes from the rock in vast quantities in two principal streams, which are quite rivers at their birth. Vernag is said to be much the same. The intelligent *baboo* who acts here as Lord Chief Justice told me that a stream of some size enters the mountains on the Jummo side, and is lost, and that here it bursts forth again. I do not know whether this is an ascertained fact, but anyhow the place Acchabul is a curious phenomenon of nature.

Such a situation for a garden did not escape the keen eye of the Mogul, and Jehanghire, taking advantage of the natural supply of water, built a pavilion and fountains. Jehanghire's pavilion forms the base of the present structure, which is not much more than a large upper chamber over the gushing stream, with rooms on each side. I believe there is a dwelling-house where the Maharajah resides. Meanwhile to the "too-too" of a bugle, and past a very respectable "present arms" of a small company of Sepoys, clad in brown *puttu*, we advance up the garden, and in the upper room are received with great cordiality by the chief of Jummo and Kashmir.

Rumbir Sing is, I should say, between forty and forty-five. He looks stout, but all natives do, from the way they wear their clothes. A pleasant, kindly-looking man, who disarmed my wrathful feelings by at once apologizing for having kept me waiting, and explaining that he had been ill. Sittings are arranged for the next day: the son, who was page to Lord Lytton, is to sit at 8 a.m., and the father at 5 p.m.; and so, after compliments, &c., the meeting ends, and we ride back to our encampment.

I have on many occasions in this diary been very hard on the ruling powers of Kashmir, but I must separate the system from the character of the ruler. In Kashmir there is a tyranny of the worst kind; and for ages the people have been ground down by their rulers. But everybody allows that the present Rajah is a kindly, well-disposed man, who has done his best to modify the system he found on his accession to power. Still, when people have been ruled with kicks and stripes oft, it is difficult at once to do better. I believe the Maharajah did send away the Vizier once, and try more pacific measures; but after a time things came to a standstill, for people would not pay except on compulsion; and so the old Vizier, with his energetic policy, was reinstated. Only everything is much milder, and punishments are tempered to the shorn Kashmiree. He is not hung for killing a cow, only imprisoned for life. *Àpropos* of cows, I hear that a great personal friend of the Maharajah's told a lady here that, as a personal favour, the chief asked him to give up eating beef, and that he had taken a pledge that he would. The Maharajah is most laborious, and holds two *durbars* a day, at which all petitions are heard. Petitions are dictated previously to the *moonshee*, who writes them out and reads them afterwards; nor is the original pleader allowed a word, so you may suppose much depends on the *moonshee*. The Maharajah's great fault is his weakness of character—perhaps good-nature—which makes him a prey to all kinds of people, religious or otherwise. He is surrounded too by members of one family, and that in itself is apt to keep things in a groove.

*8th June.*

My sittings are now over. I have had four from the son and three from the father, and in these I have been expected to paint two elaborately-got-up chiefs. I do not think I have ever been so "put to" as here. It is not the bore of having to ride two miles backwards and forwards morning and afternoon through the hot sun; but in every other place I have worked in I have always had a place where I could digest what I did, tickle up backgrounds, &c.; here I have had nothing but travelling tents. The rooms I painted in had of course an indifferent light, and everything was against me; but here I have no room at all.

The little boy, entertained principally by the Chief Justice, sat very fairly, and I hope to make a good thing by-and-bye from his study. What I shall do from the Rajah I know not; happily I have a photograph. So here I have waited five weeks for three sittings! It is too disgusting; but unless I choose to wait another fortnight I shall not get any more. What disgusts me more is that I have been unable to make any sketches of this part of

p. 234

THE CHOTA MEAN SAHIB, THIRD SON OF THE MAHARAJAH OF KASHMIR.

Kashmir, my painting things having been left at Acchabul, as it was hard to lug them backwards and forwards each day.

Kashmir in the old day was divided into two provinces: "beautiful Kashmir," and "not so beautiful Kashmir." This part was a portion of the first province. I suspect the name was given by the conquering Mogul, who looked to the number of gold *mohurs* furnished by the province. This part is very rich, being almost all under rice cultivation. But the patches of water, which tell where the rice will be by-and-bye, are not beautiful except where they reflect the flush and sheen of the sunset. The mountains too are only respectable, and have none of the marvellous grandeur of the long range of the Pir Punjal as seen from Sreenugger. Alas! since it has turned warm one seldom sees the higher peaks. (Since writing the above we have had a beautiful clear sunset, and I retract. The mountains were too lovely.)

A thunderstorm of more than usual intensity had cleared the atmosphere, and we started from Acchabul (which I see is the received way of spelling the place) at half-past six on the 8th. The mountains were all clear and splendid, and despite the heat of the sun there was a pleasant nip in the air. "We" here means Col. H——, who has joined me here, and self. We are going to make a three days' trip to see Martand, a very holy place, and just get a peep at one of the upper valleys—the Liddar. After two or three miles of paddy-field, we cross a high tableland, on one extremity of which lies the old ruins of Martand, said to date from the second century B.C., and showing considerable Greek influence, but overlaid with much rich decoration. The modern Martand, or Bawan, is over the edge of the plateau at another source of the Jhelum, which, having escaped the eye of the garden-making Jehanghire, has been turned by the pious Hindoo through two sacred tanks, and is now a holy shrine. The tanks are full of fish, a kind of tench, I should think, which it is the duty of the pilgrim to keep well fed with baked Indian corn. It is delightful to see the shoals of these dark green fish in the brilliant azure of the water. I made a sketch of the place from one corner, where squats each day an aged and very holy man, before whom the pilgrims come in flocks to prostrate themselves till their foreheads touch the ground. Unlike most holy men, this one is clean, and is moreover a very superior person, for seeing me surrounded and inconvenienced by *fakirs*, he sent his own servant to clear

BAWAN

them away. I painted him into my sketch as an acknowledgment, and when I had finished made my lowest *salaam*. The old gentleman, being probably absorbed in a contemplation of the Deity, did not respond; or are piety and good manners incompatible?

Our encampment is under some superb *chenars*, and we are soothed by the sound of falling waters,—in fact, it is delightful; only three days more, however, and I shall be sweltering in the plains.

I confess to having enjoyed Martand, despite the row of the devotees. All I saw pleased me: the picturesque figures of the *fakirs*, who rub themselves over with mud or ashes till they are quite blue; the pilgrims, with their bright dress; even the chant of the devotees, which sounds in the distance like a strange Gregorian air; the rush of the waters around; everything, in fact, but the blowing of some terrible horns, that filled the night with horror, and nearly killed my companion with rage.

I find that the devout person mentioned above is one Babadass, who was for some years the *perohit*, or father confessor to the Maharajah, and is thought very highly of by all the country.

From Martand we rode a nominal eight miles, to a place called Eismakām, and thence fourteen miles on to Palgām, at the top of the Liddar Valley. The road was awfully bad, but the landscape, especially the foreground, was delicious. Roses everywhere; not only the pale pink rose common in English hedgerows, but a pure white one, and one deep crimson. Horse-chestnuts were in full blossom, clematis hung in white clusters, while the path was lined with sweet wild thyme, cloves, wild strawberries, and other delights which reminded one of home. It was at Eismakām we bade adieu to paddy-fields, and entered into what may be called the true Upper Valley. Yet do not think that all is roses and bliss in this happy vale. The road I have previously described as awful; what epithet can I apply to the bridges? Most of the streams one can ford; some, however, were too rapid and deep, and across these the wretched inhabitants have thrown two beams, which have thin planks about 2 feet 6 inches wide nailed between them loosely, while the whole erection is balanced on piles of large stones on each end. Across several of these perilous bridges I rode with impunity; but coming to a sort of double one, in which the second rose some 3 feet higher than the first, I met with a mishap. The place was no doubt a nasty one, and I ought to have walked. My pony evidently thought so too, for he hesitated in the middle of the bridge No. 1. I urged him on,—he bungled. Over went his hind legs, after them his body, and of course his rider. Well, the water was cold, and that was the worst, for bar the slightest barking of my shins, I was, wonderful to say, not the least hurt, and the pony was also none the worse. H——, who saw us go, said it was a terrible spectacle, and that he thought at least a limb would be injured.

"Truly," said my boatman, who was with me, "the reliever of

the poor," meaning me, "must be the favoured son of Khudah!"* The only discomfort brought on me was a four mile walk in my wet clothes to keep myself from catching cold. You may be sure I shall be more careful for the future.

Palgām would no doubt be a charming place under favourable circumstances, and, under a bright sky, picturesque; but the rain-clouds rolled up the valley, and everything became miserable. Tents are not comfortable in rain, the splash of the wet does not tend to cheer one; and, to add to my discomfort, my companion was really very seedy with fever, and had to go to bed the moment he arrived.

On the whole, I am confirmed in my dislike of mountains. From a distance, with a plain leading to them, giving straight lines to contrast with their rugged peaks, they are delightful. I do not like the terrible, and the eternal pine makes the mountain-side here monotonous, as it does in Switzerland, only here the pines are finer and larger; in fact, the far-famed *deodars*. I have seen the Upper Valley of Kashmir, and have been disappointed!

On the morning of the 12th, H—— being better, we started on our return journey, and sleeping again at Eismakām, arrived at this place (Islamabad) safely, notwithstanding a ducking we got in a thunderstorm.

I am now getting ready for a journey across the Pir Punjal, which will land me at Gugerat, and thence I go by rail to Lahore. This goes by H—— to Sreenugger. Thirty-five miles to the nearest post-office!

* The name for the Deity.

## CHAPTER XVI.

### ACROSS THE PIR PUNJAL.

LEAVING Islamabad on the afternoon of the 12th June, I began my journey to Gugerat, across the Pir Punjal. I have previously explained that the worthy *baboo* who is Chief Justiceman to his Highness of Kashmir, and looks after the silkworms, had suggested my crossing the Pir, as the Jummo route was stopped by the journey of one of the Maharajah's wives. The Prime Minister said he would make my journey what he called comfortable. Nevertheless, I doubted the comfort of the journey, and my suspicions were quickly confirmed. I trust the travelling wife of His Highness is ugly, or at least that she has a tongue, and makes it sometimes hot for him, for the discomfort I have suffered on his and her account has been very great. It began the very first stage, viz., from Islamabad to Meinpore, for after the first few miles the road disappeared, and I had to slosh my way through the paddy-fields as best I could. How the coolies with my luggage managed, I know not. Even on pony-back travelling was bad enough, as the water was often up to the girths, all the paddy-fields being under water, and many an artificial stream having to be crossed. It was well dark before my camping-ground was reached. At 6 a.m. the next day I started, and before night I had done two marches, passing through Sapion, a large town, and arriving at Hirpore in a downfall of rain. I lodged here in one of the old *serais*, built by the governors of Kashmir under the Moguls as resting-places all along this route, which was the one they always affected. These *serais* are mostly in ruins now; but they contrast well even in their ruins with the mud-built bungalows of the present *régime*. At Hirpore there was a bungalow built inside the old *serai*, but it was not waterproof, and so I lodged in the loft over the stables, having under me coolies and horses, all wet and, I need not to say, reeking. From this point, three marches from Sreenugger and ditto from Islamabad, really begins the ascent of the Pir.

From it to Aliabad Serai the road is awful, in fact a path over the mountains without any care bestowed on it. The stage is put down in guide books as being eleven miles; I was five hours and a half doing it. No doubt my figure makes it impossible for the Maharajah's ponies to get over really difficult ground, and on foot I am no longer able to bound "from rock to rock;" neither did I expect to have to do so; but I must for all that, and feeling about as agile as a show bullock, I skip ponderously along, cursing the Maharajah and all his men most heartily. Sleeping at Aliabad Serai, I started at half-past four to cross the Pir, the pass over which is 11,400 feet above the sea. I should advise everybody who wishes to cross high mountains in summer, under a hot sun, to start as I did at daybreak, so as to get over before the sun melts the snow. After four miles steady uphill, but over a kind of down, with ever-more frequent indications of snow in the lower dips, at last we came to real snow, which stretched in one sheet for about a *koss*, or two miles. Owing to the stupidity of my coolie, I did not strike the regular path, so had to wade about a quarter of a mile through the snow. Riding was impossible, as you may imagine, for at every pace the poor devil of a pony sank to above his knees, neither was walking a pleasant operation. Even in the regular road the snow and the slush were terrible, for along it there is much traffic by ponies, goats, and sheep. On I struggled, slipping and cursing (the Maharajah, of course), till at last a kind of guard-house was reached, and the snow ended. Not so my trouble, however, for the downward road was much more difficult than the ascent. From the guard-house there is a beautiful view of range after range of lower hills, till at last the land gets lost in the sky in one delicate tone of lilac. Neither is foreground wanted for a sketch, for there are crowds of all sorts of picturesque folk,—Bringalees, Googurs (salt-carriers and herdsmen), with innumerable goats and ponies, all resting after their climb; but I had no time to stay, as I had what the Yankees would call a "tough" day's march before me. So after a drink of water, downwards I plunged again on foot, for riding was impossible.

On the top of the Pir there lived, in Bernier's time, a hermit, who "asked alms somewhat fiercely, suffered us to take up water in earthen cups he had ranged on a great stone, made signs with his hand importing that we should speedily march away, and grumbled at those who made a noise, because (as he said to me when I came into his cave and had a little sweetened his looks with half a roupee, which with much humility I put into his hand) a noise raiseth furious storms and tempests. 'Aurungzebe did well in following my counsel, and not permitting to make any noise; Schah Jehan always took care of the same; but Jehan Gwire once mocking at it, and causing trumpets and cymbals to sound, was like to have perished here.'"

The stone bench is still here, and the earthen vessels, though the Mogul and his splendour have disappeared. I heard something of the danger of avalanches, and the necessity of silence. I suspect these were the storms and tempests of the hermit.

From here the road (the name is a hollow mockery) is six miles, —six miles all downhill, sometimes over great boulders, sometimes over the bed of a stream, across which the snow had made a bridge (or rather the stream had made a tunnel through the snow). Climbing, jumping, and "cussing," we toiled along, then another ascent of two miles, and we were at Poshiana; and my legs ached, I can tell you, for eight miles of such walking I had not done for some time.

As I have said before, the Great Mogul usually chose this route into his favourite kingdom of Kashmir. I suspect the road was kept in better repair in his day, but even then there was considerable danger from all kinds of accidents. Bernier once made the journey in his august company, and speaking of this descent that I have just made, says: "On the day that the King went upon the mountain of Pirepenjale, which is the highest of all, and whence one begins to discover afar off the country of Kashmir, on that day, I say, that the King descended this mountain, being followed by a long row of elephants, upon which sat the women in *mikdeenbars*, one of these elephants was frighted by beholding, as the Indians would have it, such a long and steep ascent, and fell back upon him that was next, and he on the next, and so on to the fifteenth, so that not one of them being able to turn in this way, which was extremely rude and steep, they all tumbled into the precipice. It was good fortune for those poor women that the precipice itself was not very steep, so there were not more than three or four of them killed, but the fifteen elephants remained in the place. When these bulky masses do once fall, with the vast burdens they are loaded with, they never rise again, though the way be ever so fair. We saw them two days after, in passing by, and I observed some of them yet stirring the trunk."

Elephants do not often go into Kashmir, happily, but I saw many carcases of other animals on this route, some of which were dead and partially eaten, but some still alive. These were generally covered with branches, but I doubt whether they were ever got from the place where they had fallen from fatigue.

Two hours' rest was all I could allow myself at Poshiana, as there was no bungalow, but only a cattle-shed, and I had to push on for Baramgulla. So I swallowed my breakfast and sent on my traps as soon as I could. For this second march I was promised a better road. Alas! the Kashmiree idea of a good road is rather vague! It was most beautiful, and would have been delightful, had I had eyes to see it. My eyes had to look to where my horse was going, for my road was the bed of a torrent, which I crossed and recrossed at least thirty times. It was awfully hot, too, and when I arrived at Baramgulla I was pretty nearly baked. It was then 4 p.m., so that, deducting my two hours at Poshiana, I had been ten hours *en route*, and I had done something over twenty miles the while, which is not fast travelling. To-day I decided to go only one stage, and shall keep to my decision till I get to Bhimbur, for marching in the sun is more than I can stand.

We have just crossed a lower branch of the Pir, called the Ruttum Pir, eight thousand odd feet high, and we had six miles up and six miles down again. I had to foot it most of the way, and, starting at 6.45, came in for a good deal of sun, as I only arrived at a quarter to eleven. However, there is no other stage to be done, so I employ my time writing up my journal.

I find that the *Dewan's*, or Minister's, idea of making my journey comfortable was to furnish me with a *chuprassee*, whom I must pay, and a pony which I have to feed and shoe at my own expense. *Perwannas*, which cost nothing, were readily supplied; but all the expense of coolies, &c., I have had to bear, the *perwannas* stipulating that I was to have what I liked on payment. Truly the Maharajah has a *Grand Seigneur* way of doing things!

It is curious to watch the different zones of vegetable life from the top of the Pir where nothing grows, through the belt of birch-trees which hang on many a mountain-side, scarred and stripped by avalanche, to that of the more solid pine; thence to a region of delightful flowers, roses climbing to the top of tall trees, clematis, strawberry (now getting ripe), and many old favourites and friends. Then you come lower, to pomegranate and peach and pear. To-day's march has brought me to cactus and palm, in fact, to the heat of the plain, at Naoshira (not the Punjab Naoshira). I shall do my marching now at night, to avoid the heat. I started at 2 a.m. last night, to-night I go at seven; to-morrow I reach Bhimbur, I hope, and get to good roads and trains.

It has been a great grind, that 's the fact, on account of the heat of the sun. Still, there has been some pleasure of an artistic kind: sometimes some red-tailed bird would flit across one's path, or a blue creature of the kingfisher tribe would skim along the torrent, and give one an artistic shock in the midst of one's troubles. At one place, Thanna Mandi, there came a wandering poet or bard, who entertained me the whole afternoon with Kashmiree songs, some of which I copied, and will get translated. He was a filthy object, the dirtiest of the dirty; but he had the soul of a poet, and as he played his poor four-stringed instrument, he threw his head on one side, and bent over his guitar, much as first-rate performers do at home. He was grateful too, for when I left at 5 a.m., I found him waiting, and he played to me along a couple of miles of road, with his dirty legs keeping time to the twang of his music, and his nose well in the air; neither would he leave until I gave *hookham* or permission.

My good friend Major Henderson has sent me translations of two of this poet's songs. One appears to be well known as the love-song of Mohammed Gami, a Kashmir poet.

> "Like a flower-bearing plant I have become withered,
> Even I, for thy love, O Bee;
> I will wail like the nightingale,
> 'Where shall I seek thee, O Lily?'
> Deal gently with me, come to my feast;
> I will encircle thee with my arms, O Bee!
> What said I to thee that vexed thy heart with me?
> By God, I adjure thee, tell me what is in thy heart.
> O dear friend, where didst thou flee from me?
> Forsaking me, Sundar,* O Bee!"

I should like to have imported my poet as he appeared to me in his rags and filth; yet is his love-song much like such as are sung in the drawing-rooms of Belgravia. The second song is another love-song, and the name of the poet is not known.

> "Go, O bosom friend, bring me my lover, gently, gently.
> In anger he left me, sore and vexed: what offence could I have caused him?
> What is to me adornment of the person, antimony for the eyes, or any other embellishment?
> For wealth and pearls what care I? or the bells attached to my skirt?
> O friend, sit with me in the shade of a wide-spreading *chenar!*
> Let not the calumny of an enemy affect thee. I am helpless.
> For my beauteous and graceful lover a divan and couch I will prepare.
> If he is not pleased with me, for whom shall I prepare them?
> See what happened to Shuk Sanáa for the sake of the Hindoo maiden!
> He wore the sacred thread, he cherished swine with his own hands!"

The poet was a Moslem, so this devotion was equivalent to changing his religion.

At Naoshira, where, as usual, I was spending the afternoon on the flat of my back, with a coolie to fan me, it suddenly occurred to me that I had not made my will, and that it was everybody's duty to make a will; so, being in an ill humour, I set to work.

* Sundar, the name of a songstress, also means "the beautiful one."

I cannot say how it amused me while I was doing it, and what a feeling of satisfaction I enjoy now I have done! To think of one's goods and chattels, and one's familiar *chez soi*, on the Pir Punjal route, made one quite happy. Well, it is all over now, and I am at Bhimbur. The last two marches I have done by night, "by sweet Dian's beams;" and as I ascended the Anutak range, the last wave of hill that beats round the foot of the mighty mountains, I saw in the distant gloaming a blue streak, the Pir Punjal itself, which I have had so much worry to cross, and shall probably never see again. Well, thousands of men and women go over every year. It is nothing of a feat; only, if the Maharajah wishes to do honour to a stout middle-aged gentleman, he should not send him that way in the latter part of June. Here at Bhimbur it is very hot—a foretaste of what I shall find at Lahore. There is a hot wind, moreover, like the blast one feels on opening the door of a Turkish bath. Of course, there are none of the conveniences I shall find at the capital of the Punjab—no *punkahs*, or therm-antidotes, or *chics;* so that even if Lahore is hotter, it will be more tolerable. I do not propose stopping there, however; but shall go to the cool of Simla as soon as I can.

From Bhimbur I took the mail-cart, and, leaving at seven o'clock, arrived at Gugerat in time to catch the evening train for Lahore. Oh! the joy of progressing, even at the rate of eight miles an hour! The vehicle is a kind of *tonga*, a machine on two wheels drawn by a pair of horses, one in the shafts, and the other harnessed outside. The road is detestable, being *cucha*, that is, unmade; the coachman shows his contempt of civilization by preferring the ploughed fields to the regular track; and the springs are weak, or seem to be so, on my side. One of our passengers is a small bear brought from Sreenugger, who is wild with excitement and terror at his first ride in a carriage, and occasionally stampedes over the back hair and turban of my servant on to my back. Yet I must say that the sense of motion was most enjoyable. On we dashed, thump and bang! till, passing through the sleeping streets of Gugerat—literally sleeping, for all the inhabitants were laid out in *charpoys* in the open thoroughfare—we at last arrived at Gugerat Station.

"Sir," says the station-master, a *baboo*, "why does your servant beat our coolies?"

I find my irascible Noor Khan has assaulted the porter, whose friendly endeavours to put labels on the luggage he interprets into a design to examine the contents. To further get rid of his temper, sorely tried by the long journey in the back seat of a *tonga*, holding a bear, he proceeds to thrash half a dozen coolies. With the Fuller case before me, I am stern, and give him a tremendous rowing. This appeases the *baboo*. I take my tickets,—one first, two third, and a ticket for a bear.

"A what?"

"A bear."

"Don't know what that is. Can I see him?"

"Of course."

"Oh, a 'beer'!" cries the *baboo*, on seeing my tormentor. "One rupee eight annas."

So they speak English here.

The bear was a great source of anxiety to me in my carriage, but finally both arrived safely at Lahore, where happily we parted. I gave him away! But he had previously filled the catalogue of his crimes by biting me through the hand.

Here I am again in the most comfortable of houses, with everything a weary traveller could desire—*punkahs*, therm-antidotes, ice, and, above all, kindly welcome from my good friends the Plowdens. The thermometer is 92° in the house, notwithstanding all the resources of science. Outside I tremble to think what it is; yet people say it is unusually cool, and I must say that I do not find it so intolerable as I fancied I should. After all, the flesh-pots of Egypt, the society of people one likes, and a healthy state of body, would make even the burning fiery furnace tolerable. By-the-bye, the famous Three had at least the pleasure of society. Had there been only one, I fancy he would have given in.

I must have a turn at the Nawab of Bhawalpore's dress this

morning, though I confess I do not like painting in the temperature of 90°. However, to-morrow I leave for Simla, and the cool. I am rather glad I have felt Lahore in this hot weather, as I am glad I crossed the Pir, and have had the measles, &c. One looks back with pleasure to these things in after years, no doubt.

I found the Nawab of Bhawalpore, who has settled at Lahore, there to complete his education; so I had another sitting, to get the colour of his dress. Oh! these dresses, they are too irritating. This one is all *kincaub*, with a collar and large sort of shoulder-straps of purple velvet, embroidered all over with gold and pearls. With the thermometer at 90°, at six in the morning, with the window shut, a *punkah* going, no light, and a most minute bit of work, my nerves got so upset that I fear I did no good. The experience was, however, useful, for it shows me that working down in the plains during the hot weather is impossible; not from the heat—though Heaven knows that is bad enough—but from the want of light in all rooms. There is a good photograph of Bhawalpore, so with what I have done I hope to get along.

On the evening of 26th June, by 7 p.m. train, I left Lahore, where I had received most hospitable entertainment, where I left many friends, and the thermometer at 96°, despite the *punkah*, &c. We had reserved beforehand a good saloon carriage, in which there is a contrivance by which, when the train is in motion, a stream of air is passed through *tatties** into the carriage. By lying with your head close in to this apparatus, you feel tolerably comfortable for a time. But the train stops, the *tatties* do not work, and you are straightway in hell fire. I never felt so hot in my life. Still, there was enough of the freshness of the hills in my veins to enable me to stand the heat better than my brother and another man who was with me; and, with plenty of iced soda, we arrived safely, in the cool (?) of the morning, at Umballa, where carriages were waiting to take us on to Kalka, at which place you change your vehicle for the *tonga* of the hills. From Umballa to Kalka the

* *Tatties* are screens made of *cushcush* grass, which are kept wet and placed at open windows. Should there be a breeze, however hot, on passing through the *cushcush tatty* the draught becomes delightfully cool.

road is flat enough; but long before the forty miles are over you come to low hills, and on arriving at Kalka, find yourself well at the foot of the Himalaya. Thence to Simla is fifty-six miles, almost all uphill. The road has not long been opened, and seems to me to be an admirable bit of ingenious engineering. It ascends all the way gradually, until you find yourself winding along the top of high mountains and the road stretches before you for miles like a dusty thread on their tawny green sides. An eight-hours' drive in a two-wheel conveyance is trying to long legs and bulky figure, however good the road may be. You feel the jogging just where the waist ought to be, and in the knees; and when at last you see Simla, with its houses and hideous church, in the distance, you feel inclined to offer up a prayer to Mercury, who was, I believe, the God of Travellers, to help you over the last six miles.

# CHAPTER XVII.

## SIMLA.

HOW can I describe Simla itself? It lies along the top of a high hill, varying from 6,000 to 8,000 feet. In the centre of a sort of saddle is the town, with its busy bazaar, filth, and noise; on each side for miles are innumerable bungalows, nestled into the hill-side wherever there is any room to build; while over them and round them grow *deodars* and rhododendrons without number. Here and there yet lingers a blossom, the last rose of summer, to show what a glory the full bloom of these rhododendrons must be; for they are no mean bushes, but trees rising fifty or sixty feet, and the sight a month ago must have been splendid indeed.

Carriages are not admitted into Simla, and you must progress by the means provided by nature, by pony, or by *jampon*. The first two are preferred bythe males, the latter by females. Through the length of Simla runs the *Mall*. This may almost be called a road; all other ways are but narrow tracks, and go up and down from the houses without railing or barrier to protect the passer-by from going over the "cud." At night this is dangerous enough.

The day after my arrival I went to a ball at Peterhoff, the viceregal lodge, to see the beauty and fashion. I came to the conclusion that there are a great many captains. I forget what jealous husband it was who said he was glad of the Crimean War. "For now," said he, "there will be fewer captains." By "captains" he and I mean people on leave with nothing to do. This place is full of such people, who have a difficulty in passing the day. Of course the devil is busy, and provides mischief. Sad tales are told of the place, no doubt; but like all such tales, there is a great element of exaggeration therein. Of course people gamble, and—do what they ought not. They do that everywhere. The play is very high, the whist execrable, and I hope the money lost is paid. Rupees stand for shillings, gold *mohurs* (sixteen rupees) for sovereigns. Well, I suppose this is the blood-letting necessary, after the heat of the plain and the monotony of regimental duty,—excitement provided by kind Nature to restore the equilibrium of the system.

Meanwhile I have determined to stay here some time. I have never really designed my picture, and shall do it as well as I can here. I shall put my sketches of rajahs in order, and generally digest my last six months' work: to do this at my ease, I have had to take a house at a considerable expense.

The rains have set in here; the clouds come rolling up the hill in the most mysterious way, gathering far down in the valley in small masses, and gaining strength as they reach the peaks. Thick mists are common enough, but ever and anon the sun breaks through cloud and mist, lighting up with fantastic gleams alike mountain and cloud, and producing magical effects, such as no artist has yet dreamed of. In my little nest of a house (Cranagh is its name) I shall have plenty of opportunity to watch such effects, and shall try and record them to the best of my power. I feel certain that my artistic friends in England (excepting one or two) will think them the productions of a heated imagination, the result of the fleshpots and champagne of Simla.

*16th July.*

The rains had gone off in a most unexampled manner, and for the last week we have enjoyed fine weather; yet people complain and find fault. Yesterday and again to-day the clouds rolled up the hill and heavy rain set in, so I hope the grumblers are satisfied. One must get used to it. The weather-wise say that it will last more or less for two months; and last year it rained twelve days, day and night, without once clearing up. It is pouring down now. The steady drip is most distressingly monotonous, and as there is much thunder in the air, and the booming and rolling among the mountains goes on pretty well all day, it cannot be said to be a bracing climate. However, anything is better than the heat of the plains now. At Lahore, where I left it 96°, I hear they had 106° two days after. Phew! the very idea makes me moist.

The gaieties of Simla go on just the same wet or dry. Rinking is greatly on the increase, being the only exercise many men and all ladies can take. I have not yet put on the skates, but look on and talk, as it is the general rendezvous in the afternoon after 6 p.m. It is a funny sight,—young and old all hard at work; now a tiny mite raised high upon her skates, and now a portly dame with most serious countenance, supported in her feeble efforts by aides-de-camp or secretaries. There is a great crowd and constant collisions occur, and it is not an uncommon thing to see a young lady throw her arms wildly round a stranger's neck to support herself. Yet it is exercise, and brings people together.

I do not feel that my ideas are brightening in this climate. I feel constantly sleepy, and not energetic. However, work must be done, and I am getting new conceptions arranged as well as I can. I shall begin Nabha or the Viceroy this week; possibly both. My general design creeps on too. I am hesitating about giving way to my imagination entirely.* I suppose people will not quite stand an entire subversion of facts. It is an awfully tough job I have to do.

This is a story told me by one who was at Jodhpore at the time. The old Rajah of Jodhpore, Tukt Sing, was of a most amorous complexion. It is the habit in the Zenana for the Rajah to hold a *durbar* each day at midday, and he then decides which of his ladies is to attend on him and give him his food for the next twenty-four hours. Now, Tukt Sing's favourite wife was the mother of his second son, Zuroor Sing, and she was so often selected that the jealousy of the others was excited. One

* My picture will not be in the least like the real Assemblage. I have made up my mind to give up the truth of general aspect altogether, merely keeping the portraits of the chiefs and rajahs, and the order and general arrangement. Thus I hope to make a better work of art by doing a picture not of the Assemblage of Delhi, but commemorative of the Assemblage. The picture is progressing.—(Nov. 1878.)

day the amorous Tukt determined to take his Ranee out tiger-shooting with him. They were to watch for a tiger who was known to be in the neighbourhood, and who had been fed there some days. A young buffalo is tied up, and the sportsman takes his stand on a platform built into a tree, and there spends the night. Now, Tukt not only took his Ranee into his tree, but a brandy-bottle with her; indeed, if report speaks true, it is questionable which he preferred, the flesh or the spirit. So they enjoyed themselves, and became inebriated, and slept; but when the Rajah woke, the favourite was not there, and was never seen again. The tiger had taken her, they said. If he had, he must have been a very hungry one, as he ate her, bones, clothes, bangles, and all, for none of these things were ever found. He was a funny fellow, this old Tukt, and was thought to be very extravagant. When he was dying he pointed to his treasury, and said he had 80 lacs of treasure and jewels there; but when it was opened there was little more than one lac, and it was always supposed that his favourite, another and not his wife, had helped herself during his last illness.

I have just come back from doing my first rajah here, viz., Nabha. Rajah Hira Sing Bahadur is a very handsome fellow of, I suppose, forty* odd years old, with a fine curly moustache and beard. His turban is superb, and altogether painting him is a pleasant job. He is a Sikh, very different from some of the effete-looking Hindoos I have had to do. He has a fine bass voice and a kindly smile; moreover he treats one like a gentleman; but, then, he is not of the highest.

Nabha, Jheend, and Puttiala are small Sikh states, which were in the way of being snapped up by that devourer of small states, Runjeet Sing. We, however, interfered, and saved them. Unlike most natives, these chiefs were true to us to the backbone, and it was mainly owing to them that we were not turned out of India. They kept communication open between Lahore and Delhi, during the siege of the latter place, and so enabled us to devote the whole of our strength to taking that centre of revolt.

* The Rajah, I find, is only thirty-four. Rajahs age very quickly, I fear.

p. 252

H.H. HIRA SING BAHADUR, RAJAH OF NABHA.

Nabha has a bungalow here, furnished with many a glass lamp and globe of every colour. He, like most of the small maharajahs, is treated with much more respect outwardly than the bigwigs. "Omer-wa-Doulat Maharajah Sahib!" announces his entry, his rising and his sitting; whereas Sindia toddles about without ceremony, and even Oodeypore comes and goes without fuss. You see, rajahs are not different from other swells; the smaller the swell the greater airs he gives himself.

Let me record an extraordinary fact—it is a fine day to-day. The old stagers are aghast. The seasons have been turned "upside down." The rains will not come down, and the whole country will starve. So say the croakers; I take a more cheerful view of the matter, and thank Heaven that the wind (and rain) is tempered for the shorn lamb. It is wonderful, on the whole, how very lucky I am wherever I go. This has been the coolest season for many a long year.

I am very much amused at the English habits joyfully resumed by the visitors to Simla. Down in the plains they say that you always know the "Griff," or new arrival, by his morning salutation of "Fine day." It is always fine in India, except in the rainy reason. In Simla, however, the weather is the principal topic of conversation and anxiety, for the rain occupies every one's thoughts. No wonder! the health of Simla depends on it, to say nothing of the lives of millions down in the plains, where famine threatens unless the god Indra prove propitious. In Simla itself water is very scarce and bad. When there is rain, a torrent forms in what is in finc weather a dry gully in the centre of the town. This torrent quickly runs itself out, the springs dry up, and the wretched *bheesties*, or water-carriers, have to bring water from miles off. This they will not do except when forced by the *sahib*. For their own drinking they prefer any water, however impure, which is at hand, to the purest springs of Mahāssu. You see the lazy brutes, fifty at a time, sitting round the dry bed of the torrent aforesaid, and waiting patiently their turns, while three or four are employed digging with their hands holes in the bed of the stream, where, after a time, a thick muddy tea-cup full of filth percolates, which is carefully put into the skins carried by these *bheesties.* It takes hours to fill a skin; but what is time to the Hindoo?

*23rd July.*

My journal seems to get more meagre every mail. There are no religious festivals, no gorgeous processions to record; nothing more than the usual routine of an artist's life, varied by dinners and balls, much as it might be in London and Paris. More rajahs have not yet arrived, and I am still trifling with his Highness of Nabha, and occupying my leisure with painting Lady Lytton, who will take a prominent position in the picture.

It is now eight months since I painted a white face, so that it comes rather strange.

Meanwhile the rains have not really set in; we have an occasional outburst, and then it stops. The old and weather-wise are beginning to despair. If the monsoon does not really break soon, we shall have famine all over the place, which, with an impoverished exchequer and a war in the distance, is not a bright look-out for the future.

I have been very lazy personally since I have been here. I have seen none of the views, and called on none of the swells. A quiet, tranquil existence, with work, is a change for me. I hope that, after the excitement of travel, this very quiet will not cause my liver to give trouble. It is the being stuck down in one place, without change, that brings on most of the enlarged livers for which Anglo-Indians are proverbial. At present mine is much as usual; indeed, except that I do not think Simla bracing, I am as well as ever I was. I am, however, much thinner, being a stone and a half lighter than when in England.

I hear a rumour that there is to be a *durbar* of hill rajahs next month, which will be a very picturesque sight. Amongst them will be Sirmor, about whom we know something, only I fancy from what I hear that my old father rather exaggerated the size of his state in his ballad. Still, I shall try and make a sketch of one who bears so well-known a name. He is but a small fellow, and but that he has been already immortalized by one of the family, I should hardly desire to paint him in a picture where only swells are to be seen.*

Other swells are announced for the Council of the Empire, though what they are to do or say at the said Council has probably yet to be settled. The rajahs think that it is to get money out of them. Most of them have vast funds locked up, which might profitably be lent to the Paramount Power; but then the rajah could not feel it, touch it, and see it when he liked, and would think himself a poorer man. They like to have a thing, like a child, for their very own, and if they lent it, it would not be quite the same thing. The late Rana of Oodeypore was thought to be so badly off, in consequence of the depredations committed in his state by Marathas and others during the preceding reign, that his yearly tribute was remitted on his accession; yet he owned to the political agent that his predecessor had left him £60,000 hid away; and so even the poorest rajah has secret stores, the place of concealment being known to none but the rajah and one other man. At Dholepore there is believed to be such a treasure hidden, the site of which is known only by the Minister of the late Rajah, who refuses to part with the secret. He is kept in confinement, I think at Benares, but has offered £10,000 for his liberty. Yet Dholepore is but a very small state.

*29th July.*

Not much to record again this week. I have been busy every day painting Lady Lytton and her eldest girl, who will also figure in my picture. The Viceroy I have not begun; his robes have not yet arrived from Calcutta, and what is a Viceroy without his robes?

Till last night the rains have kept off. People say the crops are lost in a great part of India, and that famines are imminent. Last night and again to-day the rain has set in, and although personally very inconvenient for me, I cannot but hope that it

* See Appendix. I never got to Sirmor.

may continue. One blank cloud envelopes the whole hill, and the drip and splash of the water last all day. It is not so dark as I expected, and will not stop work.

No fresh rajahs have arrived, nor do I expect they will be fools enough to come up while the rain lasts; only this being altogether an abnormal year, one cannot tell how long anything will last.

And so I have nothing to record. One hears tales of rajahs from the officials here, which give one an idea of the kind of folk they really are. Take this: Gholab Sing was the father of the present Rajah of Kashmir, who thinks that his parent is a fish. Gholab, talking to an English friend, was boasting of his goodness. "But," said the Englishman, "you're so cruel; you flay people alive."

"Now, what a shame to say so!" cried the Rajah. "I never flayed but one person, and he was a man I really had an affection for. He constantly rebelled against me, and I as constantly forgave him; but at last I told him, 'If you rebel again, I will flay you alive.' Well, he did rebel, and I caught him; and what could I do? I was bound to keep my word, wasn't I? But even then I liked the man so much that I gave orders he should be only half-flayed. The poor fellow died, however, and I was very sorry for him!"

This of the Kashgar Envoy I do not think I have recorded. Passing through Lahore, he was asked to dine with the Lieutenant-Governor. During dinner he drank sixteen bottles of soda-water. You may imagine that he was watched with extreme interest by both Governor and staff, for if he exploded, adieu to our good relations with Kashgar. When he called for his seventeenth bottle the excitement grew intense; but the Envoy rose solemnly, and squatting down, had No. 17 poured over his hands.

Maharajah Nabha, who is still here, went to see a burlesque of "Robert Macaire" got up by the amateurs of Simla. In this there is a song sung by *Robert Macaire*:

> "When my wife, against my will,
> Goes out, I never stops her;
> But when she's gone a little way,
> I calls her back and 'whops' her."

Nabha asked the Foreign Secretary to tell him what the song meant, so Thornton translated, as well as he could, the above silly words. "We do not do that," said Nabha, gravely; "we shouldn't let our wives go out at all." He probably thinks that the above song is a picture of an English gentleman's behaviour, and that Lord Lytton continually "whops" his lady.

*5th August.*

Another week has passed, with the usual monotony of work and play. I am getting on with Lady Lytton's picture, and have begun the Viceroy. As far as his head goes he will be easy enough to do, for that is decidedly good; but his drapery is most voluminous, and being of blue velvet with a thick ermine tippet, it is apt to make the Grand-Master of the Star of India look like a bundle of clothes.

I regret to say that the first conversation I have had with Lord Lytton has been a very disagreeable one for me, for in it he informed me that reasons of state would necessitate his being seated in my picture, especially as I found it necessary to depict him without his hat. Now, I have always had my doubts about his standing while the rajahs were all seated; but, as he did it at the Grand Assembly, I thought I might do it in my picture. Then, again, for state purposes, I shall have to paint the great officers sitting by their chiefs. This will give me no end of a lot more work, but that no one seems to consider.

On Wednesday I had my last sitting of Nabha, and in the afternoon of Thursday went to bid him adieu. He was most polite, and set me on his throne of state, while he occupied a lowly chair by my side. He was not born in the purple, and was once only the head of a village, till called to the *guddee* by the death of his cousin. This accounts for his modesty and a certain manliness not found in porphyrogenitous rajahs.

The Commander-in-Chief was expected; the *dewan*, the only English-speaking member of his Highness's Court, had gone to meet him, so our conversation was necessarily very limited. Gifts in many trays were brought to me, but in the middle of the ceremony the approach of the "Chief" was announced. The trays were whisked away to serve again for his Excellency; and, hastily be-attared and be-pânned, I was bowed out, to make way for the "Gingi Lord Sahib." I met him and his suite coming down the roadway that zigzags down from the mall—the *cud*—and had a laugh with him about my being kicked out in his favour.

On coming home yesterday from reading the papers (in which, by-the-bye, there seems but little news), I found the *vakeel* of Maharajah Nabha waiting with a letter and a bag. The letter said, "His Highness herewith sends five hundred rupees as a present. Kindly accept," &c., signed by his Highness's Foreign Minister. This is the first present made me by a Rajah. I own at first I felt inclined to send it back; but then why should I? Was it intended for a civility, or was it intended that I should return it? Anyhow, I kept it: not being in the Civil Service, I shall not send it to the State Treasury; only I wish the present had been in something else, and not hard rupees.

This last week I have sent away my servant, Noor Khan, whom I have mentioned during my journey. He was a most energetic man, but frightfully jealous. He was always accusing the other servants of all sorts of crimes. Two or three times he had been guilty of most unaccountable explosions of violence; and once, as I have recorded in my journal, during my journey from Jodhpore to Oodeypore, he had got me into a mess by absenting himself for thirty-six hours. I find this is all owing to smoking opium.

Since I have been here he has had less to do, and more time to smoke; so he finally got himself into a state of excitement bordering on madness. He declared that the servants all accused him of robbing me, and that the people of the bazaar pointed their fingers at him, and said, "There goes the man who stole eight hundred rupees." He finally said he could not stand it any more: "I want a little to hang myself." And then I said, "Go."

Then the next day he repented, came and embraced my knees, and wept.

"I look on master as my God," he sobbed. "Other master I no leave till they went away from India. When I go home my friends say, 'Master left?' 'No.' 'Then master dead?' 'Master no dead.' Then they say, 'Master no dead, then you dam bad fellow!'"

I believe he had made a lot of money out of me—whether honestly or not I do not know; but anyhow he handed me 300 rupees, to be sent to a doctor in Bombay, who recommended him to me. I did not yield to his tears, and he has left.

These English-speaking bearers are great rogues, as a rule. The servants generally are much like the gondoliers and Italian servants; they exact "black mail" from all your tradesmen, under the name of *destoree*, or custom. One anna in the rupee is what they get, that is one-sixteenth, which is no bad percentage. Their English is very funny; I never heard any of them speak of a beating except as a "dam licking," and "so dam bad fellow," and so on, using the oath as a strengthening adjective. These servants have generally been brought up in regiments, where they learn the language, and, I fear, some of the vices of their masters. I need not say that I have never touched one of my servants; but I see many others do, and that it seems the habit, principally in the cavalry regiments, to use the stick freely. As excuse, I am told the servants of officers are of the worst class. Perhaps it acts both ways.

I may here state that while travelling in the native states, I have always found the person in authority very lavish with the stick. Maharajahs' coachmen freely use their whip, and many a bare black back have I seen writhing under a well-delivered blow. I have heard the coachman, if his whip was too short to reach the too active offender, commission the *syce* to perform the castigation, which he invariably did with a rope he carried to repair harness if necessary. I am told too that native officers are great users of the cane. Of course these are no precedents for us, who should set a better example. During the whole time I was in India I never heard of a civilian, or a man in any authority, using violence to a native, and I must bear evidence to the extreme forbearance displayed by such officers under trying circumstances; for when the native is stupid, his stupidity is peculiarly aggravating.

*14th August.*

Another week has passed, in which I have been occupied in painting Lord Lytton and staff. I am much pressed for time, for the head-quarters leave on Thursday for Madras, to look after the famine. Old Indians are notorious croakers, and they all croak in chorus over the danger incurred by his Excellency in leaving the temperate climate of Simla for the heat of lower India. I myself suspect that the danger is very small, though of course the inconvenience will be very great. When I left Kashmir, the doctor at Sreenugger took upon himself to croak in the same way, telling me that I ran great risks in the plain from heat apoplexy, and that I did not know what I was doing. I was also told that coffins were kept at all the stations for people who died of heat apoplexy, which was cheering news for a stout and possibly apoplectic traveller! And yet I did myself no harm, although the heat was very oppressive.

I must say that Lord Lytton does not consult his personal convenience. Of course the Viceroy travels with much more comfort than the common traveller. He fixes his own time, and everything is made to suit him. Still, he deserves great credit for the personal sacrifice he makes in taking so long a journey before the cold weather sets in.

I wonder how viceroys and people managed in the old time, when all went about in tall hats and voluminous neckties, and neither ice nor soda-water were to be had? Are we really gone off? have we got soft and luxurious? In the old time, I suspect, the weak quickly succumbed, and those that have survived to us of the old "*qui his*" are those with constitutions of iron.

Lord Lytton has certainly not an iron constitution, but he stands more work than most people, for he does not require exercise to keep him in good health. I doubt whether he ever took exercise even when young. Now he is sometimes days without going out. He writes day and night, and even while sitting to me he does business with secretaries and others. I was much struck by the business-like view he took of the questions discussed before me. Of course, I cannot talk of these, for, like the doctor or the lawyer, there are times when the artist must not betray the confidence reposed in him.

On the Viceroy's departure I shall be left with little to do. I have, however, the Commander-in-Chief and several of the Viceroy's staff left. Of course no rajahs are expected while the Viceregal sun is eclipsed. The Foreign Secretary, however, tells me that he will summon them a fortnight before the Viceroy's return, and during that time I shall have an orgie of potentates.

Meanwhile the rain keeps off, and we are having perfect weather. The wise each morning say there is rain in the air. If there is, it keeps there, as none falls; the more 's the pity, for Simla requires constant washing to make it sweet. I know no worse smell than *jamponee*, and these *jamponees*, or *jampon*-bearers, are a large class here. The *jampon* is a kind of palanquin, carried with movable cross-poles instead of only one straight one through the middle. Each *jampon* has from four to six *jamponees*, and in most establishments there are two or more *jampons*, and very often two relays of bearers to each. In fine weather the *jampon* is open, and in shape is rather like a large shoe. In bad weather or in the evening there is a waterproof square hood fixed over all, that gives it a most funereal appearance. I thank Heaven I have not had occasion to use this means of progression, which my weight would render most difficult for the *jamponee*, and enjoyment of which is, from the movement of the bearers, decidedly an acquired taste for the person inside.

The world of Simla jogs on, or rather rushes along, at its usual pace. All are bent on enjoying themselves, and champagne flows on every side. Every evening at eight the roads are full of *jampons* conveying the fair sex to their festivities. Dinners are nominally at half-past eight, and of course the evening beginning so late, the hour for returning is also deferred. The distances, too, for so small a place, are enormous. It is more than three miles from here to Peterhoff, where lives the "*Mulike Lord Sahib;*" and the "*Chota Lord Sahib,*" or Lieutenant-Governor of the Punjab, lives some half-mile farther on this side. The native town or bazaar through which you have to pass from the Viceregal *quartier* to this is sufficiently dirty and offensive to the nose. It is most thickly inhabited; and at night, coming home from dinner, one is astonished at the number of inanimate bundles lying on step, shelf, or roof, all of which represent so many sleeping men. Of course these camp-followers of head-quarters, for they are mostly of that class, make a good thing of the Simla season. The other day, going to paint at Peterhoff, I found the long verandah which runs round the house strewn with precious goods, shawls, jewels, and stuffs of all kinds, while all around squatted the inferior shopmen with other bundles of goods. Lady Lytton had signified her intention of buying some presents.

The English notices and advertisements in some of the shops are amusing. My grocer has written up in large letters, "Licensed to Retail Wonders."

Simla society is a curious study. Simla itself is like an English watering-place gone mad. Real sociability does not exist. People pair off directly they arrive at a party, as a matter of course, and the pairs, happy in their own conversation, do not trouble themselves about the general hilarity. Indeed, the *muffin* system, like that in Canada, is the order of the day. If you have not a pair, as in my case, you are likely to die of social inanition. When such a state of society exists, there must arise most frequent and terrible squabbles, especially among the fair sex, and it is difficult to find two of the dear creatures who are on friendly terms. Theatricals are much in vogue, and I was begged to get up a piece of mine, but I found it next to impossible, since Mrs. M., whom I wanted to act with Mrs. N., refused to do so, while Mrs. X. would act with neither. This would be rather amusing if it were not a bore, for my tastes are catholic, and I do not want to mix myself in either the local scandals or squabbles.

*19th August.*

The clouds have at length risen, and we are in a fine mist of rain, out of which looms and flashes thunder and lightning. Moreover, the Viceregal sun has left us for Madras, so that I am doubly in the shade.

Before he went down, I finished the head of the Viceroy, so that in case of accidents the picture is safe. I went up the day before he left to have my final sittings, and see Burne, the Private Secretary. It was a curious sight, for the final Council was sitting, and all about flitted secretaries with papers. It is odd to think that the plain-looking gentlemen there assembled should be ruling over two hundred millions of God's images!

My interview with the Secretary was somewhat unsatisfactory. They want me to put in many more Europeans, and amongst others these very Councillors. Now, beyond the work it entails, every person I put into the picture renders it so much bigger, and, as far as I can make out, it will be 30 feet already. I should have time to paint them while waiting for the Viceroy, but I tremble at the size of the work.

On Thursday, thirty-one guns announced the departure of His Excellency. At Delhi most of the chiefs had the number of the guns in their salute increased, and some—Sindia, Holkar, Kashmir, and Oodeypore—were raised up to the traditional Viceregal salute, viz., twenty-one—to their great delight. Imagine their disgust at finding by the *Gazette* that the Viceregal salute was increased ten guns, and the Empress's raised to one hundred and one; so that there was a greater distance than ever between the ruler and the ruled. This is our way of conferring favours. Notwithstanding the departure of the Viceroy, there is no cessation in the gaiety of this place. Dinners begin to pall upon me, since everywhere you get the same thing to eat; there is always the same preserved salmon or whitebait, the same soups and *entrées*, and nearly the same company. Indians suppose that the Queen and Empress always feeds on preserved meats, and when you dine with a rajah you get nothing else. Kashmir gave me eleven different kinds of preserves. Oh for a good sole or some kind of fresh fish! It is only out here that you can realize the enormous trade some houses do in this preserving business. I never could imagine how Messrs. Crosse and Blackwell manage to keep up their palace in Soho on Worcester and other sauces, which is all one sees from that establishment in England. India is the true source of their wealth, and not Worcester.

*20th August.*

The rains are off to-day, and everything is clear and beautiful. There is also a fresh touch in the air, reminding one of early autumn in England. Under these circumstances, Simla is delightful; ordinarily, it is very relaxing.

In the lull between the going of the Viceroy and the coming of my rajahs, I have undertaken to bring out a play.

This will not interfere with my work with Europeans, and anything but Europeans I despair of getting; I should have to go into the interior to get subjects to paint, and, with the rains not well on yet, it is rather hazardous travelling. I am told that the hill rajahs do not hide up their women; and it is just possible, through the influence of the Deputy Commissioner, I may be able to get some studies. I am working that official, and waiting anxiously for the result. Meanwhile to-morrow I begin the Commander-in-Chief, who has a very good soldierly head, which I shall enjoy painting.

What more can I write about Simla, where I spent three months in comfort? Everything is so English and unpicturesque that, except that the people one meets are those who rule and make our history—a fact one can hardly realize—one would fancy oneself at Margate.

One of the customs of society here is, I think, peculiar to India. Any one can call without a previous introduction. Indeed, the new arrival is expected to go round and show himself in the station, and this in the morning, for from eleven to two is the fashionable hour of reception. I cannot bring myself to leave my work and rush round, pasteboard in hand, to make new acquaintances; consequently I have got into much hot water, and am thought an uncivilized prig!

Officialism is also rampant. The new order of precedence has just been published, which, if some had their way, would have been taken down to second-class post-office clerks. In this new order everything is settled, as to India; but the visitor, however high his rank, has no precedence, except by courtesy. I do not find any mention of artists in this document, either with or without Government commission, and I am in consequence frequently left in the cold. So much the better: the hot water in which I have got may serve to warm me.

As the season goes on the weather gets refreshingly brisk. Jheend has arrived, and also Faredkote. The former will only sit in the early morning, so when I start at six for my four miles' ride to his Highness's house, which is in the farthest part of the town, it is quite fresh, and even cold. The rides back are not so agreeable, as the sun is, of course, always warm.

All these Sikh rajahs are descendants of successful free-lances of the last century. The Sikhs themselves are Jāts, cultivators of the soil. Their religion was founded by a *Guru* or holy man who wrote their scriptures, a book called the *Granth*. At the fall of the Mogul Empire, the Sikh power rose in the Punjab; but it consisted of a kind of warlike republic, composed of successful chieftains. Even Runjeet Sing, the Lion of the Punjab, never took the title of King, though he was paramount over the Land of the Five Rivers. In theory the Sikhs are all equal and belong to the *Khalsa*, or Brotherhood of the Faith. Runjeet merely assumed the headship of the *Khalsa*, and fought for God and Guru Govend.

Maharajah Jheend is a cousin of Nabha. Between them I fancy there is no love lost. Nabha's predecessor was supposed to have been not quite loyal during the second Sikh War, and the state was consequently not viewed with favour. Jheend, on the contrary, has always been treated with honour. He has been made a G.C.S.I., along with the late Puttiala, much to Sindia's disgust.

"What does the Government mean by putting such fellows on

an equality with me?" said the great Maharajah. "Why, my ancestor used to send orders to them, and never thought of writing with his own hand!"

Ah! Maharajah, think of the Peishwa's slippers!

This present Jheend is universally esteemed. He is a good ruler, a kindly old man, and, moreover, has what to me is much more important, a very fine head. He is only forty-two, but looks over fifty. His house is just like Nabha's.

Faredkote is quite a small rajah. When I arrived at Lahore, Faredkote's *vakeel* sought me out, and begged me to arrange about sittings. The Rajah was in Lahore, and offered to call on me, or send his carriage, or do anything I wished. I called on him, and found him most friendly, and he decided to come up to Simla to be painted. He has a charming son, who is a great favourite with all Simla. In native society one must never praise a child's looks, as it is thought to bring bad luck. If any one does hazard an observation that the youngster looks well or handsome, the parent assumes at once a most distressed look, and will, if he knows you well enough, give the child a blow on the cheek, to avert the ill omen. Both Jheend and Faredkote I have painted.

The Viceroy is back; the festivities of Simla still continue; and rain has fallen, at least in the plains. Here we are sadly behindhand, being some 60 inches short of our normal supply. I am told that it is cooler in the plains, and begin to think of flitting. Meanwhile I fear the journal is neglected. No rajahs are expected, and my time, during the month of September, is spent pleasantly, but, I fear I must own, unprofitably. The modern Capua has decidedly an enervating influence on my artistic energies. I managed, however, to paint both the Viceroy and Lady Lytton, with their eldest daughter, the Commander-in-Chief, and six of the viceregal staff, besides the three Sikh rajahs I have mentioned.

## CHAPTER XVIII.

### HOLY BENARES.

15*th October.*

AT length I have left Simla and its civilized gaieties and scandals, and can resume my journal with some chance of recording therein something more than the flirtation of Captain A. with Mrs. B., or the quarrels and jealousies of C. and his wife, which form the staple conversation of the modern Capua, swelled by tittle-tattle of the Viceroy and his eccentricity, and idle speculation as to the doings of the far-off Turk. And yet it is when one has left Simla that one sees the advantage of its delicious climate. On the morning of 15th October, as I rode down to the *tonga* office, nothing could have been more enjoyable than the morning air, that almost made one long for a great-coat, and rendered necessary a good warm suit, such as one wears during the English autumn. Yet at Kalka, eight hours' drive, it was decidedly warm; at Umballa, notwithstanding the shower falling, excessively stuffy; and in the railway, directly the 16th sun rose, most fearfully hot. However, as you rattle along through the flat plains of Hindostan (the Himalaya snows having been long since lost to view), the motion of the railway makes an agreeable substitute for the *punkah*, and it is only when the train stops that one perceives how hot it really is. Still, I confess the sight of the plains delights me. At each station crowds of white-muslin or linen-clad natives, jabbering, washing, smoking, and even praying, are a constant delight. I marked one evidently superior person, neatly dressed, with patent-leather shoes and gold spectacles, who at every station spread his bit of linen on the ground, took off his European shoes (which he would not have done for any *sahib*), unhooked from his nose his gold specs, and prayed most fervently. Was it ostentatious piety, to attract notice, or real religious fervour?—"*biz* or spangles?" Who shall say? But there, at each stoppage of a quarter of an hour, I was sure to see my friend, and as these opportunities occur at least every hour, he must have got through a "sight of prayers" during the day. So on we sped during the whole of that day and the next night. At Aligurh I was surprised at being recognized by a man I had not seen for twenty-two years, who was at college with me. At Allahabad I met another friend, whom I had last met at the head of the Liddar Valley at Palgam—so small is the world! Finally, at twelve o'clock on Wednesday, after a good roasting and much shaking, I arrive at the holy Ganges, and see Benares on the other bank.

I confess I was surprised during the journey to see the country look so green. It has narrowly escaped a tremendous famine, saved by only just enough rain to enable the natives to get in their cold-weather crop; yet the trees were green, and much of the ground covered with greenery of different kinds. Everywhere the ploughs were at work, drawn by patient little bullocks, scratching up the ground in the primitive way which suffices for such elementary cultivation as it has sufficed from time immemorial, and will suffice till the "three R's" are taught through the land, and India and Indian cease to be a delight to the eye.

Meanwhile I have to force my way through the squabbling and noise I have always found wherever there is any water, whether river or channel, to be crossed; and finally, having taken my seat with much dignity in by far the most primitive boat I ever entered, I have time to look around, and to see across the broad bosom of the sacred Ganges, Benares, stretching for two or three miles, with a crowd of boats at its feet, and many fine-looking buildings rising high into the sultry air. Whew! it was very hot. What beautiful *torsos* the rowers had—black as the deepest coppery bronze—showing every muscle of the chest and stomach! It is only when they stand up that one perceives the weakness of their lower limbs, which are decidedly bandy

And what oars they row with!—a bit of board nailed on to a broom-handle! The boat is steered by an enormous oar, worked beautifully by the steerer, who has to throw his whole weight on it to make it act.

At length we land, and I am conveyed in a close *gharry* through the cantonments—very like the Agra cantonment, or that of Lahore or Gwalior, for all cantonments are alike—to an hotel, which is somewhat out of the way in comfort. I confess that I go to sleep, but then I had not been in bed for three nights.

At half-past four I sally forth to see the Holy City. First, I am told there is a festival, the *Bharot Metta*, going on, where I shall see all the rich people and rajahs of Benares, and very glad I am that I arrived in time to see this truly native feast. The streets were crowded with the usual throng of picturesque figures; but what formed the beauty of the scene was the crowded housetops and balconies, where seemed to be gathered the beauty and fashion of the Hindoo Zenana, who are not generally to be seen; women with every conceivable kind of coloured drapery, in all manner of wonderful positions, who did not mind showing their faces on the anniversary of the meeting of Ram with his brother Lachsmana. Now and then we passed the balcony of some important person, rajah or rich man, where he sat in state with his family, fanned by attentive domestics, and clad in his best. Sometimes this great man was a little child, held by his mother or grandmother, and seeming to enjoy the scene with the dignity that an Oriental inherits at his birth. High over head rose the dust, mixing with the warm sunset tones, and making a delicious "flue," which would have delighted some of our French brother painters; and at length, the sun being down and the moon well up, I take boat at the Jeypore *ghât* and float down the Ganges.

It is the hour of prayer, and along the banks of the river, on planks hardly above the stream, I see dimly innumerable forms of Brahmins doing *pooja*, wrapped in devout contemplation. At one *ghât* I see a fire where they are burning the body of a Hindoo, who has been fortunate enough to gain Paradise by dying on the banks of the sacred river. From many a temple rises the sound of bells, not offensively loud, but mixed with flutes and softly-beaten tom-toms. Down the river itself float many lamps in earthenware jars, while over all shines a moon as soft and delicate, amid its white clouds, as any I can remember in far-off England. The air is cool, the sounds and sights blend harmoniously together. I forget the long journey, the heat and rattle of the railway, and rejoice that I too have been allowed to make a pilgrimage to Holy Benares.

*18th October.*

Up at five, and start at half-past, to see again by daylight what I saw first by the magic light of a silver moon. A delightfully cool drive brought me down to the Jeypore *ghât*, and again we take boat. The early-rising sun gilds the buildings along the bank, among which stand many fine palaces belonging to most of the great rajahs. There is Holkar's, where 700 pilgrims and Brahmins are daily fed; there Nipal's; there the site of Sindia's, splendid in its desolation, for the whole side of the mud-bank has given way, and tower and bastion have fallen, and lie there on the river bank. Here is the palace of the great Jey Sing, by the *ghât* from which I embark, and inside is that learned Rajah's observatory. In fact, in number the palaces almost equal those in Venice, and very much resemble them in that each consists of a solid basement, from which rises the palace proper; only at Benares the buildings rise from a high bank, and sloping down from the basements are the *ghâts*, to which even picturesque Venice has no parallel, for these *ghâts* are crowded with devotees and Brahmins doing their morning ablutions. There are 25,000 Brahmins in Benares, and over 100,000 pilgrims, who must all wash in the muddy stream, for the Ganges, like most things sacred, is offensive to the nose. But what a feast for the eye of an artist! Here a Brahmim wrapt in prayer, there a group of boys splashing about in the river; here a mixed throng of men and women, the latter in every conceivable kind of colour; and all are bathing and washing, yet without the least indecency. It is true that the wet made the drapery cling with statue-like fidelity to the rounded limbs of the bathers; but these ladies have a way of shifting one garment (and they only have one) and putting on another, without showing a portion of their own skin. The high-class Brahmin presents when nude—and he only wears when bathing the scantiest attire—a most comfortable appearance. He is always sleek, and often fat; indeed, some presented an abdominal appearance that quite put me in conceit of myself. The Brahmin is moreover fair. The women were many of them a light coffee colour, and some had most divine figures, admirably displayed by the clinging of their wet garments. But alas! few were young. Is it that the young and pretty think not of *pooja* and washing? or does the crafty Brahmin consider that his prayers and washing will do for the object of his affections, so long as he divides his attentions to her with prayers to the Mahadeva and the terrible Sati? There must be young women in Benares, as in other places. Yesterday, at the festival I have described, I saw wonderfully beautiful faces, and one in particular—a great lady, evidently—sitting in state in a balcony, with (let us hope) her husband, was one of the handsomest women I ever saw. She was sitting down, it was true; perhaps if she moved I should exclaim with *Achille Dufard* in the play, "She have bandy legs!" But none of these young women show themselves while bathing. It is true that I saw one or two reserved places, where great people can bathe unseen. Is it possible that these one or two places can suffice for all the beauty of Benares? All this was most charming to look at, but for the practical artist meant pure distraction: only an amateur could have the pluck to attempt to work in such a scene; the artist would require a month's study and careful watching, to get himself well imbued with the feeling around; and even then, which of us could do justice to what I saw in that morning's sun? I could only make some small scribbles, but shall return and have another artistic orgie to-morrow.

After a couple of hours on the water I landed, and went to see some of the temples. The great one is dedicated to Biseshwar, or Siva, the patron god of Benares, as Vishnu, or rather his incarnation Krishna, is to Matthera or Muttra. This temple is rather a collection of shrines, as, though Biseshwar, in the shape of a lingum or conical stone, occupies the place of honour, the whole Hindoo mythology is represented around. In this courtyard is the gold temple raised to Biseshwar by Runjeet Sing. Now, Runjeet was a Sikh, and believed in the *Granth*, and not in Biseshwar. He was, in fact, a dissenter, but showed his sympathy for the religion of many of his subjects by this good deed. So I have recorded how Maharajah Sindia kept Mohurrum with the Mohammedan, though a Hindoo. Fancy what a scandal it would make among the pious dissenters, if one of their body subscribed to the building of a chapel for the Romanists, or if a British magistrate were to contribute to a shrine of Siva! The Mohammedans are not so tolerant: our fanatical friend Aurungzebe destroyed Benares much as he stamped out Matthera (or Muttra), and erected the mosque, whose beautiful slender minarets are the first things that strike a newly-arrived traveller, on the ruins of the old temple to Biseshwar, and with its materials too. But though Aurungzebe's mosque is there still, the times are changed. Through some decision of our courts, the right of way to the mosque has been stopped. The Hindoos have been too strong for the Moslem. They will not allow him to use the great gate to the courtyard of his own mosque, but force him to enter through a side door. The mosque is therefore seldom used.

In all the temples I visited there was a crowd of worshippers, —men and women. They bowed and prostrated themselves before the idols, and, those that had any, poured Ganges water over the Linga; those that had none, dipped their fingers into the water and signed themselves, very much as Roman Catholics do. They then rang, or rather struck, a bell, to wake the god, "lest peradventure he slept." It is curious how much one religion that is cumbered with much ceremonial must necessarily borrow from another. All this bowing and signing and offering sacrifice one has seen a thousand times in Italy and elsewhere. At one temple, that to the Holy Cow, and one of the most picturesque, there were at least fifty bulls and cows, every whit as sleek and fat as their attendant Brahmins. Well, at all events, the Brahmins have that worship to themselves!

In England one gets to consider India as a kind of changeless fossil country, but this is not so. No country has been so terribly harried by innumerable conquerors and tyrants. Aurungzebe, who died in the beginning of the last century, seems to have destroyed more buildings than most countries ever possessed. Benares he quite destroyed; yet, notwithstanding, the priests here say that temples have existed on the present sites from time immemorial; but it is a well-known fact that none of the temples now extant are two hundred years old, that is, about the age of Kensington Old Church, lately pulled down. One sure sign of this is their extreme smallness, which is accounted for by the fact that Aurungzebe forbad any Hindoo temples to compete with mosques in splendour, and limited their size. This limit has now become the fashion, and, although our Government of course exercises no control in such matters, all the temples, modern or ancient, are wretchedly small, being all built to the scale to which they were limited by Aurungzebe, but which has now become the prescribed form.

Benares was much out of elbows generally during the reign of the Moslem bigot, and it was only the revival of Hindooism, under Sivaji and the Marathas, that saved it from falling into utter decadence. All the finest houses and temples have been built by the Maratha chiefs of that day, and are kept up by their descendants.

The Hindoo religion takes a very realistic view of the godlike offices. There is one Deity, Sakhi Binayaka, whose duty it is to record the visits of the pilgrims—*sakhi* meaning "witness-bearing;" and no pilgrimage is valid unless the pilgrim goes to this shrine and puts in an appearance by ringing the sacred bell. Again, another deity, Bhairmath, is the *kotwal* or magistrate appointed by Siva to look after everything in Benares, and there is a temple dedicated to his club, a kind of huge policeman's *bâton* in stone. There are sacred wells of the most stinking kind, which are supposed to cure all diseases; but as the bathers have to bathe in them for twelve years before they can be cured, Nature generally decides one way or the other before the period of bathing is over, and spares the priest responsibility. Thus has priestcraft overlaid the original fine idea of Brahminical religion with all kinds of absurd tradition tending to increase the power of the Brahmins, and bring money into their pockets—that is, if they have any. Yet is Hindooism anything but moribund; on the contrary, to my surprise, I hear it is converting all the wild tribes by incorporating their deities into the already crowded Hindoo mythology. They say there are three or four times more gods than mortals in Benares itself. Certainly the fervour I witnessed both yesterday and to-day, at the bathing and in the temples, was very surprising.. People I saw, both men and women, wrapt in thought, holding their nostrils to make their prayer more efficacious, and spending whole hours in religious contemplation; before smearing themselves over with ashes and ochre, to prove that *pooja* is over. I have been reading a handbook of Benares, by an English *padre*, sneering at all these things and at the foolish traditions and stories of these simple folk. If the Brahmins chose to retort, they might find much to sneer at in the religion of the *sahib.* Far be it from me to say which is the most overlaid with superstition.

Some people laugh at the poor Hindoo for his worship of idols. Intelligent Hindoos will tell you that they do not worship the image, but view it as a symbol, and that something tangible is necessary to fix the wandering mind of the worshipper; much as I remember a calculating boy requiring a slate on which he described circles all the time he was mentally calculating, to keep his eye from catching view of anything that might distract his thoughts. In India often the idol is not an object of much veneration, except to the uneducated. I saw myself a well-dressed woman make a *lingum* from Ganges mud, and pray to it for some time. When her prayers were over, she broke up the mud and threw it away!

I must conclude with an amusing story of Indian servants,

which happened to a friend of mine on leaving Simla. This lady had engaged several servants during her sojourn in the hills, and on leaving wished to discharge them. They of course all demanded *chittis* (written characters); and these characters were given. What, then, was the ladies' astonishment, on arriving at the luggage-booking office, whither she had sent her luggage the day before, to find that it had been refused as "insufficiently labelled." Insufficiently indeed! The labels were the servants' characters—"Gundha good bearer for three months," &c.; while the servants had gone off contentedly with the labels, "Mrs ——, passenger to Umballa."

*24th October.*

The only temple I visited in Benares after the dispatch of my last journal was the famous Monkey Temple. I went to it at sunset through the outskirts of the town, past many handsome houses belonging to the rajahs and swells, who seem to like to congregate in this truly Hindoo city. Some of these houses had fine gardens attached, which were kept with considerable care, and looked green and pleasant amid the heat and dust of the city. The temple itself is like most temples, a red central building, much covered with carving, standing in the centre of a cloister by the side of a tank. It is dedicated to the goddess Durga, another name for Sati, the wife of Siva. The goddess seems to have a liking for monkeys; possibly because of their repulsive likeness to human kind and especially Hindoos, for she is represented as a destroying and pitiless deity, who would delight in the lowering of man to the level of brutes. Monkeys abound in the vicinity of her fane. On the payment of a rupee, which is spent in sweet biscuits, to the call of administering Brahmins, thousands of them rush headlong into the temple: *mères de famille* with young ones clinging to them; small monkeys; large dittos, and every kind of green-grey abomination, all scrambling, kicking, and screaming. Presently they scatter in all directions, and a gigantic male appears. He is the Rajah, and woe betide any one of his subjects who comes within reach of his terrible paw! for this worthy representative of the terrible deity of the place spares neither age nor sex. It was a scene not without its comic or even moral side.

I remarked that the very young monkeys did not seem to know the use of their hands. When they fed, they took their food with their mouths like dogs. I wonder whether all monkeys do this in their wild state, and only use their hands in imitation of that great ape—man? Those that I saw, who had arrived at an age of discretion, certainly fed themselves with their hands, but then I only saw them where men could have shown them how to eat.

## CHAPTER XIX.

### DHAR—INDORE—SATNA.

ON Saturday I left Benares and its sweltering heat, and journeyed all one day and night; past Allahabad, where we were four hours late, owing to the blocking of the line through an accident; past Jubbulpore; and across the plains of Hindostan. On Sunday we see the Nagpore hills in the distance, where there is a sanitarium, Puchmurree, much frequented by the gasping English of these parts.

It is very hot, very dusty, and most disagreeable travelling. There are clouds over the hills, and we long for a shower to cool the air and lay the dust; but no rain comes, and somewhat pumped out I arrive at Khundwa (thirty hours from Benares) some three hours late. Here I am hospitably entertained by the railway magistrate. Khundwa is in the midst of a very wild country, and is the station whence the Holkar State Railway leaves the main line, and travels up the *ghâts* to Indore. Our host, after dinner—or rather supper, for we do not arrive till 10 p.m.—tells us one or two tales of the jungles around. This one, which I remember, is original. The following telegram was received at Khundwa Station: "Tiger dancing on platform. Pointsman run away. Line not clear. What for do?" The tiger was shot the next day to prove the truth of the *baboo* stationmaster's telegram.

On Monday I journey on by the Holkar State Railway, and our road lay through thick jungle—on seeing which I can well believe the above story—and very much uphill, so that the fifty-six miles to Chozal take over four hours. The line is laid all the way to Indore, except in one place, where for about two hundred yards there is nothing but sand. Here they have tried every means, both tunnelling and cutting, but everything falls in, and they are now trying to dig out the objectionable bit, and build in the gap. This little break necessitates a drive of twenty-three miles. The first part of the drive (six miles) is an ascent like the rail, after that you arrive at a level plateau, only broken by several isolated flat-topped hills, and this plateau is the richest part of Holkar's land.

Indore itself is hidden by trees, and I have not yet seen it. I drove straight to the Residency or Agency, a large strongly-built house, which played a part in the Mutiny, when, by-the-bye, Holkar narrowly escaped being hung by the uncompromising Sir H. Rose. At the door I was received by Captain Barr, who, as Sir Henry Daly, the Governor-General's agent, was at Simla, was deputed to do the honours.

My travels, however, were not over. After a good rest that night, we started the next morning for Dhar, thirty-six miles off. We "railed" to Mhow, and then drove thirty-three miles over a flat plain to our destination.

Dhar is a small remnant of what was a large Maratha state. The founder of the family was one of the original leaders of the Hindoo revival, under the great Sivaji, and ought to rank with the Guicowar of Baroda; but, unfortunately for the present representative of the family, the founder died before he consolidated his family and state, and both were much preyed on by the subsequent leaders of the Marathas, Sindia, and especially Holkar. Indeed, if the British had not interfered, Holkar would, in the most neighbourly way, have quite swallowed up Dhar.

It is a curious fact that both Sindia and Holkar of that day, although they destroyed the state of Dhar, always acknowledged the superiority of the Rajah's family, and in *durbars*, &c., at the Court of the Peishwa, occupied places of lower rank. The present Sindia and Holkar have, I fear, forgotten their origin, and would be surprised indeed if required now to give the precedence to the Rajah of Dhar, which was readily conceded by the founders of their families, Madaji Rao Sindia and Jeswant Rao Holkar.

The Maharajah is, like his state, very small, but a most cheerful and friendly little man, who received Barr and myself with the utmost cordiality, and granted me a sitting the very afternoon we arrived. He is a very good little man, and very popular among his people, who say, "The Maharajah may be small, but he has a large heart." He is, I believe, a careful and intelligent ruler.

The town of Dhar presents a comfortable and, for an Indian town, quite clean appearance. There is a fort, of course, but how unlike the feudal fortresses of Rajpootana! This is a solid walled and bastioned summit to a hill, strong enough once, before artillery had arrived at perfection, and the art of killing risen to a science.

Times are sadly changed now. In the Mutiny, when the Maharajah was a boy, the Dhar army, only a handful of men, mutinied too, purely from funk, and took refuge in this same fort. We brought up troops, and breached the walls, but by some strange carelessness allowed the mutineers to escape. There, however, is the breach, and it was only this year that the Maharajah had leave to repair our handiwork. The poor little man hid his face when we asked him why he had not rebuilt it, and said the damage we had done would cause him the outlay of a lac, and that at present he could not afford the money, even though he viewed the breach in his ancestral walls as a disgrace.

Here is a curious story—quite true. On our arrival here the *dewan*, or Minister, came, as in duty bound, to pay his respects. Talking to Barr (who is assistant agent), he said of a neighbouring rajah, "*Wultum ki bemare hai*" (He has the Wultum sickness). And what do you suppose is "Wultum"? Why, "Old Tom" gin! a common sickness among the dusky potentates.

Dhar, the Maharajah, not the place, has a passion for photographs, and has had himself taken in every conceivable position. He sent up for our amusement eight large books, in which, without exaggeration, there were fifty photographs of himself. He is proud of his family too, and hates Holkar, who, he says, is not a Maratha, but only a Bania. The Dhars are Puar Rajpoots, and belonged to the first wave of Marathaism under Sivaji, who was a scion of the Oodeypore family, and consequently a close relation of the sun.

On Friday the Maharajah, having been refused our company to dinner in consequence of our short stay, gave us some sports. We had previously surprised him at a buffalo fight, of which he seemed rather ashamed, as the present Agent of Dhar is somewhat of a serious turn, and tries to prevent any amusement of the kind. There is no such feeling with me. I confess I like to see a good fight, even between buffaloes. These in Dhar fought better than those I saw at Muttra, and came together once or twice with a great crash. I do not suppose they really hurt themselves; the buffalo is not a very plucky beast, and soon runs away. Not so the rams we saw on Friday; they were most plucky, and caring not for weight or size, got knocked head over heels in the most joyous way.

We saw too some feats of horsemanship, which to my mind were infinitely more cruel than any fair fighting, for the poor horse is bitted most cruelly, and tied in in every conceivable way. It is wonderful to see them walk across the *maidan* on their hind legs, but not beautiful; and as they approached, we saw that their mouths were full of blood, from the horrible bits employed to keep them up to their work.

After the sports I bade adieu to the Maharajah of Dhar, who did all he could for me, and presented me with a curious attar-sprinkler of silver, made at his capital, and a *tulwar*, that must have been manufactured to his size, so small is it.

On Saturday we drove back to Mhow, and again railed to Indore, and I am ready to do Holkar and Dewas this week, and, I hope, Sir Henry Daly, who ought to arrive on Thursday from Simla.

## INDORE.

On Monday, 25th October, I began my rajahs here. Dewas (junior branch) was my first. He is a youngster of about sixteen, who is at school here, being brought up under the eye of the *burra sahib;* a thin, sickly youth, cousin to Dhar, and, like him, a Puar Rajpoot. The grandfather had two sons, whom he loved equally well, and could not bear to give all his broad acres to one, leaving the other in the cold; consequently he split his property. The two Rajahs were to live at Dewas, and everything was to be fairly divided; and the saying in Dewas is that if a lemon is brought in as tribute, it must be cut in two, that each Rajah may have a share. The Dewas of the elder branch, who is a kind of half-uncle to the younger, is in disgrace. He "raised merry hell" in his portion of the property, so that it has been taken from him to be managed, and he has to live on £2,000 a year, and was not allowed to go to Delhi.

My sitter is rather a prig; he is not without brains, and fancies himself vastly.

"What is your favourite study?" I ask him.

"Political economy, for that is the study of the most use to a rajah."

He is always talking of his studies, yet two years ago he was a miserable specimen of humanity, who could not speak in the presence of the *sahib* without crying! I fancy he tries to say the right thing, and is sly. I hear some little time ago he got very drunk just to see what it was like, and had to be soundly scolded; now, therefore, he is on his P's and Q's.

"What is that great garden in London?"

"Garden! Do you mean the Crystal Palace?"

"No; I mean where there are so many animals and other things to be seen."

"Oh, the Zoological Gardens?"

"Yes, that's what I mean. Is your picture going there?" he asked.

He intends to go to England, he says. Well, he has a fine establishment of about £40,000 a year, and has had a long minority, so he may be able to gratify his tastes for a few years at least.

"When are you going to make a railway to Dewas?" I ask.

"Never!" cries my young Conservative; "for then I should lose all my transit dues on opium."

"And how about your political economy, Rajah Sahib?"

"Oh, but the transit dues on opium are very valuable."

So the Rajah is, I fear, no exception to the rule. Theory is all very well, but it requires a bold man to practise what he learns. Notwithstanding his speaking English, the little man bores me. I cannot help thinking him a humbug, and resent having fair sentiments stuffed down my throat.

On Tuesday I go to Holkar. Tukaji Rao Holkar has been ill since Delhi; he has even now fever, the result of cold, and requested me to paint him as fat as he was at the Assemblage, rather than as he is now. He prides himself on his flesh, and can, they say, eat a whole wild boar unassisted at one meal! I must say I saw but little change in his vast bulk; he looks a little greyer, but that may be that he has forgotten the dye this morning. However, he is certainly seedy, and that does not render his society or conversation any more fascinating.

I described Tukaji Rao at Delhi. I have since then seen many rajahs. His Highness is the twenty-fourth I have painted. Holkar is, however, the *beau ideal* of a rajah. He sits lolling about in his big chair while flies are brushed away by attendant slaves, and if his Rajahship leans back, a cushion is put under head or elbow; in fact, a rajah for the Surrey Theatre—"the Great Mogul called Bello"—the dream of one's youth; yet as sharp as a needle, and as cheeky and proud as the King of the Cannibal Isles with nothing on but a club and a few beads. The second day I went there the Rajah had to put on his jewels, and what a sight! It takes at least six men to dress him. There is the Hereditary Master of the Jewels, an old man with spectacles, who puts them on with the care of a real artist, while four men stand around with trays, on which are displayed jewels worth I do not know how many lacs.

"What shall I wear?" says the Rajah. "I think this handsome." And he holds up a kind of peacock made of diamonds and pearls. "Yes, that will do."

And the peacock is "offered up" to his head while he lazily turns from side to side, gazing with self-satisfied look into a glass, which originally cost eight annas (one shilling), and which,

p. 282

H.H. TUKAJI RAO HOLKAR, MAHARAJAH OF INDORE.

held by a sixth man, contrasts strangely with the jewels it is called on to reflect. Squalor and magnificence are found side by side in all these rajahs' abodes. None of them have any sense of fitness—in fact, no native has.

"We won't put on these pearls," cries the Maharajah, "for without them this looks more like a crown."

And this in India, the land of caste, changeless through succeeding ages! Why, this man's ancestor was a goatherd, and he himself, for all his airs, would cheerfully pay any sum of money to be considered a Rajpoot; and while many Brahmins stand around with clasped hands, and probably his cook is of Brahminical caste, not one of them would eat with him, Rajah though he be.

And Indore? Well, it is, like many other Indian towns, well to do and modern. Driving from the Residency to the palace, you pass through the same kind of dirty suburbs; you cross one rather good bridge over a river which, this dry year, has ceased to run, the water remaining only in pools, filthy and stinking, but thronged, nevertheless, with people washing, bathing, and praying as usual; then you pass a square, in the centre of which is a statue of the Resident before the Mutiny, Sir Robert Hamilton, erected by the grateful Holkar to the memory of the man who undoubtedly saved him from being hanged by Sir Hugh Rose. Then you are in Indore proper, a thriving, bustling city, but without any character apart from other Indian cities. Everywhere is the same feeling for decoration, some of the better houses even here having really good carving on them, but nothing is really fine or striking. You require some aid from nature to make a place really picturesque. Pile up the rocks, raise a high cliff, perch a castle on the top, and straightway you have a dream for handbook makers, whether it be Edinburgh, Heidelberg, Jodhpore, or Oodeypore. A town on a flat always starts with a disadvantage from the picturesque point of view, although of course it is easy to make it fine with broad streets and big houses. Well, Indore is on the flat, and since the streets are not broad nor the houses high, it is not picturesque or striking.

The palace in the centre of the town is not large for so wealthy a Rajah. It is irregularly built, and rises some five storeys high, but then the rooms are very low, and the windows little holes. Of course the room in which I painted the Maharajah was singularly unfit for a painting-room; what room in India is suitable for a studio?

I have done what I want from the Rajah, and am now painting Sir Henry Daly, the Governor-General's Agent here, who is one of the Europeans who are to figure in my picture by the side of the rajahs, to prove that the Assemblage was not got up entirely for my dark friends. Sir Henry is a Lieutenant-General and an officer of some distinction. He commanded the Guides through the siege of Delhi, and was there badly wounded. He is, moreover, an agreeable man of the world, and Irish, so I am *bien tombé*.

I do not know what to do after I leave this, or when I do leave it. Rewah, whom I really want to paint, has been telegraphed to, and it is just possible he may come here. If he does so, I shall, while waiting for him, go out and do Rutlam. If I have to go to Rewah, Rutlam will have to be left out. Meanwhile I am expected at Mysore.

*7th November.*

On Sunday there was a Hindoo festival,—the Dewali, when the pious Hindoo regulates his affairs, counts his rupees, and dedicates the whole to one of his innumerable deities, I forget which. When Holkar was sitting, I remarked that I had kept the Mohurrum with Sindia, and the Hooli and Gungore with the Rana of Oodeypore.

"Then," said Holkar, "you shall keep the Dewali with me." But he forgot to send for me, and I was not sorry, for there was but little to see. I walked down to the bridge to see the illuminations, which were certainly pretty. The river is very low, as I said before, and only a series of pools reflected the innumerable little lamps; but the dark spaces between, caused by the drought, rather added to the effect. Everything had its little illumination; the *molly* or gardener had his lamp in the garden, the *syce* in the stable, and so on. There was a continual bang and splatter of squib and cracker, and of course tom-toms and flutes were ceaselessly exercised, for natives love noise.

Monday I employed in painting Daly, and on Tuesday I went again to the palace, to make a study of the Bala Sahib, or the eldest son of Holkar. He is a youth of nineteen, a fine big fellow, with a good deal of "go" in him; possibly he may grow into a solid lump of inert flesh, like his father. He talks English, and wishes much to go to England. I fancy his "paternal" does not care about "shelling out" for the trip.

Holkar, they say, is a tremendous *bania*, a financier of the first water. He lends money wherever he can get good security; has his agent at Bombay, and his quiet flutter in that speculative market. Moreover, he has a way of screwing his *ryots* known to him alone, and gets more out of the land than any other chief I was talking to the head of the police (Khundwa) here, and remarked that there was no famine in Indore.

"Don't you know what the Rajah does?" said he. "He has his agent at Choral (the present terminus of the railway), who gives every distressed *ryot* his railway fare and two rupees, and ships him off to the British territory. So he saves the expense of keeping his famine-stricken *ryots*."

I fear he is not the only man who tries to shunt the responsibility of the famine, or rather scarcity (for it is not a famine yet in Malwa), on to the broad shoulders of the British administration. Down the Neemuch road (by which I passed from Oodeypore, or rather from Chitore, to Ajmere) thousands of people have passed to Neemuch, where British territory begins. They say as many as 130,000, with their beasts and household goods, are there congregated: not yet are they famine-stricken, but at any moment, should grass fail, all these people would be on our hands.

Meanwhile, during the whole time I was at Indore the sky was of the most limpid blue, and not a cloud was to be seen. The sun rose cloudless, and without a cloud he sank in the red west, hot and scorching, drying up tank and river. They cannot have rain before Christmas, and that is two months off—alas!

On Tuesday, 6th November, I left Indore with regret; for there I met capital living, pleasant people,—all, in fact, that makes life enjoyable; but I must not linger, and, considering I have painted three rajahs and the Agent to the Governor-General in a fortnight, I do not think I have done badly, especially as I had to go to Dhar, which took more than two days out of the said fortnight. I must say it was with intense regret that on Wednesday I turned up the line away from Bombay, instead of to that point of happy departure. Rewah had to be done, even though he was sixteen hours' by train out of my way; and at Rewah, or rather Satna, I arrived at half-past two on Thursday morning. Satna is the residence of the Political Agent, Major Bannerman, and is only a small modern town round the railway station. Rewah is under British administration. The Maharajah, who is of one of the most ancient families in India, is a great muddler, and wasted his substance horribly. If a Brahmin came to him and said a good prayer, the Rajah would say, "That is a good word," and give the holy man a village. And so, after a long reign, villages have become scarce, and poor Raghuraj Sing had to come to the British for 11 lacs, and place his realm under a political officer. The state of Rewah, or rather Bāghel Khand, is of vast extent, and, like all the old states, belongs in a great part to *thakoors* and feudal chiefs, who are virtually independent. The Rajah is the head of the Baghele Rajpoots, descended, like Oodeypore and Jeypore, from the sun. I do not think that the Rana of Oodeypore would quite allow either family a direct descent from the sun or Suraji; but, then, each family naturally thinks itself allied to Oodeypore, who is acknowledged head of the Rajpoots.

Orcha, whom I painted at Delhi, is the head of the Bundelis—enemy of the Bagheles. Years ago the rajah of these parts lost, one after the other, all his sons, and was so distressed that when a new one was born he sent him out into the jungle. There he was found by a holy man being suckled by a tigress, and taken home to his unnatural parent, who, on being sternly reproved, became repentant and hopeful. This son succeeded, and afterwards founded the clan of Rajpoots called "Baghele," after his nurse; *baghel* being "tiger" in the *patois* of this part of India. So, you see, the story of Romulus and Remus is repeated in Hindoostani.

There have been thirty-five rajahs in direct descent to the present one, Rajhuraj.

Baghel Khand is of course a very wild country, and full of odd customs and funny people. The resident or political agent told me that when he first arrived he had great difficulty in convincing them that justice and truth were inseparable from the British Raj. Brahmins, of course, are the great obstructives. They are the Irish of India. However, Major Bannerman hung one for murder the other day, and they have, as the Yankees say, "simmered down." Amongst the curious customs may be cited that of *bansmaree.* When two people quarrel and have words, one will go home and in cold blood cut the throat of one of his children, and the blood of that child is supposed to be on the head of the man who caused the quarrel. Another custom is a kind of *hari kari,* like the Japanese. You offend a Brahmin, and he commits *janghmaree,* that is, literally, "thigh-cutting,"—sometimes cutting his thigh, sometimes even stabbing himself in the stomach—and his blood is on you. One Brahmin actually did this in court, before the present agent; but he, a stolid and determined Scot, had him cured, and then gave him two dozen to teach him better manners.

Among all these people lives the agent, who manages Baghel Khand without a guard of any kind by day, and only one policeman by night.

I have lost no time here. The very first day, at 2 p.m., the Rajah arrived. I have described him elsewhere. If Holkar is like a rajah at the Surrey, what is Rewah like? Imagine a tall burly man, having his face painted bright red with some kind of earth. He talks English in a curious disjointed way, and can even read it. Altogether he is rather a learned man, up in the

Vedas, the Vedantas, and Vedangas, but withal a somewhat burlesque personage. His painting himself arises from his belief that he has leprosy. The doctors say he has nothing of the kind. His skin is singularly fair, his hands quite like a European's, and large and well formed. When young he was a very strong man, and he is a great *shikaree* even now, though much given to *pooja.* He says, "When tigĕr come, *pooja* must wait!"

This curious individual arrived in a *palki* with the oddest get-up, his head being bound in a handkerchief to keep the whiskers up in the fashionable manner. Behind him was the usual tagrag and bobtail always found in the suite of a maharajah. He then proceeded to dress. What the looking-glass conveys to him I cannot imagine, but with what he sees he seems much satisfied. He has more clothes than any other maharajah, and no end of jewels. His crown, a most eccentric sort of hat, is worth £40,000. He talks of it with affection, and points out each individual jewel. In fact, he is a kind of mixture of childishness and cleverness, and is moreover a very good fellow. Talking of Jallawar, he said, "He little child, and stupid."

"Silly?" said the agent.

"No; stupid. He a ass."

"Why?"

"He come to me and say, 'Maharajah well?' I say, 'I quite well.' Then he say again, 'Maharajah well?' I say, 'Quite well.' He say again, 'Maharajah quite well?' I say, 'No; Maharajah ill.' Oh, he a ass!"

The poor little Rajah was probably frightened at Maharajah Rewah's appearance, and well he might be.

"And what do you think of Maharajah Ulwar?"

"He ignorant—oh! very ignorant. Not read. He say to me, 'Where live?' I say, 'Know capital of Jeypore!' He say, 'No.' I say, 'Not know capital of Jeypore! What for want to know where I live?'"

The old sinner has thirteen wives, but only one son alive. He has had many, but they always die about two years old. In the Zenanas I fancy they stuff them with sweetmeats, and give them

p. 288

H.H. RAJHURAJ SING, MAHARAJAH OF REWAR OR BAGHEL KHAND.

no end of opium to keep them quiet. When his last child died, he did not even shave himself to prove his grief.

"What use? I bit philosopher; leave crying to women. I no cry."

They laughed here when I told them what Daly had said, that he had shaved himself for the death of his *muktēr* or minister. He had bad gout, that was all. I have had three sittings, and am off to-morrow morning at 4 a.m. It is absolutely absurd to paint so elaborate a potentate in the time: a month at least would be required to paint his coat and jewels; but I have done something like, and he at least is satisfied.

"I like much picture—oh! very much. I say, sir, I like picture. I want copy of big picture."

He has no idea of what he wishes. When at Calcutta he goes into a shop, and literally buys everything; a most burlesque old chief, but a gentleman, and very different from Holkar.

"Maharajah Holkar he say to me, 'Want to be Rajpoot.' Oh, very difficult; first Rajah Jeypore, then Jodhpore, then Oodeypore. Perhaps pay one *crore* (one million), and we talk about it."

The old fellow would take the money, no doubt, but it could never be done. He is a most staunch supporter of the British. In the Mutiny he stuck to us like a man, and he attends every *durbar*.

"Are you going to Calcutta, Maharajah?"

"Yes, I go."

"And Jeypore?"

"He not go. He very thoughtful."

"Why?"

"Because Maharajah Jummo sit higher. I say what matter? Government mean not harm. Government know. But he thoughtful: that not good word."

He has just sent me a ring, to remind me of Rewah. He told me, "When see it on finger, think of Baghel Khand. I say, sar when I sitting, I put on *durbar* face."

"What is that?"

"Like angry tiger."

"Hungry tiger?" said I, misunderstanding him.

"No, sar, not hungry; that mean passion. Angry tiger; that good word." And he proceeded to call up an expression more comic than any I ever saw.

And so I bid adieu to this eccentric but kind old man, for whom I confess I entertain a warm feeling of friendship. I fear from a business point of view he is not satisfactory. He changes his mind every minute, and is most impulsive; but he is, according to the natives' ideas, a perfect rajah. Should British capital ever flow into Baghel Khand, Rewah may become very rich. There are minerals of all kinds in the country, and untold wealth amid its vast jungles, where even elephants are yet to be found. Alas! there are no roads. Under British management these no doubt will be made, but if in the time of the present Rajah, he will no doubt squander his money, as he has done hitherto, on Brahmins and splendour. They say he has elephant-chains made of solid gold.

# CHAPTER XX.

## BOMBAY—BANGALORE—MYSORE—MADRAS.

HAVING again reached civilization, it is difficult to find anything to record in my journal; and, moreover, the last batch went away on Monday, and this has to leave on Friday morning, when I start on another journey, against the post, to Bangalore.

This place is so full of bustle and noise, that sitting here, in by far the most uncomfortable hotel I have yet been in, I can fancy myself back in Europe. But heat, and above all prickly heat, quickly recalls me to a consciousness of self and India. Happily the land-breeze does set in towards afternoon, to make things tolerable. Bombay feels generally like a hothouse, and even this delightful breeze resembles the draught of air from an open door in a Turkish bath, not cool in itself, but cooler than what one has been through all the day. Yet Bombay people like it, and even get ill when removed to a more exhilarating climate. So I find Calcutta people sicken at Lahore, and up-country folk cannot stand either Calcutta or Bombay. I myself feel quite incapable of exertion, either mentally or bodily, here. Perhaps I might get used to it, as the shrimp said to the hot water; meanwhile, like the shrimp, I am getting a good red colour all over. Never mind, to-morrow I leave for something better.

I have been painting Sir R. Temple, the Governor of Bombay, who was at Delhi as Lieutenant-Governor of Bengal. It would not do for me to paint a picture of an Indian ceremonial and leave out his marked and energetic features. I have therefore been these last three days to Malabar Point, to do his portrait.

"I have a palace at Parel," H.E. explained, "but I prefer this villa, since it's cooler."

I cannot, in such a climate as Bombay, fancy a more delightful place. It is on a headland, and has the sea on three sides, so that it catches all the cool breezes that blow. There is actually no house. There is a central bungalow, with three large sitting-rooms, and round are seven other bungalows, with sleeping accommodation, and all in a delightful garden. Each bungalow has a broad verandah, in one of which I immortalized the Governor. It is very hot even there, but after a few hours of fever-heat there comes a cheerful tinkle. You look up, and find it is the glass drops of the chandelier moving in the breeze. The tinkle becomes louder, and never is music more welcome. "Blow, gentle Zephyr, blow!" At nights, even in my hotel the wind blows steadily, and luckily it does, for when it stops you quickly wake, and toss about and fight with mosquitoes, and use bad language (shocking mine was the first night!) in vain, until Zephyr comes again, and you sleep and dream of—her?—no, but home! Very pleasant, but very ungrateful. Melvill, my former host, is away, and being left to my own devices, I have seen more of the town, or—forgive me, Bombayans—city. Around this hotel are enormous blocks of buildings, with high-pitched roof and pointed windows, built for public offices at vast cost. Well, I do not like them. They look heavy and out of place; but then they are like home, and cheer the hearts of the English here, who are very proud of their new buildings. "It was the very best butter," said (I think) the Hatter in "Alice in Wonderland." Yes, but why use it for the works of a watch? So our friends here have sent to the very best architects for designs, and the very best architects have sent designs; only those admirable gentlemen have never been out here, and know nothing of the requirements of the country or of the art that exists here, so the result is far from satisfactory; and between ourselves, I do not think the designs, even from an English point of view, are of the best. Quite good enough for India, I fancy, some people would say. On this I have my own opinion. I, being of cold and unsentimental nature, prefer the barbaric originality of some of the houses in the bazaar to the Churchwarden Gothic I see around me, though such Gothic does remind me of my beloved country and far-off home. There is something absurd in building in India houses with high-pitched roofs. In Europe such roofs were raised to cast off the snow. Fancy snow in Bombay! In India, at all events in the plains, the roofs are flat, for a good reason: the people during the hot weather invariably sleep on the tops of their houses, to catch the breeze if possible.

## BANGALORE.

*19th November.*

I left Bombay on 16th November (Friday) at half-past two. I need not say the weather was fine. Towards evening we reached the *ghâts*, or mountains, that form the edge of the vast plains forming India proper. I have been up them and down again, but each time have made the journey after dark. This time I had a chance of seeing the beauties of these mountains: strange weird forms of granite, notched and worn into all kinds of curious peaks and pinnacles, all aglow with the setting sun or violet against a golden sky; while down below are the valleys, deep blue, and fading into the plains or flats of the sea-coast. The scene was wonderful, and the traveller going up had every chance of studying its varied effects, for the ascent of the *ghâts* is very steep, being among the engineering triumphs of the age, and one which has only lately been equalled by some of the American inclines on the Pacific Railway. And so I enjoy myself much, with my head out of window to see the view and get as much air as possible, as the engine puffs slowly along. But evening must come at last, and the finest prospect fade, and I settled myself down for the night, with a hope of seeing something of Southern India at waking. When I do wake I find a flat plain and nothing else. For hours we glide along, still nothing but plain; then here and there come little mounds of boulders, as though some giants of bygone age had been collecting rocks and piling them in heaps. When the railway passes close to any of these heaps, one is astonished to see the size of the stones. At Raichore, which I reach on Saturday afternoon, there is a whole range of these rocky hills, and, moreover, a collection of low houses, iron-roofed and English-looking, inhabited by the officials of the railway. This is after more than twenty-four hours' rail. We have stopped at many stations, but, on my honour, I do not think we saw a single house, excepting the station and perhaps one or two houses near. I was told afterwards that there were towns near, but that there had been a quarrel between two engineers as to the proper course of the railway, and it had been decided to take a different course from either of those recommended, and wait for the towns to come to the railway! Well, the towns have not come, and do not seem in a hurry to come.

This is famine country, although it looks bright and green now, and fresh with growing crops. By-and-bye two Englishmen come into my carriage,—one evidently a military man, and the other a civilian. I find they are both employed on famine work. I must say I have been rather sceptical about the famine, so I asked my friends,

"Have people actually died about here?"

"By hundreds," says the military man. "When the famine first began, Government would not believe the reports of the collectors. After a time the people began to die so fast they were obliged to believe."

"What!" said I, "actually of want of food, or disease?"

"Of want of food. When I came here, the place was quite stinking with the smell of dead people, who lay along the road-side. I do not know what we should have done without the dogs and vultures."

"How did you manage to keep well amidst all this?"

"Well, I had a touch of cholera, and my assistant died of it; but it's all right now."

"And you have now plenty of food?"

"More than we want. There are fifty thousand tons of grain at head-quarters."

"Yes," said the civilian, who wore green spectacles, "so there is in my *taloog*, and much of it is rotting."

"And don't the people bury the dead?" I asked.

"Generally they do not, being too weak; and if they do, when we insist, they only put them in loose earth, which is no good."

"Not a bit," said Green Spectacles. "I nearly lost my eyesight through a fly getting into my eye, which the doctors said must have come from a dead body."

"Yes," said the other, "I don't know what we would have done without the dogs and vultures."

"And when you had grain, was there any waste?" I asked.

"I have seen the grain just thrown off the trucks amongst the people; but this was at the beginning: when we were sent down, we quickly stopped it."

"And do the people work now?"

"They wouldn't at first. They said, 'What's the use? the Queen feeds us.' But we refused to feed them unless they did something, so now they are obliged to work. Of course they don't do half the work of an ordinary coolie, you know."

"I suppose it's all over now?" said I, looking on the green and smiling landscape, so little like famine, where I see crops growing and people working.

"Yes," said he, "it's only the sick and feeble that suffer now."

"And how about the money from home?" I asked.

"We've been distributing it, and a great discussion we've had over it. Our collector is for giving it to everybody. 'John Bull mustn't be trifled with; it must be given away at once,' he says. Then some missionaries and others say some ought to be kept for charitable institutions, to provide for the future. But we've decided to give it away, and let the future look after itself. I'm very much against giving to everybody," he said. "The labouring classes are much the same as they were before, if you give them a cloth and repair their houses. It is the small holders who require the most, for they have lost all power of employing labour, and have no cattle, or houses, or seed. These are the proper objects for home charity."

I was much struck with my friend's observations. Still, one could hardly believe in such a thing. Every station was crowded with natives, all seeming to enjoy themselves, chattering and making a noise, and, as I said before, the fields looked so green and bright. That night I again spent in the train, and arrived at Arconum, where the rail branches off to Bangalore, at 4.30 a.m. Here I had to stop till 9 a.m. Then on again. Now I find the country changed for the better, and, oh, joy! at Arconum, before I start, it rains. The whole day is grey and delightful, not only because the rain lays the dust, which is most intolerable, but because the grey is so unlike India, and reminds me somehow of England and home; and the landscape too has a familiar look. There are high hills and much water; not lakes, but tanks, only so large as to look like lakes, and the whole scene with its drifting clouds and scraps of sunshine recalls the landscape of Scotland, or perhaps of North Italy about Brescia. Of course there is an occasional black figure to remind us we are in the East, and now and then a grove of palms. Yet I feel sure that if I had done a landscape of that part of the country, no one in England would have thought it was India.

All Sunday I speed on, and arrive at last at Bangalore at 7 p.m.—fifty-three hours from Bombay. This is a long way to come for one rajah; but on arriving at Bangalore, where I am most hospitably received, I hear that my journey is not at an end, and that I have eighty-seven miles' carriage drive to Mysore, where the Rajah lives. I decide on twenty-four hours' rest, which I think is well earned.

Bangalore is delightfully cool. It is one of the best stations for climate in India. After the steam of Bombay I quite revel in this temperature, and hope to get rid of my irritating prickly heat, picked up at what its inhabitants call the "First City in India."

At Bangalore I renewed my inquiries about the famine.

"Was it bad?"

"Bad? This was one of the worst places!—the dead bodies used to lie all about the cantonment. I have seen as many as thirty collected in one night out of holes and corners by the road, into which the poor creatures had crawled to die."

"It is all over now, I suppose?"

"Oh, yes, it's all over now; the crops are splendid."

"I should have liked," said I,—not out of vulgar curiosity, I hope, but because I had seen photographs of the famine-stricken, and they were such very awful specimens that I thought they must have been selected from their improbability,—"I should like," said I, "to see some famine camp;" and so I was sent to a kitchen. A large quadrangle, surrounded by a high wall, and with one large guarded door, and inside, round the wall, sheds with pens made of bamboo; and down the middle were two rows of sheds, and under the sheds and in the pens, little huddled heaps mostly asleep. "Are these animals or human beings?" I think, and then a thing comes towards me—a skeleton! It is easy to *say* a skeleton,—to realize it with all its ghastliness is impossible. The limbs with no flesh, and the joints with nothing to conceal their articulation, are horrible enough; but far more dreadful the head,—mostly shaved here,—showing not only bone but suture; and, worst, the poor ribs back and front, with the shoulder-blades sticking on as if they had been an afterthought; and the poor stomach, now full, but with skin stretched on so tight that one can fancy one can trace the organs within.

Now, this is not exaggerated in the least. I have described one; they are all the same. Add to this horrible skin diseases that would make even a Scotchman scratch himself; and imagine 490 of these beings in one relief kitchen! Yet the famine is over, and many of these are convalescent and making sheds for the rest.

The superintendent, who showed me as much of this misery as I could stand, told me that these were only bad cases—men and women who had wandered from the relief works, from a desire to escape working, and been picked up by the police.

"These," said he, pointing to the pens, "are those brought in last night. We give 'em lots to eat, but, Lord, sir! there's no satisfying 'em. They lie and steal to get more, and that's what makes them ill with fever and dysentery and diarrhœa. They 're sure to get it if they eat too much."

"Do many of them die?"

"About ten a night on an average,—sometimes as many as eighteen."

I pointed to one woman with swelled feet, and asked whether that was dropsy. "Yes, sir, that 's dropsy. That 's what they get last. When they have that bad, there 's no saving them. These are the orphans; they 're well looked after," said he, with a smile; and I saw a Sister of Charity wandering about them, who was anxious to save their bodies that she might have a turn at their souls. Then we came to the women. I was much struck by the patient silence of all those I had seen, but the women were not silent. Many of them had petitions to make. One old creature was most clamorous. "She wants to be let out, and prefers begging about in the bazaar to being here," said the superintendent. "It 's useless feeding up the old people. Give 'em as much as you like, you cannot fatten them."

"Do parents care much for their children?" I asked.

"Not much, sir. I 've known 'em steal their children's food, saying they were certain to die, and the food could do them no possible good. It 's astonishing what they 'll eat. Now, this little chap," said the superintendent, tapping a little boy on the head, "he 'll eat enough for two grown-up men, and it don't seem to do him any good either."

The superintendent is a tall stout Eurasian, who was evidently a credit to his feeding, and the contrast between him and the mite was terrible. The boy was scarcely human, squatting on the ground, and progressing in that squatting position, like a monkey. He crawled thus up to us, and laid his upturned palms on the ground, and cried. He was covered with filth, and perfectly naked: a truly horrible spectacle.

"It 's no use clothing him; he won't keep on anything. He 's mad, sir, and this is not the right place for him."

The poor boy cried on, making creases in his thin face like a hideous caricature.

"Poor boy!" said I.

"We have great trouble with him sometimes. He can be most abusive, I assure you. Would you like to see the infirmary, sir?"

But I had had enough of horrors. Infirmary! were these not infirm enough? So I left, with an impression I shall never forget. The whole thing, hideous as it was, was rendered almost grotesque by the inhuman aspect of these poor creatures. If they had been white, I could not have stood the sight a moment; as it was, I could hardly realize that I was of the same genus as these ape-like beings. And the famine is over! There were double the number here formerly, and ten times the number in other camps! Only a fourth of the famine-stricken here were men.

My host, a high official, told me that the famine had been coming on for a year, that up to August there had been no showers, and that then the bravest-hearted despaired, for all hope of rain was past. Happily in August it poured hard—a most unusual thing—and the country was saved. I saw the food being given out to these poor people. Their rice and meat to me did not look appetizing, but I was told that it was better than what they usually had. God help them! I wonder how many of them will live? They seemed all treated with kindness, though of course a small amount of discipline has to be exerted. Famine seems to deprive the poor creatures of all sense of respect or decency.

With Bangalore itself I was rather disappointed. The scenery on the way from Arconum here had been so pretty that I had anticipated finding Bangalore surrounded with hills, and highly sketchable. But the place itself is on an elevated plateau or rolling prairie; well wooded, no doubt, but without a character of its own.

On Monday night (19th November), after dinner, I start by moonlight for Mysore. Thirty miles had to be done by carriage, then twenty-seven by bullock-cart, and another thirty by carriage. I have frequently remarked that it is not pleasant for a tall man to travel by bullock-cart, and I experienced all the misery of being doubled up for eight hours. However, the longest night must end, and on day breaking I found myself driving through a pleasant country, along a good road shaded by fine trees. At about five I arrive at a place famous in history—Seringapatam. I well remember an engraving of a picture of the death of Tippoo. The usurper has fallen to the ground, still grinding his teeth, and surrounded by equally furious Sepoys; behind are tall walls and minarets, and, I think, a palm-tree; for what is a picture of India without a palm-tree? Well, Seringapatam is very unlike that picture. I had but a short glimpse of the town or fortress as I drove by, but on my return was enabled to make a longer visit. The country round about is green and flourishing, the rice nearly fit to cut, and nothing remains of the wars of years past, or indeed of the famine of the present year. Seven miles farther on we come to Mysore, so pleasantly situated among green trees, amidst which the roofs glint in so familiar a manner, that I can almost fancy myself in England.

Mysore, the capital (nominally) of the state of that name, is called after a devil. Close to the town is a hill, rising about 1,000 feet from the town level, called Chāmundi, on which is a temple sacred to Kali, the wife of Siva. She is reported to have slain here the demon Maheshawar, and this demon's name was contracted to Maisur or Mysore. Kali is of course the tutelary deity of the Rajah. Her sacred rites, including human sacrifices, used to be freely performed here; in fact, Kali is as diabolical a bogey as ever was elevated to the godhood.

Having refreshed myself after my fifteen hours' coaching, I went with Captain Wilson, His Highness's tutor, to the school to see my subject.

The school is a summer-house of the late Maharajah's, where a certain number of lads of good family are educated with the present Rajah, and here I found His Highness sitting in class, learning geography.

Chamrajendra Wodeār is a very stout lad of fourteen; he was the adopted son of the late Maharajah, and succeeded, when of course quite a child, in 1868. In Mysore there are no large landowners; probably Hyder Ali and his son swept them all away. But there is a kind of ruling clan—the Ursu—who call themselves Rajpoots, and from this clan the late Maharajah chose his successor. It was curious to see His Highness sitting with his class of less fortunate Ursus. "Turn, Fortune, turn thy wheel." Here is one suddenly made heir to 5,000,000 of subjects and 75 lacs a year, and the others have nothing. With him are his two elder brothers, fat, like him, and too old for school, whose occupation consists in looking after the fortunate youth. Among the most intelligent of the class-fellows of the Rajah was the Delwai, or hereditary Commander-in-Chief of Mysore. In old time the Delwai was a kind of Mayor of the Palace, and, besides being very powerful, had vast landed estates. Hyder and Tippoo quickly seized this nobleman's property, and the family is reduced to comparative poverty. The present Delwai is a charming boy, rather younger than the Rajah.

I was asked to put a question to the class, and heard from the Maharajah the names of the five rivers of the Punjab, the source of the Ganges, Burhampootra, and Indus, and many other things useful to rajahs. One rather forward youth readily undertook to show me the course of the Congo, though Stanley had only by that week's mail decided that much-vexed question.

The Maharajah has no pride or swagger. In the evening I went to see the boys play at cricket; they play right well, bowling round-hand, and "swiping" freely, and all but the Maharajah barefooted; they actually rink, and put their skates on their bare feet! Each boy had a long lock of hair hanging behind, while all the rest of the head is shaved; and, as they mostly wore long white raiment, they looked like a lot of demented schoolgirls when playing.

They shout and cheer in English, both at cricket and at polo, which game I witnessed the next day.

The Maharajah is certainly a most amiable lad. He does what he is told without hesitation, and is thoroughly Anglicized. Of course there was the usual struggle with the Zenana. He was taken to Ootacamund, the hill station of this part of India, quite a sickly, mealy-faced youth, and brought back bronzed and healthy.

"What!" cried the head Ranee, "I entrusted you with a Maharajah, and you bring me back a black boy!"

He is, however, quite emancipated from the influence of the Brahmins, as the following incident will prove. The Maharajah has his head shaved (all but one lock) once a month. Now the month was nearly up while I was at Mysore, and underneath the royal *pugree* there was quite a show of black hair.

"You must not paint him so," said one of the Brahmin attendants.

"Then he must shave," said I, "for I can only paint what I see."

"It cannot be! His Highness can only be shaved on a propitious day chosen by the astrologers, and they won't be hurried."

And so the discussion went on. The Maharajah said nothing. But when he was resting, he said, "Would you mind leaving the hair? I think it is better so."

His rooms in the palace are quite like a European's, and as he is brought up with every kind of healthy instruction, I trust he may turn out well. I regret the European furniture, though I fear that is unavoidable.

The palace was built by the late Rajah, who was put on the *guddee* in '99, and died only a few years ago. It contains some curious bits of Oriental work, in the way of carved ivory and silver doors and thrones, and also the most remarkable collection of atrocious pictures I have ever seen. There are portraits of all kinds of people from the time of Colonel Wellesley, strange specimens of art.

There is one throne which is viewed with religious awe. It is of solid gold, and belonged to an ancient dynasty of rajahs, from whom the family we put on the throne claim their descent. During the reign of the Moguls, the Rajahs of Mysore actually sent to get permission from the Kings of Delhi to use this throne, and Aurungzebe, after the payment of a large sum, gave them the required authority. And yet I fancy Aurungzebe's authority never reached beyond the Deccan. I was shown this throne, of which the workmanship is curious, and in parts very fine. It is supported on three beasts, two, the outer ones, supposed to be horses, while the centre one is a dragon, with red glass eyes. On his head was a sprinkling of red powder, showing that some one had recently been doing *pooja* here.

The town of Mysore was entirely destroyed by Tippoo, who transferred the Government to Seringapatam. No doubt he thought by obliterating all trace of the former Raj to consolidate his own. The family of the Rajah were kept close prisoners in the palace of the usurper, and, when we took Seringapatam, were found in the Hindoo temple, trembling for the result. The son was quite a boy when raised to the *guddee*, and it was he who built this palace. All these curious carved doors and ornamental work were done in his reign, which lasted seventy years. These show the artistic proclivities of the Southern Indian. Moreover, I saw some modern work that was extremely good; but of course, as no one now encourages it, and this young Rajah is brought up with English ideas, and will probably look down on everything Oriental, such art will in a few years cease to exist.

I left Mysore after my afternoon sitting, and drove out to Seringapatam. This well-known place, or rather fort, is surrounded on two sides by the river Cāvery. The two sides unprotected by the river have been most carefully fortified, I suspect by the French, and are very strong; in fact, to the old guns of '99 the place must have been nearly impregnable. Our attack was made on the corner at which the river bifurcates. Our batteries were placed on the farther side of the river, and across it we stormed. All this is a matter of history. The breach has been repaired, though by the new masonry its situation is still to be traced.

The town of Seringapatam owes its prosperity of a few years to the Sultans Hyder Ali and Tippoo. There was formerly but a village here, round the temple of Vishnu, from which the town takes its name,—*Sre-ranga-patana*, "City of the Sacred Sun." The richness of the country round about probably led to its adoption as the capital. The river Cāvery, unlike most of the rivers of Southern India, was even when I saw it a considerable stream, and by irrigation its waters are carried over much of the adjacent country. This year has been a time of unprecedented drought, but around Seringapatam the crops are magnificent, not only rice being grown, but sugar-canes in great abundance.

We held the city and fort for several years, but the climate was so very malarious, and the number of deaths so great, that our garrison had to be removed, and now we have only one regiment at a place about ten miles off, called French Rocks.* This unhealthiness is said to arise from the effects of the sun on the rocks in the bed of the river. Seringapatam has therefore fallen from its greatness, and only boasts the tombs of the two men who first raised it to the rank of capital of a province. But owing to the injustice of posterity, while Hyder Ali, the really great man, is nearly forgotten by the Moslems, whom he raised to power, Tippoo, who was a bigot and a tyrant, and whose conduct was almost that of a madman, still lives in their memories, and his tomb is much frequented by the pious, who can read there, in an inscription carefully preserved by English money, that he died a glorious martyr for his religion, and will live for ever in the hearts of his co-religionists.

About a mile from Seringapatam is the Durya Dowlat, or pleasure-house of Tippoo, a small palace in a pleasant garden reaching down to the river. This palace is covered with rich ornamentation, and is a most successful specimen of Moslem art. Every corner is decorated with painted arabesques and patterns, while the lower storey (did I say there were two?) contains a series of mural pictures of the triumphs of Tippoo. Here his army, with his French auxiliaries, all with moustaches, are going to the wars. Here they attack, with artillery, the English, who are forming square, though evidently getting much the worst of it. In the centre of the square is the English commander, Colonel Bailie, represented with whiskers (all the English have whiskers), in a palanquin, with his finger in his mouth, clearly quite non-

* Anybody who has read that interesting book, "The French in India," by Colonel Malleson, will recollect this place, where some of our severest struggles with the French took place.

plussed; while Tippo is painted holding a rose in his hand, calm and triumphant. On one side there is a series of portraits of Moslem swells, past and present. The whole place has been thoroughly repaired.* Probably the sun has harmonized the colours, but the effect of the decorations is most harmonious and excellent, though somewhat barbaric.†

This place has a very bad reputation for health. They say that the rocks in the bed of the Cāvery give out a miasma here too, but I suspect it is the rich paddy land, irrigated by the river, that causes fever. The Duke of Wellington lived here while he was Commissioner, and must have had many a laugh over the Indian Vernet's attempts at military art.

I continued my journey to Bangalore after I had satisfied my curiosity at Seringapatam, and in carriage and bullock-cart got through my eighty miles by 8 a.m. on the 24th. Here I rested a day, and left again on the evening of the 25th for Madras, where I arrived at 6 a.m. of the 26th. Madras is decidedly the land of palms. In no other place have I seen them grow so luxuriantly. Of the town I can only speak from a ten hours' visit. I drove along the beach; saw the catamarans and the surf; drove out a long way to pay a visit; and have come away with the impression that the distances are enormous, the houses large and handsome, the club most comfortable (the best I have

* Lord Dalhousie paid a visit to this interesting building, and wrote a minute, through which a fund was instituted for keeping the place in thorough repair.

† In Buchanan's journey through Mysore, A.D. 1800 ("Pinkerton's Voyages"), I find a curious account of the way the gilding in this palace was done. It appears no gold was used, but lead and glue. The lead is beat very fine dry, and then in water is beat up with the glue, and made into cakes. "This," says Buchanan, "can at any time be dissolved in water, and spread thin with a hair brush on common white paper. The paper must be put on a smooth plank, and rubbed with a polished stone till it acquires a metallic surface. The edges of the paper are pasted down, and the metallic surface is rubbed with the palm of the hand, which is smeared with an oil called *gurna*, and then exposed to the sun. This has to be done two days, when the paper acquires a metallic yellow colour, which, however, more resembles the hue of brass than of gold."

seen in India), and the climate decidedly hot. They say the town is very poor, and indeed it does present a rather tumble-down, dilapidated appearance; but there are numerous new official buildings, and these have at least the merit of being original, and not Gothic. There are no rich native houses such as one sees at Bombay and, I am told, at Calcutta; neither are there many rich natives in Madras, as little business is done there. On the evening of the 26th I left, and, after a very hot journey of nearly thirty-six hours, arrived at Hyderabad, and here I am at the Court of the Nizam, our faithful ally.

## CHAPTER XXI.

### HYDERABAD.

I WAS received by Sir Richard Meade, the Resident, and am still at the Residency, though Sir Richard and his family have gone out to their country house at Bolaram, about ten miles from Hyderabad, beyond Secunderabad, where we have our cantonments. The Residency is a palace, with fine lofty rooms built by a former Nizam for the then resident, about sixty years ago.

At 8 a.m. I left to pay my first visit to the Nizam, so you see I lost no time.

Our faithful allies the Nizams have always been the most independent and powerful of the chiefs of India. Like most ruling powers, they are the descendants of usurpers, the first being but lieutenants of the Emperors of Delhi. As the Mogul Empire became weakened by dissensions, and the Marathas conquered the country to the north, the Nizams asserted their own independence, and were wise enough to help us against the usurpers of Southern India, Tippoo and the French. They were gainers, for they were confirmed in their possessions; but they voluntarily gave up the Berars to pay their share of the expenses we had incurred conjointly. These provinces were to be held by us until these debts were paid, certain portions of their revenues being spent to keep up the Hyderabad contingent. The debts have long since been paid, but the Berars have been retained by us, and under our rule have greatly increased in value. The contingent is still kept up at considerable cost, while from 15 to 20 lacs surplus is yearly handed over to the Nizam. It is to regain the Berars that Sir Salar Jung made his journey to England.

Unfortunately he could not have done a more foolish thing. He was led by the friends of the Prince of Wales to believe that by advocating his rights at head-quarters he must gain the day. He ought to have known that nothing angers the Administration here so much as appeals direct to Parliament, and even publicity is disliked by the mighty officials of the Calcutta Foreign Office.

Sir Salar Jung has caught it hot. He is supposed to have been spoilt by his English friends. He has been snubbed, and struggles on in vain. Even now Hyderabad is a whirlwind of political intrigue. An English secretary of Sir Salar Jung's has been told to go, and no reason assigned. His fellow-minister died, and he has been forced to accept one who has always been acting against him. Every one is in a state of high excitement; and as I am an outsider, and have no bias for either party, I hear stories on both sides. All I can clearly make out is that since the death of the late Nizam, the English have been determined to break down the barriers of etiquette that surrounded the chief. Up to that date, even the Resident, on approaching "the presence," had to take off his shoes and squat on the floor. The last Nizam's successor was quite a small child, and the then Resident, Mr. C. B. Saunders, Sir R. Meade's predecessor, declared he intended to go into *durbar* with his shoes on, and sit on a chair. Sir Salar said it was as much as his life was worth to try any such thing, as the nobles of the Court were a set of wild Arabs and Pathans. The Resident insisted. He had a telegraph-wire laid on from the Residency to the camp at Secunderabad; the troops were then kept under arms, and an official left with orders, if he heard one gun fired, to give the signal to sack Hyderabad. Sir Salar, informed of this, said he would do what he could. He lined the streets with his own men. The Resident left, paid his visit, sat on his chair, did not take off his shoes, and was not killed.

Since then the Nizam has been accessible to all, but Sir Salar naturally thinks, as an Indian, that some of the *prestige* of his chief is gone. He is accused of having left his old enlightened ways and of wishing to retrograde; but I think there is some excuse for Sir Salar, who is sharp enough to see how gradually English manners and customs undermine Eastern dynasties. After all, though the Indian Government have taken upon themselves the guardianship, he is the real guardian of the boy, and but does his best to keep his kingdom and honours together till he comes of age. That he saved this part of India during the Mutiny there is no doubt. He may have been shrewd enough to perceive that an Indian anarchy would be worse for him than hard British rule, but he *did* stick to us. He has done, moreover, an enormous amount of good to the state. All the lawless Moslem nobles, some of whom are very powerful and rich, are completely under his thumb; the streets of Hyderabad have been broadened and modernized, though still retaining Eastern architecture, and you may, as I did this morning, drive safely along them, though every man you meet is armed with *tulwar*, gun, and innumerable pistols and knives. Much traffic seems streaming along: swells in palanquins, whose bearers have a queer chaunt (very different from my friends in Rajpootana, who only ejaculate "Hum, hum, ha, ha!"), preceded by a host of their retainers with swords and spears aloft; elephants, carriages, and foot passengers,—although it is only 8 a.m. Finally, my carriage stops at a large gate of unpainted wood. There is a pause.

"How do you do?" says a stout gentleman in brown silk, giving me his hand.

I alight, and answer his civility; but I find that the above sentence and "Quite well" are all my friend knows of English! However, he takes my arm affectionately, and we enter a garden between high walls, in which there is a pavilion. Stopping at the steps to take off his shoes, my friend leads me forward to a good-sized room, where I find the Nizam's tutor, Captain Clarke, who welcomes me, and tells me that the Nizam is putting on his coat. Then, after a minute, the little man enters, *salaams*, and shakes hands.

Mir Maboob Ali Khan (the Beloved of Ali), Nizam-al-Mulk, who has titles that would occupy three lines, is a boy of twelve, and small for his age. He has a decidedly sharp face, with eyes running upwards, like a Mongolian; his complexion is fair, and in his small white *pugree* and red velvet dress he looks like a gentleman. He is much improved since I saw him at Delhi, looking stronger and altogether bigger. Captain Clarke makes him take exercise and ride, and, above all, eat wholesome things. As a Moslem, he can eat with us English, and this makes it much easier to look after him than after a Hindoo boy, like his Highness of Mysore, who is stuffed with *ghee*, sugar, and rice in the Zenana, where we dare not penetrate, and who is not allowed by caste to eat with his tutors. This boy is most active and plucky, as I will tell you by next mail.

*5th December.*

My first visit to the Nizam was merely one of ceremony, to appoint the hour of sitting, &c.; and, having fixed for 8 a.m. the next day, I made my *salaam* and retired. I was to breakfast with the Minister, Sir Salar Jung, at ten, and have a sitting from His Excellency afterwards. In the afternoon I drove out to a dinner at Bolaram, given by the 12th in honour of the Meades. Bolaram is beyond the Secunderabad cantonment, where we have a strong division of troops to overawe the supposed discontented population of Hyderabad. It is ten miles out. The road is pretty, rising gradually 400 feet, with ridge after ridge of stony ground. Secunderabad is of course, like all other cantonments, a gathering of ghastly white barracks, which even the gold of the setting sun could hardly render picturesque. However, the hospitality of the 12th was unbounded; the dinner was followed by a dance, and the evening passed pleasantly enough. I was not home till 1.30 a.m., and, as I had not been in bed for two nights, I was not sorry to draw my mosquito-curtain round me and sleep.

Up at half-past six to go to the Nizam. The same drive through the streets, the same affable gentleman to take me by the arm, and I am in the palace again. I find the Azure,* as he is called, playing at lawn tennis. He will make really a good

* I spell this as pronounced, but I suppose it should be, more properly, "*huzoor*," meaning "the presence," or "His Highness."

p. 310

H.H. MIR MABOOB ALI KHAN, NIZAM OF HYDERABAD.

player,—hits straight and volleys well. Soon we are at work, and I find that His Highness is a most fidgety subject. In vain the gentleman who brings me in, who is a sort of chamberlain, Mustafun Jung by name, tells him stories: he cannot keep quiet; he sits on the arm of his chair or on the back—anywhere but in the right position. He is most inquisitive, wants to know about my colours, and, having selected some of my brushes, whispers something to Captain Clarke, his tutor. "Ask him yourself," says Captain C. Then Mustafun Jung whispers something to Captain C., and I perceive that the Azure wants my brushes, which I give him; and he sends for a paint-box and commences a picture of the chamberlain. I find afterwards that it is against etiquette to refuse the Azure anything, and it was this that Mustafun Jung had whispered.

The Nizam is of a most acquisitive turn of mind, and extremely careful. Salar Jung, when I told him about the brushes, said that the little man always took all the *nuzzars** presented to him, and as every one who approaches the Nizam presents a *nuzzar*—generally money—he (Sir Salar) thought his Highness had been put up to it by the women of the Zenana, but on inquiring he found the little fellow locked away all he got himself. He produced a large bunch of keys one day, with which he locks up his savings, which must be, even now, of considerable value. The desk he works at is also kept carefully locked, and one day when I looked inside I found the books, copybooks, and papers beautifully arranged. After the first sitting he called for a cloth, and himself folded up his newly-acquired brushes most carefully. He has too a great feeling for arrangement generally, ordering about the servants and boys around him with great abruptness.

In all affairs of state it is the Nizam first, and the rest nowhere. Nearly every day Sir Salar, who, as Minister, has managed the Nizam's state for the last twenty-five years, calls on the little

* *Nuzzars* are gifts given by an inferior to a superior. Sir Salar gave one to the Queen, of course; but the newspapers said "Sir Salar Jung then presented a handsome *mugger* to Her Majesty, which was graciously received.' "*Mugger*" is the Hindoostani for a crocodile—rather an unpleasant gift.

Azure. He advances to the foot of the steps, and *salaams* three times to the ground, while the Nizam stands bolt upright, with his hand raised to the top of his turban. It is a curious sight to see the grown man and powerful Minister humbling himself before the child. After twelve the Azure retires to the Zenana, and tyrannizes over 400 women, who spoil and pet him, as a matter of course. Zenana influence is the principal thing against which the tutors of one of these boy princes has to contend. When Clarke first undertook the education of this boy, only a year ago, he was a very weakly specimen of scrofulous childhood. He was always surrounded by domestics, so that he could hardly ever breathe fresh air. He was fed on sweetmeats and unwholesome things, and of course permitted to eat whatever he wanted. Little by little this evil influence has been overcome, and now the Nizam always has a good wholesome meal every morning with his tutor and any other gentleman present. He will not have any servants near him if he can help it, ordering them away with great *hauteur*. He rides, plays at lawn tennis, and is anxiously preparing for cricket. In fact, in a year or two he will be as acomplished, in games at least, as any English boy of his age. His health too, as I have said before, has wonderfully improved.

At 10 a.m., after painting the Nizam, I have been each day to breakfast with the Nizam's Minister. Everybody in London is familiar with that tall sad-looking man, with his small white turban and simple long black or dark cloth coat. Everybody agrees that Sir Salar is the best dressed native in India. Without going quite to that length, I must say that both in appearance and manners he is quite the polished gentleman. To every one he is most polite and courteous, and to me he was most friendly. As I breakfasted with him five consecutive mornings, I saw a great deal of him, and all that I saw I liked. He sometimes had his visitors in while sitting, and transacted business before me. Then, when he was interested or excited, his eyes, ordinarily so sad and heavy, would flash out and show that there was no want of spirit beneath that calm and placid exterior.

SIR SALAR JUNG.

There is one thing about Sir Salar that I thought I discovered, and that is that his confidence in himself is so strong as sometimes to deceive him. For instance, there is no doubt that he speaks English remarkably well, and has every reason to be proud of the knowledge he possesses; but I am sure that very often he does not understand what is said to him. Talking with one who seems to understand everything so well, an Englishman is apt naturally to talk as though he were speaking to another Englishman, and employ all sorts of idioms and colloquial abbreviations, which I am sure even Sir Salar does not understand, but which he is too proud to ask to have explained. I am told he always will conduct his business with the Resident in English, and I am equally certain that many of the difficulties into which he has found himself plunged have resulted therefrom.

Sir Salar's house is an irregular pile of buildings without any architectural elevation whatever. The place in which I painted him was entirely English, with pictures, books, and furniture, such as you would find in any wealthy Englishman's house. Sir Salar has, too, a gallery of pictures, about which I would rather not trust myself to speak. He has also an English library and librarian, and an Oriental library, and a *'sisti mahal*, or looking-glass hall, &c., &c.; in fact, there is court after court of reception-rooms. He has an embarrassing way of saying, "And what do you think of that picture?" otherwise I always enjoyed my visit to him very much.

I have heard now so much of the questions that agitate Hyderabad society, and have heard too both sides, that I begin to have a clear opinion of their character and importance. There is no doubt of one thing, viz., that Sir Salar has the Berars on the brain. For years he has thought of nothing else. In vain the Government here have told him that the time for the reconstruction of our treaties with the Nizams has not yet arrived. Sir Salar will not take that for an answer. He has committed the unpardonable fault of agitating at home. He has had all kinds of petitions and statements presented to all kinds of august persons unknown to the Indian Government.

Now, it must be clear to every one that the Indian Government must be paramount here, and that, if the Nizam is under them, it is wrong to communicate with those at home, except through the Foreigh Office in India. But, unfortunately, Sir Salar has been influenced by the visitors whom he has received here, some of them peers and M.P.s, and has put himself undoubtedly in the wrong. When his late colleague died, he was asked who was fit for the post, and he said there was only one person, but that he was his enemy. Well, the Government, having suffered much from Sir Salar lately, thought it was not right to leave him alone in the management of the state, so said they, "As you acknowledge there is but one person who is capable of helping you, we must perforce appoint that one person, although, as you say, he is your enemy." And so the co-Regent was appointed, and Sir Salar was much shut up. How all the squabbling will end I do not know. I fear it can only end in one way, and that not the way the Minister would wish. Meanwhile he has to put up with the co-Regent, who was here to-day, and is an elderly gentleman, with a capital head to paint, and has the name and title of Nawab-Sheemool-ool Oomrah Amir-i-Kabir Bahadoor!

Sir Salar Jung is a notable instance of the difficulties with which an educated native has to contend. He is a most able administrator,—that is allowed by all sides,—but he is not a successful diplomat. Now this is not Sir Salar's fault. He fights us in diplomacy as a native, and according to native ideas; but he talks English so well, and is so English in his seeming habits, that the English officials who have to deal with him are apt to treat him as though he were an Englishman. When, therefore, he commits a fault in our eyes, everybody is aghast, forgetting that in the eyes of the native what we consider a fault is not a fault, but even a merit. To get the better of an adversary by whatever means you can devise is the natives' idea. Truth, honour, consistency, these are English virtues, and to the natives incomprehensible. Not that I wish to accuse Sir Salar of any want of truth, but only of that suppleness to be found in every Oriental from Constantinople to Shanghai. The rulers of India are often of the unbending class, and make no allowance for such things.

Sir Salar is accused of a wish to get all the power into his own hands. "Ambition is a grievous fault, and grievously hath Salar answered it." I think it is only too probable that Sir Salar is fond of power. He has been Prime Minister since he was quite young. Ruling has been his only occupation, and no one can say he has been unsuccessful in ruling the state of Hyderabad. To give up this would be as death to him; yet, if he had been a wise man, he would have resigned for a time, and let people see that this turbulent state is not so easily managed; for Hyderabad is full of the descendants of all the wild Afghans, Pathans, and Arabs of the late Mogul Empire, who sought a field for their ambition here, under the Nizam-ul-Mulk. Thus, among the nobles that followed the Nizam to Delhi last year, I find many Arabs, and one Hindoo rajah. Sir Salar Jung himself is a pure Arab.

He told me that his ancestors came from between Jerusalem and Damascus. In the old days all these Arabs had armies of retainers, who always went armed, and were ever ready for a lawless act. Now, Sir Salar has acquired such a supremacy over them, that they are quiet; but, his influence once removed, they would quickly revert to their old ways. Two of the most powerful of these Arab chiefs Sir Salar took with him to England, to be sure of them during his absence. One is since dead; the other, an old gentleman of past eighty, I saw. He was much pleased at the notice the Pope Pio Nono had accorded him. He was just of the same age as His Holiness.

As a curious instance of the state of the society at Hyderabad, take this story. During the lifetime of the late Nizam, who hated Sir Salar, there was as Resident a certain Col. D——. Now, the Nizam was anxious to oust the Minister, and naturally wished to have the support of the Resident in doing so.

One day a lady, calling herself Mrs. D——, put herself in communication with the Nizam, through the Amir-i-Kabir, and promised to use her influence. She was told to call again, and, doing so, left with a carriage-full of rupees, when, to the horror of the conspirators, it was discovered that the lady was the wife of a chemist, who had dressed up as the Resident's wife, and had walked off with the rupees. This story was one of the reasons given for not employing this Amir-i-Kabir; but the thing happened many years ago, and if attempts at bribery were to be a bar to public employment in native states, even Sir Salar might have to plead guilty.

Etiquette is very strict here. The amount of bowing and *salaaming* at the Minister's is most embarrassing. A younger brother is not allowed to sit in the presence of his elder, and *salaams* to the ground on coming into the room. I have been told that at the Nizam's Court when a boy is born, eight wet-nurses are chosen for him, and generally succeed in killing him with over-nourishment, as might be expected. The late Nizam died in a singular and most distressing way. He had a disease, not dangerous of itself, but one which rendered a slight operation necessary; but he funked. He had all the people of the city who were afflicted with the same disease brought to him and operated on in his presence; yet he could not make up his mind, and at last mortification set in, and he died miserably.

This story of the etiquette of the Nizam's Court will, I hope, prove interesting. When the Nizam was paying a visit to Golconda, he, boy-like, ran into Sir Salar Jung's room, and found the Minister taking a *siesta.* The Minister had taken off his girdle! Now, to be in the Nizam's company without a girdle is a heinous offence, and the Minister at once handed over to the little Nizam fifteen gold *mohurs.* The next morning he sent him 1,500 rupees to complete the fine! What do you think they call this girdle, which is generally a golden kind of sword-belt? *Buggēlas,* which they say is an English word. Can it be derived from "buckles"?

The Hyderabadists are, like all natives, mad on the subject of glass chandeliers. They have them even in the mosques, and when they are tied up in muslin bags they have anything but a religious look, but rather as if the family were out of town.

Golconda, which raises in one's mind visions of diamond mines, is a town about six miles from Hyderabad, and is the state prison. Europeans are jealously excluded from its sacred precincts, except when the Nizam is there; and as the Nizam never goes there, except once, at the commencement of his reign, or when consigned there as a prisoner, I do not suppose any European had ever been there before the Resident and Captain Clarke, the other day. There is nothing, they tell me, inside. The outside, which I visited one morning, presents the appearance of a fortified hill, of which I made a sketch. As a fortress, now-a-days, it will be quite useless. The tombs about which I had heard so much are veritable whited sepulchres, and not worth a visit.

On Wednesday, 5th December, the Nizam left Hyderabad for an outing. He wished to show his grandmother, who was too ill to go to Delhi with him, what the railway was like; so he got permission, not without difficulty, to go to a garden he has at Puttemcheroo out-station, along the Hyderabad and

Bombay Railway. And what a set-out it was, all to give pleasure to an old woman and a boy! There was a special train of sixteen carriages, for the Minister and most of the Court went out, as a matter of course. The station was crowded with the great ones of the country, all with pistols, swords, and daggers. I went also to say good bye and see the little man off. The ladies had to get in at a station of their own, far removed from the vulgar gaze. They were late, of course; but, after an hour's waiting, drums beat, trumpets sound, and in walks the little Azure with great dignity, amid the low *salaams* of the notables. He shakes hands condescendingly with me, but is evidently greatly excited. Three saloon carriages, full of ladies, are hooked on, and off goes the train. And so I bad adieu to the Nizam and drove off to Bolaram, where I was hospitably entertained by the Resident, and polished off his portrait in three days. Then I started for Bombay, and after thirty hours' rail arrived at that centre of commerce. Again I am entertained by my good friend Melvill, whose hospitality is unbounded. I left him just a year ago, and return to find the Buganvilliers again in full bloom, and everything as it was when I was last here; and yet what a lot have I seen since then! I find sixty-seven names of places marked on my pocket-book as visited within the year! I have been seventy days and forty nights travelling in different conveyances—more than two months of my life! This "gives to think," as the French say.

## CHAPTER XXII.

### NOWSAREE—BOMBAY.

I DO not remain in Bombay. On the 12th I leave for Nowsaree, where I am to paint the Gackwar. It is not a long journey, but the train is slow. I start at 6.30 a.m., and arrive at 5.40. The railway, besides being slow, is most inhospitable, for during the whole of that time there is no station at which one can feed, and having brought no food with me, I find myself breakfasting at 6.30 p.m. It was, however, cool. In Bombay I shall never forget Melvill's astonished observation: "Why, the thermometer only reaches sixty-five degrees: I never remember it so low!" This was at 8 a.m.

I am rather disappointed at having to come here instead of painting the Gaekwar at Baroda itself. I have deferred making studies of elephants, camels, &c., and their trappings, since everybody said, "Oh, you'll find all that best at Baroda." So at Baroda I expected a regular orgie—a feast of colour! and now I shall not get done what I wanted, for I must not delay my departure from India for any feast whatever. I ought to have known better. Always sketch while you can, and never put off making valuable notes because people say you can do better in another place. I remember I was told that the carved work was infinitely better at Jeypore than at Gwalior. I found the contrary to be the case. Possibly the barbaric splendour of Baroda has been exaggerated. Let me think so!

Nowsaree is a town, or rather large village, of some 20,000 inhabitants, differing from other Indian villages only in that it is one of the head-quarters of Parseeism. These people, the most industrious and money-making of all the people in India, originally settled down somewhere here, and here they still are, in great numbers. It is in one of their residences that I am lodged at present. This house is perfectly new, and rather coquettish in its bright yellow and blue paint. There are two largish rooms, both of course full of chandeliers, one on the ground floor, and one, with a balcony, on the first floor. Opening from the latter is a very small room, in which I sleep; how a large Parsee family can live here I cannot imagine. There are Towers of Silence at Nowsaree, and many grim stories about them. The following one was told me as perfectly authentic, the name both of the man and of the village in which he at present resides being given.

It appears, then, that a certain Parsee was attacked with some choleraic symptoms, and through exhaustion fell into a kind of syncope. His relations thought he was dead, and off he was carried to the Tower of Silence. The priest saw his body placed on the terrible grating; the fatal door was closed; the birds swooped down on their prey. But at the first plunge of those fearful beaks the man recovered consciousness. A terrible struggle ensued; but finally he succeeded in climbing up the walls of his prison by ladders, which, they say, are always there, and he crawled back home. His family, however, would have nothing to say to him; they declared the real man was dead, and that he was an impostor. The Parsee community, too, threatened to kill him if he stayed at Nowsaree, and so the poor wretch went forth, a beggar and an outcast. One of the neighbouring villagers, however, took pity on him, and there he lives at present, and, so great is the indignation his case excited amongst the quiet country folk, no Parsee dare show himself within the precincts of that sheltering village. Such is the story told me, and generally believed here. I do not certify to its truth. It may be merely the invention of the enemy, but it is curious, and somewhat ghastly.

The morning after my arrival here, at 8 a.m., the Gaekwar came to sit. Siaji Rao Guicowar, or Gaekwar, Maharajah of Baroda, and future possessor of an income of £1,100,000 a year, was about two years ago a common village boy. He was the lucky one of three who were brought up for selection to Jumna

Bae, the Ranee of Khundi Rao Gaekwar. To realize the extraordinary changes and sudden rises that occur in native history, it will be necessary first to recount the history of the Ranee. Jumna Bae was of good family, and, being very pretty, captivated the heart of Khundi Rao, who married her when only twelve years old. If report speaks true, the Gaekwar was not above chastening even in public the object of his love, who received at least as many slaps as caresses.

However, Khundi Rao went the way of all Gaekwars, and on his death the Resident rather prematurely proclaimed Mulhar Rao, his brother, Gaekwar in his stead. This Mulhar Rao had the worst reputation. He had spent a good deal of his time in prison. At nine years old he is said to have tried to poison his nurse. At eighteen he tried to poison his brother, Khundi Rao Gaekwar. Now Khundi Rao was not over given to clemency, and would, had he had his own way, have got rid of his brother without scruple. But our Resident was horrified. "What, kill your own brother?" he cried.

"Why not?" said Khundi Rao, "since he is a wild beast, and not fit to live!"

But the Resident was firm, and Mulhar Rao was sent to prison. After nine years, through the influence of another Resident, he was so far pardoned as to be allowed to join a set of *fakirs*. And so for several more years he went about with nothing on but a bit of string, serving the deity of his choice. People have told me that they have seen him go to the Resident's in this nude state, and put on clothes in a carriage for his interview, and after his talk retire again clothes-less. All this did not tame his wild spirit. Once he tried to force his way into the presence of his brother and sovereign, but was unceremoniously turned out by Bhao Sindia, the Minister. However, the Gaekwar had no children, so his brother was next in succession, and had to be acknowledged Maharajah. As Khundi Rao predicted, we rued the day he escaped the just punishment of his misdeeds. The Resident was, moreover, premature in proclaiming him Gaekwar, for shortly after this acknowledgment it was discovered that Jumna Bae was in a fair way to increase the number of the Gaekwar's family. Here was a fix! Mulhar Rao was told that if the child proved to be a boy he would have to give up his *guddee*. Imagine Mulhar Rao's feelings! For safety's sake Jumna Bae was removed from the palace, and taken care of by an English lady. The Gaekwar in possession was furious. He used to exercise his troops round the house in which the Ranee lived, and fire his biggest guns under her window, in the hopes of producing a mishap. He is said to have tried poison. But in vain! Eight months after the death of Khundi Rao the child was born, and reported a boy. Even poor Jumna Bae was told it was a boy. The Gaekwar was in despair. At last, however, the truth came out that it was a girl. The Gaekwar is reported to have danced about the room, and to have shied his turban to the ceiling in his joy. His one object then was to get hold of the mother and child, against whom he swore all kinds of vengeance. To the mother especially, whose beauty excited his passions, he swore—I will not say what. Jumna Bae was much too wise to trust herself to the tender mercies of the Zenana. She escaped to Poona, and there lived on the magnificent sum of thirty rupees a month, allowed by the English.

Mulhar Rao's subsequent proceedings all the world knows. How he fell a prey to the charms of Luxmee Bae, a woman of low caste, and some one else's wife; how he tried to poison Col. Phayre, &c., &c. At last he was deposed. Then came the question of succession, and Jumna Bae was fetched from Poona, and thirty rupees a month, to assume the position of Ranee Regnant, and choose a Gaekwar. The present Gaekwar is her adopted son; over him and the palace she rules supreme, and whenever she goes out or in, it is amidst the cries of her servants, "Wealth and happiness, Maharanee Sahib!" and to the sound of "God save the Queen!"

The Gaekwar himself is a thick-set lad of fifteen. At first he looks stupid and stolid, but when you talk to him you quickly perceive that, though not brilliant, he is far from unintelligent. He has immense determination and energy. He

p. 323

H.H. JUMNA BAE, MAHARANEE REGNANT OF BARODA.

already speaks and reads English very well, and bids fair to be quite a model chief. He conducts his sports with the same energy he displays at his work. I got up one morning to see him wrestle. Wrestling, you must know, is a national weakness of the Gaekwars. Mulhar Rao spent prodigious sums on this amusement. Under the frugal administration of Sir Madhava Rao, the present Regent, this establishment has been very much cut down. The principal *pailwān*, or wrestler, has left in disgust, but No. 2 still remains to teach the young Gaekwar. No. 2 is a very fine man, too "beefy" according to our ideas of training, but with enormous development of shoulders and thin flanks. His struggles with the Gaekwar were a most amusing exhibition. He groaned, as if with terrible effort; he allowed himself to be thrown head over heels by the boy, and struggled ludicrously in his boyish grasp. Then some of the smaller boys came to have their lesson. It was like an enormous Newfoundland toying with a small terrier. He rolled them about, and kicked them gently over with his feet, without hurting them. However, the Gaekwar is a most muscular fellow, and I would back him against any lad of his size in his national pursuit.

There is nothing of a palace here. The house in which Jumna Bae and the Gaekwar live is unusually squalid, even for a rajah's palace. Here, on the afternoon of my first day, I went to see the Ranee. We were ushered up to a tolerably well-sized room, where we found a tall slender woman, still very pretty. Her eyes are large and well formed, her nose straight, her cheek-bones rather wide, and her mouth large and well formed, notwithstanding her inveterate habit of *pân*-eating, which has spoiled her teeth. Even while receiving us, when speaking, her cheek was bulged with a lump of *pân*. She had on a dark blue muslin *sarree*, through which one could distinctly see her olive-brown skin. Indeed, to the waist she was virtually naked, except that across her breasts she wore a rather coquettish red and gold embroidered staylette. Her hands and feet are unusually beautiful, even in this land of lovely extremities. Both are arranged with the greatest care; every nail is carefully marked, where the flesh ceases to adhere with a semicircle of henna; and on each great toe she has two rings, and one on each little toe. Nevertheless, she is singularly free from artistic retouches. Unlike the other women I have seen in India, her eyes are untouched with black; she wears no nose-ring; only in the centre of her forehead there is a beauty-mark, a kind of tattoo, of delicate blue, and on her cheek and chin a single spot of the same colour; and her jewellery, though handsome, is not garish or vulgar.

Jumna Bae is still young, only twenty-five: her manners, when she likes, are charming; with me she used her sweetest smiles, and expressed her willingness to sit as long as I liked. I hear, however, that she has the proverbial fickleness of her sex, and that she can frown as well as smile. About her there are all kinds of rumours, which I would rather not believe. Who in high position escapes the foul tongue of calumny? Tara Bae, her little daughter, born, as I have described, during the stormy times of Mulhar Rao, is a charming little creature of four or five. She cannot believe she is not a boy, and insists on being dressed like the Gaekwar. When he came here riding, she also appeared riding astride.

It is not an unusual thing for Maratha women to rise to power. There were two celebrated instances in the Holkar family, and more than one instance, too, in the royal family of Sattara. Many of these ladies have left reputations behind them which are not of the best. Tara Bae of Sattara, and Toolsah Bae, widow of Jeswant Rao Holkar, were both ladies of capricious tastes, who preferred to change the

> "Lilies and languors of virtue
> For the roses and raptures of vice."

Toolsah Bae was altogether a kind of Hindoo Messalina, and, when she was taken and beheaded on the banks of the Seepra in 1817, according to an eyewitness, "Not a foot stirred and not a voice was raised to save a woman who had never shown mercy to others."

But it is pleasant to find in the annals of the Marathas an

TARA BAE, DAUGHTER OF HER HIGHNESS THE MAHARANEE JUMNA BAE.

instance of a woman and a queen who may compare with any of her Western sisters in virtue and talent. Ahalya Bae, the account of whose life and reign may be read in Malcolm's "Central India," was the wife of the son of Mulhao Rao, the first and cleverest of the Holkar family. Her son, on succeeding his grandfather on the *guddee*, proved unworthy of his parentage, being a kind of lunatic. When he died the direct line of the Holkar family failed. But Ahalya Bae, refusing to follow the custom of her country and adopt a boy, assumed the sovereignty herself, choosing Tukajee Rao to command the armies of the state. Tukajee styled himself "Son of Mulhar Rao Holkar," and called Ahalya Bae his mother; yet she was the younger of the two.

In those days (1765) the Maratha women appear to have "rejected the custom of the Mohammedans, which is not prescribed by any of the institutions of their religion." Ahalya Bae showed herself to all, and transacted all her business in person. Her days were divided between the affairs of state and her religious duties. "I deem myself answerable to God," she used to say, "for every exercise of power." And when urged by her ministers to acts of extreme severity, was wont to exclaim, "Let us mortals beware how we destroy the works of the Almighty."

Ahalya Bae reigned at Indore thirty years. She is thus described by Malcolm: "She was of middle stature, and very thin; though at no period of her life handsome, her complexion, which was of dark olive, was clear; and her countenance is described as having been, to the last hour of her existence, agreeable, and expressive of that goodness which marked every action of her life. She was very cheerful and seldom in anger, but when provoked by wickedness or crime, the most esteemed of her attendants trembled to approach her. The mind of this extraordinary woman had been more cultivated than is usual with Hindoos. She could read and understand the *Puranas* or sacred books, which were her favourite study. She is represented as having been singularly quick and clever in the transaction of business. After her husband's death she never wore coloured clothes or any jewels, except a small necklace, and indeed remained amid every temptation unchanged in her habits or character. Flattery appears to have been lost on Ahalya Bae. A Brahmin wrote a book in her praise, which she heard read with patience; but after observing "she was a weak, sinful woman, and not deserving such fine encomiums," she directed it to be thrown into the Nerbudda, and took no further notice of its author.

"A female without vanity, a bigot without intolerance, a mind imbued with the deepest superstition, yet receiving no impressions except what promoted the happiness of those under its influence; a being exercising, in the most active and able manner, despotic power, not merely with sincere humility, but under the severest restraint that a strict conscience could impose on human action; and all this combined with the greatest indulgence for the weakness and faults of others. Such, at least, is the account which the natives of Malwa give of Ahalya Bae: with them her name is sainted, and she is styled an Avatar, or Incarnation of the Divinity."

Yet few women have had to support such sore domestic afflictions. Her husband was killed in battle when she was barely twenty. Her son, on being raised to the throne, went clearly mad, though she firmly believed him to have been possessed of an evil spirit. She had beside one daughter, Muchta Bae, who was married, and had one son, who died at Mhysir on reaching manhood. Twelve months afterwards his father died, and Muchta Bae declared immediately her intention of committing *sati* with the corpse of her husband. "No efforts (short of coercion) that a mother and a sovereign could use were untried by the virtuous Ahalya Bae to dissuade her daughter from the fatal resolution. She humbled herself to the dust before her, and entreated her as she loved her God not to leave her desolate and alone upon the earth. Muchta Bae, though affectionate, was calm and resolved.

"'You are old, mother,' she said, 'and a few years will end your pious life. My only child and husband are gone, and when you follow, life I feel will be insupportable; but the opportunity of terminating it with honour will then be past.'"

"Ahalya Bae, when she found all dissuasion unavailing, determined to witness the last dreadful scene. She walked in the procession, and stood near the pile, where she was supported by two Brahmins, who held her arms. Although obviously suffering great agony of mind, she remained tolerably firm, till the first blaze of flame made her lose all self-command; and while her shrieks increased the noise made by the exulting shouts of the multitude that stood around, she was seen to gnaw in anguish those hands she could not liberate from the persons by whom she was held. After some convulsive efforts, she so far recovered as to join in the ceremony of bathing in the Nerbudda, when the bodies were consumed."*

Where in history shall we find a more painful scene? This good woman, discharging her duties to her God and her subjects, alone and amid such terrible affliction, has no parallel in history, nor indeed, as far as I know, in fiction.

Times have changed now, and Jumna Bae has neither the education or the talent to rule. She tries to get as much power as she can over the boy Gaekwar, who, notwithstanding his dogged disposition, is most kind and obedient to the adopted mother who raised him to power. But in the state she has but little influence, neither do I think she has intellect enough to do anything but obstruct any reforms Siaji Rao may wish to carry out. With all that, Jumna Bae is a charming woman, although circumstances may prevent her ever being a great queen. I have had three sittings now from this lady, on the top of the house, under an awning. As this place is open all round, and the roof or awning only 7 feet 6 inches from the floor, one cannot fancy a worse light. Around one hears all the noises of an Indian palace,—dogs yelping, children crying, and, what is more exasperating, tom-toms and flutes making a hideous row.

Yesterday was the commemoration day of the death of Khundi Rao Gaekwar, and the tom-toming was incessant. Why should people think this objectionable noise is particularly grateful to Heaven? When the noise gets on your nerves at a time when you are endeavouring to do your best, it beats organs into fits.

I shall be here the greater part of this (17th December) week; then to Bombay for a week, and then home.

It is curious to spend one's time here at the Gaekwar's Court with men who have played a great part in the stories I have already told. This Court has ever been the scene of strange crimes. The fate of Bhao Sindia is one of the most awful on record. It was he who turned Mulhar Rao from his brother's presence. On leaving, the Gaekwar that was to be cried to the Minister, "You will live to rue this day!" So much did Bhao

* Malcolm's "Central India."

Sindia dread his vengeance, that he actually tried to commit *sati* with his master's (Khundi Rao's) body. He was by force prevented. No sooner was Mulhar Rao on the *guddee* than he threw his predecessor's Minister into prison. There he was fed on curries and highly salted and spiced food, and given only pepper-water to drink; on each of his legs was fixed 200 lbs. of chain. The unfortunate man lingered five days, and then died raving mad.

Mulhar Rao was altogether a lunatic. His brother, Khundi Rao, had during his reign built an additional storey to part of the palace, and mounted silver guns thereon. Mulhar Rao, not to be outdone, had a still higher storey built, and gold guns. His extravagance was most unbounded, but then so was his brother's, and the Residents would not believe in his madness till after the celebrated attempt to poison Colonel Phayre. Poisoning was common enough at Court,—in fact, traditional in the ruling family. Grim stories have been told of former Gaekwars. One fell a victim to toxicology, and poisoned himself in his laboratory concocting poisons for his enemies. Former residents have had their lives attempted. Sir James Outram, not a nervous man, always thought he had been poisoned at Baroda. One resident died under most suspicious circumstances. He had insulted the Gaekwar; he had refused to *salaam* to Gunputti.* Now, Baroda is a very pious place—in fact, it is called by some "The Place of Prayers," and Gunputti is the God of Baroda. Once a year, at the feast of Gunputti, the Gaekwar makes a grand procession in honour of his family deity. On that day it had been customary for the Resident to hold a parade of all the troops; and as the Gaekwar and Gunputti passed on the same elephant, the troops and the Resident saluted. Now, as the Gaekwar on this particular occasion was only playing second fiddle to Gunputti, the

* As far as I can ascertain from Moore's "Pantheon of the Hindoos," this deity is probably Gangaputri, whose birth is recorded in the above book in a minute but very unsatisfactory manner. That his father was Siva is clear; his mother is more than doubtful. He was nursed by six rajahs' daughters at the same time, and finally overthrew, after a fight of ten days, Tripurasura.—*See* Moore's "Pantheon," p. 53.

people of Baroda thought that the British Power was saluting their particular god. This a certain Resident—I forget his name—refused to do. The day after a holy man went to the then Gaekwar, and said that by prayers and magic he would destroy the Resident in three days. The Gaekwar was delighted, and, strange to say, on the third day the Resident was found dead in his bed—from apoplexy, the doctors said. The son of this holy man enjoys an estate of 20,000 rupees a year, settled on his father by the grateful chief.

This yearly worship of Gunputti has been a very sore trial to many consciences, and has now happily been stopped. The Gaekwar is made to leave the religious procession, and receive the salute of the troops in his own person.

As a pendent to the above story, let me here relate a tale that was told me in the Punjab, and very well authenticated. Some miles from Peshawur, on our side of the frontier, lies the town of Nowshera. Peshawur being most unhealthy during certain months of the year, the authorities decided to quarter certain regiments at Nowshera. These troops were accordingly marched down. Barracks were built for the troops, but the officers found it difficult to provide themselves with fitting quarters. The doctor of the regiment and two of the officers determined, therefore, to build a bungalow where they could all three chum together. They chose a site on the banks of the river, where on a small mound they found a pleasant clump of trees around an old tomb. Forthwith they proceeded to have the site cleared. The second day an old Moslem *fakir* presented himself, and asked to see the doctor *sahib* who was superintending the operations.

"Are you aware," said the *fakir*, "that you are defiling the bones of a saint?—that the tomb you are about to remove belongs to one beloved of the Prophet?"

The doctor *sahib* laughed, and said that he was not aware of the fact, but that the bones of the holy man were safe, and should not be disturbed; only the tomb must be moved.

"But the impiety of the act!" cried the *fakir*.

The doctor shrugged his shoulders.

"Will you take money? I will buy the ground—pay anything to prevent the bones of the saint being moved."

But the doctor replied that this was the only healthy site he could find for his house, that he was very sorry, but the tomb must be moved.

Whereupon the *fakir* lost his temper, and cursed the three *sahibs*, their comings in and goings out,—cursed their house and all that was theirs, and departed, shaking off the dust from his feet, amid the smiles of the soldiers.

Within the year one of these officers was killed playing polo. A short time after, the second was thrown from his buggy, and broke his neck. The doctor was ordered down to Allahabad; there, whilst canoeing with a friend, their canoes were upset. Now, the doctor was a splendid swimmer, and he and his friend struck out for the shore laughing. The friend landed safely, but the doctor, when within a few yards from the shore, threw up his hands and disappeared for ever!

A year or two after there was a flood at Nowshera. The swollen river wore out the bank on which the ill-fated house stood, and while the man who told me this story was looking on with some brother officers, suddenly the bank gave way, and the house and all therein was swept away!

This was a strange story, to say the least.

The sums of money squandered on jewels by these Baroda chiefs is almost incredible. The necklace of diamonds I painted around Siaji Rao's neck cost 40 lacs, or £400,000. The pearls are almost as valuable, several strings being as big as pigeons' eggs, and of fairish colour. Every time these jewels are seen or put on, the attendants count them with the greatest care, and Sir Madhwa Rao has had them all examined and registered, to prevent their being changed for false.

Rousselet, in his "Rajahs of India," describes the procession—at which he assisted—of the Gaekwar, after his purchase of the celebrated diamond known as the "Star of the North," which forms the centre stone of this necklace. The stone was carried to the Temple of Gunputti, and there dedicated to that deity, before the Maharajah would wear it. It cost £90,000. The flat diamond, shaped like a heart, immediately underneath is called the "Star of Dresden." It cost £45,000.

My sittings from the Ranee were rather amusing. She is utterly uneducated, and can hardly read. Of course she does not talk English. To translate I had the "Master Sahib," who tried to teach Khundi Rao English long ago. He is poetic. One day, bowing to the Ranee, he recited some Maratha poetry, which was thus translated for me: "See all the trees, how tall they are; but the palm is the tallest of trees!" The palm was of course the Ranee. And so I amused myself by talking in the same strain: "To-morrow, I regret to say, my happiness comes to an end, for I must leave the presence of beauty."

"Why don't you stop?"

"The crow must fly back to his home in the jungle, and strive to forget that it has perched on the steps of the throne."

All very foolish! But it was very hot; the beads of perspiration would run down my nose, and those wretched tom-toms would continue their cursed row, so that foolishness was permissible.

I showed my picture of the Gaekwar to the Maharanee. It is a profile.

"Why, you've only given one eye!" was the intelligent remark; "and why have you only shown two strings of pearls from the tassel of his *pugree?*"

"The rest are on the other side."

"Well, I suppose it is all right, you ought to know; but—but——"

I saw she was not satisfied, and preferred her own picture, which, being full-face, has two eyes.

I left Nowsaree and the Maharanee on the 21st, and on the morning of the 22nd safely reached Bombay.

Christmas at Bombay is indeed different from Christmas in England. Instead of snow, frost, and rain, here all is sunshine and warmth. But the warmth does not add to the homeliness. Here you have seldom the pleasant prattle of children, the mad scamper of restless youth, or the merry laugh that shows the

p. 332

H.H. SIAJI RAO, GAEKWAR (OR GUICOWAR), MAHARAJAH OF BARODA.

mind free from cares. Still, the English in Bombay do their best to keep the festive season, and if they do it sadly after the manner of their countrymen, 't is often that their minds are far away in the old country; where children are drinking the healths of their absent parents, who have become sometimes little more than a name, or old people are thinking that one more Christmas is gone cf the many that must pass before their loved one's return. Yet are the shops full of purchasers, and many a plum pudding is joyfully eaten in loving recollection of those that time has long since digested. I ate mine at my good friend Melvill's, and to me it is indeed a glad season, for now I may count my days before my return home. I have painted all the rajahs and chiefs on my list but one, and he, I know, is in Bombay waiting to be painted. My passage too is taken, and I seem to see a look in my good friend's eyes of kindly envy.

"Lucky fellow!" they say, "you are going home."

Home! Who can appreciate home so well as those who are absent? And in India what magic there is in the word!

I hope I do not triumph too much in my approaching departure, or talk too much of what I shall do, &c. But talk I assuredly do; and the kind friends who keep Christmas with me, bear with me, knowing the sensations which prompt me to talk, and laugh, and be boisterous, and which they too have indulged in; and when my last rajah arrives, I confess it is with difficulty I fix my mind on my work.

Rajah Jeswant Sing, of Ratlam, is a Rahtor descended from the seventh son of Oodi Sing, who ruled in Marwar in 1569. Rutna, the grandson of Oodi Sing, was the founder of the state of Rutlam. He had all the pluck of his family. At the battle of Futtehabad, fought between Jeswant Sing of Marwar in defence of the aged Shah Jehan against his rebel sons Aurungzebe and Morad, the doings of Rutna are "wreathed in immortal rhyme" in the "Rasa Rao Rutna." On that day well did the Rahtors maintain their reputation for courage and the fidelity (*swam dherma*) they owed the Emperor "whose salt they ate." The battle was gained through the desertion of the Mogul horse, who were bribed by the wily Aurungzebe; but, if courage were to decide a battle, the day would have ended in favour of the Rajpoots, who never lost an inch of ground, though they could not force back the vastly superior numbers of the enemy.

Jeswant next day retreated. But, on arriving at Jodhpore, "I (Bernier) cannot forbear to relate the fierce reception which the daughter of the Rana (of Oodeypore) gave to her husband, Jeswant Sing, when she heard he was nigh, and had understood what had passed in the battle: that he had fought with all possible courage; that he had but 400 of 500 men left; and at last, being no longer able to resist, had been forced to retreat. Instead of sending some one to condole him in his misfortunes, she commanded, in a dry mood, to shut the gates of the castle, and not to let this infamous man enter; that he was not her husband; that the son-in-law of the Great Rana could not have so mean a soul; that he was to remember that being grafted into so illustrious a house, he was to imitate its virtue; in a word, he was to vanquish or to die! A moment after she was of a different humour. She commanded a pile of wood to be laid, that she might burn herself; that they abused her; that her husband must be dead; that it could not be otherwise. And a little while after she seemed to change countenance, to fall into a passion, and break into a thousand reproaches against him. In short, she remained thus transported eight or nine days without being able to resolve to see her husband; till, at last, her mother coming, brought her in time to herself, comforted her by assuring her that, as soon as the Rajah had but refreshed himself, he would raise another army to fight Aurungzebe and repair his honour." Thus writes Bernier, who witnessed this battle; and he adds, "By which story one may see a pattern of the courage of the women of that country."

Jeswant Sing of Rutlam, who is the head of the Rajpoots of Malwa, may have a soul as great as his kinsman of Marwar. He is in person a stout youth of sixteen, with rather aquiline features, without much of what we painters call character in his face. He has an enormous and most elaborate *pugree*, which he says was invented by his grandfather, and which is heaped up with all kinds of jewels and ornaments. He tells me it takes two hours to tie! Salar Jung's simple *pugree* took twenty minutes. No wonder Orientals cannot take off their hats.

I got a very good photograph done of this young man, which, with my somewhat hurried sketch, will suffice for my picture. And so having finished my work on the last day of the year 1877, I embarked on board the good ship *Gwalior*. I was taken on board by my friends, and as the screw of the *Gwalior* commenced to beat the waves, the dull thuds that vibrated through the ship struck me with regret at parting with so many good people, whom I may never perchance see again to return the innumerable kindnesses I have received during my year's travel in India. But the thoughts of home quickly dissipate any such sentiments, and after one look at Bombay, dark against the setting sun, where I see lights twinkling, perhaps in well-known houses, I turn to gaze on the watery track that leads to those I love.

## CHAPTER XXIII.

### IMPRESSIONS.

"WELL, and how did you like India?" This question has been asked me very often since I returned home, and yet I have never been able to answer it with satisfaction to myself. I feel, however, that the reader who has waded through the previous chapters of this book, whom in consequence I regard as a personal friend, may perchance wish to ask the same question; nor will he be satisfied with the "Very much indeed," or "It's a wonderful country!" which sometimes has proved enough for mere acquaintances. "How do you like being Prince of Wales as far as you've got?" asks Artemus Ward, but H.R.H. does not give a very satisfactory answer, if I remember right; had he done so, I might have moulded this chapter on an august model.

Everybody is accustomed to the observation, "India is a vast place," but few can form any idea of its vastness till they have travelled across the continent that we English have somehow acquired. Do Englishmen realize the fact that it takes as long to travel from Bombay to Delhi by rail as from London to Brindisi, and from Bombay to Mysore as long again? Yet neither Mysore nor Delhi are the limits of our empire! And the races who inhabit this vast region are quite as different in their habits as those through whose country you pass in a tour across Europe.

I have, however, striven in my journals to convey some idea of the kind of people found in India. Exclusive as is a Hindoo by caste, feeling, and prejudice, it is difficult to arrive at a knowledge of his real sentiments. An Englishman and a "*sahib*" can never hope thoroughly to penetrate the thick veil that surrounds the domestic life of Natives, and it is only by their writings and their actions in contact with Europeans that he can judge at all of their characters. It is for this reason that I have very copiously quoted from Tod's translation of the Rajpoot traditions, for these have more domestic details than the wild legends of the Ramayana and Mahabharata and earlier books of Hindoo literature. From careful study of these legends and of more recent history, and from observation during my travels, I have tried to arrive at some conclusions which I venture now to submit to the public, with, I own, considerable fear lest I may be put down as a prig by those whose longer stay in the country ought to have given them more opportunities of study.

Of course the difference of religion has produced a difference in habit and character. The Moslem has still some of the swagger of a ruling race, some of the confidence always found in the followers of the creed of Mohammed. But with the exception of the province of Hyderabad, where, under the able rule of Sir Salar Jung, a Moslem state flourishes, I could not but observe that the star of the Prophet is on the wane. Already the Maratha and the Sikh assert their equality in military prowess to the Afghan and Pathan, while in administrative capacity I fancy there are at least five Hindoos in high position to one Moslem. As lawyers the Hindoos are pre-eminent, and as money-makers—bankers and general dealers—the Hindoo and Parsee are far ahead of the Mohammedan.

But in all Indians I have noticed a singular and childish unthoroughness, and in turning to history the same quality must strike a careful observer. With intellectual activity of the highest order, and with brains capable of understanding the subtlest reasoning and the nicest and most delicate quibbles of law, I should doubt any Indian's capacity for large views on any subject. Their diplomacy is so much infused with cunning as to frequently defeat itself; while their actions are hampered by a suspiciousness beyond that of any other Oriental. Their intellect seems to me that of a precocious child, their astuteness childish cunning, their suspicious disposition almost feminine. More than once the most transparent tricks have been resorted to in order to break up the strongest confederacies. Several times in history the Mogul power was checked, but the advantage lost through a false idea of treachery. A forged letter or even a word has saved the great empire of the Mogul in the hour of danger. The emperors of that house were adepts in treachery; by it they triumphed over the valour of the Rajpoots; Baber, the founder of the dynasty, employed it against Sanga of Mewar; and Aurungzebe, the cleverest of the house, was such an adept at deceit that Machiavelli was a child to him. His rise to the throne is one of the most extraordinary stories on record, and during a long reign he never forgot to employ treachery rather than force.

We have seen how the dread cry of "*Nous sommes trahis!*" demoralized a high-spirited and chivalrous nation. With the native the idea of treachery is ever present, and his imaginative temperament works the vaguest apprehensions up to the point of madness. Thus childish suspicions and proneness to intrigue seem to be in the blood of the nation; and as disloyalty and deceit, when successful, are always applauded by the national chroniclers, what wonder if a dread of treachery should always be before the eyes of the native? It is by the ideal characters, founded no doubt on truth, but embellished by the poet in song, ballad, and legend, that the character of a nation is founded. The inventions of the Round Table, the Lancelots, Tristrams, and Galahads of chivalry, produced their echoes in Chevalier Bayard and Sir Philip Sidney, and did much to raise mediæval Europe from the depth of barbarism. But Christianity tempered the warlike spirit of Europe, and if we wish to find a parallel for the traditions of India, we must look rather to the Northern legends, in which, amidst much that is fine and even tender, there is many an instance of unaccountable want of faith and cruel and indiscriminate slaughter. Fancy what Europe would have been without chivalry, which was the result of the influence of Christianity engrafted on Northern poetry, and you can imagine the state of morality in India!

And if we come down to later history, we shall find the same characteristics, for we must not forget that though brought in contact with the civilization of the west, the state of India at the present day is hardly in advance of that of Europe in the thirteenth and fourteenth centuries. The Mutiny furnished instances innumerable of this childish inconsistency, which was in many instances the result of fear of treachery. No doubt, the first regiments that mutinied were misled by artful instigators of treason. They were told about the famous greased cartridges; they were informed of the prophecy after the battle of Plassy, which limited the Raj of the East India Company to one hundred years; and they mutinied. But read the history of the rising of succeeding regiments, and see how in nearly every case it was fear of the treachery of the *sahib* that drove them to rebellion. The Poorbeah Sepoys of the time were, no doubt, a mutinous body of troops. To keep up the *physique* of the men they were recruited from the high-caste natives of Oude, and everything was conceded by their officers to their caste prejudices. That such men, brought up and nursed in all the traditions of the Hindoos, should treacherously sacrifice their English officers is not to be wondered at, since there are twenty instances at least of the like act of perfidy in the traditions which form the sole literature of the country.

When not under the influence of fear, the native is most easily governed. There is no nation imbued with a greater respect for the power over them, and assuredly no nation contented with so little apparent prosperity. Go but to any fair or religious gathering, and see the merry chattering crowd streaming along the road. From every man you receive a *salaam* and a joyous greeting, yet his worldly lot is livelong toil, and his wealth consists in his *dhotie* or loin-cloth, and the few ornaments in the ears and nose, and round the ankles and wrists of his wife, who marches contentedly behind him. But the Indian, though docile in the extreme, has the makings of a tyrant within him. Your servant is mild and obedient to you, and seems to have no spirit in his brown breast. Take some more servants into your employ, and place your mild friend over them, and see what a Frankenstein you have raised. He will beat and bully them all round, no matter what their size or strength. Your authority is on his side, and that is enough.

Again, insult or imagined insult works a native up to madness. Instances without number may be found in native history where insults have produced sad results. I have mentioned the contest between Jeichund and Pirthi Raj through an imagined affront to the last, which quarrel led to the subjugation of India by the Moslem. Oodeypore and Marwar were at war for a lengthened period because the Rana refused to eat with the chief of the Rahtors. Marwar and Jeypore rushed to arms through a joke; and although many times the chivalrous Rajpoot shed his best blood for his salt, often at the last moment has the whole wing of an army refused to fight on account of an imagined slight on its chief. Frequently I fancy the Englishman quite unintentionally gives the direst offence. I do not mean abuse to servants, and such-like: abuse to them, or indeed to any inferior, is natural enough, and to call them the "sons of owls" or "hens," or even worse, is what they are accustomed to even from their native superiors. But a native gentleman's ways are not our ways, and to his ideas the commonest conventionalities of our civilization are the grossest barbarisms. The use of a fork or spoon, or glass, that any one else has used, to the Hindoŏ is unspeakable horror. These matters will right themselves in the course of time. But breaches of etiquette, no doubt, occur, and though not noticed at the moment, rankle in the breast of the native for a long time.

One of the drollest occasions of unintentional offence I quote from Sir Thomas Roe. Jehanghire playfully seized all the supplies of presents sent out from England to Sir Thomas, and had all the boxes opened in his presence, that he might see what he liked to have presented to him. He "caused a chest of pictures to be brought, which were taken out; and there being among them one of a Venus leading a satyr by the nose, he showed it to all around him, bidding them to expound the signification of it, observing the satyr's horns, the blackness of his skin, and other particulars. Every man spoke as he thought, but the King liked none of their expositions, yet reserved his own thoughts, and asked me what it meant. I told him it was only a painter's fancy. Whereupon he said, 'Why do you bring me what you do not understand?' . . . And by what he said I had ground to believe he thought that the picture was made in derision of the people of Asia, whom he thought to be represented by the satyr, as being of their complexion; and that the Venus leading him by the nose denoted the great power the women of that country have over the men. This I relate for the information of the gentlemen of the East India Company, and of all that shall hereafter come in my place, and advise them for the future not to send into those parts things that may be liable to an ill construction, *for those people are very jealous.*"

On their religion Indians are very sensitive. There appears to be something in the air of India that leads to bigotry. The Hindoo is the strictest religionist. The smallest sin against the law of the Brahmin is visited by the terrible gods of the country with condign punishment, while in Hindoo states the prejudice against many acts that are necessary for the existence and well-being of the European is very powerful. I have seen a whole village turn out at the slaughter of a peacock or a blue jay. To kill a cow or bull is a crime which even an educated Hindoo would consider worthy of death. The Rajah of Jheend, an enlightened ruler, would cut off the hand that slew a neilghau or wild blue bull, and these prejudices are retained by many even after the society of the *sahib* has become familiar to them. I have been told of an eminent lawyer (Hindoo) in Calcutta, who, on seeing that his refusal of beef was noticed, said that he had long since overcome his religious prejudice against eaters of beef, but he had still a horror of that animal such as a Jew would have against pork But it is not only the Hindoo who is intolerant and bigoted; the Mohammedan of India is ten times as strict as any Turk I ever saw. When their religious enthusiasm is roused, either the Hindoo or the Moslem is capable of any suffering, which is looked on as a martyrdom. What they will bear for their religion is constantly brought before the eyes of the traveller in the frequent self-tortures and self-mutilations met with at every turn. The wealthy and great, even rajahs, will retire from the enjoyments of life, and lead the lives of veritable ascetics. Men of both religions were shot away from cannon during the Mutiny when they thought they were martyrs to their faith, without showing, even at the last moment, the slightest signs of fear. I have had these terrible scenes described to me by eye-witnesses, who assured me that the culprit who was about to be blown to atoms would lean with the greatest *nonchalance* against the muzzle of the cannon, and was by far the least moved of those present.

This is, then, the character of the native: childishly inconsistent, fickle, and cunning, easily elated by power, accessible to flattery but prone to take offence, bearing anything at times from those put over him, and capable of the sternest fortitude in the exercise of his religion, brave to foolhardiness yet prone to the most unaccountable panics, trusting everything to the ministers of his religion, yet placing no confidence in his fellow-man, ever fearing treachery and ingratitude.

That we English, few in number, and living so many thousand miles off, should have acquired this vast empire is one of the marvels of history. The secret lies in the contrast we present in our characters. We are the complement of the native. We owe our success to the squareness and solidity of our character, in every way the reverse of the fickle and treacherous nature of the native. Our thoroughness inspires his respect. He believes in our honesty—he has every reason to trust our courage. We give him peace such as he never enjoyed before, and insure his having justice, even against the great. There is no power that can take our place in the country. If we were to go, the flames of war would light India from the Himalaya to Cape Cormorin. I have talked with eminent natives on this subject, and they have always said, "It is peace that our nation wants. We have had no time to develope; we want education and knowledge." And they make little secret of their opinion, that when they have acquired knowleged and education we shall have to leave the country. Such is native gratitude

The mass of the people are contented with our rule, which they regard as an accomplished fact. They think we have been sent to govern them by the Gods. The belief of the Hindoo, or rather the Vishnavas, the mass of the people, is that from the beginning of the world Vishnu has ever, on being roused, thrown his spirit into some human form, who becomes an "*ouâtar*" or *avâtar* of the deity, an inspired person, whose spirit on his death returns to the God. There are many of these *avâtars* which are puerile enough,—the snake, the fish, the tortoise, the man-lion, the dwarf, the bull. All these probably denote the absorption of so many religions into the Brahminical creed.* The last, the most famous "*avâtars*" were Rama, Khrishna, and Buddha. Many Brahmins preach a fresh *avâtar* "the Raj of the English." This has been solemnly stated to me as the received belief of the larger number of Hindoos, and no doubt is a great strength to our power.

But we derive a greater hold from the divisions that exist amongst the people themselves. I cannot think that we English are loved, but the orthodox Hindoo hates us less than he hates the dissenting Sikh, and both have many reasons for preferring our rule to the rule of the Moslem. Aurungzebe's bigotry led the way to the fall of the Mogul. It was the institution of the *jezeya*, or capitation grant on all Brahmins and Hindoo devotees, that alienated the affection of the Rajpoot princes who were allies to the imperial family. It roused an intolerance among the Hindoos† that was foreign to their disposition. Their religion rather aimed at absorbing all the religions of the world. Their priests insist that both Mohammed and the Founder of our religion were alike incarnations of Vishnu. But persecution sowed the seeds of a hatred between the Moslems and Hindoos which is not yet effaced, and which, if we are wise, ought to strengthen our hands for many a year to come.

* The Brahmins convert whole tribes of the aboriginal Bheels and Shenas by incorporating their favourite idol into the circle of Hindoo Gods; they say such idols were no doubt incarnations of Vishnu. See Benares, p. 274.

† See Appendix II.

There is one side of the native's character that I have not noticed—his extreme and feminine gentleness. With children he is most admirable. In the South of Europe the same gentleness is found, but throughout India I have observed it in high and low. Most people must have noticed in the streets of London the native man-servant carrying a small child. In India everywhere the man-servant looks after the children from the moment they leave the wet-nurse. Their devotion to their charges is perfectly wonderful. As a general rule, English children in India are unruly brats, wilful to a degree, and a severe tax on the best of tempers. Yet the bearer, often a high-caste Hindoo, will watch over them and humour them with a gentleness that is entirely foreign to the Northern nature. In his relation to his master, too, the Indian servant often shows the most affectionate solicitude, and he who would cheat and pilfer on other occasions will, when his master is ailing, prove the most gentle and faithful of nurses. I have seen the youthful rajahs and princes with their tutors, and their affection—nay, tenderness—for some of these officers has been a convincing proof of the depth of the native character. Instances without number occurred during the Mutiny of personal influence exercised over the native by the European. A strange kind of mesmeric power was possessed by men like Nicholson, which the softer nature of the Hindoo seemed unable to resist. To such men the natives would always be true and loyal. Their affection for them is that of a child to its parent.

I have seen it frequently stated that we rule in India by the sword alone. No man can readily believe that the few hundred Europeans in India can hold in subjection the 240,000,000 natives except by force. No doubt our sway has originated in conquest, and what empire has not? No doubt after the Mutiny we gave the Indian nation a severe lesson. The sword of England was heavy on the wrong-doer. Our justice was rather that of the terrible Gods of the country than of that Deity whose attribute is mercy. But it is not by the sword alone that we rule. The Moguls had the power of the sword. They had the means to strike, and struck sharply and without sparing; but during their reign, lasting over two hundred years, there was no peace, neither did their power extend over nearly so much of the country as the Viceroy rules. Therefore, I am inclined to think with Sir James Stephen that we govern more by justice than by the sword. It is the moral force of our rule rather than the physical that maintains our authority. It is the high character of the nation that enables an Englishman to travel through the country as I did, and as any other Englishman can do, alone, unarmed, and without speaking the language. And this character we owe to the men who have governed, and still govern, the country.

Surely in this we English have something to be proud of. History has no parallel to our rule in India. The Romans ruled over an equal extent of country, and in somewhat the same way; but the Roman official was too prone to make hay while the sun of office was bright. No doubt the early English administrators did likewise. Ill paid, and amid a population with whom bribery was an institution, themselves more or less adventurers, our first officers in India retired with wealth sufficient to make the word Nabob a proverb. But for the last hundred years, ever since the English rule has been consolidated, the English official has been without reproach. With every facility, amid every temptation, the name of an Englishman is still in India a synonym for honesty and truth. During those hundred years the number of those who have fallen to temptation would not equal the number of one's fingers; and if an Englishman wishes to feel that his nation is something in the world, if he wishes to have the sensation of pride of the Roman, whose greatest boast was "*civis Romanus sum*," let him go to India, where all that is great and noble is associated with the name of England.

Coming as I do from an Indian family, allied to many still in the service, it ill becomes me to criticize; but I have tried to be honest in my journals, even at the risk of giving offence, and so now I cannot forbear pointing out what I consider to be the faults of our rule in India.

And in truth I have but little fault to find. If anything, we are a little too English. We are a nation without poetry. We are apt to be guided by the hard and fast line of the law, and are devoid of sentiment or enthusiasm. Now, the Indian, like the Irishman, is full of poetry and imagination, and so, like the Irishman, we have conquered his respect, but, I fear, never tried to gain his love. We have never flattered him with the gorgeous pageant of sovereignty, as did the great Mogul. Hardly can he suppose that he forms a part of that Government which he sees so firmly carried out by our iron hands. He is dazzled by display, and cannot yet understand the hard reasoning of figures, which prove that India, so gorgeous in the past, is a very poor country. In matters of religion we maintain the same dry neutrality. The Government aid neither the Hindoo nor the Moslem communities; nor do they publicly befriend the Christian. All this to the native is incomprehensible. To him a tyranny is familiar. To crawl on all-fours to the throne would be no disgrace; to be degraded or raised to power at the caprice of his Sovereign would give scope for his ambition and talent for intrigue; but to be told to stand up and be a man, and yet not to have the same position as the *sahib*; to be taught that before the law all men are equal, and yet not to be allowed his portion in the Government of the country,—such is the position we have taken, and I fear it is hardly logical. I do not say that the native is yet fit to govern. Those few natives who have passed in the Civil Service competition—and it is greatly to their credit to have done so—have, I fear, not proved as yet brilliant successes. Yet if we open the door, we should open it wide. It does not do to show the bright inside, and then shut the portal. It does not do to preserve too strictly the pride of the conquering race, and yet to preach liberality of sentiment.

It was not thus that the early rulers of the country consolidated their power. They mixed more freely with the natives, they showed more sympathy with their prejudices, and strove more to understand their characters, at the same time treating them more as their own rulers would treat them in matters of etiquette. I would not advocate the return of the lax morality of our old services,* but I would have more interchange of sociality between the two races. I would have the Englishman unbend somewhat towards the native, and be inclined to make more allowance for his prejudices, which are the inheritance of ages; in fact, not expect a native to be an Englishman.

And I am emboldened to speak in this manner, because I fear that each day we are becoming more English in India. Each year communication becomes more easy between England and her great empire in the East. Each year greater facility is offered to the English official to visit his native land, and so that official becomes more and more a camper and sojourner in India. With his eyes constantly fixed on England, he does not identify himself with the people and the country, with which he has little sympathy, and is apt to regulate his conduct by the opinions of his fellow-countrymen, rather than by the interests of the empire he is called upon to govern. Frequently, too, I fancy, India is sacrificed to the exigencies of the home Government, for those who direct our home policy have no idea of the many wants of the native, whose character they have never studied. I think I am only saying what every Indian officer would endorse, and that it is impossible for India to be well governed from Downing Street.

Meanwhile, I cannot but observe that much has already been done towards breaking down the barriers which separate the Hindoo from European civilization. Gradually caste and caste prejudice must disappear before those great levellers, the railway and the telegraph. But let us not break down such prejudices before we have given something to supply their place. Let us give the necessary time for the change we expect. The native is of an imitative nature; and to put on a mere veneering of civilization will be to him an easy matter. Let us remember that such a cleaning of the outside of the platter, such a conforming to the outward observances of society, is not sufficient. That there are many good and loyal native gentlemen in India I have no doubt,

* I have heard old officers assert that in the old time the Mutiny would have been impossible; that full intelligence of the revolt would surely have come to the authorities through their connection with the bazaars!

but I do doubt their being amongst those who seek the approbation of the English by outward observance and time-serving.

I have been frequently asked since the Afghan troubles have come upon us my opinion of the native army. I can speak best of the Punjabees, as it is that portion of our force that I had most leisure to observe.* Of these I can affirm that I rarely have seen a finer body of men, and I am also sure that they are true to their "salt." I had an opportunity of seeing and speaking with many of their officers, both native and English. I believe that the spirit of chivalry, such as I have described in my extracts from the history of the Rajpoots, exists in many of the frontier regiments. I have heard authentic accounts of their exploits. "When a body of frontier cavalry of my regiment," said an English officer of cavalry to me, "had to charge a lot of Afredees the other day, their native officer (a Sikh) suddenly let down his long hair† and cried, 'Let us show the *sahibs* that we are worthy of their salt!' His men did the like, and, headed by their *rassaldar*, delivered a brilliant charge." If such men are well led, they are capable of anything; and I am confident that, as a rule, their officers are dashing and efficient soldiers, in whom the men can trust.

And in this Afghan business the good wishes of every inhabitant of Hindostan will be on our side against the hated Afghans. Many a time have these mountaineers, since the reign of the terrible Mahmoud of Ghuznee, invaded the rich plains of India, carrying desolation and famine with them. The Mohammedan cannot have forgotten the sacking of Delhi by Nadir Shah, whose army, though nominally Persians, consisted principally of Afghans and nomads from Central Asia. The Marathas yet remember their defeat at Paniput by Ahmed Shah Abdallee, and Sindia himself would not be slow to avenge the death of the head of his family and the laming of the celebrated Madaji

* As a rule Indian regiments have a higher average standard of height than the regiments that come from England; the men do not, however, weigh so much. The Goorka regiments are an exception; they are composed of short, wiry, active mountaineers.

† When a Sikh lets down his hair, it is a sign that he intends to conquer or die.

Rao Sindia at that disastrous battle. When Tukaji Rao Holkar wished to make a truce on a subsequent occasion with Nujeeb-ud-Dowlah, to whose bravery the victory of Paniput was due, Madaji Rao said,—

"I demand for the Peishwa the country possessed by this chief and the Afghans. I demand for myself the blood of my brother, of my two nephews, and my own leg, of which I am deprived."

"He used frequently," says Sir John Malcolm, in his "Central India," "to recount the particulars of this event. He fled from the field, but was pursued to a great distance by an Afghan. His fine Deccany mare carried him a great way ahead of the strong animal upon which the soldier who had marked him for prey was mounted; but whenever he rested for an interval, however short, his enemy appeared keeping the same pace. At last his fatigued mare fell into a ditch. He was taken, spit upon, and left. He used to say that the circumstance had made so strong an impression upon his imagination that he could not for a long time sleep without seeing the Afghan and his clumsy charger pacing after him and his fine Decanny mare."

Does Sindia ever think of this?

But our army in India and the discipline of our regiments are kept up entirely by our *prestige*, and if this should suffer in any way our troops would at once become demoralized. It is necessary for us to take every precaution against any disaster, or even the rumour of a disaster. Bazaar gossip in India supplies the place of public opinion; and a story flies through the country in an incredibly short space of time. Like the social game of German gossip, the tale with an original tittle of truth gets distorted into a monstrosity. I have alluded before to the prophecy of the duration of the Raj of the East India Company. I have been assured that a belief in that prophecy had much to do with the Mutiny.* Our reputation should, like that of Cæsar's wife, be above suspicion.

* See Meadows Taylor's "Life." It is curious that the transfer of the Government of India from the East India Company to the Queen should have carried out this prophecy!

We have, then, a noble reputation to keep up. We have an inheritance of which we may well be proud. But such an inheritance has its duties as well as its advantages. By valour we acquired, by justice we have consolidated, our empire. Let us never, through the necessities of the Home Government, forget our position. Let us never, for the sake of a cry, show the weakness or vacillation, sometimes the apparent result of our representative system, lest perchance the native—not understanding our real strength, and seeing only our apparent weakness—should think with Sir Josiah Child, "that the House of Commons hardly know how to make laws for the good government of their own private families, much less for the regulating of foreign affairs or commerce!"*

In conclusion, let me say a few words about my impressions as an artist. As a field for artists, India has been of late years sadly neglected. While the more fortunate countries of the East—Turkey, Syria, Egypt, and Arabia—have been frequently depicted, India has remained almost unknown to the painter. Zoffany and Daniel, both Royal Academicians, in the old time, when the voyage alone to India was an affair of six months or more, thought it worth their while to visit the unknown land of Hind. Now in six months much of India may be seen, and yet since the time of these two artists no painter of note† has thought it worth his while to convey to his countrymen an impression of our Eastern empire. The only figure painter of eminence who has visited India for the last eighty years has been a Russian, M. Verestchagine. Ought not we painters to be rather ashamed of this? Yet India, I can assure my brother painters, is an inexhaustible field for artistic energy. It is unlike anything else ever painted. It outdoes in originality the weirdest fancies of Fortuny, Gerôme, or Decamps, for it presents not only the most original combinations of colour and form at every turn, but abounds in romantic tradition. I have striven to record some of

* See *ante* page 17.

† I must except one or two water-colour painters, who were only landscape sketchers.

these, and if I have succeeded in exciting the imagination of any of my brother labourers in the arts—if I can induce any of them to follow in my footsteps, and visit the scenes I have feebly described—I shall be rewarded for many a toilsome journey, in heat and discomfort, through the length and breadth of Imperial India.

# APPENDIX.

I.

I CANNOT refrain from printing in the Appendix of my book the following ballad written by my father, which is taken from a legend of Sirmoor. The Giri is a river flowing a few miles from Simla.

## THE NUTNEE.*

### A LEGEND OF SIMLA.

I.

In the mountains of Sirmoor spreads far and wide
  The domain of a Rajah dread,
And his palace is built on a mountain's side,
Where the Giri rushes with furious tide
  Deep in its rocky bed.

II.

On a jutting rock's summit, the palace wall
  Stands at a dizzy height;
And a stone from the topmost tower of all
Into the Giri's deep bed would fall
  In one unbroken flight.

III.

On that tower's high terrace the Rajah sits,
  And the wine they freely pour,
And the voices of mirth and the laughter-fits,
As the Rajah drinks with his favourites,
  Mix with the torrent's roar.

* NUTNEE,—The Nuts are the gipsies of India, living by jugglers' tricks and feats, to which they train children from youth. Nutnee is the feminine of Nut.

IV.

" Where lingers my Nutnee concubine?
My queen of the dance and song?
Bid her come hither to share our wine,
Her merry black eye and her voice divine
Shall the joy of this revel prolong."

V.

The Rajah a cup to her health hath quaffed,
And called her to sit by his side.
" Now tell us, while draining this goblet's draught,
How cams't thou to learn the tricks of thy craft,
And the feats of thy people the pride?"

VI.

" My training at three years old began,
I learned then the balance true;
From little to great things my lessons ran,
Till there's not a feat performed by man
That I have not learned to do.

VII.

" Amid sharp swords I can dance blindfold,
Stringing of eggs a crown:
So true is my balance, so firm my hold,
I can swing on a bamboo, and walk quite bold
On a tight rope, up or down."

VIII.

" I have seen thee walk on a rope stretched tight;
But thy courage now prove to me.
We will stretch a rope over to yonder height,
And there thou shalt walk like an angel bright,
For my people below to see."

IX.

" 'T is a dizzy height of two thousand feet,
And the torrent that roars below
Sustains not the spirit like music sweet:
Sure never hath mortal performed like feat.
The guerdon I first would know."

X.

" For guerdon thou shalt not my humour mock ;
  A bond I will seal and sign,
That if thou walk over from tower to rock,
Bearing thy infant child on thy back,
  One-half of my kingdom is thine."

XI.

" Shall the child of my heart then a Rajah be,
  And a powerful lord among men?
Then stretch the rope over, and thou shalt see
What a mother will do in her bravery,
  That meed for her child to win."

XII.

An arrow is shot from a strong hill bow
  Bearing a silken thread :
Then thicker and thicker the cords they throw,
Till over the chasm that gapes below
  The perilous bridge is spread.

XIII.

She hath girded her loins, she hath strapped the child,
  It will motionless lie in sleep.
" Salaam to thee, Rajah," she said, and smiled ;
Then sank on her knees, and in accents wild
  Thus prayed o'er the terrible deep :

XIV.

" Great God of my fathers, great God of my race,
  Life, honour, and all are Thine ;
'T is Thou givest glory, or death and disgrace ;
Oh ! be it Thy will, I Thy people should raise,
  And found here a royal line."

XV.

In hand she hath taken the balancing-pole,
  And steps on the perilous bridge :
Firm forward she goes, for high hope fills her soul.
She walks in mid-air—*Hureebôl! Hureebôl!** . .
  With her eye on the opposite ridge.

* HUREEBÔL.—The usual exclamation of great wonder ; an invocation to Huree or Krishna.

XVI.

"Back, back!" cries the Rajah, "and tempt not fate;
I wished but thy courage to try."
Still forward she walks,—the recall is too late;
So steady her step, so unflinching her gait,
All danger she seems to defy.

XVII.

Half-way she hath reached, and still safely moves
Mark the sweat on the Rajah's brow,—
Already he deems half his kingdom gone,
And his eye falls by chance on his Jobraj* son;
And where is the remedy now?

XVIII.

A Nutnee will take his inheritance,
Thus staked in a foolish whim,
And the curse of his caste, of Rajpoot Chohans,
The curse of the children born of his loins,
Will lie for ever on him.

XIX.

A thought diabolical seizes his brain:
He clenches his dagger-hilt hard;
He looks at the Nutnee girl once again,
To the rock but a dozen short steps remain;—
He severs the tightening cord!

XX.

Ah! heard you that shrill supernatural cry,
And heard you the wail from below?
Down, down like a meteor shot from the sky,
Or angel rebellious hurled from on high,
Down, deep where the waters flow,

XXI.

They have fallen, the mother and innocent child,
And are lost in the Giri's flood
But the cord on the rock-side, fresh cut and uncoiled,
Damning evidence, shows how the bold feat was spoiled,
And on whom lies the gilt of blood.

* JOBRAJ.—A rajah's heir-apparent is so called.

XXII.

The curse of all good men lies heavy on him,
  Cain-marked—void of honour and truth.
Alas! one so perfect of feature and limb,
So courageous, to be, by a damnable crime,
  Cut off in the flower of youth!

XXIII.

Can that Rajah sleep now in his palace bed,
  And list to the Giri's roar?
Hath his soul no remorse, and his conscience no dread
Of the power on earth of the murdered dead,
  Of the gods who watch over Sirmoor?

XXIV

Oh, honour, lost honour! how can he forget
  That shriek of unearthly sound?
For aye is the sun of his destiny set:
Unnerved now for action his realm is beset
  By enemies gathering round.

XXV.

A battle is lost, and the Rajah hath fled
  To his refuge, the rock-built tower:
'T is the day of the year when the Nutnee fell dead,
And the heavens look wild, and the sun sets red,
  And storm-freighted clouds dark lower.

XXVI.

A tempest is raging the whole night long,
  And frequent the lightnings flash,
And loud rolls the thunder the mountains among:
One flash! then a thunder-clap, sudden and strong!
  Hark! hark to the following crash!

XXVII.

Dark with rain is the night, all is silent now
  Save the Giri's more angry roar:
Men listen and whisper who live far below:
Some dread thing hath happened, yet none may know,
  Till morning, the fate of Sirmoor.

XXVIII.

Men look for the palace that frowned o'er the town,
They look for that guilty tower.
All into the Giri have crumbled down,
The Rajah and all his household have gone
Where his victims went before.

XXIX.

Some said that a thunderbolt shivered the rock,
From heaven in anger sent;
Some said they had felt a earthquake-shock,
That the spirits below did the earth unlock,
And dragged him to punishment.

XXX.

Not heaven nor hell, but the Nuts did this,—
Their vengeance strikes ever true:
'Mong Nuts ever sacred their secret is,
This was one of the wonderful mysteries'
Of arts which they only knew.

---

## II.

The letter from Rana Raj Sing, of Mewar, to the Emperor Aurungzebe, is so remarkable an instance of the feeling of toleration among Hindoos, that, though it is quoted by me before, I venture to insert it here *in extenso*. Recollect, it is the temporal head of the Hindoos who thus writes on the imposition of a most intolerable tax on all that he held most sacred:

"All due praise be rendered to the glory of the Almighty, and the munificence of your Majesty, which is conspicuous as the sun and moon. Although I, your well-wisher, have separated myself from your sublime presence, I am nevertheless zealous in the performance of every bounden act of obedience and loyalty. My ardent wishes and strenuous services are employed to promote the prosperity of the kings, nobles, mirzas, rajahs, and rojs of the provinces of Hindostan, and the chiefs of Æraun, Turaun, Room, and Shawm; the inhabitants of the seven climates, and all persons travelling by land and by water. This my inclination is notorious, nor can your Royal wisdom entertain a doubt thereof. Reflecting, therefore, on my former services and your Majesty's condescension, I presume to solicit the Royal attention to some circumstances in which the public as well as private welfare is greatly interested.

"I have been informed that enormous sums have been dissipated in the prosecution of the designs formed against me, your well-wisher, and that you have ordered a tribute to be levied, to satisfy exigencies of your exhausted treasury.

"May it please your Majesty, your Royal ancestor Mohamed Jelal-oo-Deen Akbar, whose throne is now in heaven, conducted the affairs of this empire in equity and firm security for the space of fifty-two years, preserving every tribe of men in ease and happiness, whether they were followers of Jesus or of Moses, of David or Mohammed; were they Brahmins, were they of the sect Dharians, which denies the eternity of matter, or of that which ascribes the existence of the world to chance,—they all equally enjoyed his countenance and favour, insomuch that his people, in gratitude for the indiscriminate protection he afforded them, distinguished him by the appellation, 'Juggut Gooroo' (Guardian of Mankind).

"His Majesty Mohamed Noor-oo-Deen Jehanghir likewise, whose dwelling is now in Paradise, extended, for a period of twenty-two years, the shadow of his protection over the heads of his people, successful, by a constant fidelity to his allies, and a vigorous exertion of his arm in business.

"Nor less did the illustrious Shah Jehan, by a propitious reign of thirty-two years, acquire to himself immortal reputation, the glorious reward of clemency and virtue.

"Such were the benevolent inclinations of your ancestors. Whilst they pursued their great and generous principles wheresoever they directed their steps, conquest and prosperity went before them; and then they reduced many countries and fortresses to their obedience. During your Majesty's reign many have been alienated from the empire, and further loss of territory must necessarily follow, since devastation and rapine now universally prevail without restraint. Your subjects are trampled underfoot, and every province of your empire is impoverished; depopulation spreads, and difficulties accumulate; and when indigence has reached the habitation of the Sovereign and his princes, what can be the condition of the nobles? As to the soldiery, they are in murmurs, the merchants complaining, the Mohammedans discontented, the Hindoos destitute, and multitudes of people, wretched even to the want of their nightly meal, are beating their heads throughout the day in rage and desperation.

"How can the dignity of the Sovereign be preserved, who employs his power in exacting heavy tributes from a people thus miserably reduced? At this juncture it is told from east to west, that the Emperor of Hindostan, jealous of the poor Hindoo devotees, will exact a tribute from Brahmins, Sanorahs, Joghies, Berawghies, Sanyasees; that, regardless of the illustrious honour of his Timurian race, he condescends to exercise his power over the solitary inoffensive anchorites! If your Majesty places any faith in those books, by distinction called divine, you will there be instructed that God is the God of all mankind, not the God of Mohammedans alone. Pagans and Mohammedans are equal in His presence, distinction of colour are of His ordination. It is He who gives existence. In your temples to His name the voice is raised in prayer; in the House of Images, where the bell is shaken, still He is the object of adoration: to vilify the religion or customs of other men is to set at naught the pleasure of the Almighty; when we deface the picture, we naturally incur the resentment of the painter; and justly has the poet said, 'Presume not to arraign or scrutinize the various works of Power Divine.'

"In fine, the tribute you demand from the Hindoos is repugnant to justice; it is equally foreign from good policy, as it must impoverish the country. Moreover, it is an innovation and an infringement of the laws of Hindostan. But if zeal for your own religion hath induced you to determine upon this measure, the demand ought, by the rules of equity, to have been made first upon Ram Sing, who is esteemed the principal among the Hindoos. Then let your well-wisher be called upon, with whom you will have less difficulty to encounter; but to torment ants and flies is unworthy of an heroic or generous mind. It is wonderful that the Ministers of your Government should have neglected to instruct your Majesty in the rule of rectitude and honour."

DALZIEL BROTHERS · Camden Press · ENGRAVERS & PRINTERS

11, *Henrietta Street, Covent Garden, W.C.*
(*Late* 193, *Piccadilly, W.*)

*June*, 1884.

# CATALOGUE OF BOOKS

PUBLISHED BY

# CHAPMAN & HALL,

LIMITED,

INCLUDING

DRAWING EXAMPLES, DIAGRAMS, MODELS,
INSTRUMENTS, ETC.

ISSUED UNDER THE AUTHORITY OF

## THE SCIENCE AND ART DEPARTMENT, SOUTH KENSINGTON,

FOR THE USE OF SCHOOLS AND ART AND SCIENCE CLASSES.

# MILITARY BIOGRAPHIES.

Messrs. CHAPMAN & HALL are preparing for publication a Series of Volumes dedicated to the Lives of Great Military Commanders.

The volumes are designed to form a set of critical Biographies, illustrative of the operations and the art of war, by writers of distinction in the profession of arms, whose competence to weigh the military qualities and deeds of the Chiefs can be accepted. Maps will, when necessary, accompany the volumes, for the convenience of students.

The aim of these volumes is to be both popular and scientific, combining the narrative of the most romantic and instructive of human lives with a clear examination of the genius of the soldier.

"FREDERICK THE GREAT," by Col. C. B. BRACKENBURY, containing Maps, is now ready, price 4s.

"MARSHAL LOUDON," by Col. MALLESON, C.S.I., will follow it; the two Lives presenting the opposing aspects of the Seven Years' War.

# BOOKS

PUBLISHED BY

# CHAPMAN & HALL, LIMITED.

*ABBOTT (EDWIN), formerly Head Master of the Philological School*—

A CONCORDANCE OF THE ORIGINAL POETICAL WORKS OF ALEXANDER POPE. Medium 8vo, 21s.

*ADAMS (FRANCIS)*—

HISTORY OF THE ELEMENTARY SCHOOL CONTEST IN ENGLAND. Demy 8vo, 6s.

*BADEN-POWELL (GEORGE)*—

STATE AID AND STATE INTERFERENCE. Illustrated by Results in Commerce and Industry. Crown 8vo, 9s.

*BARTLEY (G. C. T.)*—

A HANDY BOOK FOR GUARDIANS OF THE POOR. Crown 8vo, cloth, 3s.

THE PARISH NET: HOW IT'S DRAGGED AND WHAT IT CATCHES. Crown 8vo, cloth, 7s. 6d.

THE SEVEN AGES OF A VILLAGE PAUPER. Crown 8vo, cloth, 5s.

BAYARD: HISTORY OF THE GOOD CHEVALIER, SANS PEUR ET SANS REPROCHE. Compiled by the LOYAL SERVITEUR; translated into English from the French of Loredan Larchey. With over 200 Illustrations. Royal 8vo, 21s.

*BEESLEY (EDWARD SPENCER)*—

CATILINE, CLODIUS, AND TIBERIUS. Large crown 8vo, 6s.

*BELL (DR. JAMES), Principal of the Somerset House Laboratory*—

THE CHEMISTRY OF FOODS. With Microscopic Illustrations.

PART I. TEA, COFFEE, SUGAR, ETC. Large crown 8vo, 2s. 6d.

PART II. MILK, BUTTER, CEREALS, PREPARED STARCHES, ETC. Large Crown 8vo, 3s.

*BENNET (WILLIAM) The Late*—

KING OF THE PEAK: a Romance. With Portrait. Crown 8vo, 6s.

*BENSON (W.)*—

MANUAL OF THE SCIENCE OF COLOUR. Coloured Frontispiece and Illustrations. 12mo, cloth, 2s. 6d.

PRINCIPLES OF THE SCIENCE OF COLOUR. Small 4to, cloth, 15s.

*BINGHAM (CAPT. THE HON. D.)*—

A SELECTION FROM THE LETTERS AND DESPATCHES OF THE FIRST NAPOLEON. With Explanatory Notes. 3 vols. demy 8vo. [*In the Press.*

*BIRDWOOD (SIR GEORGE C. M.), C.S.I.*—

THE INDUSTRIAL ARTS OF INDIA. With Map and 174 Illustrations. New Edition. Demy 8vo, 14s.

*BLACKIE (JOHN STUART) F.R.S.E.*—

ALTAVONA: FACT AND FICTION FROM MY LIFE IN THE HIGHLANDS. Third Edition. Crown 8vo, 6s.

*BLAKE (EDITH OSBORNE)*—

THE REALITIES OF FREEMASONRY. Demy 8vo, 9s.

*BLATHERWICK (DR.)*—

PERSONAL RECOLLECTIONS OF PETER STONNOR, Esq. With Illustrations by JAMES GUTHRIE and A. S. BOYD. Large crown 8vo, 6s.

*BOYLE (FREDERICK)*—

ON THE BORDERLAND—BETWIXT THE REALMS OF FACT AND FANCY. Crown 8vo, 10s. 6d.

*BRADLEY (THOMAS), of the Royal Military Academy, Woolwich*—

ELEMENTS OF GEOMETRICAL DRAWING. In Two Parts, with Sixty Plates. Oblong folio, half bound, each Part 16s.

*BRAY (MRS.)*—

AUTOBIOGRAPHY OF (born 1789, died 1883). Author of the "Life of Thomas Stothard, R.A.," "The White Hoods," &c. Edited by JOHN A. KEMPE. With Portraits. Crown 8vo, 10s. 6d.

## MRS. BRAY'S NOVELS AND ROMANCES.

*New and Revised Editions, with Frontispieces. 3s. 6d. each.*

THE WHITE HOODS; a Romance of Flanders.
DE FOIX; a Romance of Bearn.
THE TALBA; or, The Moor of Portugal.
THE PROTESTANT; a Tale of the Times of Queen Mary.

NOVELS FOUNDED ON TRADITIONS OF DEVON AND CORNWALL.

FITZ OF FITZFORD; a Tale of Destiny.
HENRY DE POMEROY. [*In the Press.*
TRELAWNY OF TRELAWNE. [*In the Press.*
WARLEIGH; or, The Fatal Oak.
COURTENAY OF WALREDDON. [*In the Press.*
HARTLAND FOREST AND ROSE-TEAGUE. [*In the Press.*

MISCELLANEOUS TALES.

A FATHER'S CURSE AND A DAUGHTER'S SACRIFICE. [*In the Press.*
TRIALS OF THE HEART. [*In the Press.*

*BROADLEY (A. M.)*—

HOW WE DEFENDED ARABI AND HIS FRIENDS. A Story of Egypt and the Egyptians. Illustrated by FREDERICK VILLIERS. Second Edition. Demy 8vo. 12s.

*BUCKLAND (FRANK)*—

LOG-BOOK OF A FISHERMAN AND ZOOLOGIST. Fourth Thousand. With numerous Illustrations. Crown 8vo, 5s.

*BURCHETT (R.)*—

DEFINITIONS OF GEOMETRY. New Edition. 24mo, cloth, 5d.

LINEAR PERSPECTIVE, for the Use of Schools of Art. Twenty-first Thousand. With Illustrations. Post 8vo, cloth, 7s.

PRACTICAL GEOMETRY: The Course of Construction of Plane Geometrical Figures. With 137 Diagrams. Eighteenth Edition. Post 8vo, cloth, 5s.

*BURNAND (F. C.), B.A., Trin. Coll. Camb.*—

THE "A. D. C.;" being Personal Reminiscences of the University Amateur Dramatic Club, Cambridge. Second Edition. Demy 8vo, 12s.

*CAMPION (J. S.)*—

ON THE FRONTIER. Reminiscences of Wild Sports, Personal Adventures, and Strange Scenes. With Illustrations. Second Edition. Demy 8vo, 16s.

ON FOOT IN SPAIN. With Illustrations. Second Edition. Demy 8vo, 16s.

*CARLYLE (THOMAS)*—*See pages 18 and 19.*

CARLYLE BIRTHDAY BOOK (THE). Prepared by Permission of Mr. THOMAS CARLYLE. Small crown, 3s.

*CHAMPEAUX (ALFRED)*—

TAPESTRY. With Woodcuts. Cloth, 2s. 6d.

CHRISTIANITY AND COMMON SENSE. A Plea for the Worship of our Heavenly Father, and also for the Opening of Museums and Galleries on Sundays. By a BARRISTER. Demy 8vo, 7s. 6d.

*CHURCH (A. H.), M.A., Oxon.*—

PLAIN WORDS ABOUT WATER. Illustrated. Large crown 8vo, sewed, 6d.

FOOD: A Short Account of the Sources, Constituents, and Uses of Food. Large crown 8vo, cloth, 3s.

PRECIOUS STONES: considered in their Scientific and Artistic Relations. With Illustrations. Large crown 8vo, 2s. 6d.

*CLINTON (R. H.)*—

A COMPENDIUM OF ENGLISH HISTORY, from the Earliest Times to A.D. 1872. With Copious Quotations on the Leading Events and the Constitutional History, together with Appendices. Post 8vo, 7s. 6d.

COBDEN, RICHARD, LIFE OF. BY JOHN MORLEY. With Portrait. In 2 vols., demy 8vo, 32s.

New Edition. Portrait. Large crown 8vo, 7s. 6d.

Popular Edition, with Portrait, sewed, 1s.; cloth, 2s.

## CHAPMAN & HALL'S SERIES OF POPULAR NOVELS.

*New and Cheaper Editions of Popular Novels. Crown 8vo.*

THE RIGHT SORT. A Romance of the Shires. By MRS. EDWARD KENNARD. Illustrated, 6s.
FAUCIT OF BALLIOL. By HERMAN MERIVALE. 6s.
AN AUSTRALIAN HEROINE. By MRS. CAMPBELL PRAED. 6s.
HARD LINES. By HAWLEY SMART. 6s.
STORY OF AN AFRICAN FARM. By RALPH IRON. 5s.
NADINE. A Study of a Woman. By MRS. CAMPBELL PRAED. 5s.
TO LEEWARD. By F. MARION CRAWFORD. New Edition. 5s.

*COLENSO (FRANCES E.)*—

HISTORY OF THE ZULU WAR AND ITS ORIGIN. Assisted in those portions of the work which touch upon Military Matters by Lieut.-Colonel EDWARD DURNFORD. Demy 8vo, 18s.

*COOKERY*—

OFFICIAL HANDBOOK FOR THE NATIONAL TRAINING SCHOOL FOR COOKERY. Containing Lessons on Cookery; forming the Course of Instruction in the School. Compiled by "R. O. C." Twelfth Thousand. Large crown 8vo, 8s

HOW TO COOK FISH. A Series of Lessons in Cookery, from the Official Handbook to the National Training School for Cookery, South Kensington. Compiled by "R. O. C." Crown 8vo, sewed. 3d.

SICK-ROOM COOKERY. From the Official Handbook for the National School for Cookery, South Kensington. Compiled by "R. O. C." Crown 8vo, sewed, 6d.

*CRAIK (GEORGE LILLIE)*—

ENGLISH OF SHAKESPEARE. Illustrated in a Philological Commentary on his Julius Cæsar. Sixth Edition. Post 8vo, cloth, 5s.

OUTLINES OF THE HISTORY OF THE ENGLISH LANGUAGE. Ninth Edition. Post 8vo, cloth, 2s. 6d.

*CRAWFORD (F. MARION)*—

TO LEEWARD. New Edition. Crown 8vo, 5s.

*CRIPPS (WILFRED)*—

COLLEGE AND CORPORATION PLATE. With numerous Illustrations. Large crown 8vo, cloth, 2s. 6d.

DAME TROT AND HER PIG (The Wonderful History of). With Coloured Illustrations. Crown 4to, 3s. 6d.

*DAUBOURG (E.)*—

INTERIOR ARCHITECTURE. Doors, Vestibules, Staircases, Anterooms, Drawing, Dining, and Bed Rooms, Libraries, Bank and Newspaper Offices, Shop Fronts and Interiors. Half-imperial, cloth, £2 12s. 6d.

*DAVIDSON (ELLIS A.)*—

PRETTY ARTS FOR THE EMPLOYMENT OF LEISURE HOURS. A Book for Ladies. With Illustrations. Demy 8vo, 6s.

THE AMATEUR HOUSE CARPENTER: a Guide in Building, Making, and Repairing. With numerous Illustrations, drawn on Wood by the Author. Royal 8vo, 10s. 6d.

*DAVISON (THE MISSES)*—

TRIQUETI MARBLES IN THE ALBERT MEMORIAL CHAPEL, WINDSOR. A Series of Photographs. Dedicated by express permission to Her Majesty the Queen. The Work consists of 117 Photographs, with descriptive Letterpress, mounted on 49 sheets of cardboard, half-imperial. £10 10s.

*DAY (WILLIAM)*—

THE RACEHORSE IN TRAINING, with Hints on Racing and Racing Reform, to which is added a Chapter on Shoeing. Fourth Edition. Demy 8vo, 12s.

*D'HAUSSONVILLE (VICOMTE)*—

SALON OF MADAME NECKER. Translated by H. M. TROLLOPE. 2 vols. Crown 8vo, 18s.

*DE KONINCK (L. L.) and DIETZ (E.)*—

PRACTICAL MANUAL OF CHEMICAL ASSAYING, as applied to the Manufacture of Iron. Edited, with notes, by ROBERT MALLET. Post 8vo, cloth, 6s.

*DICKENS (CHARLES)*—*See pages 20–24.*

THE LETTERS OF CHARLES DICKENS. Edited by his Sister-in-Law and his Eldest Daughter. Two vols. uniform with "The Charles Dickens Edition" of his Works. Crown 8vo, 8s.

THE CHARLES DICKENS BIRTHDAY BOOK. Compiled and Edited by his Eldest Daughter. With Five Illustrations by his Youngest Daughter. In a handsome fcap. 4to volume, 12s.

*DIXON (W. HEPWORTH)*—

BRITISH CYPRUS. With Frontispiece. Demy 8vo, 15s.

*DRAYSON (LIEUT.-COL. A. W.)*—

THE CAUSE OF THE SUPPOSED PROPER MOTION OF THE FIXED STARS. Demy 8vo, cloth, 10s.

THE CAUSE, DATE, AND DURATION OF THE LAST GLACIAL EPOCH OF GEOLOGY. Demy 8vo, cloth, 10s.

PRACTICAL MILITARY SURVEYING AND SKETCHING. Fifth Edition. Post 8vo, cloth, 4s. 6d.

DYCE'S COLLECTION. A Catalogue of Printed Books and Manuscripts bequeathed by the REV. ALEXANDER DYCE to the South Kensington Museum. 2 vols. Royal 8vo, half-morocco, 14s.

A Collection of Paintings, Miniatures, Drawings, Engravings, Rings, and Miscellaneous Objects, bequeathed by the REV. ALEXANDER DYCE to the South Kensington Museum. Royal 8vo, half-morocco, 6s. 6d.

*DYCE (WILLIAM), R.A.*—

DRAWING-BOOK OF THE GOVERNMENT SCHOOL OF DESIGN; OR, ELEMENTARY OUTLINES OF ORNAMENT. Fifty selected Plates. Folio, sewed, 5s.; mounted, 18s.

Text to Ditto. Sewed, 6d.

*EGYPTIAN ART*—

A HISTORY OF ART IN ANCIENT EGYPT. By G. PERROT and C. CHIPIEZ. Translated by WALTER ARMSTRONG. With over 600 Illustrations. 2 vols. Royal 8vo, £2 2s.

*ELLIS (CAPTAIN A. B.)*—

THE LAND OF FETISH. Demy 8vo. 12s.

*ENGEL (CARL)*—

A DESCRIPTIVE AND ILLUSTRATED CATALOGUE OF THE MUSICAL INSTRUMENTS in the SOUTH KENSINGTON MUSEUM, preceded by an Essay on the History of Musical Instruments. Second Edition. Royal 8vo, half-morocco, 12s.

MUSICAL INSTRUMENTS. With numerous Woodcuts. Large crown 8vo, cloth, 2s. 6d.

*ESCOTT (T. H. S.)*—

PILLARS OF THE EMPIRE: Short Biographical Sketches. Demy 8vo, 10s. 6d.

*EWALD (ALEXANDER CHARLES), F.S.A.*—

REPRESENTATIVE STATESMEN: Political Studies. 2 vols. Large crown 8vo, £1 4s.

SIR ROBERT WALPOLE. A Political Biography, 1676–1745. Demy 8vo, 18s.

*FANE (VIOLET)*—

QUEEN OF THE FAIRIES (A Village Story), and other Poems. Crown 8vo, 6s.

ANTHONY BABINGTON: a Drama. Crown 8vo, 6s.

*FEARNLEY (W.)*—

LESSONS IN HORSE JUDGING, AND THE SUMMERING OF HUNTERS. With Illustrations. Crown 8vo, 4s.

*FITZ-PATRICK (W. J.)*—

LIFE OF CHARLES LEVER. 2 vols. Demy 8vo, 30s.

*FLEMING (GEORGE), F.R.C.S.*—

ANIMAL PLAGUES: THEIR HISTORY, NATURE, AND PREVENTION. 8vo, cloth, 15s.

PRACTICAL HORSE-SHOEING. With 37 Illustrations. Second Edition, enlarged. 8vo, sewed, 2s.

RABIES AND HYDROPHOBIA: THEIR HISTORY, NATURE, CAUSES, SYMPTOMS, AND PREVENTION. With 8 Illustrations. 8vo, cloth, 15s.

A MANUAL OF VETERINARY SANITARY SCIENCE AND POLICE. With 33 Illustrations. 2 vols. Demy 8vo, 36s.

*FORSTER (JOHN), M.P. for Berwick*—

THE CHRONICLE OF JAMES I., KING OF ARAGON, SURNAMED THE CONQUEROR. Written by Himself. Translated from the Catalan by the late JOHN FORSTER, M.P. for Berwick. With an Historical Introduction by DON PASCUAL DE GAYANGOS. 2 vols. Royal 8vo, 28s.

*FORSTER (JOHN)*—

THE LIFE OF CHARLES DICKENS. With Portraits and other Illustrations. 15th Thousand. 3 vols. 8vo, cloth, £2 2s.

THE LIFE OF CHARLES DICKENS. Uniform with the Illustrated Library Edition of Dickens's Works. 2 vols. Demy 8vo, £1 8s.

THE LIFE OF CHARLES DICKENS. Uniform with the Library Edition. Post 8vo, 10s. 6d.

THE LIFE OF CHARLES DICKENS. Uniform with the "C. D." Edition. With Numerous Illustrations. 2 vols. 7s.

THE LIFE OF CHARLES DICKENS. Uniform with the Household Edition. With Illustrations by F. BARNARD. Crown 4to, cloth, 5s.

WALTER SAVAGE LANDOR: a Biography, 1775–1864. With Portrait. A New and Revised Edition. Demy 8vo, 12s.

*FORTNIGHTLY REVIEW*—

FORTNIGHTLY REVIEW.—First Series, May, 1865, to Dec. 1866. 6 vols. Cloth, 13s. each.

New Series, 1867 to 1872. In Half-yearly Volumes. Cloth, 13s. each.

From January, 1873, to the present time, in Half-yearly Volumes. Cloth, 16s. each.

CONTENTS OF FORTNIGHTLY REVIEW. From the commencement to end of 1878. Sewed, 2s.

*FORTNUM (C. D. E.)*—

A DESCRIPTIVE AND ILLUSTRATED CATALOGUE OF THE BRONZES OF EUROPEAN ORIGIN in the SOUTH KENSINGTON MUSEUM, with an Introductory Notice. Royal 8vo, half-morocco, £1 10s.

A DESCRIPTIVE AND ILLUSTRATED CATALOGUE OF MAIOLICA, HISPANO-MORESCO, PERSIAN, DAMASCUS, AND RHODIAN WARES in the SOUTH KENSINGTON MUSEUM. Royal 8vo, half-morocco, £2.

MAIOLICA. With numerous Woodcuts. Large crown 8vo, cloth, 2s. 6d.

BRONZES. With numerous Woodcuts. Large crown 8vo, cloth, 2s. 6d.

*FRANCATELLI (C. E.)*—

ROYAL CONFECTIONER: English and Foreign. A Practical Treatise. New and Cheap Edition. With Illustrations. Crown 8vo, 5s.

*FRANKS (A. W.)*—

JAPANESE POTTERY. Being a Native Report. Numerous Illustrations and Marks. Large crown 8vo, cloth, 2s. 6d.

*GALLENGA (ANTONIO)*—

IBERIAN REMINISCENCES. Fifteen Years' Travelling Impressions of Spain and Portugal. With a Map. 2 vols. Demy 8vo, 32s.

A SUMMER TOUR IN RUSSIA. With a Map. Demy 8vo, 14s.

*GORST (J. E.), Q.C., M.P.*—

An ELECTION MANUAL. Containing the Parliamentary Elections (Corrupt and Illegal Practices) Act, 1883, with Notes. New Edition. Crown 8vo, 2s. 6d.

*GRIFFIN (SIR LEPEL HENRY), K.C.S.I.*—

THE GREAT REPUBLIC. Crown 8vo. [*In the Press.*

*GRIFFITHS (MAJOR ARTHUR), H.M. Inspector of Prisons*—

CHRONICLES OF NEWGATE. Illustrated. New Edition. Demy 8vo, 16s.

MEMORIALS OF MILLBANK. With Illustrations. New Edition. Demy 8vo. [*In the Press.*

*HALL (SIDNEY)*—

A TRAVELLING ATLAS OF THE ENGLISH COUNTIES. Fifty Maps, coloured. New Edition, including the Railways, corrected up to the present date. Demy 8vo, in roan tuck, 10s. 6d.

*HARDY (LADY DUFFUS)*—

DOWN SOUTH. Demy 8vo. 14s.

THROUGH CITIES AND PRAIRIE LANDS. Sketches of an American Tour. Demy 8vo, 14s.

*HATTON (JOSEPH) and HARVEY (REV. M.)*—

NEWFOUNDLAND. The Oldest British Colony. Its History, Past and Present, and its Prospects in the Future. Illustrated from Photographs and Sketches specially made for this work. Demy 8vo, 18s.

TO-DAY IN AMERICA. Studies for the Old World and the New. 2 vols. Crown 8vo, 18s.

*HEAPHY (MUSGRAVE)*—

GLIMPSES AND GLEAMS. Crown 8vo, 5s.

*HILDEBRAND (HANS)*—
INDUSTRIAL ARTS OF SCANDINAVIA IN THE PAGAN TIME. Illustrated. Large crown 8vo, 2s. 6d.

*HILL (MISS G.)*—
THE PLEASURES AND PROFITS OF OUR LITTLE POULTRY FARM. Small crown 8vo, 3s.

*HITCHMAN (FRANCIS)*—
THE PUBLIC LIFE OF THE EARL OF BEACONSFIELD. 2 vols. Demy 8vo, £1 12s.

*HOLBEIN*—
TWELVE HEADS AFTER HOLBEIN. Selected from Drawings in Her Majesty's Collection at Windsor. Reproduced in Autotype, in portfolio. £1 16s.

*HOLLINGSHEAD (JOHN)*—
FOOTLIGHTS. Crown 8vo. 7s. 6d.

*HOVELACQUE (ABEL)*—
THE SCIENCE OF LANGUAGE: LINGUISTICS, PHILOLOGY, AND ETYMOLOGY. With Maps. Large crown 8vo, cloth, 5s.

HOW I BECAME A SPORTSMAN. By "AVON." Crown 8vo. 6s.

*HUMPHRIS (H. D.)*—
PRINCIPLES OF PERSPECTIVE. Illustrated in a Series of Examples. Oblong folio, half-bound, and Text 8vo, cloth, £1 1s.

HUNT-ROOM STORIES AND YACHTING YARNS. By "WANDERER," the Author of "Across Country," "Fair Diana," &c. With Illustrations by EDGAR GIBERNE. Demy 8vo. 12s.

*IRON (RALPH)*—
THE STORY OF AN AFRICAN FARM. New Edition. Crown 8vo, 5s.

JAMES I., KING OF ARAGON (THE CHRONICLE OF), SURNAMED THE CONQUEROR. Written by Himself. Translated from the Catalan by the late JOHN FORSTER, M.P. for Berwick. With an Historical Introduction by DON PASCUAL DE GAYANGOS. 2 vols. Royal 8vo. 28s.

*JARRY (GENERAL)*—
OUTPOST DUTY. Translated, with TREATISES ON MILITARY RECONNAISSANCE AND ON ROAD-MAKING. By Major-Gen. W. C. E. NAPIER. Third Edition. Crown 8vo, 5s.

*JEANS (W. T.)*—
CREATORS OF THE AGE OF STEEL. Memoirs of Sir W. Siemens, Sir H. Bessemer, Sir J. Whitworth, Sir J. Brown, and other Inventors. Crown 8vo, 7s. 6d.

*JOHNSON (DR. SAMUEL)*—
LIFE AND CONVERSATIONS. By A. MAIN. Crown 8vo, 10s. 6d.

*JONES (CAPTAIN DOUGLAS), R.A.*—
NOTES ON MILITARY LAW. Crown 8vo, 4s.

JONES COLLECTION (HANDBOOK OF THE) IN THE SOUTH KENSINGTON MUSEUM. Illustrated. Large crown 8vo, 2s. 6d.

*KEMPIS (THOMAS À)*—
OF THE IMITATION OF CHRIST. Four Books. Beautifully Illustrated Edition. Demy 8vo, 16s.

*KENT (CHARLES)*—
HUMOUR AND PATHOS OF CHARLES DICKENS, WITH ILLUSTRATIONS OF HIS MASTERY OF THE TERRIBLE AND PICTURESQUE. Portrait. Crown 8vo. 6s.

*KLACZKO (M. JULIAN)*—
TWO CHANCELLORS: PRINCE GORTCHAKOF AND PRINCE BISMARCK. Translated by MRS. TAIT. New and cheaper Edition, 6s.

LACORDAIRE'S CONFERENCES. JESUS CHRIST, GOD, AND GOD AND MAN. New Edition in 1 vol. Crown 8vo, 6s.

*LAVELEYE (EMILE DE)*—

THE ELEMENTS OF POLITICAL ECONOMY. Translated by W. POLLARD B.A., St. John's College, Oxford. Crown 8vo, 6s.

*LEFÈVRE (ANDRÉ)*—

PHILOSOPHY, Historical and Critical. Translated, with an Introduction, by A. W. KEANE, B.A. Large crown 8vo, 7s. 6d.

*LETOURNEAU (DR. CHARLES)*—

SOCIOLOGY. Based upon Ethnology. Translated by HENRY M. TROLLOPE. Large crown 8vo, 10s.

BIOLOGY. Translated by WILLIAM MACCALL. With Illustrations. Large crown 8vo, 6s.

*LILLY (W. S.)*—

ANCIENT RELIGION AND MODERN THOUGHT. One vol. demy 8vo, 12s.

*LOW (C. R.)*—

SOLDIERS OF THE VICTORIAN AGE. 2 vols. Demy 8vo, £1 10s.

*LUCAS (CAPTAIN)*—

THE ZULUS AND THE BRITISH FRONTIER. Demy 8vo, 16s.

CAMP LIFE AND SPORT IN SOUTH AFRICA. With Episodes in Kaffir Warfare. With Illustrations. Demy 8vo. 12s.

*LYTTON (ROBERT, EARL)*—

POETICAL WORKS—

FABLES IN SONG. 2 vols. Fcap. 8vo, 12s.
THE WANDERER. Fcap. 8vo, 6s.
POEMS, HISTORICAL AND CHARACTERISTIC. Fcap. 6s.

*MACEWEN (CONSTANCE)*—

ROUGH DIAMONDS; OR, SKETCHES FROM REAL LIFE. Crown 8vo, 3s. 6d.

*MALLET (DR. J. W.)*—

COTTON: THE CHEMICAL, &c., CONDITIONS OF ITS SUCCESSFUL CULTIVATION. Post 8vo, cloth, 7s. 6d.

*MALLET (ROBERT)*—

PRACTICAL MANUAL OF CHEMICAL ASSAYING, as applied to the Manufacture of Iron. By L. L. DE KONINCK and E. DIETZ. Edited, with notes, by ROBERT MALLET. Post 8vo, cloth, 6s.

GREAT NEAPOLITAN EARTHQUAKE OF 1857. First Principles of Observational Seismology, as developed in the Report to the Royal Society of London. Maps and numerous Illustrations. 2 vols. Royal 8vo, cloth, £3 3s.

*MASKELL (WILLIAM)*—

A DESCRIPTION OF THE IVORIES, ANCIENT AND MEDIÆVAL, in the SOUTH KENSINGTON MUSEUM, with a Preface. With numerous Photographs and Woodcuts. Royal 8vo, half-morocco, £1 1s.

IVORIES: ANCIENT AND MEDIÆVAL. With numerous Woodcuts. Large crown 8vo, cloth, 2s. 6d.

HANDBOOK TO THE DYCE AND FORSTER COLLECTIONS. With Illustrations. Large crown 8vo, cloth, 2s. 6d.

*McCOAN (J. CARLILE)*—

OUR NEW PROTECTORATE. TURKEY IN ASIA: ITS GEOGRAPHY, RACES, RESOURCES, AND GOVERNMENT. With Map. 2 vols. Large crown 8vo, £1 4s.

*MEREDITH (GEORGE)*—

MODERN LOVE AND POEMS OF THE ENGLISH ROADSIDE, WITH POEMS AND BALLADS. Fcap. cloth, 6s.

*MERIVALE (HERMAN CHARLES)*—

BINKO'S BLUES. A Tale for Children of all Growths. Illustrated by EDGAR GIBERNE. Small crown 8vo, 5s.

THE WHITE PILGRIM, and other Poems. Crown 8vo, 9s.

FAUCIT OF BALLIOL. Crown 8vo, 6s.

MILITARY BIOGRAPHIES.

FREDERICK THE GREAT. By COL. C. B. BRACKENBURY; containing Maps and Portrait Crown 8vo, 4s.

MARSHAL LOUDON. By COL. MALLESON, C.S.I., will follow it, the two Lives presenting the opposing aspects of the Seven Years' War. [*In the Press.*

*MOLESWORTH (W. NASSAU)*—

HISTORY OF ENGLAND FROM THE YEAR 1830 TO THE RESIGNATION OF THE GLADSTONE MINISTRY, 1874. 3 vols. Crown 8vo, 18s.

ABRIDGED EDITION. Large crown, 7s. 6d.

*MORLEY (HENRY)*—

ENGLISH WRITERS. Vol. I. Part I. THE CELTS AND ANGLO-SAXONS. With an Introductory Sketch of the Four Periods of English Literature. Part II. FROM THE CONQUEST TO CHAUCER. (Making 2 vols.) 8vo, cloth, £1 2s.

Vol. II. Part I. FROM CHAUCER TO DUNBAR. 8vo, cloth, 12s.

TABLES OF ENGLISH LITERATURE. Containing 20 Charts. Second Edition, with Index. Royal 4to, cloth, 12s.
In Three Parts. Parts I. and II., containing Three Charts, each 1s. 6d.
Part III., containing 14 Charts, 7s. Part III. also kept in Sections, 1, 2, and 5, 1s. 6d. each; 3 and 4 together, 3s. *** The Charts sold separately.

*MORLEY (JOHN)*—

LIFE OF RICHARD COBDEN. With Portrait. Popular Edition. 4to, sewed, 1s. Bound in cloth, 2s.

LIFE AND CORRESPONDENCE OF RICHARD COBDEN. Fourth Thousand. 2 vols. Demy 8vo, £1 12s.

DIDEROT AND THE ENCYCLOPÆDISTS. 2 vols. Demy 8vo, £1 6s.

**NEW UNIFORM EDITION.**

LIFE OF RICHARD COBDEN. With Portrait. Large crown 8vo, 7s. 6d.

VOLTAIRE. Large crown 8vo, 6s.

ROUSSEAU. Large crown 8vo, 9s.

DIDEROT AND THE ENCYCLOPÆDISTS. Large crown 8vo, 12s.

CRITICAL MISCELLANIES. First Series. Large crown 8vo, 6s.

CRITICAL MISCELLANIES. Second Series. [*In the Press.*

ON COMPROMISE. New Edition. Large crown 8vo, 3s. 6d.

STRUGGLE FOR NATIONAL EDUCATION. Third Edition. Demy 8vo, cloth, 3s.

*MUNTZ (EUGÈNE), From the French of*—

RAPHAEL: HIS LIFE, WORKS, AND TIMES. Edited by W. ARMSTRONG. Illustrated with 155 Wood Engravings and 41 Full-page Plates. Imperial 8vo, 36s.

*MURPHY (J. M.)*—

RAMBLES IN NORTH-WEST AMERICA. With Frontispiece and Map. 8vo, 16s.

*MURRAY (ANDREW), F.L.S.*—

ECONOMIC ENTOMOLOGY. APTERA. With numerous Illustrations. Large crown 8vo, 7s. 6d.

*NAPIER (MAJ.-GEN. W. C. E.)*—

TRANSLATION OF GEN. JARRY'S OUTPOST DUTY. With TREATISES ON MILITARY RECONNAISSANCE AND ON ROAD-MAKING. Third Edition. Crown 8vo, 5s.

NAPOLEON. A Selection from the Letters and Despatches of the First Napoleon. With Explanatory Notes by Captain the Hon. D. BINGHAM. 3 vols. demy 8vo. [*In the Press.*

*NECKER (MADAME)*—

THE SALON OF MADAME NECKER. By VICOMTE D'HAUSSONVILLE. Translated by H. M. TROLLOPE. 2 vols. Crown 8vo, 18s.

*NESBITT (ALEXANDER)*—

GLASS. Illustrated. Large crown 8vo, cloth, 2s. 6d.

*NEVINSON (HENRY)*—

A SKETCH OF HERDER AND HIS TIMES. With a Portrait. Demy 8vo, 14s.

*NEWTON (E. TULLEY), F.G.S.*—

THE TYPICAL PARTS IN THE SKELETONS OF A CAT, DUCK, AND CODFISH, being a Catalogue with Comparative Description arranged in a Tabular form. Demy 8vo, cloth, 3s.

*NORMAN (C. B.), late of the 90th Light Infantry and Bengal Staff Corps*—

TONKIN; OR, FRANCE IN THE FAR EAST. Demy 8vo, with Maps, 14s.

*OLIVER (PROFESSOR), F.R.S., &c.*—

ILLUSTRATIONS OF THE PRINCIPAL NATURAL ORDERS OF THE VEGETABLE KINGDOM, PREPARED FOR THE SCIENCE AND ART DEPARTMENT, SOUTH KENSINGTON. With 109 Plates. Oblong 8vo, plain, 16s.; coloured, £1 6s.

*OXENHAM (REV. H. N.)*—

SHORT STUDIES IN ECCLESIASTICAL HISTORY AND BIOGRAPHY. Demy 8vo. [*May 15th.*

*PERROT (GEORGES) and CHIPIEZ (CHARLES)*—

CHALDÆA AND ASSYRIA, A HISTORY OF ART IN. Translated by WALTER ARMSTRONG, B.A. Oxon. With 452 Illustrations. 2 vols. Demy 8vo. Uniform with "Ancient Egyptian Art." 42s.

ANCIENT EGYPT, A HISTORY OF ART IN. Translated from the French by W. ARMSTRONG. With over 600 Illustrations. 2 vols. Imperial 8vo, 42s.

*PITT-TAYLOR (FRANK)*—

THE CANTERBURY TALES. Being Selections from the Tales of GEOFFREY CHAUCER rendered into Modern English, with close adherence to the language of the Poet. With Frontispiece. Crown 8vo, 6s.

*POLLEN (J. H.)*—

ANCIENT AND MODERN FURNITURE AND WOODWORK IN THE SOUTH KENSINGTON MUSEUM. With an Introduction, and Illustrated with numerous Coloured Photographs and Woodcuts. Royal 8vo, half-morocco, £1 1s.

GOLD AND SILVER SMITH'S WORK. With numerous Woodcuts. Large crown 8vo, cloth, 2s. 6d.

ANCIENT AND MODERN FURNITURE AND WOODWORK. With numerous Woodcuts. Large crown 8vo, cloth, 2s. 6d.

*POLLOK (LIEUT.-COLONEL)*—

SPORT IN BRITISH BURMAH, ASSAM, AND THE CASSYAH AND JYNTIAH HILLS. With Notes of Sport in the Hilly Districts of the Northern Division, Madras Presidency. With Illustrations and 2 Maps. 2 vols. Demy 8vo, £1 4s.

*POYNTER (E. J.), R.A.*—
TEN LECTURES ON ART. Second Edition. Large crown 8vo, 9s.

*PRAED (MRS. CAMPBELL)*—
AN AUSTRALIAN HEROINE. Cheap Edition. Crown 8vo, 6s.
NADINE. Cheap Edition. Crown 8vo, 5s.
MOLOCH. Cheap Edition. [*In the Press.*

*PRINSEP (VAL), A.R.A.*—
IMPERIAL INDIA. Containing numerous Illustrations and Maps made during a Tour to the Courts of the Principal Rajahs and Princes of India. Second Edition. Demy 8vo, £1 1s.

*PUCKETT (R. CAMPBELL), Ph.D., Bonn University*—
SCIOGRAPHY; or, Radial Projection of Shadows. Third Edition. Crown 8vo, cloth, 6s.

*RAMSDEN (LADY GWENDOLEN)*—
A BIRTHDAY BOOK. Illustrated. Containing 46 Illustrations from Original Drawings, and numerous other Illustrations. Royal 8vo, 21s.

*REDGRAVE (GILBERT)*—
OUTLINES OF HISTORIC ORNAMENT. Translated from the German and edited by. With numerous Illustrations. Crown 8vo. 4s.

*REDGRAVE (GILBERT R.)*—
MANUAL OF DESIGN, compiled from the Writings and Addresses of RICHARD REDGRAVE, R.A. With Woodcuts. Large crown 8vo, cloth, 2s. 6d.

*REDGRAVE (RICHARD)*—
MANUAL AND CATECHISM ON COLOUR. 24mo, cloth, 9d.

*REDGRAVE (SAMUEL)*—
A DESCRIPTIVE CATALOGUE OF THE HISTORICAL COLLECTION OF WATER-COLOUR PAINTINGS IN THE SOUTH KENSINGTON MUSEUM. With numerous Chromo-lithographs and other Illustrations. Royal 8vo, £1 1s.

*RENAN (ERNEST)*—
RECOLLECTIONS OF MY YOUTH. Translated from the original French by C. B. PITMAN, and revised by MADAME RENAN. Crown 8vo, 8s.

*RIANO (JUAN F.)*—
THE INDUSTRIAL ARTS IN SPAIN. Illustrated. Large crown 8vo, cloth, 4s.

*ROBINSON (JAMES F.)*—
BRITISH BEE FARMING. Its Profits and Pleasures. Large crown 8vo, 5s.

*ROBINSON (J. C.)*—
ITALIAN SCULPTURE OF THE MIDDLE AGES AND PERIOD OF THE REVIVAL OF ART. With 20 Engravings. Royal 8vo, cloth, 7s. 6d.

*ROBSON (GEORGE)*—
ELEMENTARY BUILDING CONSTRUCTION. Illustrated by a Design for an Entrance Lodge and Gate. 15 Plates. Oblong folio, sewed, 8s.

*ROBSON (REV. J. H.), M.A., LL.M.*—
AN ELEMENTARY TREATISE ON ALGEBRA. Post 8vo, 6s.

*ROCK (THE VERY REV. CANON), D.D.*—
ON TEXTILE FABRICS. A Descriptive and Illustrated Catalogue of the Collection of Church Vestments, Dresses, Silk Stuffs, Needlework, and Tapestries in the South Kensington Museum. Royal 8vo, half-morocco, £1 11s. 6d.

*ROCK (THE VERY REV. CANON), D.D.*—

TEXTILE FABRICS. With numerous Woodcuts. Large crown 8vo, cloth, 2s. 6d.

*ROLAND (ARTHUR)*—

FARMING FOR PLEASURE AND PROFIT. Edited by WILLIAM ABLETT. 8 vols. Large crown 8vo, 5s. each.
DAIRY-FARMING, MANAGEMENT OF COWS, &c.
POULTRY-KEEPING.
TREE-PLANTING, FOR ORNAMENTATION OR PROFIT.
STOCK-KEEPING AND CATTLE-REARING.
DRAINAGE OF LAND, IRRIGATION, MANURES, &c.
ROOT-GROWING, HOPS, &c.
MANAGEMENT OF GRASS LANDS.
MARKET GARDENING.

*RUSDEN (G. W.), for many years Clerk of the Parliament in Victoria*—

A HISTORY OF AUSTRALIA. With a Coloured Map. 3 Vols. Demy 8vo, 50s.

A HISTORY OF NEW ZEALAND. 3 vols. Demy 8vo. with Maps, 50s.

*SALUSBURY (PHILIP H. B.)*—

TWO MONTHS WITH TCHERNAIEFF IN SERVIA. Large crown 8vo, 9s.

*SCOTT-STEVENSON (MRS.)*—

ON SUMMER SEAS. Including the Mediterranean, the Ægean, the Ionian, and the Euxine, and a voyage down the Danube. With a Map. Demy 8vo, 16s.

OUR HOME IN CYPRUS. With a Map and Illustrations. Third Edition. Demy 8vo, 14s.

OUR RIDE THROUGH ASIA MINOR. With Map. Demy 8vo, 18s.

*SHEPHERD (MAJOR), R.E.*—

PRAIRIE EXPERIENCES. With Illustrations. Demy 8vo. [*In the Press.*

*SIMMONDS (T. L.)*—

ANIMAL PRODUCTS: their Preparation, Commercial Uses, and Value. With numerous Illustrations. Large crown 8vo, 7s. 6d.

*SMART (HAWLEY)*—

SALVAGE. A Collection of Stories. Crown 8vo, 10s. 6d.

HARD LINES. 1 vol. Crown 8vo, 6s.

*SMITH (MAJOR R. MURDOCK), R.E.*—

PERSIAN ART. Second Edition, with additional Illustrations. Large crown 8vo, 2s.

*ST. CLAIR (S. G. B.)*—

TWELVE YEARS' RESIDENCE IN BULGARIA. Revised Edition. Crown 8vo, 9s.

*STORY (W. W.)*—

ROBA DI ROMA. Seventh Edition, with Additions and Portrait. Crown 8vo, cloth, 10s. 6d.

CASTLE ST. ANGELO. With Illustrations. Crown 8vo, 10s. 6d.

*SUTCLIFFE (JOHN)*—

THE SCULPTOR AND ART STUDENT'S GUIDE to the Proportions of the Human Form, with Measurements in feet and inches of Full-Grown Figures of Both Sexes and of Various Ages. By Dr. G. SCHADOW, Member of the Academies, Stockholm, Dresden, Rome, &c. &c. Translated by J. J. WRIGHT. Plates reproduced by J. SUTCLIFFE. Oblong folio, 31s. 6d.

*TANNER (PROFESSOR), F.C.S.*—

HOLT CASTLE; or, Threefold Interest in Land. Crown 8vo, 4s. 6d.

JACK'S EDUCATION; OR, HOW HE LEARNT FARMING. Second Edition. Crown 8vo, 3s. 6d.

*TOPINARD (DR. PAUL)*—
ANTHROPOLOGY. With a Preface by Professor PAUL BROCA. With numerous Illustrations. Large crown 8vo, 7s. 6d.

*TRAILL (H. D.)*—
THE NEW LUCIAN. Being a Series of Dialogues of the Dead. Demy 8vo, 12s.

*TROLLOPE (ANTHONY)*—
AYALA'S ANGEL. Crown 8vo. 6s.
LIFE OF CICERO. 2 vols. 8vo. £1 4s.
THE CHRONICLES OF BARSETSHIRE. A Uniform Edition, in 8 vols., large crown 8vo, handsomely printed, each vol. containing Frontispiece. 6s. each.

THE WARDEN and BARCHESTER TOWERS. 2 vols.
DR. THORNE.
FRAMLEY PARSONAGE.
THE SMALL HOUSE AT ALLINGTON. 2 vols.
LAST CHRONICLE OF BARSET. 2 vols.

*UNIVERSAL*—
UNIVERSAL CATALOGUE OF BOOKS ON ART. Compiled for the use of the National Art Library, and the Schools of Art in the United Kingdom. In 2 vols. Crown 4to, half-morocco, £2 2s.
Supplemental Volume to Ditto.

*VERON (EUGENE)*—
ÆSTHETICS. Translated by W. H. ARMSTRONG. Large crown 8vo, 7s. 6d.

*WALE (REV. HENRY JOHN), M.A.*—
MY GRANDFATHER'S POCKET BOOK, from 1701 to 1796. Author of "Sword and Surplice." Demy 8vo, 12s.

*WATSON (ALFRED E. T.)*
SKETCHES IN THE HUNTING FIELD. Illustrated by JOHN STURGESS. Cheap Edition. Crown 8vo, 6s.

*WESTWOOD (J. O.), M.A., F.L.S., &c.*—
CATALOGUE OF THE FICTILE IVORIES IN THE SOUTH KENSINGTON MUSEUM. With an Account of the Continental Collections of Classical and Mediæval Ivories. Royal 8vo, half-morocco, £1 4s.

*WHEELER (G. P.)*—
VISIT OF THE PRINCE OF WALES. A Chronicle of H.R.H.'s Journeyings in India, Ceylon, Spain, and Portugal. Large crown 8vo, 12s.

WHIST—
THE HANDS AT WHIST. By AQUARIUS. 32mo, cloth gilt, 1s.
EASY WHIST. 32mo, cloth gilt, 1s.
ADVANCED WHST. 32mo, cloth gilt, 1s.

*WHITE (WALTER)*—
HOLIDAYS IN TYROL: Kufstein, Klobenstein, and Paneveggio. Large crown 8vo, 14s.
A MONTH IN YORKSHIRE. Post 8vo. With a Map. Fifth Edition. 4s.
A LONDONER'S WALK TO THE LAND'S END, AND A TRIP TO THE SCILLY ISLES. Post 8vo. With 4 Maps. Third Edition. 4s.

*WILDFOWLER*—
SHOOTING, YACHTING, AND SEA-FISHING TRIPS, at Home and on the Continent. Second Series. By "WILDFOWLER," "SNAPSHOT." 2 vols. Crown 8vo, £1 1s.
SHOOTING AND FISHING TRIPS IN ENGLAND, FRANCE, ALSACE, BELGIUM, HOLLAND, AND BAVARIA. New Edition, with Illustrations. Large crown 8vo, 8s.

WILL-O'-THE-WISPS, THE. Translated from the German of Marie Petersen by CHARLOTTE J. HART. With Illustrations. Crown 8vo, 7s. 6d.

*WORNUM (R. N.)*—

ANALYSIS OF ORNAMENT: THE CHARACTERISTICS OF STYLES. An Introduction to the Study of the History of Ornamental Art. With many Illustrations. Ninth Edition. Royal 8vo, cloth, 8s.

*WORSAAE (J. J. A.)*—

INDUSTRIAL ARTS OF DENMARK, FROM THE EARLIEST TIMES TO THE DANISH CONQUEST OF ENGLAND. With Maps and Illustrations. Crown 8vo, 3s. 6d.

*WYLDE (ATHERTON)*—

MY CHIEF AND I; OR, SIX MONTHS IN NATAL AFTER THE LANGALIBALELE OUTBREAK. With Portrait of Colonel Durnford, and Illustrations. Demy 8vo, 14s.

*YEO (DR. J. BURNEY)*—

HEALTH RESORTS AND THEIR USES: BEING Vacation Studies in various Health Resorts. Crown 8vo, 8s.

*YOUNGE (C. D.)*—

PARALLEL LIVES OF ANCIENT AND MODERN HEROES. New Edition. 12mo, cloth, 4s. 6d.

---

## SOUTH KENSINGTON MUSEUM DESCRIPTIVE AND ILLUSTRATED CATALOGUES.

*Royal 8vo, half-bound.*

BRONZES OF EUROPEAN ORIGIN. By C. D. E. FORTNUM. £1 10s.

DYCE'S COLLECTION OF PRINTED BOOKS AND MANUSCRIPTS. 2 vols. 14s.

DYCE'S COLLECTION OF PAINTINGS, ENGRAVINGS, &c. 6s. 6d.

FURNITURE AND WOODWORK, ANCIENT AND MODERN. By J. H. POLLEN. £1 1s.

GLASS VESSELS. By A. NESBITT. 18s.

GOLD AND SILVER SMITH'S WORK. By J. G. POLLEN. £1 6s.

IVORIES, ANCIENT AND MEDIÆVAL. By W. MASKELL. 21s.

IVORIES, FICTILE. By J. O. WESTWOOD. £1 4s.

MAIOLICA, HISPANO-MORESCO, PERSIAN, DAMASCUS AND RHODIAN WARES. BY C. D. E. FORTNUM. £2.

MUSICAL INSTRUMENTS. By C. ENGEL. 12s.

SCULPTURE, ITALIAN SCULPTURE OF THE MIDDLE AGES. BY J. C. ROBINSON. Cloth, 7s. 6d.

SWISS COINS. By R. S. POOLE. £2 10s.

TEXTILE FABRICS. By Rev. D. ROCK. £1 11s. 6d.

WATER-COLOUR PAINTING. By S. REDGRAVE. £1 1s.

UNIVERSAL CATALOGUE OF BOOKS ON ART. 2 vols. Small 4to, £1 1s. each.

UNIVERSAL CATALOGUE OF BOOKS ON ART. Supplementary vol.

## SOUTH KENSINGTON MUSEUM SCIENCE AND ART HANDBOOKS.

*Published for the Committee of the Council on Education.*

ART IN RUSSIA. Forming a New Volume of the South Kensington Art Handbooks. With numerous Illustrations. Crown 8vo. [*In the Press.*

FRENCH POTTERY. Forming a New Volume of the South Kensington Art Handbooks. With Illustrations. Crown 8vo. [*In the Press.*

INDUSTRIAL ARTS OF DENMARK. From the Earliest Times to the Danish Conquest of England. By J. J. A. WORSAAE, Hon. F.S.A., M.R.I.A., &c. &c. With Map and Woodcuts. Large crown 8vo, 3s. 6d.

INDUSTRIAL ARTS OF SCANDINAVIA IN THE PAGAN TIME. By HANS HILDEBRAND, Royal Antiquary of Sweden. Woodcuts. Large crown 8vo, 2s. 6d.

PRECIOUS STONES. By PROFESSOR CHURCH. With Illustrations. Large crown 8vo, 2s. 6d.

INDUSTRIAL ARTS OF INDIA. By Sir GEORGE C. M. BIRDWOOD, C.S.I. With Map and 174 Illustrations. Demy 8vo, 14s.

HANDBOOK TO THE DYCE AND FORSTER COLLECTIONS. By W. MASKELL. With Illustrations. Large crown 8vo, 2s. 6d.

INDUSTRIAL ARTS IN SPAIN. By JUAN F. RIANO. Illustrated. Large crown 8vo, 4s.

GLASS. By ALEXANDER NESBITT. Illustrated. Large crown 8vo, 2s. 6d.

GOLD AND SILVER SMITH'S WORK. By JOHN HUNGERFORD POLLEN. With numerous Woodcuts. Large crown 8vo, 2s. 6d.

TAPESTRY. By ALFRED CHAMPEAUX. With Woodcuts. 2s. 6d.

BRONZES. By C. DRURY E. FORTNUM, F.S.A. With numerous Woodcuts. Large crown 8vo, 2s. 6d.

PLAIN WORDS ABOUT WATER. By A. H. CHURCH, M.A., Oxon. Illustrated. Large crown 8vo, sewed, 6d.

ANIMAL PRODUCTS: their Preparation, Commercial Uses, and Value. By T. L. SIMMONDS. With numerous Illustrations. Large crown 8vo, 7s. 6d.

FOOD: A Short Account of the Sources, Constituents, and Uses of Food; intended chiefly as a Guide to the Food Collection in the Bethnal Green Museum. By A. H. CHURCH, M.A., Oxon. Large crown 8vo, 3s.

SCIENCE CONFERENCES. Delivered at the South Kensington Museum. 2 vols. Crown 8vo, 6s. each.
VOL. I.—Physics and Mechanics.
VOL. II.—Chemistry, Biology, Physical Geography, Geology, Mineralogy, and Meteorology.

ECONOMIC ENTOMOLOGY. By ANDREW MURRAY, F.L.S. APTERA. With numerous Illustrations. Large crown 8vo, 7s. 6d.

JAPANESE POTTERY. Being a Native Report. Edited by A. W. FRANKS. Numerous Illustrations and Marks. Large crown 8vo, 2s. 6d.

HANDBOOK TO THE SPECIAL LOAN COLLECTION of Scientific Apparatus. Large crown 8vo, 3s.

INDUSTRIAL ARTS: Historical Sketches. With 242 Illustrations. Large crown 8vo, 3s.

TEXTILE FABRICS. By the Very Rev. DANIEL ROCK, D.D. With numerous Woodcuts. Large crown 8vo, 2s. 6d.

JONES COLLECTION IN THE SOUTH KENSINGTON MUSEUM. With Portrait and Illustrations. Large crown 8vo, 2s. 6d.

SOUTH KENSINGTON MUSEUM SCIENCE & ART HANDBOOKS—*Continued.*

COLLEGE AND CORPORATION PLATE. By WILFRED CRIPPS. With numerous Illustrations. Large crown 8vo, cloth, 2s. 6d.

IVORIES: ANCIENT AND MEDIÆVAL. By WILLIAM MASKELL. With numerous Woodcuts. Large crown 8vo, 2s. 6d.

ANCIENT AND MODERN FURNITURE AND WOODWORK. By JOHN HUNGERFORD POLLEN. With numerous Woodcuts. Large crown 8vo, 2s. 6d.

MAIOLICA. By C. DRURY E. FORTNUM, F.S.A. With numerous Woodcuts. Large crown 8vo, 2s. 6d.

THE CHEMISTRY OF FOODS. With Microscopic Illustrations. By JAMES BELL, Principal of the Somerset House Laboratory.
Part I.—Tea, Coffee, Cocoa, Sugar, &c. Large crown 8vo, 2s. 6d.
Part II.—Milk, Butter, Cereals, Prepared Starches, &c. Large crown 8vo, 2s. 6d.

MUSICAL INSTRUMENTS. By CARL ENGEL. With numerous Woodcuts. Large crown 8vo, 2s. 6d.

MANUAL OF DESIGN, compiled from the Writings and Addresses of RICHARD REDGRAVE, R.A. By GILBERT R. REDGRAVE. With Woodcuts. Large crown 8vo, 2s. 6d.

PERSIAN ART. By MAJOR R. MURDOCK SMITH, R.E. Second Edition, with additional Illustrations. Large crown 8vo, 2s.

FREE EVENING LECTURES. Delivered in connection with the Special Loan Collection of Scientific Apparatus, 1876. Large crown 8vo, 8s.

# CARLYLE'S (THOMAS) WORKS.

## CHEAP AND UNIFORM EDITION.

*In 23 vols., Crown 8vo, cloth, £7 5s.*

THE FRENCH REVOLUTION: A History. 2 vols., 12s.

OLIVER CROMWELL'S LETTERS AND SPEECHES, with Elucidations, &c. 3 vols., 18s.

LIVES OF SCHILLER AND JOHN STERLING. 1 vol., 6s.

CRITICAL AND MISCELLANEOUS ESSAYS. 4 vols., £1 4s.

SARTOR RESARTUS AND LECTURES ON HEROES. 1 vol., 6s.

LATTER-DAY PAMPHLETS. 1 vol., 6s.

CHARTISM AND PAST AND PRESENT. 1 vol., 6s.

TRANSLATIONS FROM THE GERMAN OF MUSÆUS, TIECK, AND RICHTER. 1 vol., 6s.

WILHELM MEISTER, by Göthe. A Translation 2 vols., 12s.

HISTORY OF FRIEDRICH THE SECOND, called Frederick the Great. 7 vols., £2 9s.

## SIXPENNY EDITION.

*4to, sewed.*

SARTOR RESARTUS. Eightieth Thousand.

HEROES AND HERO WORSHIP.

ESSAYS: BURNS, JOHNSON, SCOTT, THE DIAMOND NECKLACE.

*The above are also to be had in 1 vol., in cloth, 2s. 6d.*

CARLYLE'S (THOMAS) WORKS—*Continued.*

## LIBRARY EDITION COMPLETE.

**Handsomely printed in 34 vols., demy 8vo, cloth, £15.**

---

SARTOR RESARTUS. The Life and Opinions of Herr Teufelsdröckh. With a Portrait, 7s. 6d.

THE FRENCH REVOLUTION. A History. 3 vols., each 9s.

LIFE OF FREDERICK SCHILLER AND EXAMINATION OF HIS WORKS. With Supplement of 1872. Portrait and Plates, 9s.

CRITICAL AND MISCELLANEOUS ESSAYS. With Portrait. 6 vols., each 9s.

ON HEROES, HERO WORSHIP, AND THE HEROIC IN HISTORY. 7s. 6d.

PAST AND PRESENT. 9s.

OLIVER CROMWELL'S LETTERS AND SPEECHES. With Portraits. 5 vols., each 9s.

LATTER-DAY PAMPHLETS. 9s.

LIFE OF JOHN STERLING. With Portrait, 9s.

HISTORY OF FREDERICK THE SECOND. 10 vols., each 9s.

TRANSLATIONS FROM THE GERMAN. 3 vols., each 9s.

EARLY KINGS OF NORWAY; ESSAY ON THE PORTRAITS OF JOHN KNOX; AND GENERAL INDEX. With Portrait Illustrations. 8vo, cloth, 9s.

---

## PEOPLE'S EDITION.

*In 37 vols., small Crown 8vo. Price 2s. each vol., bound in cloth; or in sets of 37 vols. in 19, cloth gilt, for £3 14s.*

SARTOR RESARTUS.

FRENCH REVOLUTION. 3 vols.

LIFE OF JOHN STERLING.

OLIVER CROMWELL'S LETTERS AND SPEECHES. 5 vols.

ON HEROES AND HERO WORSHIP.

PAST AND PRESENT.

CRITICAL AND MISCELLANEOUS ESSAYS. 7 vols.

LATTER-DAY PAMPHLETS.

LIFE OF SCHILLER.

FREDERICK THE GREAT. 10 vols.

WILHELM MEISTER. 3 vols.

TRANSLATIONS FROM MUSÆUS, TIECK, AND RICHTER. 2 vols.

THE EARLY KINGS OF NORWAY; Essay on the Portraits of Knox; and General Index.

# DICKENS'S (CHARLES) WORKS.

## ORIGINAL EDITIONS.

*In Demy 8vo.*

THE MYSTERY OF EDWIN DROOD. With Illustrations by S. L. Fildes, and a Portrait engraved by Baker. Cloth, 7s. 6d.

OUR MUTUAL FRIEND. With Forty Illustrations by Marcus Stone. Cloth, £1 1s.

THE PICKWICK PAPERS. With Forty-three Illustrations by Seymour and Phiz. Cloth, £1 1s.

NICHOLAS NICKLEBY. With Forty Illustrations by Phiz. Cloth, £1 1s.

SKETCHES BY "BOZ." With Forty Illustrations by George Cruikshank. Cloth, £1 1s.

MARTIN CHUZZLEWIT. With Forty Illustrations by Phiz. Cloth, £1 1s.

DOMBEY AND SON. With Forty Illustrations by Phiz. Cloth, £1 1s.

DAVID COPPERFIELD. With Forty Illustrations by Phiz. Cloth, £1 1s.

BLEAK HOUSE. With Forty Illustrations by Phiz. Cloth, £1 1s.

LITTLE DORRIT. With Forty Illustrations by Phiz. Cloth, £1 1s.

THE OLD CURIOSITY SHOP. With Seventy-five Illustrations by George Cattermole and H. K. Browne. A New Edition. Uniform with the other volumes, £1 1s.

BARNABY RUDGE: a Tale of the Riots of 'Eighty. With Seventy-eight Illustrations by George Cattermole and H. K. Browne. Uniform with the other volumes, £1 1s.

CHRISTMAS BOOKS: Containing—The Christmas Carol; The Cricket on the Hearth; The Chimes; The Battle of Life; The Haunted House. With all the original Illustrations. Cloth, 12s.

OLIVER TWIST and TALE OF TWO CITIES. In one volume. Cloth, £1 1s.

OLIVER TWIST. Separately. With Twenty-four Illustrations by George Cruikshank. Cloth, 11s.

A TALE OF TWO CITIES. Separately. With Sixteen Illustrations by Phiz. Cloth, 9s.

*** *The remainder of Dickens's Works were not originally printed in Demy 8vo.*

DICKENS'S (CHARLES) WORKS—*Continued.*

## LIBRARY EDITION.

*In Post 8vo. With the Original Illustrations, 30 vols., cloth, £12.*

| | | | s. | d. |
|---|---|---|---|---|
| PICKWICK PAPERS ... ... ... ... ... | 43 Illustrns., | 2 vols. | 16 | 0 |
| NICHOLAS NICKLEBY ... ... ... ... | 39 ,, | 2 vols. | 16 | 0 |
| MARTIN CHUZZLEWIT ... ... ... ... | 40 ,, | 2 vols. | 16 | 0 |
| OLD CURIOSITY SHOP & REPRINTED PIECES | 36 ,, | 2 vols. | 16 | 0 |
| BARNABY RUDGE and HARD TIMES ... ... | 36 ,, | 2 vols. | 16 | 0 |
| BLEAK HOUSE... ... ... ... ... ... | 40 ,, | 2 vols. | 16 | 0 |
| LITTLE DORRIT ... ... ... ... ... | 40 ,, | 2 vols. | 16 | 0 |
| DOMBEY AND SON ... ... ... ... ... | 38 ,, | 2 vols. | 16 | 0 |
| DAVID COPPERFIELD ... ... ... ... | 38 ,, | 2 vols. | 16 | 0 |
| OUR MUTUAL FRIEND ... ... ... ... | 40 ,, | 2 vols. | 16 | 0 |
| SKETCHES BY "BOZ" ... ... ... ... | 39 ,, | 1 vol. | 8 | 0 |
| OLIVER TWIST ... ... ... ... ... | 24 ,, | 1 vol. | 8 | 0 |
| CHRISTMAS BOOKS ... ... ... ... ... | 17 ,, | 1 vol. | 8 | 0 |
| A TALE OF TWO CITIES ... ... ... ... | 16 ,, | 1 vol. | 8 | 0 |
| GREAT EXPECTATIONS ... ... ... ... | 8 ,, | 1 vol. | 8 | 0 |
| PICTURES FROM ITALY & AMERICAN NOTES | 8 ,, | 1 vol. | 8 | 0 |
| UNCOMMERCIAL TRAVELLER ... ... .. | 8 ,, | 1 vol. | 8 | 0 |
| CHILD'S HISTORY OF ENGLAND ... ... | 8 ,, | 1 vol. | 8 | 0 |
| EDWIN DROOD and MISCELLANIES ... ... | 12 ,, | 1 vol. | 8 | 0 |
| CHRISTMAS STORIES from "Household Words," &c. | 14 ,, | 1 vol. | 8 | 0 |

THE LIFE OF CHARLES DICKENS. By JOHN FORSTER. With Illustrations. Uniform with this Edition. 1 vol. 10s. 6d.

## THE "CHARLES DICKENS" EDITION.

*In Crown 8vo. In 21 vols., cloth, with Illustrations, £3 16s.*

| | | s. | d. |
|---|---|---|---|
| PICKWICK PAPERS ... ... ... ... ... ... | 8 Illustrations ... | 4 | 0 |
| MARTIN CHUZZLEWIT ... ... ... ... ... | 8 ,, ... | 4 | 0 |
| DOMBEY AND SON ... ... ... ... ... | 8 ,, ... | 4 | 0 |
| NICHOLAS NICKLEBY ... ... ... ... ... | 8 ,, ... | 4 | 0 |
| DAVID COPPERFIELD ... ... ... ... ... | 8 ,, ... | 4 | 0 |
| BLEAK HOUSE ... ... ... ... ... ... | 8 ,, ... | 4 | 0 |
| LITTLE DORRIT ... ... ... ... ... ... | 8 ,, ... | 4 | 0 |
| OUR MUTUAL FRIEND... ... ... ... ... | 8 ,, ... | 4 | 0 |
| BARNABY RUDGE... ... ... .. ... ... | 8 ,, ... | 3 | 6 |
| OLD CURIOSITY SHOP ... ... ... ... ... | 8 ,, ... | 3 | 6 |
| A CHILD'S HISTORY OF ENGLAND ... ... | 4 ,, ... | 3 | 6 |
| EDWIN DROOD and OTHER STORIES ... ... | 8 ,, ... | 3 | 6 |
| CHRISTMAS STORIES, from "Household Words" ... | 8 ,, ... | 3 | 6 |
| SKETCHES BY "BOZ" ... ... ... ... ... | 8 ,, ... | 3 | 6 |
| AMERICAN NOTES and REPRINTED PIECES ... | 8 ,, ... | 3 | 6 |
| CHRISTMAS BOOKS ... ... ... ... ... | 8 ,, ... | 3 | 6 |
| OLIVER TWIST ... ... ... ... ... ... | 8 ,, ... | 3 | 6 |
| GREAT EXPECTATIONS... ... ... ... ... | 8 ,, ... | 3 | 6 |
| TALE OF TWO CITIES ... ... ... ... ... | 8 ,, ... | 3 | 0 |
| HARD TIMES and PICTURES FROM ITALY ... | 8 ,, ... | 3 | 0 |
| UNCOMMERCIAL TRAVELLER ... ... ... | 4 ,, ... | 3 | 0 |
| THE LIFE OF CHARLES DICKENS. Numerous Illustrations. | 2 vols. | 7 | 0 |
| THE LETTERS OF CHARLES DICKENS .. ... ... | ...2 vols. | 8 | 0 |

DICKENS'S (CHARLES) WORKS—*Continued.*

## THE ILLUSTRATED LIBRARY EDITION.

*Complete in 30 Volumes. Demy 8vo, 10s. each; or set, £15.*

This Edition is printed on a finer paper and in a larger type than has been employed in any previous edition. The type has been cast especially for it, and the page is of a size to admit of the introduction of all the original illustrations.

No such attractive issue has been made of the writings of Mr. Dickens, which, various as have been the forms of publication adapted to the demands of an ever widely-increasing popularity, have never yet been worthily presented in a really handsome library form.

The collection comprises all the minor writings it was Mr. Dickens's wish to preserve.

SKETCHES BY "BOZ." With 40 Illustrations by George Cruikshank.

PICKWICK PAPERS. 2 vols. With 42 Illustrations by Phiz.

OLIVER TWIST. With 24 Illustrations by Cruikshank.

NICHOLAS NICKLEBY. 2 vols. With 40 Illustrations by Phiz.

OLD CURIOSITY SHOP and REPRINTED PIECES. 2 vols. With Illustrations by Cattermole, &c.

BARNABY RUDGE and HARD TIMES. 2 vols. With Illustrations by Cattermole, &c.

MARTIN CHUZZLEWIT. 2 vols. With 4 Illustrations by Phiz.

AMERICAN NOTES and PICTURES FROM ITALY. 1 vol. With 8 Illustrations.

DOMBEY AND SON. 2 vols. With 40 Illustrations by Phiz.

DAVID COPPERFIELD. 2 vols. With 40 Illustrations by Phiz.

BLEAK HOUSE. 2 vols. With 40 Illustrations by Phiz.

LITTLE DORRIT. 2 vols. With 40 Illustrations by Phiz.

A TALE OF TWO CITIES. With 16 Illustrations by Phiz.

THE UNCOMMERCIAL TRAVELLER. With 8 Illustrations by Marcus Stone.

GREAT EXPECTATIONS. With 8 Illustrations by Marcus Stone.

OUR MUTUAL FRIEND. 2 vols. With 40 Illustrations by Marcus Stone.

CHRISTMAS BOOKS. With 17 Illustrations by Sir Edwin Landseer, R.A., Maclise, R.A., &c. &c.

HISTORY OF ENGLAND. With 8 Illustrations by Marcus Stone.

CHRISTMAS STORIES. (From "Household Words" and "All the Year Round.") With 14 Illustrations.

EDWIN DROOD AND OTHER STORIES. With 12 Illustrations by S. L. Fildes.

DICKENS'S (CHARLES) WORKS—*Continued.*

## HOUSEHOLD EDITION.

*Complete in 22 Volumes. Crown 4to, cloth, £4 8s. 6d.*

MARTIN CHUZZLEWIT, with 59 Illustrations, cloth, 5s.
DAVID COPPERFIELD, with 60 Illustrations and a Portrait, cloth, 5s.
BLEAK HOUSE, with 61 Illustrations, cloth, 5s.
LITTLE DORRIT, with 58 Illustrations, cloth, 5s.
PICKWICK PAPERS, with 56 Illustrations, cloth, 5s.
OUR MUTUAL FRIEND, with 58 Illustrations, cloth, 5s.
NICHOLAS NICKLEBY, with 59 Illustrations, cloth, 5s.
DOMBEY AND SON, with 61 Illustrations, cloth, 5s.
EDWIN DROOD; REPRINTED PIECES; and other Stories, with 30 Illustrations, cloth, 5s.
THE LIFE OF DICKENS. By JOHN FORSTER. With 40 Illustrations. Cloth, 5s.
BARNABY RUDGE, with 46 Illustrations, cloth, 4s.
OLD CURIOSITY SHOP, with 32 Illustrations, cloth, 4s.
CHRISTMAS STORIES, with 23 Illustrations, cloth, 4s.
OLIVER TWIST, with 28 Illustrations, cloth, 3s.
GREAT EXPECTATIONS, with 26 Illustrations, cloth, 3s.
SKETCHES BY "BOZ," with 36 Illustrations, cloth, 3s.
UNCOMMERCIAL TRAVELLER, with 26 Illustrations, cloth, 3s.
CHRISTMAS BOOKS, with 28 Illustrations, cloth, 3s.
THE HISTORY OF ENGLAND, with 15 Illustrations, cloth, 3s.
AMERICAN NOTES and PICTURES FROM ITALY, with 18 Illustrations, cloth, 3s.
A TALE OF TWO CITIES, with 25 Illustrations, cloth, 3s.
HARD TIMES, with 20 Illustrations, cloth, 2s. 6d.

## MR. DICKENS'S READINGS.

*Fcap. 8vo, sewed.*

CHRISTMAS CAROL IN PROSE. 1s.
CRICKET ON THE HEARTH. 1s.
CHIMES: A GOBLIN STORY. 1s.
STORY OF LITTLE DOMBEY. 1s.
POOR TRAVELLER, BOOTS AT THE HOLLY-TREE INN, and MRS. GAMP. 1s.

---

A CHRISTMAS CAROL, with the Original Coloured Plates, being a reprint of the Original Edition. Small 8vo, red cloth, gilt edges, 5s.

# *List of Books, Drawing Examples, Diagrams, Models, Instruments, etc.,*

INCLUDING

THOSE ISSUED UNDER THE AUTHORITY OF THE SCIENCE AND ART DEPARTMENT, SOUTH KENSINGTON, FOR THE USE OF SCHOOLS AND ART AND SCIENCE CLASSES.

---

CATALOGUE OF MODERN WORKS ON SCIENCE AND TECHNOLOGY. 8vo, sewed, 1s.

*BENSON (W.)*—

PRINCIPLES OF THE SCIENCE OF COLOUR. Small 4to, cloth, 15s.

MANUAL OF THE SCIENCE OF COLOUR. Coloured Frontispiece and Illustrations. 12mo, cloth, 2s. 6d.

*BRADLEY (THOMAS), of the Royal Military Academy, Woolwich*—

ELEMENTS OF GEOMETRICAL DRAWING. In Two Parts, with 60 Plates. Oblong folio, half-bound, each part 16s.

Selections (from the above) of 20 Plates, for the use of the Royal Military Academy, Woolwich. Oblong folio, half-bound, 16s.

*BURCHETT*—

LINEAR PERSPECTIVE. With Illustrations. Post 8vo, 7s.

PRACTICAL GEOMETRY. Post 8vo, 5s.

DEFINITIONS OF GEOMETRY. Third Edition. 24mo, sewed, 5d.

*CARROLL (JOHN)*—

FREEHAND DRAWING LESSONS FOR THE BLACK BOARD. 6s.

*CUBLEY (W. H.)*—

A SYSTEM OF ELEMENTARY DRAWING. With Illustrations and Examples. Imperial 4to, sewed, 3s. 6d.

*DAVISON (ELLIS A.)*—

DRAWING FOR ELEMENTARY SCHOOLS. Post 8vo, 3s.

MODEL DRAWING. 12mo, 3s.

THE AMATEUR HOUSE CARPENTER: A Guide in Building, Making, and Repairing. With numerous Illustrations, drawn on Wood by the Author. Demy 8vo, 10s. 6d.

*DELAMOTTE (P. H.)*—

PROGRESSIVE DRAWING-BOOK FOR BEGINNERS. 12mo, 3s. 6d.

*DYCE*—

DRAWING-BOOK OF THE GOVERNMENT SCHOOL OF DESIGN: ELEMENTARY OUTLINES OF ORNAMENT. 50 Plates. Small folio, sewed, 5s.: mounted, 18s.

INTRODUCTION TO DITTO. Fcap. 8vo, 6d.

*FOSTER (VERE)*—

DRAWING-BOOKS:

(*a*) Twenty-four Numbers, at 1d. each.

(*b*) Forty-six Numbers, at 3d. each. The set *b* includes the subjects in *a*.

DRAWING-CARDS:

Freehand Drawing: First Grade, Sets I., II., III., 1s. each.
Second Grade, Set I., 2s.

*HENSLOW (PROFESSOR)*—

ILLUSTRATIONS TO BE EMPLOYED IN THE PRACTICAL LESSONS ON BOTANY. Prepared for South Kensington Museum. Post 8vo, sewed, 6d.

*JACOBSTHAL (E.)*—

GRAMMATIK DER ORNAMENTE, in 7 Parts of 20 Plates each. Unmounted, £3 13s. 6d.; mounted on cardboard, £11 4s. The Parts can be had separately.

*JEWITT*—

HANDBOOK OF PRACTICAL PERSPECTIVE. 18mo, cloth, 1s. 6d.

*KENNEDY (JOHN)*—

FIRST GRADE PRACTICAL GEOMETRY. 12mo, 6d.

FREEHAND DRAWING-BOOK. 16mo, 1s.

*LINDLEY (JOHN)*—

SYMMETRY OF VEGETATION: Principles to be Observed in the Delineation of Plants. 12mo, sewed, 1s.

*MARSHALL*—

HUMAN BODY. Text and Plates reduced from the large Diagrams. 2 vols., £1 1s.

*NEWTON (E. TULLEY), F.G.S.*—

THE TYPICAL PARTS IN THE SKELETONS OF A CAT, DUCK, AND CODFISH, being a Catalogue with Comparative Descriptions arranged in a Tabular Form. Demy 8vo, 3s.

*OLIVER (PROFESSOR)*—

ILLUSTRATIONS OF THE VEGETABLE KINGDOM. 109 Plates. Oblong 8vo, cloth. Plain, 16s.; coloured, £1 6s.

*POYNTER (E. J.), R.A., issued under the superintendence of*—

ELEMENTARY, FREEHAND, ORNAMENT:

Book I. Simple Geometrical Forms, 6d.

„ II. Conventionalised Floral Forms, &c., 6d.

*POYNTER (E. J.), R.A.—Continued.*

FREEHAND—FIRST GRADE:

Book I. Simple Objects and Ornament, 6d.
,, II. Various Objects, 6d.
,, III. Objects and Architectural Ornaments, 6d.
,, IV. Architectural Ornament, 6d.
,, V. Objects of Glass and Pottery, 6d.
,, VI. Common Objects, 6d.

FREEHAND—SECOND GRADE:

Book I. Various Forms of Anthermion, &c., 1s.
,, II. Greek, Roman, and Venetian, 1s.
,, III. Italian Renaissance, 1s.
,, IV. Roman, Italian, Japanese, &c. 1s.

THE SOUTH KENSINGTON DRAWING CARDS, Containing the same examples as the books:
Elementary Freehand Cards. Four packets, 9d. each.
First Grade Freehand Cards. Six packets, 1s. each.
Second Grade Freehand Cards. Four packets, 1s. 6d. each

*REDGRAVE—*

MANUAL AND CATECHISM ON COLOUR. Fifth Edition. 24mo, sewed, 9d.

*ROBSON (GEORGE)—*

ELEMENTARY BUILDING CONSTRUCTION. Oblong folio, sewed, 8s.

*WALLIS (GEORGE)—*

DRAWING-BOOK. Oblong, sewed, 3s. 6d.; mounted, 8s.

*WORNUM (R. N.)—*

THE CHARACTERISTICS OF STYLES: An Introduction to the Study of the History of Ornamental Art. Royal 8vo, 8s.

DRAWING FOR YOUNG CHILDREN. Containing 150 Copies. 16mo, cloth, 3s. 6d.

ELEMENTARY DRAWING COPY-BOOKS, for the Use of Children from four years old and upwards, in Schools and Families. Compiled by a Student certificated by the Science and Art Department as an Art Teacher. Seven Books in 4to, sewed:

Book I. Letters, 8d.
,, II. Ditto, 8d.
,, III. Geometrical and Ornamental Forms, 8d.
Book IV. Objects, 8d.
,, V. Leaves, 8d.
,, VI. Birds, Animals, &c., 8d.
,, VII. Leaves, Flowers, and Sprays, 8d.

*** Or in Sets of Seven Books, 4s. 6d.

ENGINEER AND MACHINIST DRAWING-BOOK, 16 Parts, 71 Plates. Folio, £1 12s.; mounted, £3 4s.

PRINCIPLES OF DECORATIVE ART. Folio, sewed, 1s.

DIAGRAM OF THE COLOURS OF THE SPECTRUM, with Explanatory Letterpress, on roller, 10s. 6d.

## COPIES FOR OUTLINE DRAWING:

LARGE FREEHAND EXAMPLES FOR CLASS TEACHING. Specially prepared under the authority of the Science and Art Department. Six Sheets. Size 60 by 40. 9s.

DYCE'S ELEMENTARY OUTLINES OF ORNAMENT, 50 Selected Plates, mounted back and front, 18s.; unmounted, sewed, 5s.

WEITBRICHT'S OUTLINES OF ORNAMENT, reproduced by Herman, 12 Plates, mounted back and front, 8s. 6d.; unmounted, 2s.

MORGHEN'S OUTLINES OF THE HUMAN FIGURE, reproduced by Herman, 20 Plates, mounted back and front, 15s.; unmounted, 3s. 4d.

TARSIA, from Gruner, Four Plates, mounted, 3s. 6d., unmounted, 7d.

ALBERTOLLI'S FOLIAGE, Four Plates, mounted, 3s. 6d.; unmounted, 5d.

OUTLINE OF TRAJAN FRIEZE, mounted, 1s.

WALLIS'S DRAWING-BOOK, mounted, 8s., unmounted, 3s. 6d.

OUTLINE DRAWINGS OF FLOWERS, Eight Plates, mounted, 3s. 6d. unmounted, 8d.

## COPIES FOR SHADED DRAWING:

COURSE OF DESIGN. By CH. BARGUE (French), 20 Sheets, £2 9s.

ARCHITECTURAL STUDIES. By J. B. TRIPON. 10 Plates, £1.

MECHANICAL STUDIES. By J. B. TRIPON. 15s. per dozen.

FOLIATED SCROLL FROM THE VATICAN, unmounted, 5d.; mounted, 1s. 3d.

TWELVE HEADS after Holbein, selected from his Drawings in Her Majesty's Collection at Windsor. Reproduced in Autotype. Half imperial, £1 16s.

LESSONS IN SEPIA, 9s. per dozen.

## COLOURED EXAMPLES:

A SMALL DIAGRAM OF COLOUR, mounted, 1s. 6d.; unmounted, 9d.

COTMAN'S PENCIL LANDSCAPES (set of 9), mounted, 15s.

,, SEPIA DRAWINGS (set of 5), mounted, £1.

ALLONGE'S LANDSCAPES IN CHARCOAL (Six), at 4s. each, or the set, £1 4s.

## SOLID MODELS, &c.:

*Box of Models, £1 4s.

A Stand with a universal joint, to show the solid models, &c., £1 18s.

*One Wire Quadrangle, with a circle and cross within it, and one straight wire. One solid cube. One Skeleton Wire Cube. One Sphere. One Cone. One Cylinder. One Hexagonal Prism. £2 2s.

Skeleton Cube in wood, 3s. 6d.

18-inch Skeleton Cube in wood, 12s.

*Three objects of *form* in Pottery:
Indian Jar,
Celadon Jar, } 18s. 6d.
Bottle,

*Five selected Vases in Majolica Ware, £2 11s.

*Three selected Vases in Earthenware, 18s.

Imperial Deal Frames, glazed, without sunk rings, 10s. each.

*Davidson's Smaller Solid Models, in Box, £2, containing—

| | | |
|---|---|---|
| 2 Square Slabs. | Octagon Prism. | Triangular Prism |
| 9 Oblong Blocks (steps). | Cylinder. | Pyramid, Equilateral. |
| 2 Cubes. | Cone. | Pyramid, Isosceles. |
| Square Blocks. | Jointed Cross. | Square Block. |

* Models, &c., entered as sets, can only be supplied in sets.

## SOLID MODELS, &c.—*Continued.*

* Davidson's Advanced Drawing Models, £9.—The following is a brief description of the Models:—An Obelisk—composed of 2 Octagonal Slabs, 26 and 20 inches across, and each 3 inches high; 1 Cube, 12 inches edge; 1 Monolith (forming the body of the obelisk) 3 feet high; 1 Pyramid, 6 inches base; the complete object is thus nearly 5 feet high. A Market Cross—composed of 3 Slabs, 24, 18, and 12 inches across, and each 3 inches high; 1 Upright, 3 feet high; 2 Cross Arms, united by mortise and tenon joints; complete height, 3 feet 9 inches. A Step-Ladder, 23 inches high. A Kitchen Table, 14½ inches high. A Chair to correspond. A Four-legged Stool, with projecting top and cross rails, height 14 inches. A Tub, with handles and projecting hoops, and the divisions between the staves plainly marked. A strong Trestle, 18 inches high. A Hollow Cylinder, 9 inches in diameter, and 12 inches long, divided lengthwise. A Hollow Sphere, 9 inches in diameter, divided into semi-spheres, one of which is again divided into quarters; the semi-sphere, when placed on the cylinder, gives the form and principles of shading a dome, whilst one of the quarters placed on half the cylinder forms a niche.

*Davidson's Apparatus for Teaching Practical Geometry (22 models), £5.

*Binn's Models for Illustrating the Elementary Principles of Orthographic Projection as applied to Mechanical Drawing, in box, £1 10s.

Miller's Class Drawing Models.—These Models are particularly adapted for teaching large classes; the stand is very strong, and the universal joint will hold the Models in any position. *Wood Models*: Square Prism, 12 inches side, 18 inches high; Hexagonal Prism, 14 inches side, 18 inches high; Cube, 14 inches side: Cylinder, 13 inches diameter, 16 inches high; Hexagon Pyramid, 14 inches diameter, 22½ inches side; Square Pyramid, 14 inches side, 22½ inches side; Cone, 13 inches diameter, 22½ inches side; Skeleton Cube, 19 inches solid wood 1¾ inch square; Intersecting Circles, 19 inches solid wood 2¼ by 1½ inches. *Wire Models*: Triangular Prism, 17 inches side, 22 inches high; Square Prism, 14 inches side, 20 inches high: Hexagonal Prism, 16 inches diameter, 21 inches high; Cylinder, 14 inches diameter, 21 inches high; Hexagon Pyramid, 18 inches diameter, 24 inches high; Square Pyramid, 17 inches side, 24 inches high; Cone, 17 inches side, 24 inches high; Skeleton Cube, 19 inches side; Intersecting Circles, 19 inches side; Plain Circle, 19 inches side; Plain Square, 19 inches side. Table, 27 inches by 21½ inches. Stand. The set complete, £14 13s.

Vulcanite Set Square, 5s.

Large Compasses, with chalk-holder, 5s.

*Slip, two set squares and T square, 5s.

*Parkes's Case of Instruments, containing 6-inch compasses with pen and pencil leg, 5s.

*Prize Instrument Case, with 6-inch compasses pen and pencil leg, 2 small compasses, pen and scale, 18s.

6-inch Compasses, with shifting pen and point, 4s. 6d.

---

# LARGE DIAGRAMS.

## ASTRONOMICAL:

TWELVE SHEETS. By JOHN DREW, Ph. Dr., F.R.S.A. Prepared for the Committee of Council on Education. Sheets, £2 8s.; on rollers and varnished, £4 4s.

## BOTANICAL:

NINE SHEETS. Illustrating a Practical Method of Teaching Botany. By Professor HENSLOW, F.L.S. £2; on rollers and varnished, £3 3s.

| CLASS. | DIVISION. | SECTION. | DIAGRAM. |
|---|---|---|---|
| Dicotyledon .. | Angiospermous .. | Thalamifloral .. | 1 |
| | | Calycifloral .. | 2 & 3 |
| | | Corollifloral .. | 4 |
| | | Incomplete .. | 5 |
| | Gymnospermous .. | .. .. | 6 |
| Monocotyledons .. | Petaloid .. | Superior .. | 7 |
| | | Inferior .. | 8 |
| | Glumaceous .. | .. .. | 9 |

* **Models, &c., entered as sets, can only be supplied in sets.**

## BUILDING CONSTRUCTION:

TEN SHEETS. By WILLIAM J. GLENNY, Professor of Drawing, King's College. In sets, £1 1s.

LAXTON'S EXAMPLES OF BUILDING CONSTRUCTION IN TWO DIVISIONS, containing 32 Imperial Plates, £1.

BUSBRIDGE'S DRAWINGS OF BUILDING CONSTRUCTION. 11 Sheets. 2s. 9d. Mounted, 5s. 6d.

## GEOLOGICAL:

DIAGRAM OF BRITISH STRATA. By H. W. BRISTOW, F.R.S., F.G.S. A Sheet, 4s.; on roller and varnished, 7s. 6d.

## MECHANICAL:

DIAGRAMS OF THE MECHANICAL POWERS, AND THEIR APPLICATIONS IN MACHINERY AND THE ARTS GENERALLY. By Dr. JOHN ANDERSON.

8 Diagrams, highly coloured on stout paper, 3 feet 6 inches by 2 feet 6 inches. Sheets £1 per set; mounted on rollers, £2.

DIAGRAMS OF THE STEAM-ENGINE. By Professor GOODEVE and Professor SHELLEY. Stout paper, 40 inches by 27 inches, highly coloured.

Sets of 41 Diagrams (52½ Sheets), £6 6s.; varnished and mounted on rollers, £11 11s.

MACHINE DETAILS. By Professor UNWIN. 16 Coloured Diagrams. Sheets, £2 2s.; mounted on rollers and varnished, £3 14s.

SELECTED EXAMPLES OF MACHINES, OF IRON AND WOOD (French). By STANISLAS PETTIT. 60 Sheets, £3 5s.; 13s. per dozen.

BUSBRIDGE'S DRAWINGS OF MACHINE CONSTRUCTION. 50 Sheets, 12s. 6d. Mounted, £1 5s.

## PHYSIOLOGICAL:

ELEVEN SHEETS. Illustrating Human Physiology, Life Size and Coloured from Nature. Prepared under the direction of JOHN MARSHALL, F.R.S., F.R.C.S., &c. Each Sheet, 12s. 6d. On canvas and rollers, varnished, £1 1s.

1. THE SKELETON AND LIGAMENTS.
2. THE MUSCLES, JOINTS, AND ANIMAL MECHANICS.
3. THE VISCERA IN POSITION.—THE STRUCTURE OF THE LUNGS.
4. THE ORGANS OF CIRCULATION.
5. THE LYMPHATICS OR ABSORBENTS.
6. THE ORGANS OF DIGESTION.
7. THE BRAIN AND NERVES.—THE ORGANS OF THE VOICE.
8. THE ORGANS OF THE SENSES.
9. THE ORGANS OF THE SENSES.
10. THE MICROSCOPIC STRUCTURE OF THE TEXTURES AND ORGANS.
11. THE MICROSCOPIC STRUCTURE OF THE TEXTURES AND ORGANS.

---

HUMAN BODY, LIFE SIZE. BY JOHN MARSHALL, F.R.S., F.R.C.S. Each Sheet, 12s. 6d.; on canvas and rollers, varnished, £1 1s. Explanatory Key, 1s.

1. THE SKELETON, Front View.
2. THE MUSCLES, Front View.
3. THE SKELETON, Back View.
4. THE MUSCLES, Back View
5. THE SKELETON, Side View.
6. THE MUSCLES, Side View.
7. THE FEMALE SKELETON, Front View.

## ZOOLOGICAL:

TEN SHEETS. Illustrating the Classification of Animals. By ROBERT PATTERSON. £2; on canvas and rollers, varnished, £3 10s.

The same, reduced in size on Royal paper, in 9 Sheets, uncoloured, 12s.

---

## PHYSIOLOGY AND ANATOMY OF THE HONEY BEE.

Two Diagrams. 7s. 6d.

# A History of Art in Chaldæa & Assyria.

BY GEORGES PERROT AND CHARLES CHIPIEZ.

Translated by WALTER ARMSTRONG, B.A., Oxon. With 452 Illustrations. 2 vols. royal 8vo, £2 2s.

"It is profusely illustrated, not merely with representations of the actual remains preserved in the British Museum, the Louvre, and elsewhere, but also with ingenious conjectural representations of the principal buildings from which those remains have been taken. To Englishmen familiar with the magnificent collection of Assyrian antiquities preserved in the British Museum the volume should be especially welcome. We may further mention that an English translation by Mr. Walter Armstrong, with the numerous illustrations of the original, has just been published by Messrs. Chapman and Hall."—*Times.*

"The only dissatisfaction that we can feel in turning over the two beautiful volumes in illustration of Chaldæan and Assyrian Art, by MM. Perrot and Chipiez, is in the reflection, that in this, as in so many other publications of a similar scope and nature, it is a foreign name that we see on the title page, and a translation only which we can lay to our national credit. The predominance of really important works on Archæology which have to be translated for the larger reading public of England, and the comparative scarcity of original English works of a similar calibre, is a reproach to us which we would fain see removed . . . it is most frequently to French and German writers that we are indebted for the best light and the most interesting criticisms on the arts of antiquity. Mr. Armstrong s translation is very well done.'—*Builder.*

"The work is a valuable addition to archæological literature, and the thanks of the whole civilised world are due to the authors who have so carefully compiled the history of the arts of two peoples, often forgotten, but who were in reality the founders of Western civilisation."—*Graphic.*

# History of Ancient Egyptian Art.

BY GEORGES PERROT AND CHARLES CHIPIEZ.

Translated from the French by W. ARMSTRONG. Containing 616 Engravings, drawn after the Original, or from Authentic Documents. 2 vols. imperial 8vo, £2 2s.

"The study of Egyptology is one which grows from day to day, and which has now reached such proportions as to demand arrangement and selection almost more than increased collection of material. The well-known volumes of MM. Perrot and Chipiez supply this requirement to an extent which had never hitherto been attempted, and which, before the latest researches of Mariette and Maspero, would have been impossible. Without waiting for the illustrious authors to complete their great undertaking, Mr. W. Armstrong has very properly seized their first instalment, and has presented to the English public all that has yet appeared of a most useful and fascinating work. To translate such a book, however, is a task that needs the revision of a specialist, and this Mr. Armstrong has felt, for he has not sent out his version to the world without the sanction of Dr. Birch and Mr. Reginald Stuart Poole. The result is in every way satisfactory to his readers. Mr. Armstrong adds, in an appendix, a description of that startling discovery which occurred just after the French original of these volumes left the press—namely, the finding of 38 royal mummies, with their sepulchral furniture, in a subterranean chamber at Thebes. It forms a brilliant ending to a work of great value and beauty."—*Pall Mall Gazette.*

The *Saturday Review*, speaking of the French edition, says: "To say that this magnificent work is the best history of Egyptian art that we possess, is to state one of the least of its titles to the admiration of all lovers of antiquity, Egyptian or other. No previous work can be compared with it for method or completeness. . . . . Not only are the best engravings from the older authorities utilised, but numerous unpublished designs have been inserted. M. Chipiez has added greatly to the value of a work, in which the trained eye of the architect is everywhere visible, by his restorations of various buildings and modes of construction; and the engravings in colours of the wall paintings are a noticeable feature in a work which is in every way remarkable. This history of Egyptian art is an invaluable treasure-house for the student; and, we may add, there are few more delightful volumes for the cultivated idle who live at ease to turn over—every page is full of artistic interest."

CHARLES DICKENS AND EVANS,] [CRYSTAL PALACE PRESS.